AF477234

Advances in Artificial Intelligence: Reviews

S. Yurish
Editor

Advances in Artificial Intelligence: Reviews

Book Series, Volume 1

International Frequency Sensor Association Publishing

S. Yurish, *Editor*
Advances in Artificial Intelligence: Reviews,
Book Series, Vol. 1

Published by IFSA Publishing, S. L., 2019
E-mail (for print book orders and customer service enquires):
ifsa.books@sensorsportal.com

Visit our Home Page on http://www.sensorsportal.com

ISBN: 978-84-09-09016-7
e-ISBN: 978-84-09-09015-0
BN-20190515-XX
BIC: UYQ

Contents

11. Artificial Intelligence Approaches Applied to Arabic Digits, Letters and Isolated Words Recognition 293

Preface

According to recent market study, the artificial intelligence market was valued at USD 16.06 billion in 2017 and is expected to reach USD 190.61 billion by 2025, at a CAGR of 36.62% during the forecast period.

Artificial Intelligences currently transforming the manufacturing industry. Virtual reality, automation, Internet of Things (IoT), and robotics are some important features of AI that are benefitting the manufacturing industry.

Artificial intelligence has been one of the fastest-growing technologies in recent years. The market growth is mainly driven by factors such as the increasing adoption of cloud-based applications and services, growing big data, and increasing demand for intelligent virtual assistants. Various end-use industries have also employed artificial intelligence such as retail and business analysis that has also boosted the demand in this market. The major restraint for the market is the limited number of artificial intelligence technology experts. The Book Series on '*Advances in Artificial Intelligence: Reviews*' has been launched with the aim to fill-in this gap. It is the 10th '*Advances*' Book Series published by IFSA Publishing in various research areas.

The first book volume from the '*Advances in Artificial Intelligence: Reviews*' Book Series contains 11 chapters written by 21 contributors from academia and industry from 10 countries: Algeria, Germany, India, Iran, Israel, Russia, Slovenia, South Africa, Tunisia and USA.

This book covers many different timely topics related to artificial intelligence and its applications. All chapters have the same structure: first, an introduction to specific topic under study; second, particular field description including sensing or/and measuring applications. Each of chapter is ending by well selected list of references with books, journals, conference proceedings and web sites.

I hope that readers will enjoy this book and that can be a valuable tool for those who is involved in research and development of various artificial intelligent based systems.

I shall gratefully receive any advices, comments, suggestions and notes from readers to make the next volume of '*Advances in Artificial Intelligence: Reviews*' very interesting and useful.

Sergey Y. Yurish

Editor

Contributors

Hayder T. A. Al-Ali
Don State Technical University, Rostov on Don, Russia

Ghassan H. A. Al-Farhan
Don State Technical University, Rostov on Don, Russia

M. Clement Joe Anand
Hindustan Institute of Technology and Science, Chennai, Tamil Nadu 603103, India

Janani Bharatraj
Hindustan Institute of Technology and Science, Chennai, Tamil Nadu 603103, India

Salah Bouhouche
Research Center in Industrial Technologies CRTI, Algiers, Algeria

Lotfi Boussaid
EµE Lab, Ecole Nationale d'Ingénieurs de Monastir (ENIM), University of Monastir, Monastir, Tunisia
E-mail: lotfi.boussaid@enim.rnu.tn

Younghwan Chae
Centre for Asset and Integrity Management (C-AIM), Department of Mechanical and Aeronautical Engineering, University of Pretoria, Pretoria, South Africa

Mohamed Hassine
LARATSI Lab, Ecole Nationale d'Ingénieurs de Monastir, (ENIM), University of Monastir, Monastir, Tunisia
E-mail: Hassinemohamed60@yahoo.com

Rafaat Hussein
State University of New York, New York, USA

Izidor Mlakar
Faculty of Electrical Engineering and Computer Science, University of Maribor, Slovenia

Stella Moehrle
Institute for Nuclear and Energy Technologies, Karlsruhe Institute of Technology (KIT), Germany

Wolfgang Raskob
Institute for Nuclear and Energy Technologies, Karlsruhe Institute of Technology (KIT), Germany

Matej Rojc
Faculty of Electrical Engineering and Computer Science, University of Maribor, Slovenia

Mina Salim
Assistant Professor, Faculty of Electrical and Computer Engineering, University of Tabriz, Tabriz, Iran
E-mail: m.salim@tabrizu.ac.ir

Yuliya A. Shokova
Don State Technical University, Rostov on Don, Russia

Ofer Strichman
Information Systems Engineering, IE, Technion, Haifa, Israel
E-mail: ofers@ie.technion.ac.il

Abdullah Uz Tansel
Department of Computer Science, Graduate Center, CUNY, USA
Baruch College, CUNY, USA and Pattaya Campus, Thammasat University, Thailand

Michael Veksler
Information Systems Engineering, IE, Technion, Haifa, Israel
E-mail: mveksler@tx.technion.ac.il

Daniel N. Wilke
Centre for Asset and Integrity Management (C-AIM), Department of Mechanical and Aeronautical Engineering, University of Pretoria, Pretoria, South Africa

Di Wu
  Department of Computer Science, Graduate Center, CUNY, USA

Marina Yu. Zvezdina
  Don State Technical University, Rostov on Don, Russia

Chapter 1

Learning General Constraints in CSP

Michael Veksler, Ofer Strichman

1.1. Introduction

Numerous industrial and academic decision and/or optimization problems can be modeled naturally as a Constraint Satisfaction Problems (CSP) [1]. Indeed, problems in scheduling, planning, verification, test generation and more are solved regularly with such tools. The common definition of this problem refers to a set of variables over finite and discrete domains, and a set of constraints over these variables. The decision variant of the CSP (we only refer to this variant in the chapter and ignore the optimization variant) is to find whether there exists an assignment to the variables from their respective domains that satisfies all the constraints, and emit such an assignment as output if indeed such an assignment exists. For example, we can define five variables $x_1,\ldots,x_5$, each with the domains $\{1..5\}$ and ask whether the constraint AllDifferent $(x_1,\ldots,x_5) \wedge x_3 < x_1$ is satisfiable, where AllDifferent is a constraint requiring its input variables to be assigned different values. There is a common set of constraints that is supported by many CSP solvers called FlatZinc [2], which includes over a hundred constraint types, including Boolean connectives. The decision variant of the CSP is NP-complete. While theoretically it has the same expressive power as propositional satisfiability (SAT) [3], its rich modeling language leads to easier, more succinct modeling, and furthermore, certain types of constraints can be solved efficiently (polynomially) whereas solving their translation to propositional logic is exponential. In practice the benefit of these two differences is not always apparent, because frequently the modeling is done once and then instances are generated

Michael Veksler
Information Systems Engineering, IE, Technion, Haifa, Israel

automatically and do not need to be readable; furthermore, in practice almost all CSPs combine many types of constraints that at least some of them cannot be solved efficiently, hence the NP-hardness of the problem is evident in practice. The tremendous progress in efficient SAT solving as of the introduction of the SAT solver Chaff [4] in 2001 has led to the development of several competitive CSP solvers (at the time they were developed) that translate the input CSP to SAT, e.g., see [5].

The ability of CSP solvers to *learn* new constraints during the solving process possibly shortens run-time by an exponential factor (see, e.g., [6]). Learning in a limited form was present in early CSP solvers, where it was called *nogood learning* [7]. Nogoods are defined as partial assignments that cannot be extended to a full solution. Later *generalized nogoods* [6] (g-nogoods for short) were proposed, which allow *non-assignments* as well, e.g., a g-nogood ($x \nleftarrow 1, y \leftarrow 1$) means that an assignment in which x is assigned anything but 1 and y is assigned 1 cannot be extended to a solution. This formalism is convenient for representing knowledge obtained during the search for a solution. The g-nogood above, for example, can result from removing 1 from the domain of x, which leads the solver to remove 1 from the domain of y. G-nogoods may be exponentially stronger than nogoods, as shown in [6]. Another extension is $c-$ nogoods [26], which are like g-nogoods, but a literal can reify a general constraint. $c-$ nogoods are implemented in MINION [9] for a few types of constraints.

A more general and succinct representation of learned knowledge is in the form of *signed clauses*. Such clauses are disjunctions of *signed literals*, where a signed literal has the form $v \in D$ or $v \notin D$ (called positive and negative signed literals, respectively), where v is a variable and D is a domain. Beckert et al. [10] studied the satisfiability problem of signed CNF, i.e., satisfiability of a conjunction of signed clauses. Their inference system is based on simplification rules and a rule for binary resolution of signed clauses:

$$\frac{((v \in A) \vee X) \quad ((v \in B) \vee Y)}{(v \in (A \cap B) \vee X \vee Y)} \quad \text{[Signed Resolution}(v)] , \quad (1.1)$$

where X and Y consist of a disjunction of zero or more literals, A and B are sets of values, and v is called the *pivot* variable. Note that in case v is Boolean and A, B are complementary Boolean domains (e.g.,

$A = \{0\}, B = \{1\}$) then this rule simplifies to the standard resolution rule for propositional clauses that is used in SAT, namely the consequent becomes $(X \vee Y)$.

As we showed in [11], we used this rule in our CSP solver HCSP (short for HaifaCSP)[2], as part of a general learning scheme based on signed clauses. Using a special inference rule for each type of non-clausal constraint, HCSP inferred a signed clause e that *explains* a propagation by that constraint. This means that e is implied by the constraint, but at the same time is strong enough to make the same propagation as the constraint, at the same state. Using such explanations in combination with rule (1.1) for resolving signed clauses, HCSP can generate a signed *conflict clause* via *conflict analysis*. By construction this clause is *asserting* (i.e., it necessarily leads to additional propagation after backtracking). In contrast to the CSP solver EFC [6], which generates a g-nogood *eagerly* for each removed *value*, HCSP generates a signed explanation clause *lazily*, only as part of conflict analysis. Lazy learning of g-nogoods was also implemented on top of MINION [9]. In [12] propositional explanations are generated for highly active constraints. There has also been work on extending explanations with new Boolean variables, which encode equalities and inequalities [13, 14], lazy model expansion [15] where the formula is lazily grounded (i.e., not related to conflicts), learning non-ground rules in the context of answer-set programming [16], and constraint-specific inference [17], such as partial sums in the case of linear constraints. In all these works there is no direct inference between general constraints.

In this chapter we study a different learning scheme, which is based on inference rules with non-clausal consequents. Non-clausal learning has been studied before in the context of several first-order quantifier-free theories: Pseudo-Boolean constraints (see, e.g., Section 22.6.4 in [18] and [19]), difference constraints [20], and integer linear constraints, e.g., [21, 22]. The congruence-closure algorithm for equality logic with uninterpreted functions, which is implemented in most SMT solvers, can also be seen as inferring non-clausal constraints, since it infers new equalities. In all of these cases such learning was shown to improve the search, which motivated us to develop such a scheme for CSP, that is strongly tied to the conflict-analysis procedure. What we suggest here is very general, as it can be used with most of the constraints that are

---

[2] In [11] it was still called PCS, for Proof-producing Constraint Solver

supported by modern CSP solvers, and allows non-clausal inference between different types of constraints.

Our main goal in introducing this scheme is to learn a conflict constraint that is logically stronger and not harder to compute than its clausal counterpart. The emphasis is on the first of these goals as it may improve the search itself. To that end, we propose a generic inference rule called *Combine* that for many popular (pairs of) constraints indeed fulfills these two goals. For example, suppose that a CSP has Boolean variables x, y_1, y_2, y_3, and two constraints ($\oplus$ denotes XOR)

$$c_1 \doteq x \oplus y_1 \oplus y_3 = 0 \qquad c_2 \doteq x \oplus y_2 \oplus y_3 = 0$$

At a state defined by

$$x \in \{0,1\} \quad y_1 \in \{1\} \quad y_2 \in \{0\} \quad y_3 \in \{0\},$$

c_1 propagates $x \in \{1\}$, and then c_2 detects a contradiction. Without going into the details of how clausal explanation works (this will be the subject of Section 1.2.3), in this case it produces the explanation clause

$$(y_1 \in \{0\} \vee y_2 \in \{1\} \vee y_3 \in \{1\}),$$

whereas our rule *Combine* produces

$$y_1 \oplus y_2 = 0,$$

which is logically stronger. One may argue that this consequent is easy to infer without any general pattern, but the point about our rule is that, in addition to the fact that it is general:

- The consequent is in the form of a disjunction where each of the literals has at least *one variable less* than the original premises;

- The inference is guaranteed to be strong enough to contradict the current state;

- It frequently generates consequents that are *difficult to infer otherwise* in an ad-hoc manner;

- The consequent is the *strongest possible* in a well-defined sense, as we will prove in Lemma 1.2.

The example above had two premises of the same type (xor), but we also use the rule for inferring combinations of constraints of different types, such as $y_1 \leq x$ with $[x, y_2] \not\subseteq [a,b]$ (here [a,b] denotes a range between two constants a and b). For some combinations of premises, however, we do not use *Combine* since the result is too complicated to derive or too computationally expensive to support. In such cases we revert to clausal explanations.

Our experimental results indicate that indeed the new scheme is better than clausal explanation. For reference, we also compared HCSP to Mistral [23], CPX [24] and iZplus [25], where the last two won the second and first places, respectively, in the 'free-search, single-core' track of the 2014 'MiniZinc Challenge' [26] (a CSP competition). HCSP performs better than these tools in terms of average run-time and the number of instances it is able to complete within the given time limit, although in optimization problems iZplus typically finds better solutions. HCSP performs an order of magnitude less backtracks than Mistral and three orders of magnitudes less backtracks than CPX, which proves that the constraints it learns are far more effective in pruning the search.

Our contributions in this chapter can be summarized as follows:

- A new learning scheme based on inference of general constraints;

- New inference rules for some popular pairs of constraints, used by this scheme;

- A new scheme for developing inference rules, called *Combine*;

- A fallback solution for the case when a pair of constraints are not directly supported.;

- A new competitive CSP solver, HCSP, that is based on this learning scheme;

- An empirical study comparing HCSP with other leading solvers.

Compared to the proceedings version of this article [27], we added here more background material about our solver, a more elaborate discussion of conflict analysis in SAT solvers, and soundness proofs of several inference rules derived from *Combine*. We left some of the longer and more tedious proofs out – those can be found in a technical report [28].

The rest of the chapter is structured as follows. The next section covers background material, including the learning framework that we use and clausal explanations [11]. Sections 1.3 and 1.4 describe the new set of inference rules, the requirements from them and the proofs that they fulfill these requirements. In Section 1.3 we also explain how we use clausal explanations as a fallback solution when we are unable to infer a general constraint that satisfies the required properties. We conclude in Section 1.5 with an empirical evaluation and some proposals for future research.

1.2. Background

A CSP is a 3-tuple $\phi = <V, D, C>$, where $V = \langle v_1, \ldots, v_n \rangle$ is the set of problem variables, $D = \langle D_1, \ldots, D_n \rangle$ is the set of their respective domains and C is the set of constraints over these variables. An assignment α satisfies a CSP ϕ if it satisfies all the constraints in C and $\forall v_i \in V . \alpha(v_i) \in D_i$. A CSP is unsatisfiable if there is no assignment that satisfies it.

For a CSP solver to support a constraint type, it needs to be able to identify whether constraints of that type are satisfied by a particular assignment to their variables, and to detect what is implied by that constraint in a given state. The algorithm that implements these capabilities is called a *propagator* of the constraint. More formally:

Definition 1.1 (Propagator). *Given a constraint c, a propagator for c is an algorithm satisfying the following requirements:*

- *In a state corresponding to a full assignment, it returns* false *if and only if c contradicts the assignment;*

- *Otherwise, if it returns* false*, then the current state contradicts c;*

- *Otherwise, it may remove (but not add) elements from the domains of some of the variables that c refers to. None of the removed elements is supported by c in the current state.*

As an example, consider a constraint $c \doteq x \leq y$ and a state $x \in \{1,2\}, y \in \{0,1\}$. Then a propagator of c can remove '2' from the domain of x and '0' from the domain of y, leading to a new state

$x \in \{1\}, y \in \{1\}$. Had the domain of x been $\{2,3\}$ the propagator may return false. An ideal propagator has the following property:

Definition 1.2 (Precise propagator). A precise propagator *is a propagator that:*

- *returns* false if and only if c *contradicts the current state.*

- *removes* all *elements from the variables that c refers to, that are not supported by c in the current state.*

Specifically, precise propagators guarantee Global Arc Consistency (GAC), which means that every value in the domain of each variable has support in the constraints in which it participates. Not all implemented propagators are precise because of complexity. These are called *imprecise* propagators. From the perspective of logic, focusing on the role of the propagator as deciding whether c is consistent with the current state, all propagators are *sound*, but only the precise ones are also *complete*. We emphasize that the incompleteness of some of the propagators does not imply incompleteness of the CSP solver, because of the first requirement in Definition 1.1.

1.2.1. Essentials of HCSP

Our solver HCSP supports all the constraint types specified in the FlatZinc format [2]. The engine of HCSP adopts classical ideas from the CSP and SAT literature. We assume the reader is mostly familiar with those, and only mention several highlights briefly. It makes a *decision* (variable ordering) by selecting a variable with the highest ratio of *score* to domain-size, where *score* is calculated similarly to Chaff's VSIDS technique [29]. This can be seen as a variant of the *dom / wdeg* strategy [30]. The value is initially chosen to be the minimal value in the domain, and after that according to the last assigned value, a technique that is typically referred to by the name *phase saving* in SAT [31]. It includes *restarts, learning,* and *deletion* of learnt-constraints with low activity.

The HCSP has *precise* propagators for the following types of constraints (where x_i denote variables, b_i Boolean variables, a_i constants, and $\Diamond \in \{=, \leq, \geq\}$): $x_0 = x_1, x_0 = -x_1$, $x_0 \Diamond abs(x_1)$, $x_0 \Diamond x_1 + x_2$ (with wrap on overflow)[3], $x_0 \leq x_1 * x_2$, $x_0 \geq x_1 * x_2$, $x_0 = \min(x_1, x_2, \ldots)$, $x_0 = \max(x_1, x_2, \ldots)$, $x_0 = (b_0 ? x_2 : x_3)$, $x \neq 0 \leftrightarrow y = z$, $x_0 \in Set \leftrightarrow x_1 < x_2$, $x_0 - x_1 \geq a_0$, $(x_0 + a_0 \leq x_1 \vee x_1 + a_1 \geq x_0)$, $x_0 \neq x_1$, AllDifferent$(x_0, x_1, \ldots)$, $[x_0, x_1 + a_0] \subseteq [a_1, a_2]$, $[x_0, x_1 + a_0] \not\subseteq [a_1, a_2]$, $a_0 * x_0 + a_1 * x_1 + \ldots \geq a_k$, signed-clauses, and a disjunction of any of the above when there are no shared variables. It has *imprecise* propagators for $x_0 = x_1 * x_2$, $x_0 = x_1 / x_2$, $x_0 = x_1 \% x_2$, $x_0 = pow(x_1, x_2)$, and table constraints. Complex constraints modeled by a language such as XCSP [32] are rewritten into more basic ones. The rest of this section is focused on the learning mechanism.

1.2.2. Conflict Analysis

An *implication graph* $G(N, E)$ is a directed acyclic graph in which each node $n \in N$ represents a literal (a variable domain) and each edge $c \in E$ represents a constraint. Incoming edges to a node n can only be labeled with the same constraint. Let $(n_1, n), \ldots, (n_k, n)$ be the incoming edges of n, all of which are labeled with a constraint c. This represents the fact that starting with domains $n_1, \ldots, n_k$ the propagator of c inferred the domain in n. The constraint c is called the *antecedent* of n. Each node is also associated with the *decision level* in which the domain reduction occurred. When an implication graph ends with a conflict (a node labeled with $\perp$), it is called a *conflict graph*. We will follow a convention by which this graph is depicted with the roots at the left and the sink at the right, and the horizontal position of a node indicates the time it occurred. Examples of conflict graphs can be seen in Fig. 1.1 (the reader is advised to ignore at this stage the distinction between filled and empty nodes in that figure). HCSP analyzes the conflict graph in order to learn a new constraint, called accordingly a *conflict constraint* (or a conflict *clause* in SAT). A conflict constraint is called *asserting* if there exists a backtrack level in which this constraint necessarily leads to additional propagation. The conflict-analysis function, AnalyzeConflict, indeed computes this level and returns it to the solver, which backtracks accordingly.

---

[3] More precisely, in the case of $x_0 = x_1 + x_2 + \ldots$ HCSP propagates precisely only if the size of the representation of the domains is smaller than some threshold. This size is larger if the domains of the variables are fragmented

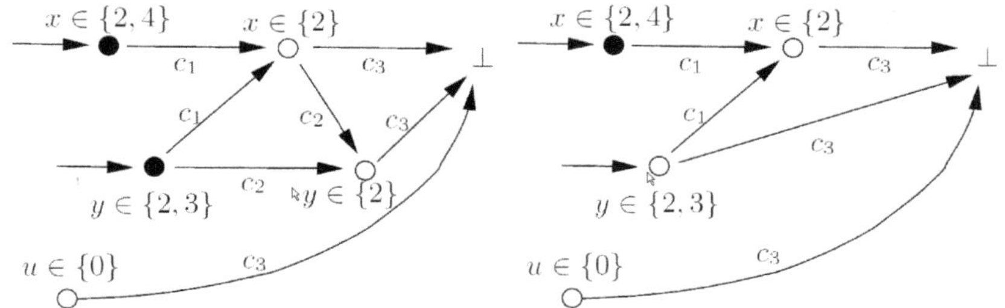

Fig. 1.1. A partial conflict graph based on the constraints in (1.2). '0' represents nodes in the set F. The left and right drawings are before and after relaxation, respectively. Relaxation discovers that the domain reduction by c_2 is unnecessary for conflicting the constraint *Cons* (c_3 in this case).

Conflict-analysis and learning in HCSP is based on the familiar pattern of traversing backward the conflict graph and computing an asserting constraint. Conflict-analysis was used in CSP before, but only while assuming that the constraints are signed clauses, as in MVS [33], or made into signed clauses via explanations (to be described in Section 1.2.3), as in [34, 35]. The conflict-analysis in HCSP is not restricted to clausal inference, and includes various adaptations and optimizations as we describe now. Algorithm 1 shows pseudo-code of AnalyzeConflict as implemented in HCSP. It maintains a set of nodes F, which is initialized to the set of nodes that contradict the input constraint cc. In line 4 it performs a *relaxation* of F. Relaxation appeared first in our technical report [35]; A similar idea appeared also in [36]. Relaxation means that each node in F is 'pushed' to the left as long as the constraint *Cons* remains conflicting. Generally this is possible when domain reductions are redundant, as demonstrated in the following example.

Example 1.1. *Consider the constraints*

$$c_1 \doteq y \geq x \quad c_2 \doteq x \geq y \quad c_3 \doteq x > y + u \tag{1.2}$$

and the conflict graph in Fig. 1.1 (left).

In Algorithm 1, initially $Cons = c_3$, *and hence after line 2* $F = \{x \in \{2\}, y \in \{2\}, u \in \{0\}\}$ *(those are marked with empty circles). Relaxation in line 4 replaces in* F *the node* $y \in \{2\}$ *with the node* $y \in \{2,3\}$, *because the new* F *also contradicts the current constraint*

Cons. Fig. 1.1 (right) shows this. The reason that this is possible is that the domain reduction by c_2 is redundant in the current state, because when $u = 0$, c_3 is capable of removing this value by itself. Such cases appear frequently, because the order in which constraints are processed is not optimal.

Algorithm 1. `AnalyzeConflict` receives as input the currently conflicting constraint, learns a new constraint *Cons* which is asserting (i.e., necessarily leads to further propagation), and returns the backtrack level. `Infer`, the subject of Sections 1.3-1.4, infers a new constraint. `GetNewSet` computes the new set of nodes F, as explained in the text.

1: **function** ANALYZECONFLICT (constraint cc) $\triangleright cc = $ conflicting constraint

2:     $F \leftarrow$ the set of nodes contradicting cc;

3:     $Cons \leftarrow cc$;

4:     $F \leftarrow$RELAX $(F, Cons)$;

5:     **while** !STOP $(F, Cons)$ **do** $\triangleright$ stop if $Cons$ is asserting or UNSAT detected

6:         $pivot \leftarrow$ node of F that was propagated last;

7:         $antecedent \leftarrow$ incoming constraint of $pivot$;

8:         $Cons \leftarrow$ INFER $(Cons, antecedent, pivot, F)$;

9:         $F \leftarrow$ GetNewSet$(F, pivot)$;

10:         Remove from F nodes referring to variables not in $Cons$.

11:         $F \leftarrow$ RELAX $(F, Cons)$; $\triangleright$ Go left as long as F contradicts $Cons$

12:     Add $Cons$ to the constraints database;

13:     **return** ASSERTINGLEVEL $(Cons, F)$; $\triangleright$ the backtracking level, or -1 if UNSAT

14: **function** GETNEWSET(node-set F, node $pivot$)

15:     $F \leftarrow (F \setminus \{pivot\}) \cup$ parents of $pivot$;

16:     $F \leftarrow$ DISTINCT (F); $\triangleright$ Chooses right-most node of each variable in F

17:     Return F;

Relaxation is necessary for several reasons: a) Preventing a situation in which the learned clause is still conflicting immediately after backtracking, instead of being asserting, b) In Section 1.4.3 we rely on relaxation in the development of some of the inference rules, and c) Our experiments show that without it many more cases fall back to clausal explanations, because relaxation enables to circumvent them.

Let us return to the description of Algorithm 1. In lines 5-9 `AnalyzeConflict` gradually updates the constraint $Cons$. It does so by traversing the conflict graph backwards (i.e., going left, from the conflict node towards the decision node) while updating F and the constraint $Cons$ such that the following loop invariants are maintained:

1. ***Invar1.*** $Cons$ contradicts the domains defined by F, and is able to detect it via propagation.[4]

2. ***Invar2.*** No two nodes in F refer to the same variable.

It should be clear that these invariants are maintained at the entry to the loop, because of the definition of F, $Cons$, and relaxation. `Infer` and `GetNewSet` are targeted towards maintaining it as will be evident later. The traversal stops in line 5 once the function stop detects that $Cons$ is asserting, or that it conflicts the domains at decision level 0. In the latter case the function AssertingLevel returns -1 to the solver, which accordingly declares the CSP to be unsatisfiable. In line 8 the current constraint $Cons$ is replaced with a constraint that is inferred from $Cons$ itself and the antecedent constraint of a node in F. The function `Infer` is the main contribution of this chapter and will be discussed in later sections.

Let us now shift our focus to `GetNewSet`, which updates the set F. Initially it replaces *pivot* with its parents. In case there is more than one node in F representing the same variable, in line 16 the function distinct leaves only the right-most one. There may be multiple entries of a variable in F because a parent of *pivot* may represent a variable that already labels a different node in F owing to relaxation (line 11 in a previous iteration.

1.2.3. Clausal Explanations

Generic explanations were used in the past (e.g., [6, 9]) for learning of g-nogoods. The scheme we describe here uses inference rules specialized for each constraint type, resulting in signed clauses. Such clausal explanations are important in our context both for understanding the alternative mechanism that we used in [11] (we use it as one of the points

---

[4] Detection is not a given, because not all constraints have a precise propagator – see Definition 1.2.

of reference for comparing the results), and because we still use it as a fallback solution when, e.g., we reach pairs of constraints for which we do not have an inference rule. Let us begin by formally defining the notion of explanation.

Definition 1.3 (Clausal explanation). *Let $l_1,\ldots,l_n$ be signed literals at the current state (each literal represents the current domain of a variable), and let c be a constraint that propagates the new signed literal l, i.e., $(l_1 \wedge \ldots \wedge l_n \wedge c) \rightarrow l$. Then a clause e is an explanation of this propagation if the following two conditions hold:*

$$c \rightarrow e, \tag{1.3}$$

$$(l_1 \wedge \cdots \wedge l_n \wedge e) \rightarrow l \tag{1.4}$$

Eq. (1.3) guarantees that the new clause e is logically implied by an existing constraint, hence we do not lose soundness. Eq. (1.4) guarantees that it is still strong enough to imply the same literal. It is always possible to derive an explanation from a constraint, regardless of the constraint type [11].

Example 1.2. *The following rule from [11] provides a clausal explanation for an inequality constraint:*

$$\frac{x \leq y}{x \in (-\infty, m] \vee y \in [m+1, \infty)} \; (LE(m)), \tag{1.5}$$

where m is a parameter instantiating it (the rule is sound for any m). It is perhaps more intuitive to rewrite the consequent as $x > m \rightarrow y \geq m+1$, which is obviously implied by the premise for any m. Note that the consequent is a signed clause. Now consider two literals:

$$l_1 \doteq (x \in [1,3]), l_2 \doteq (y \in [0,2])$$

and the constraint

$$c \doteq x \leq y,$$

which implies in the context of l_1, l_2 the literal

$$l \doteq x \in [1,2]$$

(note that $y \in [1,2]$ is also propagated, but we build an explanation for a particular implied literal). Using (1.5) with $m = \max(y) = 2$ we obtain the explanation

$$e \doteq (x \in (-\infty, 2] \vee y \in [3,\infty))$$

and indeed (1.3) and (1.4) hold, since $c \to e$ and $(l_1 \wedge l_2 \wedge e) \to l$. In [11] alternatives to choosing $m = \max(y)$ are discussed.

In [11] we showed how HCSP generates a signed conflict clause with an inference system based on signed resolution (1.1), that is reminiscent of how SAT solvers use binary resolution. Explanations are used for bridging between non-clausal constraints and a signed clause (as in the example above), and (1.1) is used for resolving signed clauses.

Example 1.3. *The following demonstrates conflict analysis with clausal explanations. In addition to (1.5), we will use a variant of this rule for strict inequality:*

$$\frac{x < y}{x \in (-\infty, m-1] \vee y \in [m+1, \infty)} \ (L(m)) \tag{1.6}$$

We will use the observation that if $c \to e$, then $(l \vee c) \to (l \vee e)$, to handle disjunctions. Let $D_x = \{0,1\}$, $D_y = \{0,1\}$, $D_z = \{0..100\}$, and

$$c_1 \doteq (z = 9 \vee x < y) \quad c_2 \doteq (z = 10 \vee x \geq y).$$

The conflict graph on the Fig. 1.2 shows the decision ($D_z = \{0\}$), and then that c_1 propagates $D_x = \{0\}$, $D_y = \{1\}$ in this order, and finally that c_2 detects a conflict. Now $F = \{z \in \{0\}, x \in \{0\}, y \in \{1\}\}$ and $pivot = \{y \in \{1\}\}$. Then c_2 generates the explanation

$$(z \in \{10\} \vee x \in [1,\infty) \vee y \in (-\infty, 0]),$$

based on LE(0) (see (1.5)), and c_1 generates the explanation

$$(z \in \{9\} \vee y \in [1,\infty) \vee x \in (-\infty, -1]),$$

based on L(0) (see (1.6)). Resolving the two explanations on y yields

$$(z \in \{9,10\} \vee x \notin \{0\}) \tag{1.7}$$

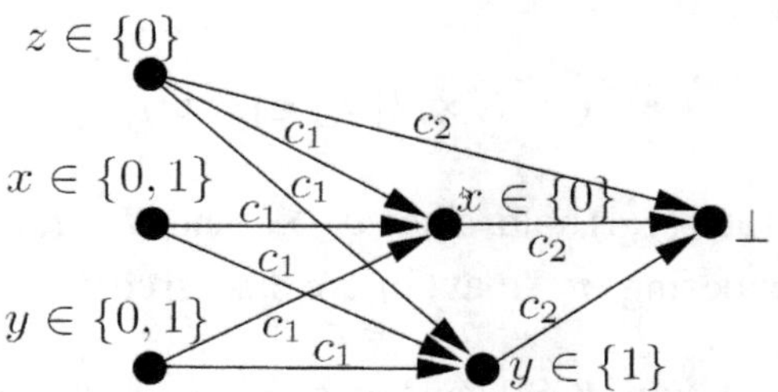

Fig. 1.2. The conflict graph.

Now pivot $= x \in \{0\}$. c_1 *explains the propagation of x with the clause*

$$(z \in \{9\} \vee y \in [2,\infty) \vee x \in (-\infty,0]),$$

based on L(1). Resolving it with (1.7) on x yields

$$(z \in \{9,10\} \vee x \in (-\infty,-1] \vee y \in [2,\infty)) \tag{1.8}$$

Now F is equal to the three nodes on the left. (1.8) is now asserting, since e.g., at the previous decision level $z \in \{9,10\}$ is implied.

1.3. Non-clausal Inference: Requirements

In Algorithm 1 Infer takes as input the constraints $Cons(x,\vec{y})$ and $antecedent(x,\vec{y})$ with a joint variable x that appears at the node *pivot* , and some set of variables $\vec{y}$, which may or may not be common to both[5]. It outputs a new constraint over $x,\vec{y}$ that is assigned back into $Cons$. In what follows we will use $c_1(x,\vec{y})$ to denote $Cons(x,\vec{y})$,

---

[5] It is of course not necessarily the case that they share all the variables, but the description is simplified if we do not consider the shared and unshared variables separately, without sacrificing correctness

$c_2(x,\vec{y})$ to denote *antecedent*$(x,\vec{y})$, and $c^*(x,\vec{y})$ to denote the output constraint. We also define

$$c_{1\wedge2}(x,\vec{y}) \doteq c_1(x,\vec{y}) \wedge c_2(x,\vec{y})$$

Typically, we will discard the parameters and write $c_1, c_2, c^*, c_{1\wedge2}$ instead.

Our first requirement from c^* is that it preserves soundness:

$$c_{1\wedge2} \rightarrow c^* \tag{1.9}$$

This guarantees that the constraint eventually learned in line 12 is inferred via sound derivations, and is hence implied by the original CSP.

Let D_x', D_y' denote the domains of $x, \vec{y}$ right before the propagation of c_1. Also, let $\vdash_{cp}$ denote the *provability relation* by constraint propagation, i.e., $\phi \vdash_{cp} \psi$ denotes that starting with a set of constraints and domains ϕ, the set of literals ψ is derivable through constraint propagation. Then to preserve *Invar1* (see Section 1.2), our second requirement from c^* is:

$$c^*, D_x', D_y' \vdash_{cp} \perp \tag{1.10}$$

In words, constraint propagation is capable of detecting unsatisfiability based on c^*, D_x', and D_y'. Finally, we aspire to find the strongest c^* that satisfies the above requirements, and which is easy to propagate.

1.4. Non-clausal Inference: Rules and Their Proofs

Rules R1-R7 in Table 1.1 are triples $\langle c_1, c_2, c^* \rangle$ that satisfy the two requirements (1.9) and (1.10). Rules R8 and R9 satisfy (1.9) but not necessarily (1.10). We use them to infer constraints, and then test whether they happen to satisfy (1.10). In addition, we use the following meta-rule for handling disjunctions:

$$\frac{(A \vee c_1) \quad (B \vee c_2)}{A \vee B \vee c^*} \tag{1.11}$$

If $\langle c_1, c_2, c^* \rangle$ satisfies (1.9) and (1.10), then so does (1.11). Detailed proofs for all of these rules can be found in a technical report extending this article [28].

Table 1.1. Triples $\langle c_1, c_2, c^* \rangle$ that we use for deriving conflict constraints. R1-R7 satisfy both (1.9) and (1.10), whereas R8-R9 are only guaranteed to satisfy (1.9). When using them we *test* if they also satisfy (1.10). The various min , max operators refer to the domain values at the point in time in which the rule is activated.

	c_1, c_2	c^*
R1	$x \in X_1 \vee A_1(\vec{y})$, $x \in X_2 \vee A_2(\vec{y})$	$x \in (X_1 \cap X_2) \vee A_1(\vec{y}) \vee A_2(\vec{y})$
R2	$y_1 \leq x - k_1$, $x \leq y_2 - k_2$	$(x \in [k_1 + m_1, m_2 - k_2]) \vee$ $([y_1, y_2 - k_2 - k_1] \not\subseteq [m_1, m_2 - k_2 - k_1])$ with $m_1 = \min(D'_{y_1}), m_2 = \max(D'_{y_2})$
R3	$y_1 \leq x$, $[x, y_2] \not\subseteq [a, b]$	$(a > x \geq \min(D'_{y_1})) \vee ([y_1, y_2] \not\subseteq [\min(D'_{y_1}), b])$
R4	$x \leq y_1 - k_1$, $[y_2, x - k_2] \not\subseteq [a, b]$	$(\max(D'_{y_1})\text{-}k_1 \geq x > b + k_2) \vee$ $[y_2, y_1\text{-}k_1\text{-}k_2] \not\subseteq [a, \max(b, \max(D'_{y_1})\text{-}k_1\text{-}k_2)]$
R5	$[y_1, x] \not\subseteq [a_1, b_1]$, $[x, y_2] \not\subseteq [a_2, b_2]$	$(a_2 > x > b_1) \vee ([y_1, y_2] \not\subseteq [a_1, b_2])$
R6	$[x, y] \not\subseteq [a_1, b_1]$, $[y, x] \not\subseteq [a_2, b_2]$	$(x \in (D'_y \setminus ([a_1, b_1] \cup [a_2, b_2]))) \vee$ $y \notin (D'_y \cup [a_1, b_1] \cup [a_2, b_2]))$
R7	$xor(x, \vec{y})$, $xor(x, \vec{z})$	$xor(\vec{y}, \vec{z}, 1)$
R8	$y \leq x + k_1$, $x \leq y + k_2$	$\begin{cases} -k_1 \leq x - y \leq k_2 & \text{if } k_1 + k_2 \geq 0 \\ \bot & \text{otherwise} \end{cases}$
R9	$ax + \sum_{i=1}^n a_i y_i \geq k_1$, $-ax + \sum_{i=1}^n b_i y_i \geq k_2$	$\sum_{i=1}^n (a_i + b_i) y_i \geq k_1 + k_2$

Example 1.4. *We now show two examples in which the rules lead to stronger learning than explanation-based learning*

- *Recall example 1.3, which yielded the conflict clause (1.8). Given the same conflict graph but using the meta rule (1.11) with pivot y, we learn instead $z \in \{9,10\}$, which is clearly stronger. Here is the derivation:*

$$c_1 \doteq (z=9 \vee x<y) \quad c_2 \doteq (z=10 \vee x \geq y)$$

According to rule (1.11)

$$\frac{c_1 \doteq (z=9 \vee x<y) \quad c_2 \doteq (z=10 \vee x \geq y)}{z=9 \vee z=10 \vee c*},$$

where in this case $c* \equiv false$. This last fact is detected trivially by our solver, but it can also be detected by applying rule R8 with $k_1 = 0$, $k_2 = -1$.

- *Consider the domains*

$$x \in \{7,10\}, y_1 \in \{8\}, y_2 \in \{8,9\}$$

and constraints

$$c_1 \doteq (z \in \{1\} \vee y_1 \leq x) \quad c_2 \doteq (z \in \{1\} \vee x \leq y_2)$$

Suppose we make a decision $z \in \{0\}$. Then c_1 propagates $x \in \{10\}$ and c_2 detects a conflict. Using rule R2 with $k_1 = k_2 = 0$, and the meta rule (1.11) we obtain:

$$(z \in \{1\} \vee x \in [8,9] \vee [y_1, y_2] \not\subseteq [8,9]) \tag{1.12}$$

Using explanations instead, c_2 's explanation via LE(9) is

$$(z \in \{1\} \vee x \in (-\infty, 9] \vee y_2 \in [10, \infty)),$$

c_1 's explanation via LE(7) is

$$(z \in \{1\} \vee y_1 \in (-\infty, 7] \vee x \in [8, \infty]),$$

and resolving these explanations on the pivot x yields

$$(z \in \{1\} \vee x \in [8,9] \vee y_1 \in (-\infty, 7] \vee y_2 \in [10, \infty)) \qquad (1.13)$$

Note that the right two disjuncts of (1.13) are equal to $y_1 \le 7 \vee y_2 \ge 10$, whereas the predicate $[y_1, y_2] \not\subseteq [8,9]$ in (1.12) is equal to $(y_1 \le 7 \vee y_2 \ge 10) \wedge y_1 \le y_2$, which is stronger. This is because if $y_1 > y_2$ then $[y_1, y_2] = \varnothing$, and $\varnothing \subseteq [8,9]$).

Most of the entries in the table were developed by instantiating a general inference rule called *Combine* (see Section 1.4.1 below), which satisfies these requirements. In some other cases instantiating it turned out to be too complicated and we found c^* without it. Section 1.4.3 includes proofs for some of these other rules.

In some cases plain conjunction is the best alternative we found. For example, the conjunction of $x \ne y$ and $x \ne z$ can be efficiently propagated and if, later, in conflict analysis, the constraint $y \ne z$ is encountered, then it is possible to infer $\text{AllDifferent}(x, y, z)$. This is stronger that what *Combine* can infer.

`Infer` uses explanation-based inference (see Section 1.2.3) as a fallback solution. This is necessary because not all combinations of rule types are supported, not all propagators are precise (i.e., logically complete) and not all rules are precise (see R8, R9 in the table). Pseudocode of `Infer`, which is rather self-explanatory, appears in Algorithm 2.

Algorithm 2. `Infer` infers a new constraint c^* from c_1, c_2, which satisfies (1.9) and (1.10), the requirements listed in Section 1.3.

```
function INFER(constraint c₁, constraint c₂, node pivot, node-set F)
    F' = GETNEWSET (F, pivot);
    if the combination of c₁, c₂ is supported then
        con = Combine (c₁,c₂, pivot);            ▷ One of the rules in Table 1.
        if F', con ⊢cp ⊥ then return con;         ▷ con satisfies Invar1
    e₁ ← explain(c₁, parents(pivot), pivot);    ▷ Fallback: use explanations.
    e₂ ← explain(c₂, F, ⊥);
    return resolve(e₁,e₂,pivot);                 ▷ Signed resolution
```

1.4.1. A Generic Inference Rule: *Combine*

Let S be some set of values. Then it is not hard to see that the following is a contradiction for any constraint $c(x, \vec{y})$:

$$c(x,\vec{y}) \wedge x \in S \wedge \forall x' \in S.\, \neg c(x', \vec{y}), \tag{1.14}$$

or, equivalently, that the following implication is valid:

$$c(x,\vec{y}) \to (x \notin S \vee \exists x' \in S.\, c(x', \vec{y})) \tag{1.15}$$

Let $\mathcal{X}$ denote the set of values of x which have no support in $D'_{\vec{y}}$:

$$\mathcal{X} = \{x' \mid \forall \vec{y}' \in D'_{\vec{y}} .\, \neg c_{1 \wedge 2}(x', \vec{y}')\} \tag{1.16}$$

Instantiating (1.15) with $c_{1 \wedge 2}$ for c and with $\mathcal{X}$ for S yields the inference rule that we call *Combine*:

$$\frac{c_{1 \wedge 2}(x, \vec{y})}{(x \notin \mathcal{X} \vee \exists x' \in \mathcal{X}.c_{1 \wedge 2}(x', \vec{y}))} \;\; (Combine) \tag{1.17}$$

Since (1.17) is just an instantiation of (1.15), then (1.17) is clearly sound, and hence (1.9) is satisfied. To satisfy (1.10) we first prove logical entailment ($\vDash$), which is weaker than the requirement of (1.10) for provability ($\vdash_{cp}$).

Lemma 1.1. *For* $c^* \doteq (x \notin \mathcal{X} \vee \exists x' \in \mathcal{X}.c_{1 \wedge 2}(x', \vec{y}))$, *the following relation holds:* $c^*, D_x', D'_{\vec{y}} \vDash \bot$.

Proof. Falsely assume that c^* is satisfied for an assignment of values $a \in D_x', \vec{b} \in D'_{\vec{y}}$ to $x, \vec{y}$, respectively. Consider the two disjuncts of c^*:

- Suppose $x \notin \mathcal{X}$ is satisfied. Considering the definition of $\mathcal{X}$ in (1.16), this implies that a is supported in $c_{1 \wedge 2}$, or formally

$$\exists \vec{y}' \in D'_{\vec{y}}.c_{1 \wedge 2}(a, \vec{y}') \tag{1.18}$$

Based on *Invar1* we know that $c_{1\wedge2}(x,\vec{y}), D_x', D_{\neg y}' \vDash \perp$, and hence $\forall x \in D_x' \neg \exists \vec{y} \in D_{\neg y}'. c_{1\wedge2}(x,\vec{y})$, and particularly for $x = a$, $\neg \exists \vec{y} \in D_{\neg y}'. c_{1\wedge2}(a,\vec{y})$, which contradicts (1.18).

- Now suppose $\exists x' {\in} \mathcal{X}. c_{1\wedge2}(x',\vec{y})$ is satisfied. Expanding $\mathcal{X}$ and substituting $\vec{y}$ with its assignment $\vec{b}$ yields

$$\exists x'. \forall \vec{y}' \in D_{\neg y}'. \neg c_{1\wedge2}(x',\vec{y}') \wedge c_{1\wedge2}(x',\vec{b})$$

Since $\vec{b} \in D_{\neg y}'$ and $\neg c_{1\wedge2}(x',\vec{y}')$ is satisfied for all $\vec{y}' \in D_{\neg y}'$, then it is satisfied for $\vec{y}' = \vec{b}$. This implies a contradiction: $\exists x'. \neg c_{1\wedge2}(x',\vec{b}) \wedge c_{1\wedge2}(x',\vec{b})$.

Hence, $x \in D_x', \vec{y} \in D_{\neg y}'$ falsifies c^*, which completes our proof.

It is trivial to see that this lemma implies (1.10) when $\vdash_{cp}$ is precise constraint propagation. When imprecise propagation is involved, e.g., $\vdash_{cp}$ is defined by bounds consistency [37], HCSP checks whether the constraint happens to be conflicting, and if not it falls back to clausal explanation.

1.4.1.1. The relative strength of *Combine*.

We prove below two observations about the strength of *Combine*:

- There is no alternative to $\mathcal{X}$ for replacing S in (1.15) that makes the resulting constraint stronger,

- The signed clause that we obtain through the explanation mechanism – see Section 1.2.3 – cannot yield a stronger consequent.

Lemma 1.2. *Consider all possible formulas of the form $\psi(x,\vec{y}) \equiv (x \notin P \vee \varphi(\vec{y}))$, for a given set P. The strongest possible $\varphi(\vec{y})$, which meets all the requirements is $\exists x' \in P. c_{1\wedge2}(x',\vec{y})$. In other* *words, for any* $\varphi(\vec{y})$ *which makes* $\psi(x,\vec{y})$ *meet the requirements, the following is satisfied:*

$$\exists x' \in P.c_{1\wedge 2}(x',\vec{y}) \vDash \varphi(\vec{y})$$

Proof. By negation, assume that there is an assignment $\vec{b}$ to $\vec{y}$ which satisfies $\exists x' \in P.c_{1\wedge 2}(x',\vec{b})$ but not $\varphi(\vec{b})$. This means that there is an $a \in P$ which satisfies $c_{1\wedge 2}(a,\vec{b})$ when $\neg\varphi(\vec{b})$. Because $c_{1\wedge 2}(a,\vec{b})$ is satisfied, (1.9) mandate that $\psi(a,\vec{b})$ should also be satisfied. According to the definition of ψ we conclude that either $a \notin P$ or $\varphi(\vec{b})$ have to be satisfied. But since $\neg\varphi(\vec{b})$ and, as defined, $a \in P$ we conclude that ψ is unsatisfied with $a,\vec{b}$. This conflict the initial assumption. This leads to the conclusion that if $\exists x' \in P.c_{1\wedge 2}(x',\vec{y})$ is satisfied, then $\varphi(\vec{y})$ must also be satisfied.

Note that this lemma refers to P, and not $\mathcal{X}$. This means that it does not rule out the possibility where $\exists x' \in P.c_{1\wedge 2}(x',\vec{y})$ is stronger than $\exists x' \in \mathcal{X}.c_{1\wedge 2}(x',\vec{y})$. It is quite possible that the smaller the set P is and the weaker the literal $x \notin P$ is, the stronger $\exists x' \in P.c_{1\wedge 2}(x',\vec{y})$ becomes.

Lemma 1.3. *Consider all possible* $\psi(x,\vec{y}) \equiv (x \notin P \vee \exists x' \in P.c_{1\wedge 2}(\vec{y}))$ *which satisfy the requirements.* P *must satisfy*

$$D_x' \subseteq P$$

Proof. By negation assume that $D_x' \not\subseteq P$, i.e., there is a value a such that $a \in D_x'$ and $a \notin P$. Consider how this affects (1.10). According to (1.10)

$$x \notin P \vee \exists x' \in P.c_{1\wedge 2}(x',\vec{y}), D_x', D_y' \vdash_{cp} \bot$$

Since $a \in D_x'$ then we can replace x with a in the above formula, and get

$$a \notin P \vee \exists x' \in P.c_{1\wedge 2}(x',\vec{y}), D_y' \vdash_{cp} \bot$$

But since a was defined such that $a \notin P$ then the above formula becomes

$$\text{true} \vee \exists x' \in P.c_{1 \wedge 2}(x', \vec{y}), D'_y \vdash_{cp} \bot$$

This basically says $\text{true} \vdash_{cp} \bot$, which is impossible. It implies that the assumption that $D_x' \not\subseteq P$ is incorrect.

Lemma 1.4. *Consider all possible* $\psi(x, \vec{y}) \equiv (x \notin P \vee \exists x' \in P.c_{1 \wedge 2}(\vec{y}))$ *which satisfy the requirements.* P *must satisfy*

$$P \subseteq \mathcal{X},$$

where $\mathcal{X}$ *was defined above as*

$$\mathcal{X} = \left\{ x' \mid \forall \vec{y}' \in D'_y . \left[\neg c_{1 \wedge 2}(x', \vec{y}') \right] \right\}$$

Proof. According to the definition of $\mathcal{X}$, the lemma can be reformulated as

$$\forall a \in P \; \forall \vec{y}' \in D'_y . \left[\neg c_{1 \wedge 2}(a, \vec{y}') \right]$$

Assume, by negation, that this is not correct. In other words there are $a \in P$ and $\vec{b} \in D'_y$ such that $c_{1 \wedge 2}(a, \vec{b})$. We will show that this conflicts (1.10). From (1.10) we know that

$$x \notin P \vee \exists x' \in P.c_{1 \wedge 2}(x', \vec{y}), D_x', D'_y \vdash_{cp} \bot$$

Since $\vec{b} \in D'_y$, the formula above implies

$$x \notin P \vee \exists x' \in P.c_{1 \wedge 2}(x', \vec{b}), D_x' \vdash_{cp} \bot$$

Assuming $\vdash_{cp}$ is precise this implies

$$\forall x \in D_x' . \neg \left[x \notin P \vee \exists x' \in P.c_{1 \wedge 2}(x', \vec{b}) \right]$$

We now push the negation down, and get

$$\forall x \in D_x'.\left[x \in P \wedge \forall x' \in P.\neg c_{1\wedge 2}(x',\vec{b}) \right]$$

First, we see that this implies $D_x' \subseteq P$. Since x is independent in the formula we conclude that

$$\forall x' \in P.\neg c_{1\wedge 2}(x',\vec{b})$$

Now we go back to $a \in P$ and $\vec{b} \in D_y'$ which guarantee $c_{1\wedge 2}(a,\vec{b})$, and combine it with the formula above. This means that we can assign $x' = a$, which leads to $\neg c_{1\wedge 2}(a,\vec{b})$, which conflicts with the guarantee of $c_{1\wedge 2}(a,\vec{b})$. This means that our assumption that the lemma is incorrect was wrong, hence $P \subseteq \mathcal{X}$.

This lemma implies that the literal $x \notin \mathcal{X}$ is the strongest possible. This does not imply anything regarding the strength of the second part of the formula, i.e., $\exists x' \in \mathcal{X}.\left[c_{1\wedge 2}(x',\vec{y}) \right]$ may be weakened by strengthening $x \notin P$. Also note that the previous lemmas bound P to $D_x' \subseteq P \subseteq \mathcal{X}$.

Theorem 1.1. *There is no alternative $\psi(x,\vec{y})$, different than c^*, which is stronger than c^* with $\mathcal{X}$. In other words*

$$\psi(x,\vec{y}) \not\equiv \left[x \notin \mathcal{X} \vee \exists x' \in \mathcal{X}.c_{1\wedge 2}(x',\vec{y}) \right]$$

$$\Downarrow$$

$$\left(\psi(x,\vec{y}) \not\models \left[x \notin \mathcal{X} \vee \exists x' \in \mathcal{X}.c_{1\wedge 2}(x',\vec{y}) \right] \right)$$

Proof. Recall that we require that $\psi(x,\vec{y})$ to be of the form $x \notin P \vee \varphi(\vec{y})$. Lemma 1.2 shows that for a given P, the strongest possible $\varphi(\vec{y})$ is $\exists x' \in P.c_{1\wedge 2}(x',\vec{y})$. This leaves us to prove that

$$x \notin P \vee \exists x' \in P.c_{1\wedge 2}(x',\vec{y})$$

is not stronger than

$$x \notin \mathcal{X} \vee \exists x' \in \mathcal{X}.c_{1\wedge 2}(x',\vec{y})$$

According to Lemma 1.4 because P complies with the given requirements then $P \subseteq \mathcal{X}$. If $P = \mathcal{X}$ the two formulas are equivalent and neither are stronger, otherwise $P \subset \mathcal{X}$. Assume that $P \subset \mathcal{X}$, this means that there is a such that $a \in \mathcal{X}$ and $a \notin P$. As a result, for $x = a$ the literal $x \notin P$ is true and the literal $x \notin \mathcal{X}$ is false. In this situation the P based formula, i.e., $x \notin P \vee \exists x' \in P.c_{1 \wedge 2}(x', \vec{y})$ is true, but the $\mathcal{X}$ based formula depends solely on

$$\exists x' \in \mathcal{X}.c_{1 \wedge 2}(x', \vec{y})$$

We look for a case where this formula is falsified when $x = a$. It can be falsified, i.e., not a tautology, since otherwise this would conflict (1.10). This means that there is an assignment $\vec{b}$ to $\vec{y}$ such that the formula is falsified. We have found $x = a$ and $y = \vec{b}$ for which the P-based formula is satisfied and the $\mathcal{X}$-based formula is falsified. This means that the P-based formula is not stronger than the $\mathcal{X}$-based formula. Because the P-based formula is the strongest possible form of $x \notin P \vee \varphi(\vec{y})$, any $\psi(x, \vec{y})$ that satisfies the requirements is not stronger than

$$x \notin \mathcal{X} \vee \exists x' \in \mathcal{X}.c_{1 \wedge 2}(x, \vec{y})$$

Note that this theorem does not say that, with $\mathcal{X}$, the resulting constraint is stronger than any other possibility; it says that no other constraint is stronger. In other words, there need not be a strict ordering of constraints.

1.4.2. Selected Rules Based on Instantiating *Combine*

We now instantiate *Combine* (1.17) with several specific constraints of interest. The derivations rely on various properties of the domains before propagation D_x', D_y' and right after it D_x'', D_y''. By definition

$$c_1, D_x', D_y' \vdash_{cp} (x \in D_x'' \wedge y \in D_y'') \tag{1.19}$$

We make the following observations about these domains:

1. The domain of x, and possibly domains of variables in $\vec{y}$, are reduced by c_1:

$$D_x'' \subset D_x', \quad D_y'' \subseteq D_y'. \tag{1.20}$$

2. Owing to *Invar1*, in the context of D_x'', D_y'', c_2 detects a conflict:

$$c_2(x, \vec{y}), D_x'', D_y'' \vdash_{cp} \bot. \tag{1.21}$$

3. c_1 cannot detect a conflict on its own in the context of D_x', D_y':

$$c_1, D_x', D_y' \nvdash_{cp} \bot. \tag{1.22}$$

We now use these observations when instantiating *Combine*.

Rule R1: $c_1 \doteq x \in X_1 \vee A_1(\vec{y}) \qquad c_2 \doteq x \in X_2 \vee A_2(\vec{y})$

A_1 and A_2 are disjunctions of zero or more literals over the variables of $\vec{y}$. Expanding $c_{1 \wedge 2}$ in (1.16) yields

$$\mathcal{X} = \{x' \mid \forall \vec{y}' \in D_y'. (x' \not\in X_1 \wedge \neg A_1(\vec{y})) \vee (x' \not\in X_2 \wedge \neg A_2(\vec{y}))\}$$

From (1.19) and (1.20) we know that $c_1(x, \vec{y}), D_x', D_y' \vdash_{cp} x \in D_x''$ and $D_x' \neq D_x''$, which implies that $A_1(\vec{y}), D_y' \models \bot$, and consequently simplifies the above to

$$\mathcal{X} = \{x' \mid \forall \vec{y}' \in D_y'.' \not\in X_1 \vee (x' \not\in X_2 \wedge \neg A_2(\vec{y}))\}$$

Note that the propagation of c_1 in the context of D_y', D_x' results in $D_x'' = X_1 \cap D_x'$ and $D_y' = D_y''$. Since $D_y' = D_y''$ and, according to (1.21), $c_2(x, \vec{y}), D_x'', D_y'' \vdash_{cp} \bot$, then $A_2(\vec{y}), D_y' \models \bot$. This means that $\forall \vec{y}' \in D_y'.\neg A_2(\vec{y})$, which simplifies the above formula to

$$\mathcal{X} = \{x' \mid \forall \vec{y}' \in D_y'.' \not\in X_1 \vee x' \not\in X_2\}$$

Since the inner part does not depend on $\vec{y}$ we can further simplify it to

$$\mathcal{X} = \{x' \mid x' \notin X_1 \vee x' \notin X_2\}$$

Using this definition of $\mathcal{X}$ we examine c^*:

$$c^*(x, D'_{\bar{y}}) = (x \in (X_1 \cap X_2) \vee \exists x' \notin (X_1 \cap X_2).c_{1 \wedge 2}(x', \vec{y}))$$

Let $A' = \exists x' \notin (X_1 \cap X_2).c_{1 \wedge 2}(x', \vec{y})$. This simplifies the above to

$$c^*(x, D'_{\bar{y}}) = (x \in (X_1 \cap X_2) \vee A') \tag{1.23}$$

We split the quantifier in A' into three cases:

$$A' = (\exists x' \in (X_1 \setminus X_2).c_{1 \wedge 2}(x', \vec{y}) \vee,$$

$$\exists x' \in (X_2 \setminus X_1).c_{1 \wedge 2}(x', \vec{y}) \vee,$$

$$\exists x' \notin (X_2 \cup X_1).c_{1 \wedge 2}(x', \vec{y}))$$

After taking the definitions of $c_{1 \wedge 2}$, c_1, and c_2 into account:

$$A' = (\exists x' \in (X_1 \setminus X_2).A_2(\vec{y}) \vee,$$

$$\exists x' \in (X_2 \setminus X_1).A_1(\vec{y}) \vee,$$

$$\exists x' \notin (X_2 \cup X_1).A_1(\vec{y}) \wedge A_2(\vec{y}))$$

Next, we eliminate the $\exists$ quantifier and get

$$A' = ((X_1 \setminus X_2 \neq \varnothing \wedge A_2(\vec{y})) \vee,$$

$$(X_2 \setminus X_1 \neq \varnothing \wedge A_1(\vec{y})) \vee,$$

$$((X_2 \cup X_1)^C \neq \varnothing \wedge A_1(\vec{y}) \wedge A_2(\vec{y})))$$

We simplify this further by showing that $X_1 \setminus X_2 \neq \varnothing$ and $X_2 \setminus X_1 \neq \varnothing$, which leads to $A' = (A_1(\vec{y}) \vee A_2(\vec{y}))$. According to (1.19), (1.20), $(x \in X_1 \vee A_1(\vec{y})), D'_x, D'_{\bar{y}} \vDash x \in D''_x$, where $D''_x \subset D'_x$, which implies that $A_1(\vec{y}), D'_{\bar{y}} \vDash \perp$. Similarly $(x \in X_1 \vee A_1(\vec{y})), D''_x, D'_{\bar{y}} \vDash \perp$

implies that $A_2(\vec{y}), D'_{\vec{y}} \models \perp$. These facts show that A_1 and A_2 are falsified in this context, meaning that we can focus only on $x \in X_1$ and $x \in X_2$ parts of c_1 and c_2 there. For the following we assume that $\vdash_{cp}$ for signed-clauses is precise, i.e., $\psi \models \phi$ iff $\psi \vdash_{cp} \phi$.

- $X_2 \setminus X_1 \neq \varnothing$. Because $c_2(x,\vec{y}), D_x', D'_{\vec{y}} \not\vdash_{cp} \perp$ and $\vdash_{cp}$ is assumed to be precise then there is an assignment $a \in D_x'$, $\vec{b} \in D'_{\vec{y}}$ such that $c_2(a,\vec{b})$ is satisfied. Since $A_2(\vec{y}), D'_{\vec{y}} \models \perp$ and $\vec{b} \in D'_{\vec{y}}$ we know that $A_2(\vec{b}) \models \perp$, which implies that $a \in X_2$. Further, since $(c_1(x,\vec{y}) \wedge c_2(x,\vec{y})), D_x', D'_{\vec{y}} \models \perp$ and $c_2(a,\vec{b})$ is satisfied then $c_1(a,\vec{b}) \models \perp$, i.e., $(a \in X_1 \vee A_1(\vec{b})), D'_{\vec{y}} \models \perp$. This leads to $a \notin X_1$, which together with $c \in X_2$ implies $X_2 \setminus X_1 \neq \varnothing$.

- $X_1 \setminus X_2 \neq \varnothing$. Because $c_1(x,\vec{y}), D_x', D'_{\vec{y}} \not\models \perp$ and since $A_1(\vec{y}), D'_{\vec{y}} \models \perp$ we know that there is at least one element $a \in D_x'$ such that $a \in X_1$. Again, since $(c_1(a,\vec{y}) \wedge c_2(a,\vec{y})), D'_{\vec{y}} \models \perp$ and $c_1(a,\vec{y}), D'_{\vec{y}} \not\models \perp$ then we know that $c_2(a,\vec{y}), D'_{\vec{y}} \models \perp$. This implies that $a \in X_2 \models \perp$, i.e., $a \notin X_2$. Since $a \notin X_2$ and $a \in X_1$ then it follows that $X_1 \setminus X_2 \neq \varnothing$.

These two facts simplify A' to

$$A' = (A_2(\vec{y}) \vee A_1(\vec{y})),$$

and correspondingly, according to (1.23),

$$c^*(x,\vec{y}) = (x \in (X_1 \cap X_2) \vee A_1(\vec{y}) \vee A_2(\vec{y})) \qquad (1.24)$$

Note the equivalence of (1.24) and the result of signed resolution in (1.1).

Rule R2: $c_1 \doteq y_2 - x \geq k_2 \qquad c_2 \doteq x - y_1 \geq k_1$

Expanding $c_{1 \wedge 2}$ in (1.16) yields

$$\mathcal{X} = \left\{ x \mid \forall \vec{y}' \in D'_y . \left[y_2 - x < k_2 \vee x - y_1 < k_1 \right] \right\} =$$

$$= \left\{ x \mid \max(D_{y_2}') - x < k_2 \vee x - \min(D_{y_1}') < k_1 \right\} =$$

$$= \left\{ x \mid \max(D_{y_2}') - k_2 < x \vee x < k_1 + \min(D_{y_1}') \right\}$$

The complement of $\mathcal{X}$ can be written as

$$\mathcal{X}^c = \left[k_1 + \min(D_{y_1}'), \max(D_{y_2}') - k_2 \right] \tag{1.25}$$

Recall (1.16): $x \notin \mathcal{X} \vee \exists x' \in \mathcal{X} . c_{1 \wedge 2}(x', \vec{y})$. The right disjunct is equal to:

$$\exists x' . x' \in \mathcal{X} \wedge \left[y_2 - x' \geq k_2 \wedge x' - y_1 \geq k_1 \right] =$$

$$= \exists x' . x' \in \mathcal{X} \wedge \left[y_2 - k_2 \geq x' \geq y_1 + k_1 \right] =$$

$$= \exists x' . x' \in \mathcal{X} \wedge x' \in \left[y_1 + k_1, y_2 - k_2 \right] \tag{1.26}$$

We use (1.25) to rewrite (1.26):

$$\exists x' . x' \notin \left[k_1 + \min(D_{y_1}'), \max(D_{y_2}') - k_2 \right] \wedge x' \in \left[y_1 + k_1, y_2 - k_2 \right],$$

which implies

$$\left[y_1 + k_1, y_2 - k_2 \right] \not\subseteq \left[k_1 + \min(D_{y_1}'), \max(D_{y_2}') - k_2 \right] =$$

$$= \left[y_1, y_2 - k_2 - k_1 \right] \not\subseteq \left[\min(D_{y_1}'), \max(D_{y_2}') - k_2 - k_1 \right]$$

Hence, the rule is

$$\frac{y_2 - x \geq k_2 \qquad x - y_1 \geq k_1}{\begin{array}{c} (x \in \left[k_1 + \min(D_{y_1}'), \max(D_{y_2}') - k_2 \right] \vee \\[6pt] \left[y_1, y_2 - k_2 - k_1 \right] \not\subseteq \left[\min(D_{y_1}'), \max(D_{y_2}') - k_2 - k_1 \right]) \end{array}} \tag{1.27}$$

Rule R6: $c_1 \doteq [x,y] \not\subseteq [a_1,b_1]$ $\qquad$ $c_2 \doteq [y,x] \not\subseteq [a_2,b_2]$

We have $c_1 \wedge c_2 \rightarrow x = y$, because otherwise, e.g., if $x < y$, then c_2 is trivially false. Since $x = y$ then their joint value cannot be contained in either of the ranges $[a_1,b_1],[a_2,b_2]$. Hence,

$$c_{1 \wedge 2} = (x = y) \wedge x \not\in [a_1,b_1] \wedge x \not\in [a_2,b_2], \qquad (1.28)$$

which implies

$$\mathcal{X} = \{x' \,|\, \forall y \in D_y \,'. \, x \neq y \vee x \in [a_1,b_1] \vee x \in [a_2,b_2]]\} =$$

$$= D_y \,'^C \cup [a_1,b_1] \cup [a_2,b_2]$$

The consequent of *Combine* is

$$c^* = (x \not\in \mathcal{X} \vee \exists x \in \mathcal{X}. \, x = y \wedge x \not\in [a_1,b_1] \wedge x \not\in [a_2,b_2]) =$$

$$= (x \not\in \mathcal{X} \vee (y \in \mathcal{X} \wedge y \not\in [a_1,b_1] \wedge y \not\in [a_2,b_2])) =$$

$$= (x \not\in \mathcal{X} \vee ((y \in [a_1,b_1] \vee y \in [a_2,b_2] \vee y \not\in D_y \,') \wedge y \not\in [a_1,b_1] \wedge y \not\in [a_2,b_2])) =$$

$$= (x \not\in \mathcal{X} \vee (y \not\in D_y \,' \wedge y \not\in [a_1,b_1] \wedge y \not\in [a_2,b_2])) =$$

$$= (x \in (D_y \,' \setminus ([a_1,b_1] \cup [a_2,b_2])) \vee y \not\in (D_y \,' \cup [a_1,b_1] \cup [a_2,b_2]))$$

Hence, the resulting rule in this case is

$$\frac{[x,y] \not\subseteq [a_1,b_1] \qquad [y,x] \not\subseteq [a_2,b_2]}{(x \in (D_y \,' \setminus ([a_1,b_1] \cup [a_2,b_2])) \vee y \not\in (D_y \,' \cup [a_1,b_1] \cup [a_2,b_2]))} \quad (1.29)$$

Rule R7: $c_1 \doteq xor(x,\vec{y})$ $\qquad$ $c_2 \doteq xor(x,\vec{z})$

Here $\vec{y} \doteq y_1,\ldots,y_n$ and $\vec{z} \doteq z_1,\ldots,z_m$. We assume that $\vec{y}$ and $\vec{z}$ are fully assigned and x is not; we further assume that, without lose of generality, c_1 propagates the value of x and c_2 detects a conflict.

Under these assumptions it is clear that c_1 and c_2 cannot be simultaneously satisfied by either $x = 0$ or $x = 1$, and hence by definition $X = \{0,1\}$, and Combine amounts to:

$$\frac{xor(x,\vec{y}) \qquad xor(x,\vec{z})}{x \notin \{0,1\} \vee \exists x' \in \{0,1\}.\left[xor(x',\vec{y}) \wedge xor(x',\vec{z})\right]}$$

We can replace $x \notin \{0,1\}$ with false and obtain:

$$\frac{xor(x,\vec{y}) \qquad xor(x,\vec{z})}{\exists x'.\left[xor(x',\vec{y}) \wedge xor(x',\vec{z})\right]}$$

It is not hard to see that the consequent is equivalent to $xor(\vec{y}) = xor(\vec{z})$, and hence also to $xor(\vec{y},\vec{z},1)$, which brings us to the desired rule:

$$\frac{xor(x,\vec{y}) \qquad xor(x,\vec{z})}{xor(\vec{y},\vec{z},1)}$$

Note that variables that are shared by $\vec{y}$ and $\vec{z}$ can be removed from the *xor* predicate without changing its value.

1.4.3. Selected Rules not Based on *Combine*

We now describe several rules that are not based on *Combine*.

Rule R3: $c_1 \doteq y_1 \leq x \qquad c_2 \doteq [x,y_2] \not\subseteq [a,b]$

We assume that at the point of conflict, replacing c_2 with $x \leq y_2$ makes $c_{1 \wedge 2}$ too weak to detect the conflict. Otherwise we simply use rule R2. Based on this assumption, which we denote by ψ, we now develop $\mathcal{X}$. ψ means that $[x,y_2] \not\subseteq [a,b]$ removes at least one value from $D_x{}'$ more than $x \leq y_2$. The extra value removed α should satisfy

$$\alpha \leq \max(D_{y_2}{}') \wedge \forall y_2 \in D_{y_2}{}'.[\alpha,y_2] \subseteq [a,b]$$

This means that

$$\alpha \leq \max(D_{y_2}') \wedge [\alpha, \max(D_{y_2}')] \subseteq [a,b]$$

From this we conclude that

$$a \leq \alpha \leq \max(D_{y_2}') \leq b$$

We require that neither constraints detect a conflict by themselves with D_{y_1}', D_{y_2}', and D_x', but when propagated consecutively they reach a conflict. This means that there is at least one value $\alpha \in D_x'$ such that

$$\exists y_1 \in D_{y_1}'.y_1 \leq \alpha \wedge$$
$$\forall y_2 \in D_{y_2}'.[\alpha, y_2] \subseteq [a,b]$$

This can be simplified to

$$\min(D_{y_1}') \leq \alpha \wedge [\alpha, \max(D_{y_2}')] \subseteq [a,b]$$

If such α exists then it can be equal to $\max(D_x')$ such that

$$\min(D_{y_1}') \leq \max(D_x') \wedge [\max(D_x'), \max(D_{y_2}')] \subseteq [a,b]$$

To summarize, we have concluded that

$$a \leq \max(D_{y_2}') \leq b \wedge \min(D_{y_1}') \leq \max(D_x') \wedge [\max(D_x'),$$
$$\max(D_{y_2}')] \subseteq [a,b]$$

The interval expression can be expanded such that

$$a \leq \max(D_{y_2}') \leq b \wedge \min(D_{y_1}') \leq \max(D_x') \wedge (\max(D_x') > \max(D_{y_2}') \vee$$
$$(a \leq \max(D_x') \wedge \max(D_{y_2}') \leq b))$$

This is simplified to

$$a \leq \max(D_{y_2}') \leq b \wedge \min(D_{y_1}') \leq \max(D_x') \wedge (\max(D_x') > \max(D_{y_2}') \vee$$
$$a \leq \max(D_x'))$$

Since $a \leq \max(D_{y_2}')$ then if $\max(D_x') > \max(D_{y_2}')$ is satisfied then $\max(D_x') > \max(D_{y_2}') \geq a$, i.e., $D_x' \geq a$, is implied. This means that $\max(D_x') > \max(D_{y_2}')$ is redundant in the above expression, generating:

$$a \leq \max(D_{y_2}') \leq b \wedge \min(D_{y_1}') \leq \max(D_x') \wedge a \leq \max(D_x')$$

We will depict this as

$$\psi' \triangleq (a \leq \max(D_{y_2}') \leq b \wedge \min(D_{y_1}') \leq \max(D_x') \wedge a \leq \max(D_x')) \quad (1.30)$$

We require that the resulting constraint be of the form

$$x \notin \mathcal{X} \vee [y_1, y_2] \nsubseteq [a^*, b^*]$$

and meet the soundness and completeness requirements. First we look for $\mathcal{X}$ which is defined by

$$\mathcal{X} = \left\{ x' \mid \forall y_1 \in D_{y_1}' \forall y_2 \in D_{y_2}'. [y_1 > x' \vee [x', y_2] \subseteq [a, b]] \right\}$$

We expand the interval operator to

$$\mathcal{X} = \left\{ x' \mid \forall y_1 \in D_{y_1}' \forall y_2 \in D_{y_2}'. [y_1 > x' \vee x' > y_2 \vee (a \leq x' \wedge y_2 \leq b)] \right\}$$

Since y_1 is bounded only from below and y_2 only from above then we can safely rewrite this expression for the worse cases of y_1 and y_2 which are $\min(D_{y_1}')$ and $\max(D_{y_2}')$:

$$\mathcal{X} = \left\{ x' \mid \min(D_{y_1}') > x' \vee x' > \max(D_{y_2}') \vee (a \leq x' \wedge \max(D_{y_2}') \leq b) \right\}$$

From the initial assumptions, as expressed by Equation (1.30), we know that $\max(D_{y_2}') \leq b$ is true. From, this we conclude that that $(a \leq x' \wedge \max(D_{y_2}') \leq b)$ can be simplified to $a \leq x'$. This yields

$$\mathcal{X} = \left\{ x' \mid \min(D_{y_1}') > x' \vee x' > \max(D_{y_2}') \vee a \leq x' \right\}$$

Equation (1.30) also states that $a \leq \max(D_{y_2}')$ which makes $x' > \max(D_{y_2}')$ redundant in $x' > \max(D_{y_2}') \vee a \leq x$. So the expression becomes

$$\mathcal{X} = \{x' \mid x' < \min(D_{y_1}') \vee a \leq x'\} \tag{1.31}$$

We propose the following consequent:

$$c^* \doteq x \notin \mathcal{X} \vee [y_1, y_2] \not\subseteq [\min(D_{y_1}'), b] = \tag{1.32}$$

$$= a > x \geq \min(D_{y_1}') \vee [y_1, y_2] \not\subseteq [\min(D_{y_1}'), b] \tag{1.33}$$

Note that c^* still follows our general pattern, by which the pivot is separated and not referred-to by the other disjunct. Since we cannot rely on the correctness of the general rule, we now prove that (1.33) satisfies (1.9) and (1.10):

- Eq. (1.9): Falsely assume the contrary, i.e., there are x, y_1, y_2 such that

$$a \leq \max(D_{y_2}') \leq b \wedge \min(D_{y_1}') \leq \max(D_x') \wedge a \leq \max(D_x') \wedge y_1 \leq x \wedge$$

$$[x, y_2] \not\subseteq [a, b] \wedge x \in \mathcal{X} \wedge [y_1, y_2] \subseteq [\min(D_{y_1}'), b]$$

Expanding $\mathcal{X}$ yields

$$a \leq \max(D_{y_2}') \leq b \wedge \min(D_{y_1}') \leq \max(D_x') \wedge a \leq \max(D_x') \wedge y_1 \leq x \wedge$$

$$[x, y_2] \not\subseteq [a, b] \wedge (x < \min(D_{y_1}') \vee a \leq x) \wedge [y_1, y_2] \subseteq [\min(D_{y_1}'), b]$$

If $x < \min(D_{y_1}')$ then $y_1 \leq x$ implies $y_1 < \min(D_{y_1}')$ which conflicts $[y_1, y_2] \subseteq [\min(D_{y_1}'), b]$. Otherwise, $x \geq a$ and $[x, y_2] \not\subseteq [a, b]$ implies $y_2 > b$ which conflicts $[y_1, y_2] \subseteq [\min(D_{y_1}'), b]$.

- Eq. (1.10): We need to check that

$$\psi' \to (x \notin \mathcal{X} \vee [y_1, y_2] \not\subseteq [\min(D_{y_1}'), b], D_x', D_{y_1}'D_{y_2}' \vdash \varnothing),$$

where ψ' is an expression defined by Equation (1.30). Falsely assume that

$$\psi' \to \exists x \in D_x' \exists y_1 \in D_{y_1}' \exists y_2 \in D_{y_2}'. x \notin \mathcal{X} \vee [y_1, y_2] \not\subseteq [\min(D_{y_1}'), b]$$

The part of x can be simplified such that

$$\psi' \to \exists y_1 \in D_{y_1}' \exists y_2 \in D_{y_2}'. D_x' \setminus \mathcal{X} \neq \varnothing \vee [y_1, y_2] \not\subseteq [\min(D_{y_1}'), b]$$

But according to the construction of $\mathcal{X}$ we know that $D_x' \setminus \mathcal{X} = \varnothing$, so the expression is further simplified to

$$\psi' \to \exists y_1 \in D_{y_1}' \exists y_2 \in D_{y_2}'. [y_1, y_2] \not\subseteq [\min(D_{y_1}'), b]$$

or

$$\psi' \to \exists y_1 \in D_{y_1}' \exists y_2 \in D_{y_2}'. y_1 \leq y_2 \wedge (y_1 < \min(D_{y_1}') \vee b < y_2)$$

Since y_1 is bounded only from above and y_2 is bounded from below then we can replace y_1 with $\min(D_{y_1}')$ and y_2 with $\max(D_{y_2}')$:

$$\psi' \to [\min(D_{y_1}') \leq \max(D_{y_2}') \wedge$$
$$(\min(D_{y_1}') < \min(D_{y_1}') \vee b < \max(D_{y_2}'))]$$

$\min(D_{y_1}') < \min(D_{y_1}')$ is clearly false, and from the definition of ψ' we know that $b < \max(D_{y_2}')$ is false. This falsifies $\min(D_{y_1}') < \min(D_{y_1}') \vee b < \max(D_{y_2}')$ from the expression, hence the whole expression is also falsified. Hence our assumption was wrong, i.e., (1.10) is not violated.

To summarize, the rule is

$$\frac{y_1 \leq x \qquad [x, y_2] \not\subseteq [a, b]}{a > x \geq \min(D_{y_1}') \vee [y_1, y_2] \not\subseteq [\min(D_{y_1}'), b]} \tag{1.34}$$

Rule R8: $c_1 \doteq (y \leq x + k_1)$ $\qquad$ $c_2 = (x \leq y + k_2)$

Isolating $x - y$ on both sides yields $c_{1 \wedge 2}(x, y) = -k_1 \leq x - y \leq k_2$, which is false if $k_1 + k_2 < 0$. Since it is simply a conjunction of the input constraints, then (1.9) and (1.10) are satisfied trivially.

1.5. Experimental Results

We performed two sets of experiments as described below. All experiments were ran on a 4 core Intel Xeon 2.5 GHz.

The 2009 CSP solver competition benchmarks. Here we used a subset of benchmarks of the Fourth International CSP Solver competition [9] (this was the last CSP competition, before the MiniZinc challenge started). Specifically out of over 7000 in the competition's satisfiability benchmark-set, we focused on the 2162 benchmarks that have at least one comparison operator from $\{<, \leq, \geq, >\}$ (the reason being that the rules in Table 1.1 refer to combinations of constraints based on these operators and constraints that are consequents of these rules). The CPU time limit was set to 1200 seconds. Out-of-memory and time-outs are called 'fails' in the discussion below.

We compared three different settings: (1) HCSP with general constraints learning based on *Combine* (from here on – HCSP), (2) HCSP using only clause-based learning with explanations, as described in Section 1.2 (from here on – Explain)[6], and (3) Mistral [23] latest version (1.550). Fig. 1.3 compares these three engines. Memory was limited to 1 GiB. Number of fails in HCSP was 25 % less than Mistral. Number of fails of HCSP was 4.9 % less than Explain.

Fig. 1.4 compares the number of backtracks considering only non-failing runs in all solvers (log-scale). The average number of backtracks in HCSP is 2045, in Explain 4389, and in Mistral 49562. This drastic difference in the average backtrack-count indicates that the cost of learning is compensated-for by a better search.

---

[6] We emphasize that this is a far-improved engine in comparison to [34], owing to numerous optimizations that are beyond the scope of the current chapter.

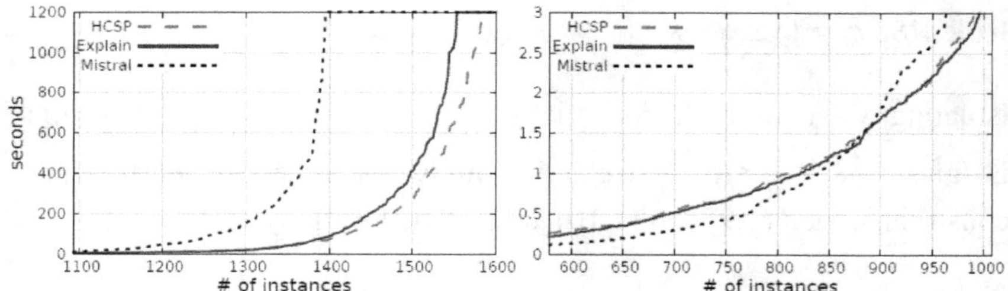

Fig. 1.3. Number of instances solved within the given time limit comparing HCSP, Explain, and Mistral. (left) Shows the time in linear scale; (right) A zoom-in of the left figure showing the cross-over between Mistral and HCSP occurring after 1-2 seconds.

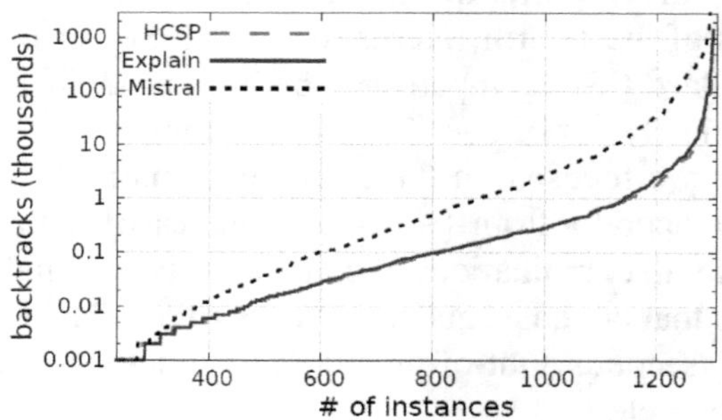

Fig 1.4. Number of backtracks considering only non-failing runs in all solvers (log-scale).

We also checked whether the difference between HCSP and Explain is affected by whether the instance is satisfiable or not. Table 1.2 summarizes this comparison.

Table 1.2. Comparing the impact of non-clausal inference on SAT and UNSAT instances. The backtracks and time refer only to instances solved by both tools. In all measures, the UNSAT cases are more affected.

	Solved		Backtracks		Time	
	SAT	UNSAT	SAT	UNSAT	SAT	UNSAT
Explain	944	666	12963.8	19211.3	41.8	47.8
HCSP	951	678	8008.1	11052.7	39.6	45.2
Difference	0.7 %	1.8 %	-38.3 %	-42.5 %	-5.3 %	-5.5 %

MiniZinc benchmarks. Given the recent results of the MiniZinc challenge, we compared HCSP and Explain to CPX and iZplus, which won the second and first places, respectively, of the 'free-search/single-core' track of the MiniZinc challenge [26]7. iZplus is based on the iZ-C constraint programming library, and includes stochastic local search for optimization problems. CPX is based on lazy clause generation (i.e., lazy reduction to SAT). We used all the 100 benchmarks of the competition, 75 of which are optimization problems. The time-limit was set to 1800 s, and the memory limit to 3 GB. All benchmarks were converted to the FlatZinc format prior to benchmarking. Tables 1.3 and 1.4 summarize the results. More detailed results can be found in [38].

Table 1.3. Comparing HCSP to other tools on optimization problems.

	Time (avg.)	*Time* (med.)	*Backtracks*	*Success*	*Opt.*	*Wins*
HCSP	1278.7	1800	**23048.1**	**70**	25	35
Explain	1312.3	1800	23150	**70**	25	39
CPX	1335.0	1800	140120.3	65	20	30
iZplus	**1275.1**	1800		66	25	**59**

Table 1.4. Comparing HCSP to other tools on satisfiability problems.

	Time (avg.)	*Time* (med.)	*Backtracks*	*Success*
HCSP	**43.1**	**1.9**	**1827.6**	**25**
Explain	211.2	5.8	1935	23
CPX	496.1	45.4	342709.3	20
iZplus	354.2	7.1		22

The columns should be interpreted as follows: *time* (avg. and median) – the number of seconds in all benchmarks, including time-out and memout cases (in which the time-out of 1800 s was assumed); *backtracks* – the number of backtracks in benchmarks in which *all* engines finished successfully *before* the time-out (i.e., in the case of Table 1.3 which is dedicated to the 75 optimization problems, all engines

---

[7] An early version of HCSP also participated in that competition and reached the 5th place. Since then we improved HCSP in multiple ways, including better data-structures and specialized code (instead of generic) to generate explanations for 'element' global constraints (an element constraint has the form var_vector[var_i] = var_0).

found the optimal value)[8]; *success* – the number of instances solved within time and memory limits, and in the case of optimization problems found a feasible solution (but not necessarily optimal); In Table 1.3 we also have *Opt.* – the number of instances, out of the 75 optimization problems, in which the solver reached optimality and proved it; and *wins* – the number of optimization instances in which the solver reached the best value among the four contenders (ties are counted).

The results show that in the optimization problems iZplus has more wins than HCSP and a slightly smaller run-time in the instances that all solvers solved, and in all other criteria HCSP is better (the *wins* column depends on the contenders. If HCSP and Explain are on their own, the former wins 65 times and the latter only 62). It is likely that iZplus's wins are due to its local search part that improves the objective function once a solution is found, a component that HCSP does not have. It is worth noting that CPX requires on average more than three orders of magnitude more backtracks compared to HCSP, which we attribute to the fact that CPX learns purely through SAT, and is limited to clauses it already generated. These clauses are not necessarily optimal for conflict analysis. Overall in these experiments 40 % of the cases explanation was used as a fall-back solution.

1.6. Conclusion and Future Work

We have presented a new learning scheme based on inference of general constraints. We presented the development of various inference rules that are necessary for this scheme, but it is clear that there is still a lot of work in deriving such rules for additional popular pairs of constraints which are currently not supported and force HCSP into a fallback solution. In addition, currently learning general constraints is incompatible with producing machine-checkable proofs in case the formula is unsatisfiable, in contrast to our earlier explanation-based method [11] (i.e., in [11] we presented a method for producing a signed-resolution proof in case the formula is unsatisfiable, which relies on clausal explanations). HCSP is written in C++, contains 23k lines of non-comment code, and its architecture enables the addition of new constraints and new rules without changing the core solver. It is free software available from [18] under the GPL license.

---

[8] iZplus , a closed-source program, does not print this information

References

[1]. R. Dechter, Constraint Processing, *Morgan Kaufmann*, 2003.

[2]. N. Nethercote, P. J. Stuckey, R. Becket, S. Brand, G. J. Duck, G. Tack, MiniZinc: Towards a standard cp modelling language, in *Proceedings of the International Conference Principles and Practice of Constraint Programming (CP'07)*, 2007, pp. 529-543.

[3]. Handbook of Satisfiability, A. Biere, M. Heule, H. van Maaren, T.Walsh, (Eds.), Frontiers in Artificial Intelligence and Applications, Vol. 185, *IOS Press*, 2009.

[4]. M. W. Moskewicz, C. F. Madigan, Y. Zhao, L. Zhang, S. Malik, Chaff: Engineering an efficient SAT solver, in *Proceedings of the 38th Design Automation Conference (DAC'2001)*, 2001, pp. 530-535.

[5]. D. L. Berre, I. Lynce, CSP2SAT4J: A simple CSP to SAT translator, System description, in *Proceedings of the 2nd International Competition of CSP and Max-CSP Solvers,* 2015.

[6]. G. Katsirelos, F. Bacchus, Generalized nogoods in CSPs, in *Proceedings of the 20th National Conference on Artificial intelligence (AAAI'05)*, 2005, pp. 390-396.

[7]. R. Dechter, Enhancement schemes for constraint processing: Backjumping, learning, and cutset decomposition, *Artif. Intell.*, Vol. 41, Issue 3, 1990, pp. 273-312.

[8]. N. C. Moore, C-learning: Further generalised g-nogood learning, in *Proceedings of the Annual ERCIM Workshop on Constraint Solving and Constraint Logic Programming (CSCLP'11)*, 2011.

[9]. I. P. Gent, I. Miguel, N. C. A. Moore, Lazy explanations for constraint propagators, in *Proceedings of the 12th International Symposium Practical Aspects of Declarative Languages (PADL'10)*, 2010, pp. 217-233.

[10]. B. Beckert, R. Hähnle, F. Manyá, The SAT problem of signed CNF formulas, in Labelled Deduction, *Springer*, 2000, pp. 59-80.

[11]. M. Veksler, O. Strichman, A proof-producing CSP solver, in *Proceedings of the 24th Conference on Artificial Intelligence (AAAI'2010)*, 2010.

[12]. I. Abío, P. J. Stuckey, Conflict directed lazy decomposition, in *Proceedings of the 18th International Conference Principles and Practice of Constraint Programming (CP'2012)*, Québec City, QC, Canada, October 8-12, 2012, pp. 70-85.

[13]. G. Katsirelos, F. Bacchus, Unrestricted nogood recording in CSP search, in *Proceedings of the 9th International Conference Principles and Practice of Constraint Programming (CP'2003)*, Kinsale, Ireland, September 29 – October 3, 2003, pp. 873-877.

[14]. O. Ohrimenko, P. J. Stuckey, M. Codish, Propagation via lazy clause generation, *Constraints*, Vol. 14, Issue 3, 2009, pp. 357-391.

[15]. B. de Cat, M. Denecker, M. Bruynooghe, P. J. Stuckey, Lazy model expansion: Interleaving grounding with search, *J. Artif. Intell. Res. (JAIR)*, Vol. 52, 2015, pp. 235-286.

[16]. A. Weinzierl, Learning non-ground rules for answer-set solving, in *Proceedings of the 2ⁿᵈ Workshop on Grounding and Transformations for Theories With Variables (GTTV'13)*, 2013.

[17]. P. J. S. Geoffrey Chu, Structure based extended resolution for constraint programming, http://arxiv.org/abs/1306.4418

[18]. A. Biere, Bounded model checking, in Handbook of Satisfiability, A. Biere, M. Heule, H. van Maaren, T. Walsh, (Eds.), Frontiers in Artificial Intelligence and Applications, Vol. 185, *IOS Press*, 2009, pp. 457-481.

[19]. H. E. Dixon, M. L. Ginsberg, Inference methods for a pseudo-boolean satisfiability solver, in *Proceedings of the 18ᵗʰ National Conference on Artificial Intelligence and Fourteenth Conference on Innovative Applications of Artificial Intelligence (AAAI'02)*, Edmonton, Alberta, Canada, 2002, pp. 635-640.

[20]. S. Cotton, O. Maler, Fast and flexible difference constraint propagation for DPLL(T), in *Proceedings of the International Conference on Theory and Applications of Satisfiability Testing (SAT'06)*, 2006, pp. 170-183.

[21]. D. Jovanovic, L. M. de Moura, Cutting to the chase – solving linear integer arithmetic, *J. Autom. Reasoning*, Vol. 51, Issue 1, 2013, pp. 79-108.

[22]. R. Nieuwenhuis, The intsat method for integer linear programming, in *Proceedings of the Principles and Practice of Constraint Programming 20th International Conference (CP'2014)*, Lyon, France, September 8-12, 2014, pp. 574-589.

[23]. E. Hebrard, Mistral, a constraints satisfiaction library, in *Proceedings of the 3ʳᵈ International CSP Solver Competition*, 2008, pp. 31-40.

[24]. Opturion, Opturion CPX – tool description, http://www.minizinc.org/challenge2014/description_opturion_cpx.txt

[25]. T. Fujiwara, iZplus – tool description, http://www.minizinc.org/challenge2014/description_izplus.txt

[26]. MiniZinc, Minizinc challenge, http://www.minizinc.org/challenge2014/

[27]. M. Veksler, O. Strichman, Learning general constraint, in *Proceedings of the Integration of AI and OR Techniques in Constraint Programming 12ᵗʰ International Conference (CPAIOR'15)*, Barcelona, Spain, May 18-22, 2015, pp. 410-426.

[28]. M. Veksler, O. Strichman, Learning non-clausal constraints in CSP (long version), Tech. Rep. IE/IS-2014-05, *Technion, Industrial Engineering*, 2014.

[29]. M. Moskewicz, C. Madigan, Y. Zhao, L. Zhang, S. Malik, Chaff: Engineering an efficient SAT solver, in *Proceedings of the Design Automation Conference (DAC'01)*, 2001.

[30]. F. Boussemart, F. Hemery, C. Lecoutre, L. Sais, Boosting systematic search by weighting constraints, in *Proceedings of the 16ᵗʰ European Conference on Artificial Intelligence (ECAI'04)*, 2004, pp. 146-150.

[31]. O. Strichman, Tuning SAT checkers for bounded model checking, in *Proceedings of the 12ᵗʰ International Conference Computer Aided Verification (CAV'2000)*, Chicago, IL, USA, July 15-19, 2000, pp. 480-494.

[32]. CSP-competition, in *Proceedings of the 4th International CSP Solver Competition*, http://www.cril.univ-artois.fr/CSC09/

[33]. C. Liu, A. Kuehlmann, M. W. Moskewicz, CAMA: A multi-valued satisfiability solver, in *Proceedings of the International Conference on Computer Aided Design (ICCAD'03)*, 2003, pp. 326-333.

[34]. M. Veksler, O. Strichman, A Proof-producing CSP Solver (a proof supplement), Tech. Rep. IE/IS-2010-02, *Industrial Engineering, Technion*, Haifa, Israel, Jan 2010.

[35]. T. Feydy, P. J. Stuckey, Lazy clause generation reengineered, in *Proceedings of the Principles and Practice of Constraint Programming 15th International Conference (CP'2009)*, pp. 352-366.

[36]. S. Jain, A. Sabharwal, M. Sellmann, A general nogood-learning framework for pseudo-boolean multi-valued SAT, in *Proceedings of the Twenty-Fifth AAAI Conference on Artificial Intelligence (AAAI'11)*, San Francisco, California, USA, August 7-11, 2011.

[37]. C. W. Choi, W. Harvey, J. H. M. Lee, P. J. Stuckey, Finite domain bounds consistency revisited, in *Proceedings of the Australian Conference on Artificial Intelligence (AI'06)*, pp. 49-58.

[38]. HCSP, The HCSP Constraint Solver Web Page: http://ie.technion.ac.il/~ofers/HCSP/index.html

Chapter 2

Sub-dimensional Surrogates to Solve High Dimensional Optimization Problems in Machine Learning

Younghwan Chae, Daniel N. Wilke

2.1. Introduction

High dimensional optimization problems, $f: \mathbb{R}^n \to \mathbb{R}, n >> 100$, are either solved by successively solving a series of one-dimensional problems, which includes classical gradient-based optimizers, or by successively searching in the full n-dimensional space as is usually done by evolutionary approaches [1]. As a consequence surrogate-assisted optimization [2-5] for high dimensional optimization problems has received limited attention, and is considered to be computationally intractable [4]. Recent attempts to address some of these challenges include constructing multiple multivariate linear interpolation models over different sub-spaces of a 16 dimensional design domain [6], to predict low cycle fatigue life. Constrained Optimization By Radial basis function Approximation (COBRA) has been used to solve a 124 dimensional vehicle dynamics problem subjected to 68 black-box inequality constraints [7]. The construction of surrogate models can be enhanced with gradient information, e.g. weighted gradient-enhanced kriging (WGEK) [8] has been used to combine a number of sub-domain models to solve a 108 design variable problem for the inverse design of a transonic wing [9]. In turn, DYnamic COordinate search Response Surface models (DYCORS) construct surrogate models for the full dimension but only selects a subset of variables to be perturbed for

Younghwan Chae
Centre for Asset and Integrity Management (C-AIM), Department of Mechanical and Aeronautical Engineering, University of Pretoria, Pretoria, South Africa

additional DOE points to extend surrogate-based optimization to 200 dimensional problems [10].

As an alternative way to solve optimization problems in sub-spaces, the successive one-dimensional updates of coordinate descent (CD), random coordinate descent (RCD) [11] and cyclic coordinate descent (CCD) [12-15] has been extended to block coordinate descent (BCD) by selecting a subset or block of variables [16, 17] to update. That is a high dimensional problem solved by successively solving sub-dimensional problems. In evolutionary optimization, this concept was introduced as cooperative searches by Potter and Jong (1994) [18], and dynamically dimensioned searches (DDS) by Tolson and Shoemaker (2007) [19]. Renewed interest into CD and BCD has been sparked by success in various applications in statistical learning [20, 21] and machine learning [22].

Research into CD and BCD has been largely limited to direct optimization of objective functions with limited work on surrogate-based optimization, which are limited to the work by Werth et al. (2017) [23] that divides high-dimensional optimization problems into low-dimensional sub-problems using the monotony and non-linearity tests to solve 1000 dimensional problems. A sub-dimensional surrogate model can be optimized using appropriate optimizers that may include gradient-based, gradient-free or evolutionary optimizers [10, 24]. A number of research questions in sub-dimensional searches remains, which includes:

1. Selection of sub-dimensional spaces: cyclically, randomly, elastic nets [25], DM-HDMR [26], monotony [23], non-linearity [23], random decomposition method (DECC-G) [1] and the self-adaptive decomposition method [27];

2. Number of variables to define the sub-space;

3. Which sub-space to select;

4. Appropriate test problems.

In this study, we investigate in particular the utility of the gradient vector to select sub-dimensional spaces for a vanilla algorithm that incorporates no heuristics. The availability of analytical gradients is becoming standard with automatic differentiation numerical libraries such as Pytorch and Tensorflow [28, 29]. We demonstrate that the gradient vector allows for sensible selection of sub-space over which to construct surrogate models for 500 dimensional test problems that include Ackley and Sum of squares, in both their original description frames and rotated description frames. We include the performance of CD and steepest gradient descent (SGD) as baseline strategies. Various potential heuristics are proposed based on the lessons learned from the test problems. Lastly, the sub-dimensional surrogate strategy was implemented to train the Iris dataset with 11, 51, and 507 weight variables in order to compare the relationships between the training errors and test errors for a various number of dimensions for sub-dimensional surrogates.

2.2. Sub-dimensional Surrogates

Given a function $f: \mathbb{R}^n \to \mathbb{R}$, we may construct an $m \leq n$ dimensional surrogate function $\tilde{f}_k: \mathbb{R}^m \to \mathbb{R}$ that approximates $f: \mathbb{R}^m \to \mathbb{R}$ with the remaining variables x_k^{n-m} kept fixed. Numerous approaches have been proposed for CD and BCD strategies to select the m variables, which could be used to construct an m-dimensional surrogate. These include cyclically, randomly, elastic nets [25], DM-HDMR [26], monotony [23], non-linearity [23], random decomposition method (DECC-G) [1] and the self-adaptive decomposition method [27]. In this study, we investigate the gradient vector to serve as a selection strategy, with gradients that are becoming more and more accessible with the likes of automatic differentiation frameworks such as Tensorflow and PyTorch that are used extensively in statistical learning, machine learning, deep learning, data science and numerical modelling.

2.2.1. Sub-dimensional Greedy Surrogates

Given the current best solution x^k, we compute the gradient $\nabla f(x_k)$ and select the m gradient components with the largest magnitudes to select the sub-space $\mathbb{R}^m$ in which we construct our m-dimensional surrogates, i.e. we construct greedy m-dimensional surrogates following the four steps:

1. Compute $\nabla f(x_k) \in \mathbb{R}^n$;

2. Select the $m \leq n$ variables, $\boldsymbol{m}$, associated with the m largest components of $\nabla f(x_k)$;

3. Sample the m-dimensional sub-space to obtain p new samples, while keeping the other variables $\boldsymbol{x}_k^{n-m}$ fixed;

4. Using the p sampled designs, construct the sub-dimensional surrogate $\tilde{f}_k \colon \mathbb{R}^m \to \mathbb{R}$;

5. Find the minimizer $\boldsymbol{x}_k^{m*} \in \mathbb{R}^m$ by minimizing $\tilde{f}_k$;

6. Update $\boldsymbol{x}_{k+1}^m = \boldsymbol{x}_k^{m*}$ to construct $\boldsymbol{x}_{k+1} \in \mathbb{R}^n$;

7. Repeat steps 1 - 6 until convergence or maximum iterations is reached.

As this is one of the first papers to investigate sub-dimensional surrogates to solve high dimensional problems, *our aim is not to propose state of the art algorithms but rather to investigate the potential merits of sub-dimensional surrogates to solve high dimensional problems.* In particular, we want to investigate the merits of using the gradient vector as a variable selection strategy. Hence, we only consider a base (or vanilla) algorithm without the incorporation of heuristics for this study. This is done to allow us to explore the merits of solving sub-dimensional surrogates, with a gradient-based selection criterion. Although we do not include heuristics, we do offer a number of avenues that could be pursued to include heuristics that offers a substantial improvement on the performance of the current study that could be explored in future studies.

2.2.1.1. Construction of Sub-dimensional Surrogates

At the kth iterate, given that $\boldsymbol{x}_k^{n-m} \in \mathbb{R}^{n-m}$ remains fixed, we construct an m-dimensional surrogate $\tilde{f}_k \colon \mathbb{R}^m \to \mathbb{R}$. It is evident that information density over which we construct a surrogate is critical i.e. larger domains require more sampling points for the same accuracy. Although this is important, we simplify our study by fixing the sampling of surrogate domain $\boldsymbol{D}_s$ to 120 % of the original bound constrained domain $\boldsymbol{D} = \{x_i^{min} \leq D_i \in \mathbb{R} \leq x_i^{max}, i \in \boldsymbol{m}\}$. The bound constraints are however imposed to be the size of the original domain, this is to ensure we have a proper surrogate description at the bounds of the problem.

We, therefore, sample the sub-dimensional surrogate domain using Latin Hypercube Sampling (LHS) [30] using $\boldsymbol{p}$ points. For the surrogate construction, we transform $\boldsymbol{D} = \{x_i^{min} \leq D_i \in \mathbb{R} \leq x_i^{max}, i \in \boldsymbol{m}\}$ to $\boldsymbol{N} = \{0 \leq N_i \in \mathbb{R} \leq 1, i \in \boldsymbol{m}\}$. Hence, before evaluating the surrogate, we first transform $\boldsymbol{x} \in \boldsymbol{D}_s$ to $\boldsymbol{z} \in \boldsymbol{N}$.

In this study, we construct radial basis function (RBF) surrogate supplemented by a bias and linear polynomials [31, 32].

$$\tilde{f}(x) = [1, x]\begin{bmatrix} c_1 \\ c_2 \\ \vdots \\ c_p \end{bmatrix} + \sum_{i=1}^{p} \lambda_i \phi_i(x), \qquad (2.1)$$

using the cubic radial basis function

$$\phi(r_i(x)) = r_i(x)^3, r_i = \|x - x_i\|_2, \qquad (2.2)$$

where $r_i(x)$ is the Euclidean distance x to the center x_i of the ith basis function. Given $p = m$ sampled LHS designs $X \in \mathbb{R}^{m \times p}$, with their associated function evaluations, f, the unknown RBF weights λ and polynomial coefficients c are then solved from the following square system of equations

$$\begin{bmatrix} \Phi & P \\ P & 0 \end{bmatrix} \begin{bmatrix} \lambda \\ c \end{bmatrix} = \begin{bmatrix} f \\ 0 \end{bmatrix}, \qquad (2.3)$$

to obtain an interpolation based RBF approximation. Here, $\Phi^{p \times p}$ denotes the matrix with each ith row $\varphi_i(x_j)$ for

$$x_j \in X_j, j = 1, \ldots, p.$$

The cubic basis functions together with low order polynomials have been demonstrated by Regis and Shoemaker (2013) [10] and Ilievski et al. (2016) [33] of which the linear polynomial tail ensures for unique solutions if and only if the rank of the matrix P is $1 + n$ to obtain an invertible coefficient matrix in Eq. (2.3) [31].

2.2.1.2. Sub-dimensional Surrogate Minimization

The sub-dimensional surrogates (or 'sub-surrogates' for compactness) are then minimized using the Nelder-Mead algorithm [34] by using MATLAB (2015) [35] built-in optimization algorithm *fminsearch* from 10 random initial starting points within the feasible domain. Although we are solving 500-dimensional problems in this study for which Nelder-Mead is intractable, our sub-dimensional surrogates are limited to 1, 2 and 4-dimensions. The optimization is conducted from 9 random starting points, with the tenth point as the current best point.

The sub-dimensional minimizer $z_k^{m*} \in N$ is then transformed to $x_k^{m*} \in D$ and the solution for the next iterate constructed $x_{k+1} \in \mathbb{R}^n$.

2.3. Numerical Study Online

In this study, we first consider two well-known test problems, listed in Table 2.1, with $n = 500$ (MATLAB codes for the test problems supplied by Surjanovic and Bingham (2013) [36]). We also include the performance of steepest gradient descent (SGD) and coordinate descent (CD) algorithms. In addition, we include results for the problems formulated in their proposed reference frame, as well as in an arbitrary rotated reference frame. This is to investigate the performance when the formulated functions are separable as well as when there is a strong interaction between the variables. That is the function $f(x)$ expressed in the original coordinate system $x \in \mathbb{R}^n$ is related to the arbitrary rotated function $\hat{f}(\hat{x})$ as follows $\hat{x} = Qx$, where $Q \in Orth^+$ is an arbitrary proper orthogonal matrix, i.e. $det(Q) = 1$ (see Fig. 2.1). In this study, Q is constructed following a simple series expansion of an exponential map $Q = I + W + (1/2)WW + (1/6)WWW +...$ as outlined by Moler and Van Loan (2003) [37], where $W = \frac{\alpha\pi}{180}(A - A^T)$ and A is a random $n \times n$ matrix, with each entry a random number between -0.5 and 0.5.

Table 2.1. Prescribed domain and the global minimum function values for the two test functions.

Function	x_{min}	x_{max}	$f(x^*)$
Ackley	-32.768	32.768	0
Sum of squares	-5.12	5.12	0

Although the problems under consideration are test problems, some of them are representative of actual objective functions often encountered in machine learning and deep learning. In particular, the Ackley function is a good candidate for a typical state of the art deep network, namely ResNet-56 [38], as depicted in Fig. 2.2. It is well known that objective function surfaces in machine learning often have large domains with low gradients and curvatures, which surround higher curvature domains of the manifold [39].

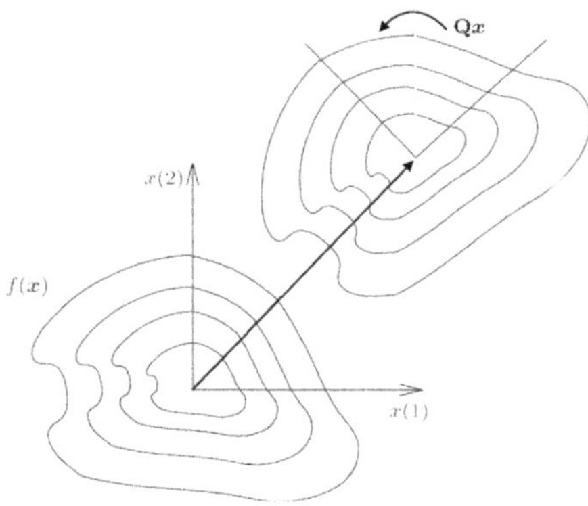

Fig. 2.1. A function and the same function arbitrarily rotated to affect the variable interaction.

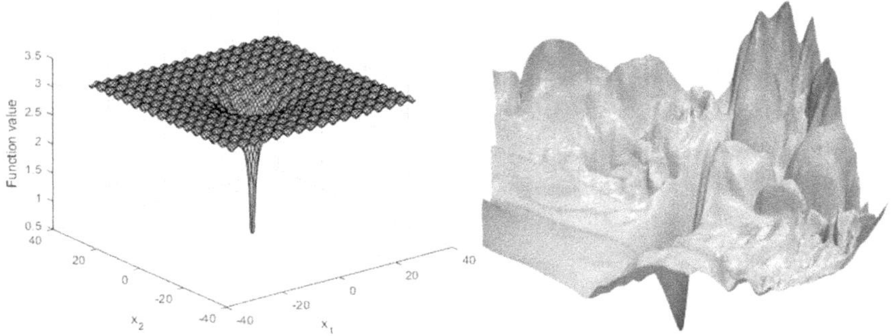

Fig. 2.2. The Ackley function in 2-D (left) and the loss surfaces of ResNet-56 (right) [38], both functions are depicted on a log-scale for the function values.

The remaining test problem, Sum of squares is representative of general ellipsoidal bowl-shaped optimization problem that is coercive. This test problem is representative of classical regularization or penalization that results in a coercive function given a sufficiently large regularization parameter. We conclude our numerical study with the neural network training a deep neural network on the Iris dataset to convey the basic findings of the potential impact of this approach on machine learning when considering not only a training set performance but also the test set performance for generalization of the trained result. Note that for the two test problems, the gradients were computed analytically to resemble gradients from automatic differentiation packages such as Tensorflow or Pytorch.

To allow for a systematic study, for both SGD and CD at every iteration, a fixed number of function evaluations were taken along the descent direction using Latin hypercube samplings (LHS) of the actual function. The update to the minimum function value was considered as the update step at every iteration. Hence, the number of function evaluations per iteration for SGD and CD matches the number of points sampled per iteration for a sub-dimensional surrogate approach to generate surrogate models. For CD, the highest magnitude partial derivative in the gradient is chosen as the coordinate to update. Lastly, the sampling domain is chosen to be 20 % larger than the surrogate optimization domain along the descent direction.

Surrogate optimizers are denoted 1-D, 2-D, and 4-D, while SGD1 and SGD2 denote SGD sampling the univariate function along only the descent direction or sampling the univariate function along the entire sub-domain, i.e. along ascent and descent of the univariate function. Similarly, CD1 and CD2 respectively denote sampling along the descent direction or sampling over the entire domain of the univariate function. It is important to note, that differences between 1-D and CD2 are only due to the surrogate being minimized in 1-D using the same sampling points as CD2.

We limit the maximum number of function evaluations to 10^5, for the sub-dimension $m = 1$, 2 and 4, using $p = 8$, 16, 32 and 64 LHS sampling points per iteration. As we do not vary the size of the surrogate domain, the information density for each surrogate remains constant at every iteration.

The expected values for each test problem were computed over 30 runs. The initial guesses were taken randomly from the prescribed domains for each test problem as listed in Table 2.1.

2.4. Results

The results for our two test functions, Ackley and Sum of squares are discussed in this section. Although it is expected for SGD to perform exactly the same for the unrotated and rotated problems, observed differences are due to the stochastic sampling along the search directions.

2.4.1. Ackley Results

In particular, the results of the various optimizers on the Ackley function are shown in Fig. 2.3(a)-(d). It is clear that as the number of sampling points increases, the higher sub-dimensional surrogates are better defined and the respective variance of the 30 averaged solutions decrease, e.g. for the 4-dimensional sub-surrogate the averaged response using $p = 16$ sampling points is more smooth than the $p = 8$ LHS points.

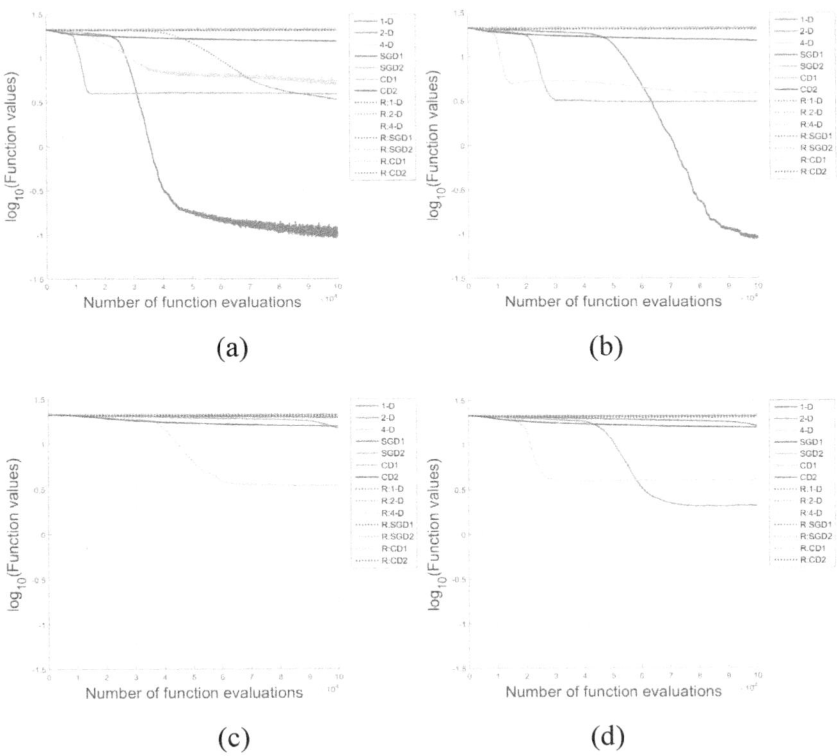

Fig. 2.3. Ackley function sampled with (a) $p = 8$, (b) $p = 16$, (c) $p = 32$, and (d) $p = 64$ data points at each iteration for unrotated (solid line) and rotated problem (dashed line) reference frames for the problem description.

For $p = 8$ sampling points, the initial performance of the 2-dimensional sub-surrogate model performs the best. The performance stagnates in the limit as the accuracy of the surrogate is reached, since we do not reduce the volume of the domain over which the surrogate is constructed. The 1-D surrogates have a much higher sampling density and consequently result in a significantly more accurate surrogate that is limited to a single dimension.

For p = 16 sampling points, the initial performance of the 4-dimensional sub-surrogate model now performs the best, i.e. the higher sampling density results in a much more reliable surrogate to guide the optimizer. In fact, using $p = 16$ points for 4-dimensional sub-surrogate outperforms the 2-D sub-surrogate sampled using both $p = 8$ and $p = 16$ points. As expected, the performance stagnates in the limit as the accuracy of the surrogates reaches a limit, since we do not reduce the domain over which the surrogates are constructed. It is also evident that the surrogates become more accurate in the limit as more samples points are used, however in most cases to reach this accuracy a larger number of total function evaluations are required. The exceptions here are the 4-dimensional sub-surrogate that obtains better solutions using fewer total function evaluations when sampling $p = 16$ points as apposed to $p = 8$ samples, whereas $p = 32$ and $p = 64$ results in better solutions but requires significantly more total function evaluations to reach the same accuracy as $p = 8$ and $p = 16$ sampling points.

For p = 32 and 64 sampling points, it is evident that the required number of function evaluations to reach a specific accuracy is significantly more. The total improvement of the solution in the limit due to a better-resolved surrogate is also marginal. In turn, reducing the problem dimension from 4-D to 2-D, and 2-D to 1-D significantly improves the accuracy of the sub-dimensional surrogates in the limit. This study clearly demonstrates that surrogates do not only have to be either one-dimensional or full-dimensional, but sub-dimensional surrogates are powerful in that they allow for an alternative mechanism between exploration and exploitation, as well as adjusting sampling density given a fixed number of points. This adds an additional mechanism to control the sampling density, which traditionally consisted of:

1. Sampling using more points to better resolve a surrogate;

2. Sampling over a sub-domain (but in the same sub-space) is closely related to using more sampling points over sub-domain of the same volume, which this study complements with a significant third mechanism;

3. Reducing the sub-dimension of the surrogate, which significantly enhances the limit accuracy of the surrogate.

We consider a second test function to demonstrate that a significant amount of work is still required as the performance of Ackley, which seems to be well suited to a number of machine learning and deep learning objective functions, does not necessarily apply to all test problems. We, therefore, consider a second test problem namely the Sum of squares function that is a coercive function (as $\|x\|_2 \to \infty$, $f(x) \to \infty$), which is distinct from the noisy flat planes of the Ackley test function.

2.4.2. Sum of Squares Results

The results of the various optimizers on the Sum of squares function are shown in Fig. 2.4 (a)-(d). Two significantly different characteristic changes are evident. It is clear that coordinate descent performs much better on Sum of squares than Ackley.

For $p = 8$ sampling points, the initial performance of SGD1 (descent direction domain sampling) and SGD2 (full domain sampling) and the 2-dimensional sub-surrogate models perform the best, which is followed by the 4-dimensional and 1-dimensional sub-surrogate models. The performance stagnates in the limit as the accuracy of the surrogate is reached.

For $p = 16$ sampling points, the initial performance of both CDs and 1-dimensional sub-surrogate models are similar, with a significant improvement in the lowest error of the 1-dimensional sub-surrogate model. The initial performance of the 4-D sub-surrogate model significantly outperforms the 2-D sub-surrogate but it stagnates quicker than 2-D sub-surrogate model.

For $p = 32$ and 64 sampling points, it is evident that the 2-D benefits from more sampling points to obtain lower minima due to a higher sampling density. Importantly, the 4-D sub-surrogate has the best initial performance of all the strategies, while the 1-D sub-surrogate sampled using 64-points has the best overall final performance. Note the larger the number of sampling points becomes the less iterations are achieved for a fixed number of function evaluations. Hence, the graphs look stretched as the rate of decrease in the model errors affecting the function value is slower than the rate of convergence of function value due to new models at each iteration.

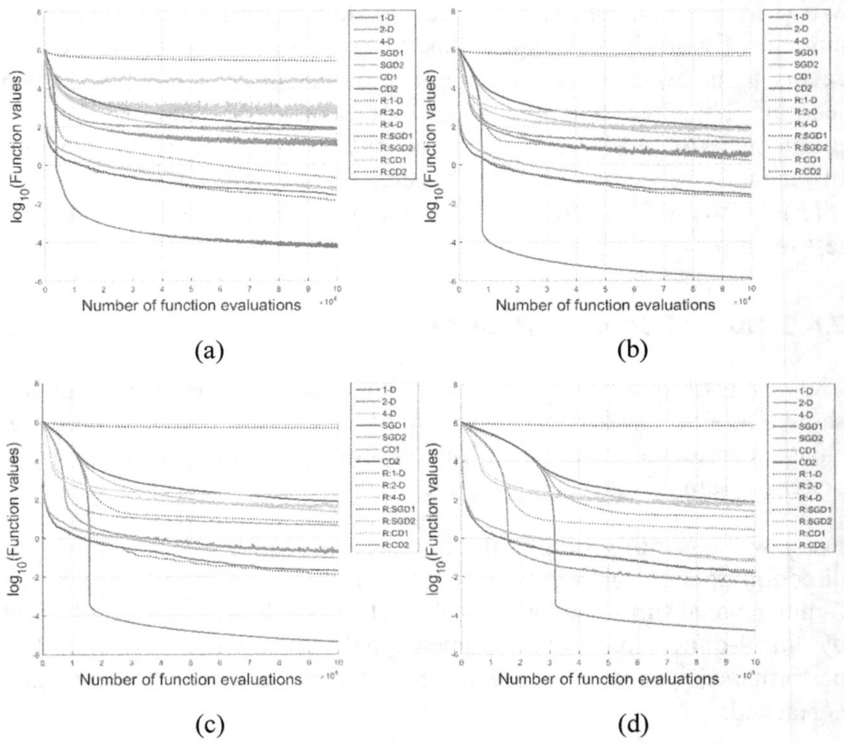

Fig. 2.4. Sum of squares function sampled with (a) $p = 8$, (b) $p = 16$, (c) $p = 32$, and (d) $p = 64$ data points at each iteration for unrotated (solid line) and rotated problem (dashed line) reference frames for the problem description.

Although the performance of the various algorithms on Sum of squares is significantly different to Ackley, the noteworthy observations based on Ackley are still evident on Sum of squares, i.e. higher dimensional surrogates have significantly better initial performance and reducing the surrogate sub-space significantly increases the sampling density.

For unrotated (solid) and rotated (dashed) Sum of squares descriptions, it is clear that by increasing the interaction amongst the variables, the performance in general degrades. That said, it is important to note that the severity is more pronounced for the lower dimensional surrogates and alleviated for the higher dimensional surrogates. This is a critical observation: *searching in sub-dimensions makes the optimization strategy less sensitive to stronger interaction or coupling amongst the variables.*

Evidently, higher sub-dimensional surrogates allow for better exploration and initial improvement, while lower dimensional surrogates allow for surrogates that are better resolved. This opens up a new area of research to explore algorithms and heuristics that can be developed to explore and exploit the benefits and trade-offs of sub-dimensional surrogates.

2.4.3. Discussion on Higher Versus Lower Dimensional Searches on Initial Performance

We demonstrate that on all the test problems considered, the 4-D performs best, followed by 2-D, followed by 1-D sub-surrogates in Fig. 2.5 (a)-(b).

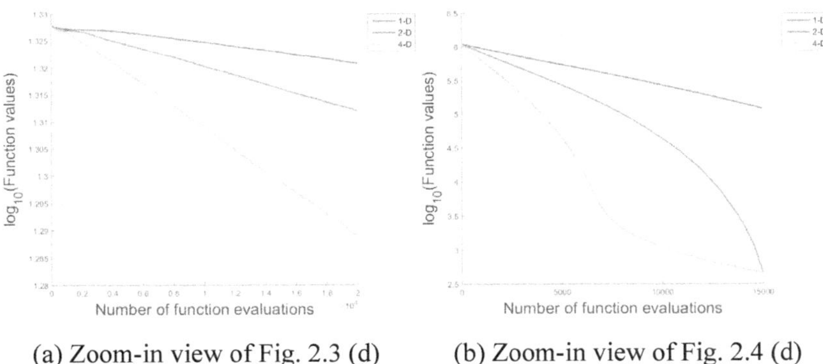

(a) Zoom-in view of Fig. 2.3 (d)   (b) Zoom-in view of Fig. 2.4 (d)

Fig. 2.5. Performance differences between surrogate sub-dimensions when sampling using $p = 64$ points on (a) Ackley, and (b) Sum of squares.

This clearly informs desirable characteristics for heuristics to be developed for sub-dimensional surrogates, i.e. initial searches should be high dimensional, while lower the dimensionality of the searches should be reduced as improvements are made. This is in addition to simple heuristics that would have significantly improved the performance of our sub-dimensional surrogates in this study but at the cost of obscuring insights due to the heuristic performance dominating the foundational algorithmic performance. For example, choosing the best solution not only from the best surrogate solutions but also from the best-sampled solutions. This would have completely hidden any indication of the quality of the surrogate surface. This just again emphasizes the importance of using a vanilla sub-dimensional surrogate strategy in initial investigations. We emphasize again this study does not propose a state of the art algorithm but clearly highlights insight and focus points for potential heuristics in this domain of sub-dimensional surrogates.

2.5. Lessons Learned and Sensible Heuristics

Performance of the proposed vanilla flavored sub-dimensional surrogates can be significantly improved by incorporating sensible heuristics. Based on the findings of our study, we outline a number of potentially sensible heuristics as well as what they should aim to achieve.

2.5.1. Surrogate Dimensionality Heuristic

This study proposes sub-dimensionality of surrogates as a new domain of research. This study clearly indicates that higher dimensional sub-surrogates offer better exploration and faster convergence but suffers from low sampling density. This can be alleviated by decreasing the sampling domain, increasing the number of samples, and as shown in the results of this study reducing the dimensionality of the domain over which the sub-dimensional surrogate is constructed.

Heuristics that identifies when to rather construct as a lower dimensional surrogate is very important. The benefits of such a heuristic are demonstrated in Fig. 2.6 (a) and (b) for the Ackley and Sum of squares test functions, where we start off initially with the 4-D sub-surrogate that is then reduced to 2-D and finally 1-D for a sampling density of 16-points per sub-dimensional surrogate.

2.5.2. Sampling Dimensions Heuristic or Strategy

Strategies to identify appropriate sub-dimensions for the construction of the surrogates also plays a critical role. In this study, we considered a basic and effectively greedy strategy, where we selected the partial derivatives of the gradient vector that is the highest magnitude. We demonstrate the importance of a selection heuristic and selection strategy by considering the random selection of a sub-space for the 1-D (denoted rand:1-D), 2-D (denoted rand:2-D) and 4-D (denoted rand:4-D) sub-surrogates for Ackley and Sum of squares which are depicted in Figs. 2.7(a)-(d) – 2.8(a)-(d).

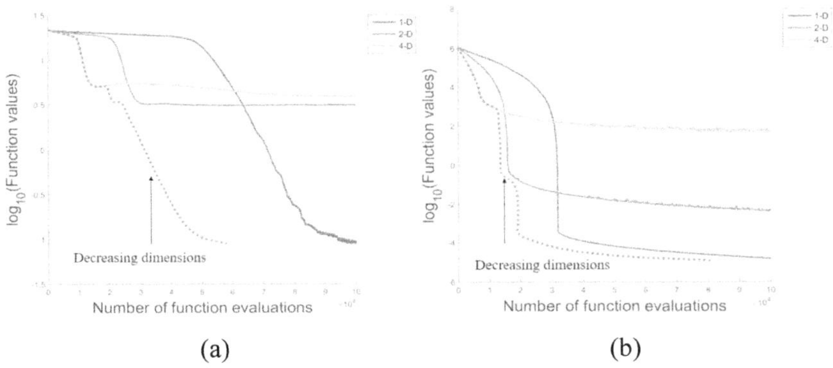

(a)   (b)

Fig. 2.6. Decreasing sub-surrogate dimensions for (a) Ackley ($p = 16$) and (b) Sum of squares ($p = 64$) from 4-D to 2-D to 1-D.

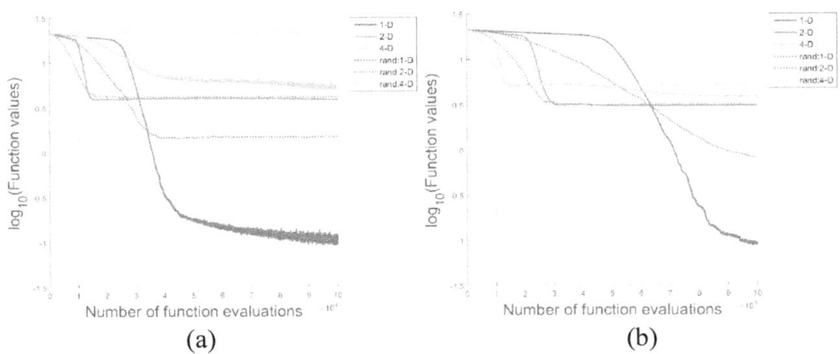

(a)   (b)

Fig. 2.7. Ackley function sampled with (a) $p = 8$, (b) $p = 16$, (c) $p = 32$, and (d) $p = 64$ data points at each iteration. Sub-dimensional variable selection (1-D, 2-D and 4-D) is based on the gradient vector or randomly selected (rand:1D, rand:2D and rand:4D).

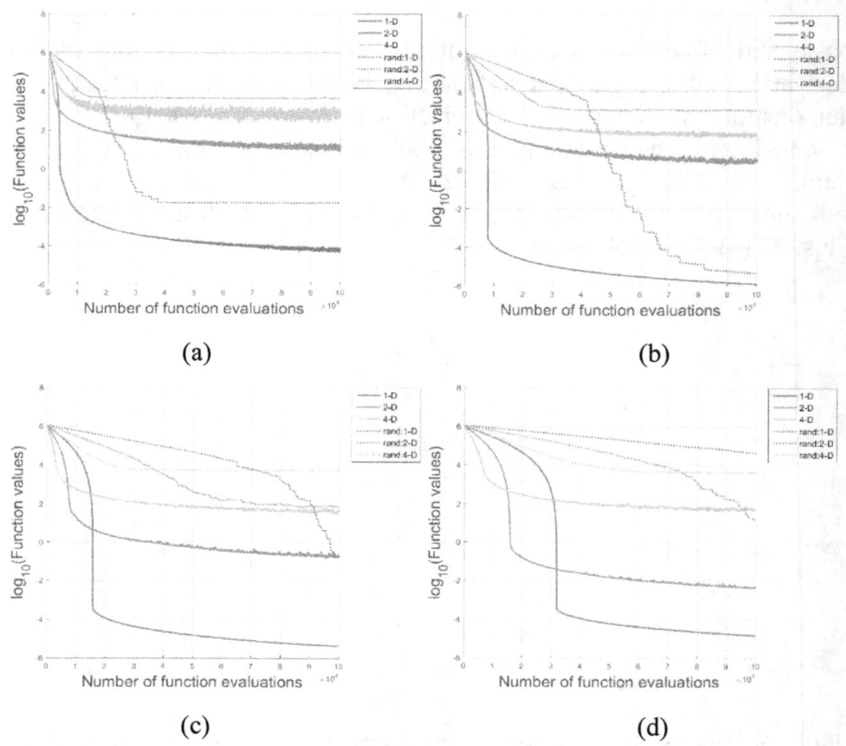

Fig. 2.8. Sum of squares function sampled with (a) $p = 8$, (b) $p = 16$, (c) $p = 32$, and (d) $p = 64$ data points at each iteration. Sub-dimensional variable selection (1-D, 2-D, and 4-D) is based on the gradient vector or randomly selected (rand:1D, rand:2D and rand:4D).

For the Ackley function, it is evident that the lower the sub-surrogate dimension the more sensitive the solution to variable interaction and the more care should be exercised to select sub-dimensions. In turn, the 2-D and 4-D sub-dimensional surrogates were less affected. In addition, it is clear that there is room for improvement in using the magnitude of gradient components for the 2-D and 4-D sub-dimensional surrogates, as the randomly selected sub-dimensions had better initial performance than the sub-dimensions selected on the gradient criteria on Ackley function.

That said for the Sum of squares function, the gradient component magnitude strategy significantly outperformed the randomly selected sub-dimensions for the 1-D, 2-D and 4-D sub-dimensional surrogates.

There is significant room for improvement on our investigated greedy gradient component magnitude strategy to identify appropriate sub-dimensions for future research.

2.5.3. Sampling Quantity Heuristic

The number of sampling points can be increased e.g. doubled by going from 8 to 16 to 32 and 64 to obtain the performance depicted in Fig. 2.9(a) and (b) for Ackley and Sum of squares. It is evident from Fig. 2.6(a) and (b) that reducing the dimensionality seems to be a much more beneficial strategy to increase sampling density than increasing the number of points. That said, increasing the number of points allows for a finer grained control of the sampling density, i.e. a slight increase in the number of sampling points may supply enough information and allow for a useful higher dimensional surrogate to be constructed.

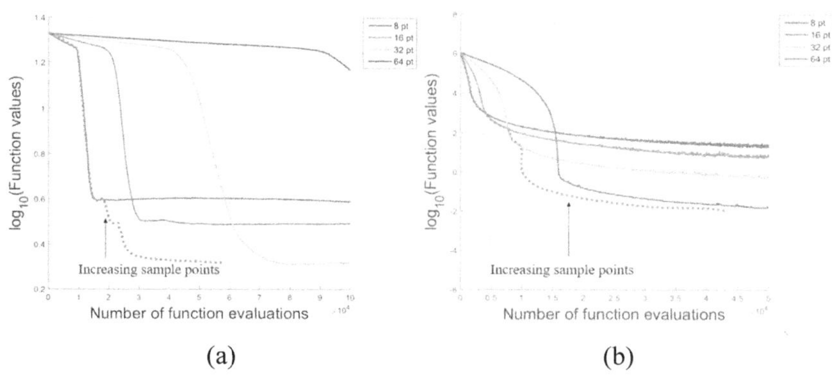

Fig. 2.9. Increasing the number of sampling points for (a) Ackley and (b) Sum of squares for the 4-D sub-surrogate.

2.5.4. Sampling Domain Heuristic

Closely related to the sampling quantity is the sampling volume for a given sub-dimension. Reducing the sampling volume too aggressively results in a localized search early on, while reducing the sampling volume too slowly may waste significant computational resources. Again, the sampling allows for finer control of sampling density. In this study, we always constructed surrogates over the entire domain, however, Fig. 2.10(a) and (b) depict the potential benefits of sampling an appropriate sub-domain. This was conducted by multiplying a dynamically changing scaling factor c_k with the distances from the current point x_k to the boundaries of the surrogates.

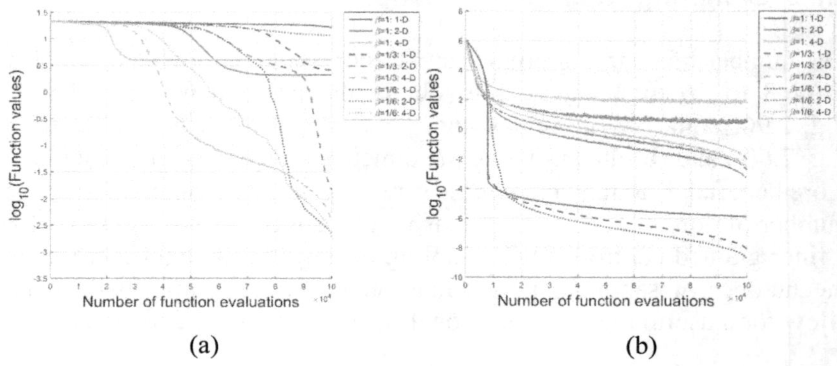

(a) (b)

Fig. 2.10. Decreasing the sampling volume for (a) Ackley ($p = 16$ points) and (b) Sum of squares ($p = 32$ points).

The expression for c_k is given by

$$c_k = \left(\sqrt{m}\right)^{-1}(1 - 10^{-10})\left(1 - \left(\frac{feval_k}{feval_{max}}\right)^{\beta}\right) + 10^{-10}, \quad (2.4)$$

2.6. Neural Network Training

We now demonstrate that the behavior and performance observed on our test problems are related to actual machine learning problems. Towards this aim we consider three neural network architectures to solve the Iris dataset that has 4 input variables and 3 output variables for which the gradients were computed using backpropagation.

We consider 3 problems of neural network (NN) with single hidden layer:

1. 1 node in the hidden layer resulted in a $(4+1)1+(1+1)3 = 11$ variable problem;

2. 6 nodes in the hidden layer resulted in a $(4+1)6+(6+1)3 = 51$ variable problem;

3. 63 nodes in the hidden layer resulted in a (4 + 1)63 + (63 + 1)3 = 507 variable problem.

All variables are initialized between -1 and 1. For training the network problems, a heuristic method is implemented such that the optimization range is not fixed between -1 and 1 but the range may slide dynamically along with the current solution x_k so that x_k always remains at the centre of the range. This method allows for the sampling density to be constant while the domain over which we samples may change.

The training errors are indicated with solid lines and the test errors are indicated by dotted lines for 11, 51 and 507-D in Figs. 2.11-2.13.

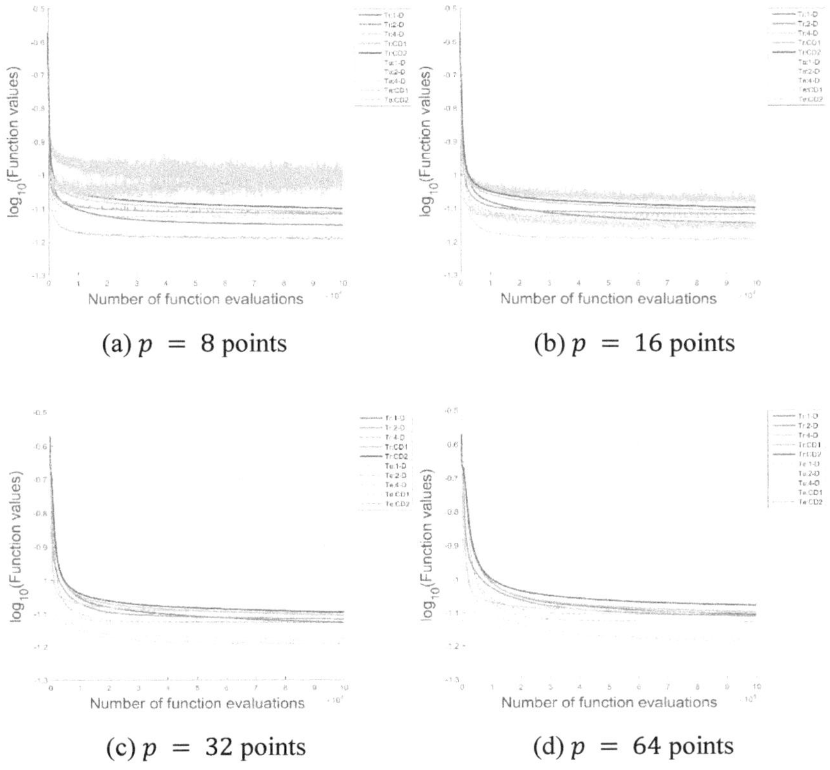

(a) $p = 8$ points

(b) $p = 16$ points

(c) $p = 32$ points

(d) $p = 64$ points

Fig. 2.11. Training Iris data set with the gradient-based variable selection approach for 11-D.

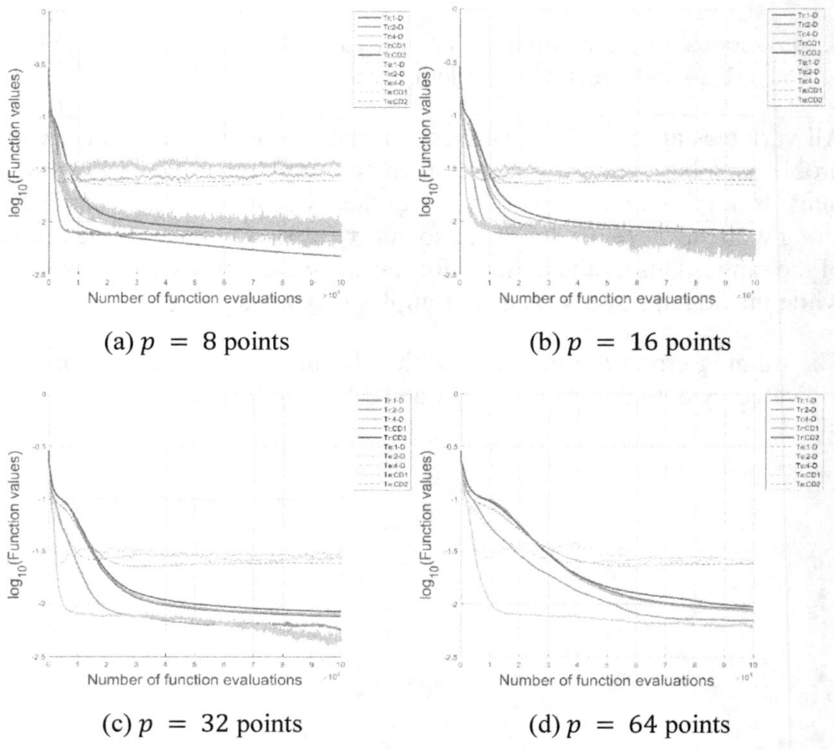

(a) $p = 8$ points

(b) $p = 16$ points

(c) $p = 32$ points

(d) $p = 64$ points

Fig. 2.12. Training Iris data set with the gradient-based variable selection approach for 51-D.

The results for the 11-D problem are similar to the results obtained for the test problems. The multi-dimension surrogate search outperforms the univariate searches in terms of computational cost and generality as both the 2-D and 4-D achieve significantly improved test errors for $p = 32$ and 64 sampling points (see Fig. 2.11 (c) and (d)). In fact, 2-D achieved the best performance using $p = 8$ and $p = 16$ points, while 4-D saw significant improvement going from $p = 16$ to $p = 32$ points. Both training and test errors of the 4-D are significantly higher when lower number of sampling points were used (Fig. 2.11 (a)), however, as the number of points increase, the lower the minimum (Fig. 2.11 (d)).

The trend between 51-D and 507-D are similar due to the simplicity of the problem due to overfitting (see Figs. 2.12-2.13). It needs to be emphasized that the test errors for both CD and 1-D sub-surrogate

approaches are insensitive to the number of sampling points but for 2-D
and 4-D sub-surrogate approaches, increasing the number of sampling
points noticeably increases convergence rate with decreases in both
training and test errors.

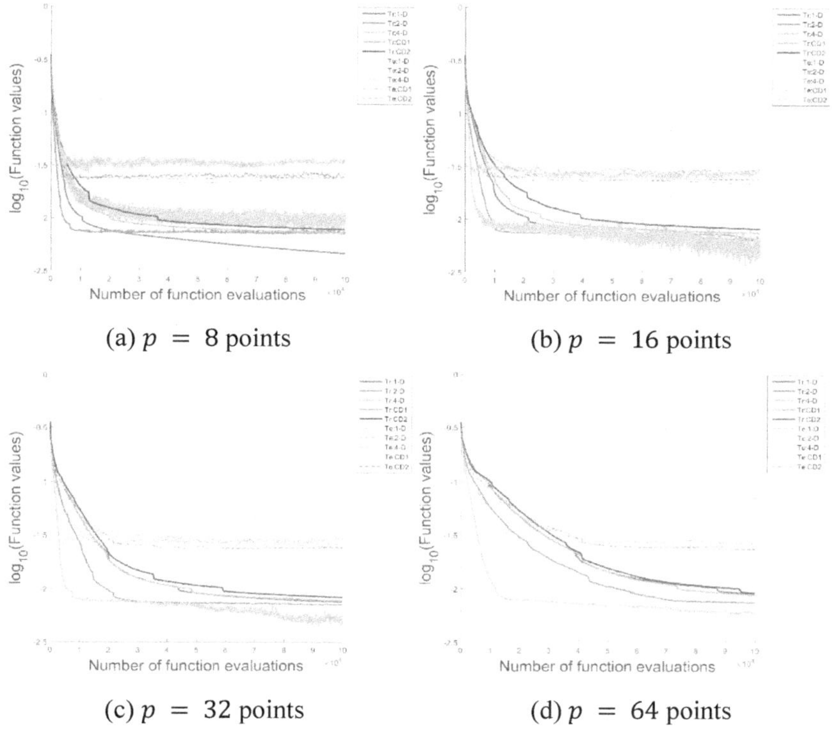

(a) $p = 8$ points

(b) $p = 16$ points

(c) $p = 32$ points

(d) $p = 64$ points

Fig. 2.13. Training Iris data set with the gradient-based variable selection
approach for 507-D.

2.7. Conclusions

Currently surrogates are constructed for either 1-dimensions, i.e. line
searches or full-dimensional, i.e. standard surrogates. This study
proposes sub-dimensional surrogates, i.e. constructing surrogates in
sub-dimensions between 1-dimension and the full-dimensions. We
demonstrated that there is merit in exploring this research domain using
merely a vanilla sub-dimensional surrogate strategy, without any

heuristics, yes, we even omitted the obvious ones on purpose. This was done to ensure we investigate and learn from our investigation to gain further insight into this new research domain of surrogate construction, namely, sub-dimensional surrogates. We demonstrate that sub-dimensional surrogates are a viable approach to extend surrogate-based optimization to even higher dimensions on two test problems as formulated and randomly rotated to increase the variable interaction. Higher sub-dimensions allow for better initial improvement and exploration that are less sensitive to variable interactions, while lower sub-dimensions allow for better exploitation and are more sensitive to variable interactions. This study introduces two new domains for heuristics in surrogate construction namely sub-dimensions to control sampling density and heuristics to identify appropriate sub-dimensional spaces.

Based on our findings, we have identified the following areas of future research, which are to develop heuristics that:

1. Identify when to reduce the dimensionality of the sub-dimensional surrogate;

2. Identifying appropriate sub-dimensions;

3. Scale the number of samples and sampling domain (sub-space) given the sub-dimension.

We concluded our study by showing that the carefully selected test problems for our study are related to actual cost functions encountered in machine learning by training three neural nets on a well-known test problem in machine learning, namely the Iris data set.

Acknowledgments

This research was supported by the National Research Foundation (NRF), South Africa and the Center for Asset Integrity Management (C-AIM), Department of Mechanical and Aeronautical Engineering, University of Pretoria, Pretoria, South Africa.

References

[1] Z. Yang, K. Tang, X. Yao, Large scale evolutionary optimization using cooperative coevolution, *Inf. Sci.*, Vol. 178, Issue 15, 2008, pp. 2985-2999.

[2] N. V. Queipo, R. T. Haftka, W. Shyy, T. Goel, R. Vaidyanathan, P. Kevin Tucker, Surrogate-based analysis and optimization, *Prog. Aerosp. Sci.*, Vol. 41, Issue 1, 2005, pp. 1-28.

[3] W. Shyy, Y. C. Cho, W. Du, A. Gupta, C. C. Tseng, A. M. Sastry, Surrogate-based modeling and dimension reduction techniques for multi-scale mechanics problems, *Acta Mech. Sin. Xuebao*, Vol. 27, Issue 6, 2011, pp. 845-865.

[4] S. Shan, G. G. Wang, Survey of modeling and optimization strategies to solve high-dimensional design problems with computationally-expensive black-box functions, *Struct. Multidiscip. Optim.*, Vol. 41, Issue 2, 2010, pp. 219-241.

[5] M. Kubicek, E. Minisci, M. Cisternino, High dimensional sensitivity analysis using surrogate modeling and high dimensional model representation, *Int. J. Uncertain. Quantif.*, Vol. 5, Issue 5, 2015, pp. 393-414.

[6] K. Kang, I. Lee, D. Kim, Efficient Metamodeling Strategy using Multivariate Linear Interpolation for High Dimensional Problems, in *Proceedings of the 12th World Congress Struct. Multidisciplinary Optim. (WCSMO'17)*, June 2017, pp. 1-6.

[7] R. G. Regis, Constrained optimization by radial basis function interpolation for high-dimensional expensive black-box problems with infeasible initial points, *Eng. Optim.*, Vol. 46, Issue 2, 2014, pp. 218-243.

[8] Z. H. Han, S. Görtz, R. Zimmermann, Improving variable-fidelity surrogate modeling via gradient-enhanced kriging and a generalized hybrid bridge function, *Aerosp. Sci. Technol.*, Vol. 25, Issue 1, 2013, pp. 177-189.

[9] Z.-H. Han, Y. Zhang, C.-X. Song, K.-S. Zhang, Weighted gradient-enhanced kriging for high-dimensional surrogate modeling and design optimization, *AIAA J.*, Vol. 55, Issue 12, 2017, pp. 4330-4346.

[10] R. G. Regis, C. A. Shoemaker, Combining radial basis function surrogates and dynamic coordinate search in high-dimensional expensive black-box optimization, *Eng. Optim.*, Vol. 45, Issue 5, 2013, pp. 529-555.

[11] Y. Nesterov, Efficiency of coordinate descent methods on huge-scale optimization problems, *SIAM J. Optim.*, Vol. 22, Issue 2, 2012, pp. 341-362.

[12] A. A. Canutescu, R. L. Dunbrack, Cyclic coordinate descent: A robotics algorithm for protein loop closure, *Protein Sci.*, 2003.

[13] K. Sauer, C. Bouman, A local update strategy for iterative reconstruction from projections, *IEEE Trans. Signal Process.*, Vol. 41, Issue 2, 1993, pp. 534-548.

[14] D. Bertsekas, Nonlinear Programming, *Athena Scientific*, 1999.

[15] S. J. Wright, Coordinate descent algorithms, *Math. Program.*, Vol. 151, Issue 1, 2015, pp. 3-34.

[16] Z. Q. Luo, P. Tseng, A coordinate gradient descent method for nonsmooth separable minimization, *J. Optim. Theory Appl.*, Vol. 72, 2002.

[17] P. Richtárik, Iteration complexity of randomized block-coordinate descent methods for minimizing a composite function, *arXiv:1107.2848*, 2011.

[18] M. A. Potter, K. A. Jong, A cooperative coevolutionary approach to function optimization, in *Proceedings of the International Conference on Parallel Problem Solving from Nature (PPSN'94)*, 1994, pp. 249-257.

[19] B. A. Tolson, C. A. Shoemaker, Dynamically dimensioned search algorithm for computationally efficient watershed model calibration, *Water Resour. Res.*, Vol. 43, Issue 1, 2007, pp. 1-16.

[20] J. Friedman, T. Hastie, R. Tibshirani, Sparse inverse covariance estimation with the graphical lasso, *Biostatistics*, Vol. 9, Issue 3, 2008, pp. 432-441.

[21] J. Friedman, T. Hastie, R. Tibshirani, Regularization paths for generalized linear models via coordinate descent, *J. Stat. Softw.*, Vol. 33, Issue 1, 2010, pp. 1-22.

[22] K.-W. Chang, C.-J. Hsieh, C.-J. Lin, Coordinate descent method for large-scale L2-loss linear support vector machines, *J. Mach. Learn. Res.*, Vol. 9, 2008, pp. 1369-1398.

[23] B. Werth, E. Pitzer, M. Affenzeller, Enabling High-dimensional Surrogate-assisted Optimization by Using Sliding Windows, in *Proceedings of the Genet. Evol. Comput. Conference (GECCO'17)*, 2017, pp. 1630-1637.

[24] C. Sun, Y. Jin, R. Cheng, J. Ding, J. Zeng, Surrogate-Assisted Cooperative Swarm Optimization of High-Dimensional Expensive Problems, *IEEE Trans. Evol. Comput.*, Vol. 21, Issue 4, 2017, pp. 644-660.

[25] H. Zou, T. Hastie, Regularization and variable selection via the elastic net, *J. R. Stat. Soc. Ser. B Stat. Methodol.*, Vol. 67, Issue 2, 2005, pp. 301-320.

[26] S. Mahdavi, M. E. Shiri, S. Rahnamayan, Cooperative Co-evolution with a new decomposition method for large-scale optimization, in *Proceedings of the IEEE Congress Evol. Comput. (CEC'14)*, 2014, pp. 1285-1292.

[27] Z. Yang, K. Tang, X. Yao, Multilevel cooperative coevolution for large scale optimization, in *Proceedings of the IEEE Congr. Evol. Comput. (CEC'08)*, 2008, pp. 1663-1670.

[28] A. Paszke *et al.*, Automatic differentiation in PyTorch, *Adv. Neural Inf. Process. Syst.*, Vol. 30, 2017, pp. 1-4.

[29] N. Shukla, Machine Learning with TensorFlow, *Manning*, 2018.

[30] M. D. McKay, R. J. Beckman, W. J. Conover, A comparison of three methods for selecting values of input variables in the analysis of output from a computer code, *Technometrics*, Vol. 21, Issue 2, 2000, pp. 239-245.

[31] M. J. D. Powell, The theory of radial basis function approximation in 1990, in Advances in Numerical Analysis, Vol. I, (Edited by W. Light), Clarendon Press, Oxford, 1992, pp. 105-210.

[32] M. J. D. Powell, Five lectures on radial basis functions, *IMM Lect.*, 2004, p. 27.

[33] I. Ilievski, T. Akhtar, J. Feng, C. A. Shoemaker, Efficient hyperparameter optimization of deep learning algorithms using deterministic RBF surrogates, *arXiv:1607.08316*, 2016.

[34] J. A. Nelder, R. Mead, A simplex method for function minimization, *Comput. J.*, Vol. 7, Issue 4, 1965, pp. 308-313.

[35] MATLAB, Version 8.6.0.267246, *The MathWorks Inc.*, 2015.

[36] S. Surjanovic, D. Bingham, Virtual Library of Simulation Experiments: Test Functions and Datasets, http://www.sfu.ca/~ssurjaIssue

[37] C. Moler, C. Van Loan, Nineteen dubious ways to compute the exponential of a matrix, twenty-five years later, *SIAM Rev.*, Vol. 45, Issue 1, 2003, pp. 3-49.

[38] H. Li, Z. Xu, G. Taylor, C. Studer, T. Goldstein, Visualizing the loss landscape of neural nets, *arXiv:1712.09913*, 2017.

[39] I. J. Goodfellow, O. Vinyals, A. M. Saxe, Qualitatively characterizing neural network optimization problems, *arXiv1412.6544*, 2014.

Chapter 3

Reusing Strategies for Decision Support in Disaster Management – A Case-based High-level Petri Net Approach

Stella Moehrle, Wolfgang Raskob

3.1. Introduction

Disasters are characterized by serious disruptions of society's functionality involving human, material, economic, and/or environmental losses, and particularly by exceeding society's capacity to cope with its own resources [1]. Disaster management is "the organization, planning and application of measures preparing for, responding to and recovering from disasters" [2]. There are several models that explain the key elements of disaster management from different points of view. The most common approach is the division into the four phases 'mitigation', 'preparedness', 'response', and 'recovery' [3]. This research is dedicated to the 'preparedness' phase which aims at facilitating response and recovery by, for example, developing decision support methods and software solutions or, in general, by promoting readiness. The method presented is mainly elaborated through nuclear emergencies.

Decision-making in the event of a disaster is complicated by various factors such as the uncertainty on what is happening and the limited time frame available to identify appropriate strategies for countering such events. A *strategy* is understood as a combination of several measures aiming at specific objectives. In the case of nuclear accidents, for instance, objectives are to reduce the level of radiation exposure to humans and, in the longer term, to return to normal living conditions.

Stella Moehrle
Institute for Nuclear and Energy Technologies, Karlsruhe Institute of Technology (KIT), Germany

Computerized support for disaster management is a vital research topic which is reflected, for example, by the annually held Conference on Information Systems for Crisis Response and Management [4] or the various knowledge management systems developed over the last decades [5]. When explicitly looking for decision-supporting solutions for disaster management, the focus varies from scheduling [6] to mobile support [7] to humanitarian relief [8]. Furthermore, different event types such as floods [9] or environmental [10] and technological emergencies [11] have been investigated.

In respect of nuclear emergencies, JRodos [12], Argos [13] or the NARAC [14] system are among the well-known and operationally used decision support systems. These systems prepare decisive information for constructing a strategy with each new event, e.g., projections of the radiological situation, and analyses of the effectiveness of combined measures. However, as regards emergency management, there are still some issues that became particularly apparent during the Fukushima Daiichi Nuclear Power Plant Accident and that have been discussed in several reports and papers (e.g. International Atomic Energy Agency (IAEA), 2015; Investigation Committee on the Accident at Fukushima Nuclear Power Stations of Tokyo Electric Power Company, 2012; The Fukushima Nuclear Accident Independent Investigation Commission, 2012). Some of these are: (i) Uncertainty in respect of initial information and simulation results; (ii) Complexity of strategy building. Above all, there is a lack of practical experience with regard to appropriate strategies and their implementation, especially in the long-term. (iii) Preparedness and, above all, the structured integration of existing knowledge and experience in the decision process. Mainly with regard to (ii), preparing scenarios and strategies in advance of an accident would help to save time and avoid mistakes in the event of an incident. We suggest a case-based decision support method that identifies strategies for response and recovery on the basis of experience and expert knowledge and in particular prepared strategies that are adaptable to the current circumstances. Here, the strategies are subject to a High-level Petri net (HLPN) model to be included in the case-based decision support system. Hence, the suggested strategies are stored in a structured manner and are executable as well as analyzable.

The presented method is independent of the underlying *event* and hence the occurrence of the incident that triggers the necessity of building and implementing a strategy. However, the concrete implementation of the case-based decision support method requires an in-depth analysis of the underlying triggering incident. The timely structuring of a nuclear accident taking into account the status of release of radioactive material could not be applied to earthquakes, for example. Information on release is crucial for decision-making in nuclear emergency management and would not be relevant in the case of natural disasters.

Our case-based decision support method particularly addresses issues that became apparent during the Fukushima Daiichi Nuclear Power Plant Accident and aims at complementing existing decision support systems (i) In times of high uncertainty; (ii) By suggesting coherent strategies; (iii) By structuring and storing experience and existing knowledge to be reused in a current event, and especially (iv) By preparing scenarios in advance of an event as well as (v) By promoting computerized strategy support and analysis possibilities. To sum up, the method pursues a different approach than do current decision support systems or methods that are mainly simulation-based or based on multi-criteria decision analysis (e.g. [18]).

Fig. 3.1 illustrates an overview of the decision support method which relies on Case-based Reasoning (CBR), a problem-solving paradigm that utilizes knowledge of previously experienced problematic situations to solve a current problem [19]. Here, the description of a problem, the corresponding strategies for problem solving, their effectiveness, and further decision-supporting information build a case in the case base. Scenarios i.e., fictitious events following the same structure as a historical event, enhance the case base. The idea is to determine different accidents and appropriate strategies in advance to store them in the case base and to make them reusable in the case of a current event.

CBR and especially the decision-supporting method can be described as a cycle process that consists of four phases. After identifying and describing the problem to be solved, the first step is to retrieve the most similar case or cases from a case base. The second step is to reuse the strategies of the similar cases involving possibly the merging of several strategies and the adaptation to current circumstances. Besides numerical adaptations according to effectiveness parameters such as waste or costs, several potentially appropriate strategies should be merged to cover all objects possibly endangered. The suggested solution will be revised by the user and possibly tested or adjusted. Finally, the case base is updated by retaining the new case with its confirmed solution in the case base. In general, each phase involves several tasks with various methods to be realized [19]. Besides the specific knowledge in the cases, general domain-dependent knowledge supports each phase of the CBR cycle.

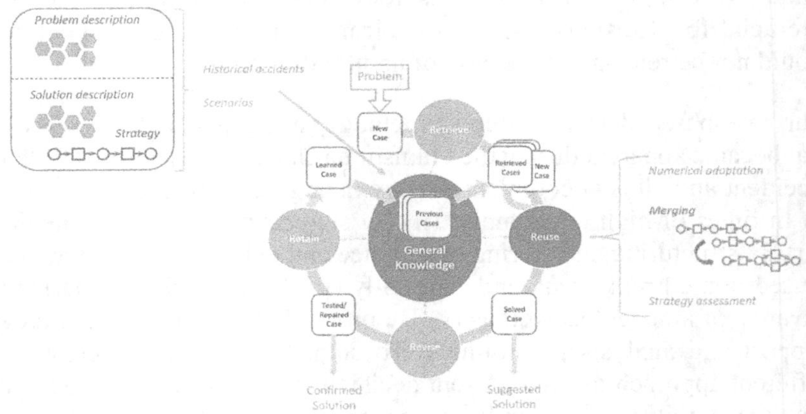

Fig. 3.1. Overview of the decision-supporting method with a special focus on strategy modeling and reuse in the framework of case-based reasoning. The CBR cycle is based on [19].

Research on CBR is manifold (e.g. [20-23]), for example in the context of disaster management as a special field of application (e.g. [24-30]). CBR can be used when solutions are difficult to obtain and when storage makes sense for later reuse. It can also be used in exceptional situations when causal models would reach their limits and in domains that are not fully understood and where the use of similarity offers possibilities to reason [31]. Similar situations may also offer a framework for evaluating solutions and specifically for avoiding mistakes of the past [31] or mistakes that have already been thought through. The latter mainly refers to scenario construction which is part of the method proposed. In general, CBR is intuitively comprehensible and transparent and the proximity to human problem-solving is advantageous in respect of accepting the decision-supporting method.

The strategies stored in the case base are subject to a HLPN model to capture the implementation order, provide analysis possibilities, and support their automated reuse in the course of a current event. Petri nets essentially provide means to describe a course of action formally and unambiguously and are applied successfully in various fields, inter alia in disaster management. The combination with CBR is promising since

(i) Suggestions on strategies are based on experience and expert knowledge; (ii) Strategies are stored in a structured manner and are executable as well as analyzable; and (iii) The approach supports preparedness and provides means to improve by integrating more knowledge.

In Fig. 3.1, the parts of the method presented in the following are highlighted in green. Previous publications particularly focus on the case base and retrieval [32, 33]. First research on the reuse step has already been published [34, 35], and further results are presented in the sections below.

The structure of the book chapter is as follows: First, (high-level) Petri nets are introduced, and their research and benefits in the field of disaster management are discussed. Next, the research questions are presented, and an overview is given of the structure of the entire method, the focus of this publication, and the added value. An introduction to the strategy model is then followed by a presentation of the reuse step and predominantly of the merging of several strategies as well as by examples and a discussion of the Petri net approach and future work.

3.2. Petri Nets and Their Application in Disaster Management

Petri nets are a graphical and mathematical modeling tool useful for describing and analyzing information processing systems as well as for visual communication [36]. They originate from the early work of Carl Adam Petri [37]. A Petri net [36] is a tuple

$$PN = (P, T, F, W, M_0),$$

where:

- P and T are the non-empty finite sets of places and transitions,

- $P \cap T = \emptyset$,

- $F \subseteq (P \times T) \cup (T \times P)$ is called a flow relation of PN. The elements of F are called arcs,

- $W: F \rightarrow \mathbb{N}$ is the weight function,

- $M_0: P \rightarrow \mathbb{N}$ is the initial marking.

Places are represented by circles, transitions by rectangles, and arcs are labeled by weights. The state of the system, which is called a marking $M: P \rightarrow \mathbb{N}$, is reflected by the distribution of tokens, represented by black dots, over places. The input and output places of transitions are defined as follows:

- $\bullet t = \{p|(p,t) \in F\}$ is called the set of input places of transition t,

- $t \bullet = \{p|(t,p) \in F\}$ is called the set of output places of transition t.

The dynamics of the system can be described by marking changes caused by firing a transition. A transition t is enabled if and only if each input place p contains at least $w(p,t)$ tokens where $w(p,t)$ denotes the weight of the arc from p to t. The firing of t removes $w(p,t)$ tokens from each input place p and adds $w(t,p)$ tokens to each output place p of t where $w(t,p)$ is the weight of the arc from t to p.

There are different types of nets, namely low- and high-level Petri nets. In low-level nets, such as the classical Petri nets introduced above, tokens are indistinguishable. In HLPNs [38], tokens have individual characteristics and therefore can be distinguished. Here, places and transitions are defined with respect to different token types. Further well-known extensions of low-level nets are according to time and hierarchy to structure large models [39]. HLPNs allow for a more compact description than low-level nets and for practical applications, they are preferred to the latter [40].

Petri nets are interesting for a variety of application fields such as performance evaluation, manufacturing/industrial control systems, distributed software systems or decision models [36]. They are used for various emergency management applications: generalized stochastic Petri nets are used e.g. for modeling traffic accident rescue processes [41], and stochastic Petri nets are applied for performance analyses of coal mine emergency processes [42], emergency response decision-making processes [43], and urban response [44]. Colored Petri nets, in particular, are used to model emergency plan business processes [45] and emergency response in the course of chemical accidents with continuous places and transitions [46]. They are used in combination with a queuing system for resource use [47] and in the framework of critical infrastructure protection [48] or for modeling the patients flow in an emergency medical department [49]. Further application examples of Petri nets are emergency management modeling in railway stations [50], modeling of industrial fire management processes [51] or accident modeling [52] where the difficulty is to transfer text into a formal model [53]. Moreover, Petri nets have a huge potential in the field of risk analysis and accident modeling with the possibility of expressing common concepts in Petri net formalisms [54]. Petri nets are particularly used in nuclear power plant emergency management, which aims at reducing the number of false evacuations [55].

The Petri net applications presented so far focus on specific emergency response processes (i.e., in the framework of a specific accident scenario) for performance analysis or for execution support. The research questions addressed in this book chapter have a different focus which will be discussed in the following. The papers by [45-47] are thematically close to our approach. They report on working with HLPNs and distinguishable tokens according to different resource types and the level of the fire state [46]. The application domain of nuclear emergencies can be found in [55] who models a specific emergency management process addressing actions within a nuclear power plant with the help of low-level Petri nets.

3.3. Research Questions

The research presented in this book chapter has a different focus than related work on Petri nets in disaster management. Above all, the following question is addressed: **How can strategies for disaster management be modeled considering following requirements?**

(i)   **Independence from the type of event.** This requirement originated from research in the field of natural disasters and analyses of different types of events allowing now to transfer the model to nuclear emergencies as well. The focus on nuclear emergencies originated from the participation in the European project PREPARE [56] where a close collaboration with experts took place providing the possibility of data collection.

(ii)   **Capturing the implementation order of measures.** In general, measures cannot be executed in an arbitrary order. Examples in the nuclear field can be found in the Handbook for Assisting in the Management of Contaminated Inhabited Areas in Europe Following a Radiological Emergency [57] where decontamination measures are listed that may have timely or logical constraints with regard to the implementation order.

(iii) **Comprising short- and long-term decisions as well as possible event developments.** Being part of the preparedness phase of disaster management, this work aims at providing support for response and recovery and hence short- and long-term decisions.

(iv) **Capturing the effects of measures.** This requirement is important for the comparability of strategies.

(v) **Capturing crucial factors influencing decisions on measures.** This requirement particularly refers to the learning capability of CBR. The crucial factors are important for identifying similar cases from the case base. Some of them are important for the reuse step as well.

(vi) **Allowing performance analysis**, which is important for the assessment of strategies. Hence, simulation possibilities are of great value.

(vii) **Supporting a graphical representation of strategies** facilitating user understanding. A structured storage and possibilities for automatic processing are of first priority. A graphical presentation would mainly be useful for communication and manual adaptation of strategies, if desired. The latter would be future work.

(viii) **Facilitating automatic processing** which is important for the reuse step of CBR.

(ix) **Allowing easy extensibility.** The modeling capabilities should not be limited. This work does not claim to have integrated all decisive factors but rather focuses on a general model for strategies.

Studies on related work, reports on the flood in 2002 in Germany [58, 59], the German fire department regulation 100 (FwDV 100) [60] dealing with leadership and command in emergency operations command and control systems as well as research within the PREPARE project resulted in the requirements listed so far. The fire department regulations particularly guide situation assessment which is based on locality, time, weather, damage, damaged objects, the extent of damage as well as resources determining the planning process and the resulting measures. In this work, location, context of event or the initial situation are primarily covered by the retrieval step of CBR.

Petri nets are regarded as an appropriate tool answering the research question and meeting the requirements presented before. They allow for a mathematical representation of strategies and provide analysis capabilities of structure and dynamic behavior [61]. Furthermore, they have a good graphical representation. Petri nets are applied successfully in various fields, particularly in the areas of emergency and disaster management as well as accident modeling, as can be seen in the literature review. The modeling of strategies including measures, events, and decisive information leads to various states and an increasing complexity. Hence, HLPNs are preferred over low-level Petri nets allowing for a compact, generic, and clear representation of strategies.

Petri nets are also used in the context of CBR e.g., for establishing a database where case retrieval is based on similarity calculations between markings [62]. In addition, they serve as a means for gaining parameters that can be used in the case retrieval [63] or are used to model cases [64], [65]. Again, specific implementations, purposes, and application domains differ from what is studied and presented in this book chapter. The following section summarizes the structure of the entire method, the focus of this publication, and the added value.

3.4. Case- and HLPN-based Decision Support

The structure of the main components is as follows:

(i) A case of the case base is subject to a case model that consists of a problem and solution model. The solution model includes the strategy model [32]. Strategies are instances of the strategy model.

(ii) The problem model is an n-tuple of attributes where specific attributes are used for the retrieval step of CBR [32]. The strategies of the k most similar cases (k can be a fixed number or the number of cases whose similarity values exceed a certain threshold) may be reused. Reuse includes numerical adaptation, merging of several strategies, and strategy assessment.

The application domain is disaster management and above all the development of a decision-supporting method for response and recovery promoting the reuse of already compiled knowledge and particularly preparedness. This work builds on previous studies, focusing now on the strategy model and on the reuse step. The strategy model, which is based on HLPNs, allows a structured storage of strategies, automatization of the reuse step of CBR as well as analyses concerning effectiveness parameters. The strategy model is an inherent part of the case model whose graphical representation possibilities may be used to promote user understanding and manual adaptation.

To the best of the authors' knowledge, the above presented integration of HLPNs in a case-based decision-supporting method is new in disaster management. In particular, the authors promote a novel research direction, namely case-based decision support in nuclear emergency management [32], [33], [66-68]. The following section presents the developed strategy model.

3.5. Strategy Model

The strategy model is based on ISO/IEC 15909 [69] with the final published version in 2004 [70]. Moreover, the labeling of transitions [36] is integrated. The strategies in the case base are instances of the strategy model. In consideration of the requirements listed before, the following **assumptions** are made:

(i)   The model contains two active components with different behaviors: measures and events.

(ii) Events cause the endangerment of specific objects. In respect of nuclear emergency management, objects may also be surfaces that have been contaminated. Here, 'endangerment' needs to be understood in a wider sense.

(iii) Measures are decided upon and implemented because of an event and its resulting endangered objects.

(iv) Measures reduce the endangerment of the objects and do not create endangerment.

(v)   Measures consume resources.

Definition 3.1. HLPN-based strategy model.

The strategy model S is a tuple

$$S = (P, T, Dom, Type, Pre, Post, M_0),$$

where:

(i) P is the finite set of places.

(ii) $T = T_m \cup T_e$ is a finite set of transitions where T_m denotes the set of measures and T_e denotes the set of events. It holds that $P \cap T = \emptyset$. Moreover, there are finite sets of labels for measures Σ_m and events Σ_e and labeling functions

$$L_k: T_k \rightarrow \Sigma_k, k \in \{m, e\},$$

which assign labels to the transitions from a predefined domain.

(iii) $Dom = \{B \times [0,1], R, \{\cdot\}\}$ is a set of domains where each element of *Dom* is called a type. The first type B is a predefined set of endangered objects. The interval $[0,1]$ indicates the degree of endangerment expressed as real number between 0 and 1. With reference to a contaminated surface, 1 indicates 100 % contamination and 0 indicates a successful decontamination[1]. The second type R is a predefined set of resources. The type $\{\cdot\}$ does not have any characteristics.

(iv) $Type: P \cup T \rightarrow Dom$ is a function used to assign types to places and to determine transition modes. A transition mode is a pair comprising the transition and a value taken from the transition's type.

(v) $Pre, Post: TRANS \rightarrow \mu PLACE$ are pre- and post-mappings with

$$TRANS = \{(t, m) | t \in T, m \in Type(t)\},$$

$$PLACE = \{(p, g) | p \in P, g \in Type(p)\},$$

$\mu PLACE$ is the set of multisets over the set $PLACE$.

(vi) $M_0 \in \mu PLACE$ is the initial marking of the net.

---

[1] A successful decontamination does not necessarily correspond to a pre-release status but rather to the achievement of specific effectiveness values and the restoration of a worth-living environment

For $(t, m) \in TRANS$, the pre- and post-mappings can be written as symbolic sums of elements of *PLACE* scaled by their multiplicities:

$$Pre(t, m) = P_\mu = \sum_{x \in PLACE} P_\mu(x)'x, \, P_\mu \in \mu PLACE,$$

and $Post(t, m)$ respectively. $P_\mu(x)$ denotes the multiplicity of $x \in PLACE$ in the multiset P_μ.

Denote $M \in \mu PLACE$ a marking. A transition mode $(t, m) \in TRANS$ is enabled at a marking M if and only if

$$Pre(t, m) \leq M$$

A finite multiset of transition modes $T_\mu \in \mu TRANS$[1] is enabled at a marking M if and only if

$$Pre(T_\mu) = \sum_{(t,m) \in TRANS} T_\mu(t, m) Pre(t, m) \leq M$$

All transition modes in T_μ are concurrently enabled if T_μ is enabled and there are enough tokens on the input places satisfying the linear combination of the pre-mappings for each transition mode in T_μ. Given that T_μ is enabled at M a step, denoted by $M \xrightarrow{T_\mu} M'$, may occur resulting in a new marking M'

$$M' = M - Pre(T_\mu) + Post(T_\mu)$$

Let

$$TRANS|T_m = \{(t, m) | t \in T_m, m \in Type(t)\},$$

$$TRANS|T_e = \{(t, m) | t \in T_e, m \in Type(t)\}$$

Assumptions (ii) and (iv) can be formalized as follows:

Let $(t, m) \in TRANS$ with $m = (b, y) \in B \times [0,1]$. For all $\left(p_1, (b, y_{pre})\right) \in Pre(t, m)$ and $\left(p_2, (b, y_{post})\right) \in Post(t, m)$ it holds

$$y_{pre} \leq y_{post} \; if \; (t, m) \in TRANS|T_e, \tag{3.1}$$

$$y_{pre} \geq y_{post} \; if \; (t, m) \in TRANS|T_m \tag{3.2}$$

---

[1] $\mu TRANS$ is the set of multisets over the set *TRANS*

Note that $\{\cdot\}$ is equivalent to $(p, (b, 0))$ and (p, b) for any $p \in P$ and $b \in B$. The first inequality formalizes assumption (ii): events may create endangerment. The second inequality refers to assumption (ii): measures may reduce endangerment.

Assumption (v), which refers to the consumption of resources, can be formalized as follows:

Let $(t, m) \in TRANS|T_m, P_\mu = Pre(t, m)$ and $P_{\tilde{\mu}} = Post(t, m)$. There exists at least one $x = (p, r) \in P_\mu{}^1$ with $r \in R$ for which it holds that

$$x \in P_{\tilde{\mu}} \text{ and } P_\mu(x) \geq P_{\tilde{\mu}}(x) \text{ or } x \notin P_{\tilde{\mu}} \tag{3.3}$$

The latter indicates a complete consumption of resources.

The tokens contain information on endangered objects and their endangerment as well as on resources. The implementation of a strategy corresponds to a run of an instance of the strategy model.

3.6. Reuse of Prepared Strategies for Decision Support

Assume that k similar cases are retrieved from the case base to solve a current problem. The specification of k is not a subject of this research. Hence, k strategies are available to be reused. Measures are directed towards specific objects. Hence, the objects are significant when choosing a measure. If a strategy of a retrieved case does not cover all objects currently endangered, another strategy directed towards the missing objects possibly provides additional decision support. The question is how to combine these strategies to cover all endangered objects? Computerized support may facilitate the reuse.

For the sake of clarity, the following **assumptions** are made:

(i)   Each net has exactly one initial node and one final node. The initial and final nodes are places of type $\{\cdot\}$.

(ii) Endangerment is produced and reduced completely in each net.

(iii) Resources are completely consumed in each net.

---

[1] x is a member of the multiset P_μ denoted by $x \in P_\mu$ if $P_\mu(x) > 0$

In the course of merging, we mainly focus on the following situations starting with two strategies to be merged. We assume a joint event resulting in endangered objects:

(i) Both strategies in each case cover disjoint subsets of endangered objects.

   a. They do not have any measures in common. This case particularly would result in concurrently implemented measures.

   b. They share the same measure. This case enhances the set of transition modes and essentially refers to the case when a measure is directed towards different endangered objects. The demanded resources rise accordingly.

(ii) Both strategies are directed towards the same endangered objects. The strategies do not have any measure in common resulting in a choice of measures for specific objects.

These cases may be combined and generalized arbitrarily. The purpose of merging is to identify possible strategies in case a single strategy would only cover part of the problem. The latter primarily refers to the objects currently endangered. Furthermore, in case the addressed objects are the same but different strategies are available, the choice of measures should be identified. Hence, *merging* of two strategies and hence two Petri nets is conducted at their common equally labeled transitions including corresponding pre- and post-mappings and may result in an extension of place types and transition modes.

The way of merging depends on the application context and the intention behind e.g., merging business processes due to organization merging [71] via specific merge points (places). Bottom-up process synthesis is another related research area (see [72] for a literature review) where systems are composed of incomplete sub-systems (modules) with the prominent application area of manufacturing systems [73]. For synthesis, places are merged [74, 75] as well as common transitions, places and paths [76]. Petri nets are synthesized from modules that are modeled by strongly connected state machines [77], colored Petri nets [78], generalized Petri nets [79], labeled partial orders/scenarios [80, 81] or state-based models [73]. [81, 82] particularly embed process synthesis in the disaster response field by modeling adaptive disaster response processes, in which the behavior is synthesized by scenarios at run-time.

Here, transitions (places) are merged if they are labeled equally and have equally labeled predecessors. In general, synthesis techniques may be susceptible to a possible loss of control in behavior of the composed system [72]. A further related research area is the composition of Petri nets [83-86] either via common places, transitions, and arcs or specific nodes. The literature review is intentionally restricted to Petri nets as modeling language. Furthermore, research on pre-merging activities such as identifying correspondences between processes is excluded as well. A wider literature review can be found in [35].

Merging in our context focuses on (i) combining several strategies that cover subsets of objects currently endangered, (ii) providing runs taking into account newly combined endangered objects, and (iii) preserving the original runs of the nets.

Let S_1 and S_2 be two strategies

$$S_i = (P_i, T_i, Dom_i, Type_i, Pre_i, Post_i, M_{0,i})$$

with

$$Pre_i, Post_i: TRANS_i \rightarrow \mu PLACE_i,$$

and $L_{m,i}$, $L_{e,i}$ the labeling functions of $S_i, i \in \{1,2\}$. In the following, transitions are referred to by their labels

$$T_i := \{L_{k,i}(t) | t \in T_i, k \in \{m, e\}\}, i \in \{1,2\}$$

Denote $start \in P_i$ and $end \in P_i, i \in \{1,2\}$ the start and end nodes of the nets.

The merging of the two nets is based on merging the transitions with the same labels, the nodes *start* and *end*, and places that are involved in the pre-and post-mappings of the merged transitions. In the following, the merging of two transitions is investigated further, especially the merged places involved.

Let $t_1 \in T_1$ and $t_2 \in T_2$ with $t_1 = t_2$. Denote

$$TRANS|t_i = \{(t_i, m) | m \in Type(t_i)\}, i \in \{1,2\},$$

$$\tilde{P}_i^{pre} = \{p \in P_i | (p, Type(p)) \in Pre(TRANS|t_i)\},$$

and

$$\tilde{P}_i^{post} = \{p \in P_i | (p, Type(p)) \in Post(TRANS|t_i)\}, i \in \{1,2\},$$

the places involved in the pre- and post-mappings of t_1 and t_2. Two places $p_1 \in \tilde{P}_1^{pre}$ and $p_2 \in \tilde{P}_2^{pre}$ are merged if $Type(p_1)$ and $Type(p_2)$ both belong either to the endangered objects and their endangerment, resources or do not have any characteristics. The merging generates a new place $p \in P^M$ which denotes the set of all new places originating from merging a place of P_1 with a place of P_2. The same applies to places that belong to $\tilde{P}_i^{post}, i \in \{1,2\}$. *Start* and *end* nodes are always merged.

Let

$$I: P_1 \times P_2 \rightarrow P^M,$$

a bijective function assigning places $p_1 \in P_1$ and $p_2 \in P_2$ to a place $p \in P^M$. Denote

$$\pi_i: P_1 \times P_2 \rightarrow P_i,$$

the i-th projection mapping, $i \in \{1,2\}$, and

$$\tilde{P}_i = \{p \in P_i | \exists \bar{p} \in P^M : \pi_i(I^{-1}(\bar{p})) = p\}, i \in \{1,2\},$$

the places of S_1 and S_2 that are merged.

Definition 3.2. Merged nets.

Let S_1 and S_2 be two strategies with

$$S_i = (P_i, T_i, Dom_i, Type_i, Pre_i, Post_i, M_{0,i}), i \in \{1,2\}$$

The merged nets result in

$$S = (P, T, Dom, Type, Pre, Post, M_0),$$

where:

(i) $\quad P = (P_1 \cup P_2 \cup P^M) \backslash (\tilde{P}_1 \cup \tilde{P}_2),$

(ii) $\quad T = T_1 \cup T_2,$

(iii) $\quad Dom = Dom_1 \cup Dom_2,$

(iv) $\quad Type(p) =$

$$= \begin{cases} Type_i(p), p \in P_i \backslash \tilde{P}_i, i \in \{1,2\} \\ Type_1(\pi_1(I^{-1}(p))) \cup Type_2(\pi_2(I^{-1}(p))), p \in P^M \end{cases}$$

(v) $\quad Type(t) = \begin{cases} Type_i(t), t \in T_i, t \notin T_1 \cap T_2, i \in \{1,2\} \\ Type_1(t) \cup Type_2(t), t \in T_1 \cap T_2 \end{cases},$

(vi) $\quad TRANS = TRANS_1 \cup TRANS_2,$

(vii) $\quad Pre, Post: TRANS \rightarrow \mu PLACE$ with

$$PLACE = \{(p,g)|p \in P, g \in Type(g)\},$$

and for $(t,m) \in TRANS \backslash TRANS_j$

$$Pre(t,m) = \widetilde{Pre}_i(t,m), \qquad (3.4)$$

$i \neq j, i, j \in \{1,2\}$ with

$$\widetilde{Pre}_i(t,m) = \sum_{\substack{(p,g)\in PLACE \\ p \notin P^M}} P_\mu^i(p,g)'(p,g) +$$

$$+ \sum_{\substack{(p,g)\in PLACE \\ p \in P^M}} P_\mu^i\big(\pi_i(I^{-1}(p)), g\big)'(p,g),$$

with $P_\mu^i = Pre_i(t,m)$ and for $(t,m) \in TRANS_1 \cap TRANS_2$

$$Pre(t,m) = Pre_1(t,m) \vee Pre_2(t,m) \qquad (3.5)$$

The same applies to *Post*, respectively.

(viii) $\quad M_0 = M_{0,1} + M_{0,2}$

3.7. Example

For illustrating the merging approach, CPN Tools[1], a modeling and simulation tool for Colored Petri Nets (CPNs), is used. CPNs belong to

---

[1] http://cpntools.org/

the class of HLPNs and is characterized by the combination of PNs and programming languages [87]. The CPN modeling language particularly conforms to the ISO/IEC standard the definition of the strategy model is based on.

Assume three similar cases retrieved from the case base and hence three strategies available for solving the current problem situation. The first strategy (Fig. 3.2) is targeted towards 'playground' and 'dairy cow', suggesting 'topsoil removal' and 'cover with clean soil' as well as 'clean feeding'. The first two measures can be implemented concurrently to the last measure.

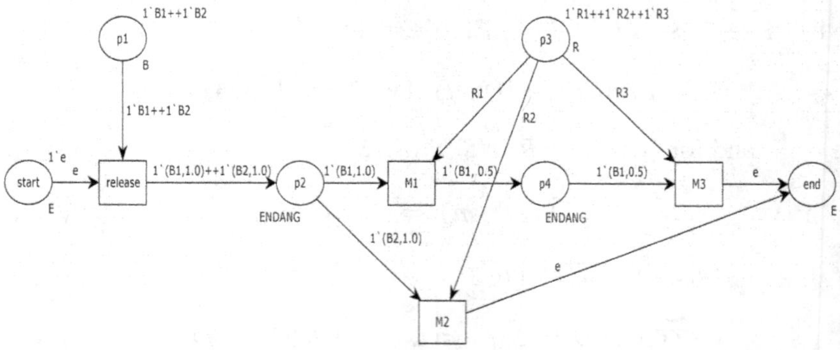

Fig. 3.2. Strategy directed towards $B1$ = playground and $B2$ = dairy cow. $M1$ = topsoil removal, $M2$ = clean feeding, $M3$ = cover with clean soil. $E = \{e\}$, $B = \{B1, B2\}$, $DEG = [0,1]$, $ENDANG = B \times DEG$, $R = \{R1, R2, R3\}$.

The second strategy (Fig. 3.3) suggests 'topsoil removal' and 'plant and shrub removal' to decontaminate the playground. Both measures are implemented sequentially.

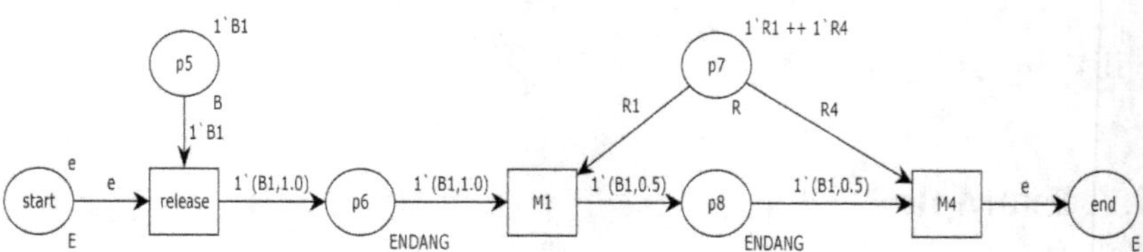

Fig. 3.3. Strategy directed towards $B1$ = playground. $M1$ = topsoil removal, $M4$ = plant and shrub removal. $E = \{e\}$, $B = \{B1, B2\}$, $DEG = [0,1]$, $ENDANG = B \times DEG$, $R = \{R1, R4\}$.

The third strategy (Fig. 3.4) is directed towards 'park' and suggests 'ploughing' and 'cover with clean soil', both implemented sequentially.

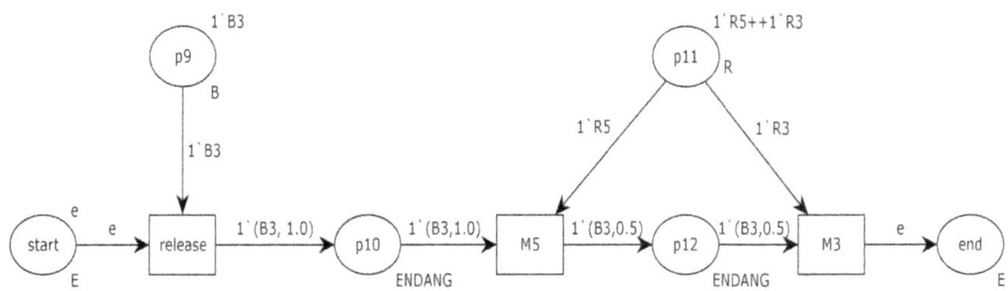

Fig. 3.4. Strategy directed towards 'park'. *M5* = ploughing, *M3* = cover with clean soil. *E = {e}, B = {B3}, DEG = [0,1], ENDANG = B × DEG, R = {R5, R3}.*

To begin with, the first two strategies are merged (Fig. 3.5).

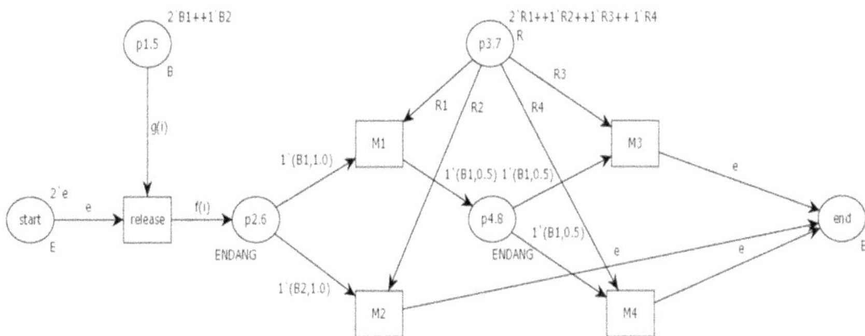

Fig. 3.5. Merging of strategies illustrated in Figs. 3.2 and 3.3 based on common transitions 'release' and *M1*. *B1* = playground, *B2* = dairy cows, *M1* = topsoil removal, *M2* = clean feeding, *M3* = cover with clean soil, *M4* = tree and shrub removal. *E = {e}, B = {B1, B2}, DEG = [0,1], ENDANG = B × DEG, R = {R1, R2, R3, R4}.*

The common transitions are 'release' and *M1* = topsoil removal. Hence the places involved in the pre- and post-mapping are merged accordingly. The resulting strategy offers a choice of measures with regard to the endangered object 'playground'. After topsoil removal (*M1*), either 'cover with clean soil' or 'plant and shrub removal' can be implemented. The set of endangered objects is not extended in the course of merging and hence there is no new combination of endangered objects. The functions *g* and *f* with *B1* = playground and *B2* = dairy cow reflect the possible runs:

$$g(i) = \begin{cases} 1`B1 + 1`B2, i = 1 \\ 1`B1, i = 2 \end{cases}$$

$$f(i) = \begin{cases} 1`(B1,1.0) + 1`(B2,1.0), i = 1 \\ 1`(B1,1.0), i = 2 \end{cases}$$

Fig. 3.6 illustrates the final merged net and merging the net of Fig. 3.5 and Fig. 3.4, respectively.

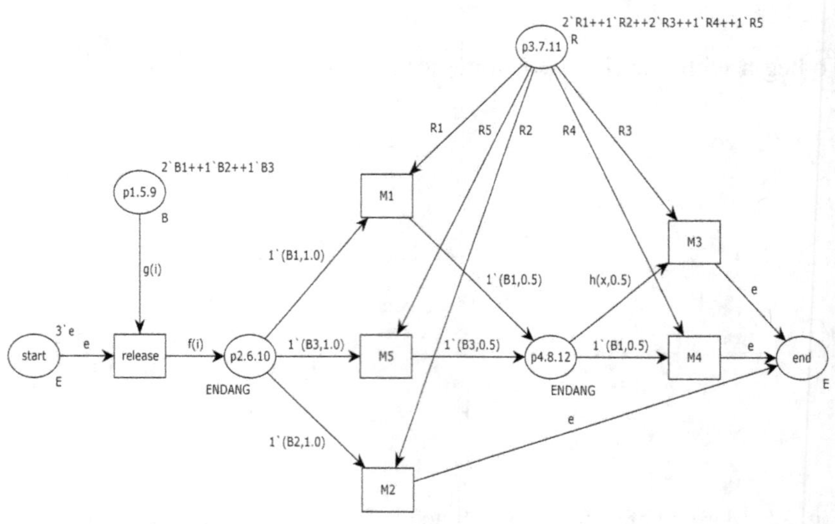

Fig. 3.6. Net resulting from merging nets illustrated in Figs. 3.5 and 3.4 and hence all three strategies available. Merging is based on merging 'release', *M1*, and *M3*. *B1* = playground, *B2* = dairy cows, *B3* = park, *M1* = topsoil removal, *M2* = clean feeding, *M3* = cover with clean soil, *M4* = tree and shrub removal, *M5* = ploughing. *E* = {*e*}, *B* = {*B1, B2, B3*}, *DEG* = [0,1], *ENDANG* = *B* × *DEG, R* = {*R1, R2, R3, R4, R5*}.

The merging is based on the common transitions 'release', *M1* and *M3*. The set of endangered objects is enhanced by *B3* = park where new combinations of endangered objects are possible now:

$$
g(i) = \begin{cases} 1`B1 + 1`B2, i \ = \ 1, \\ 1`B1, i \ = \ 2, \\ 1`B3, i \ = \ 3, \\ 1`B1 + 1`B2 + 1`B3, i \ = \ 4, \\ 1`B1 + 1`B3, i \ = \ 5, \end{cases}
$$

$$
f(i) = \begin{cases} 1`(B1,1.0) + 1`(B2,1.0), i \ = \ 1, \\ 1`(B1,1.0), i \ = \ 2, \\ 1`(B3,1.0), i \ = \ 3, \\ 1`(B1,1.0) + 1`(B2,1.0) + 1`(B3,1.0), i \ = \ 4, \\ 1`(B1,1.0) + 1`(B3,1.0), i \ = \ 5 \end{cases}
$$

The measure *M3* is directed towards 'playground' and 'park' and hence the user may choose between *M3* and *M4* with regard to 'playground':

$$
h(x, 0.5) = \begin{cases} 1`(B1,0.5), x \ = \ B1, \\ 1`(B3,0.5), x \ = \ B3 \end{cases}
$$

3.8. Discussion and Future Work

This chapter presents the reuse step of a case-based decision support method for disaster management. A case of the case base is subject to a case model that consists of a problem and solution model. The solution model includes a strategy model which is the subject of this publication and which is particularly based on High-level Petri nets. Strategies stored in the cases are instances of the strategy model.

Basically, the strategy model includes two types of transitions which are events that trigger the endangerment of objects and measures that reduce the endangerment. The tokens contain information on the object endangered and its degree of endangerment. The latter is modified during a run. This chapter above all focuses on the semantic model to present the basic ideas. In the example section, a possible graphical representation is introduced.

The strategies of the *k* most similar cases (*k* can be a fixed number or the number of cases whose similarity values exceed a certain threshold) may be reused. Reuse includes numerical adaptation, merging of several strategies, and strategy assessment. The merging is particularly presented in this chapter, in case each strategy retrieved only covers part of the problem description of the query and a subset of the current endangered objects, respectively. Merging aims at identifying strategies that cover all endangered objects specified in the query. The basic ideas are to merge the common transitions and their pre- and post-mappings. We specifically assume a predefined set of transition labels. The merging preserves the original runs of the Petri nets and identifies possible new runs for newly combined endangered objects.

Process-oriented approaches are very promising for disaster management although many requirements of this specific application field have not been addressed so far, among others a lack of disaster response management-related elements in the modeling languages [88]. Other research gaps refer to methods and tools for process analysis and simulation at design time, tools to transform models into executable process specifications, integration of resource management during process enactment, adaptation of processes at runtime, and evaluation [88].

Processes are often used to model emergency management measures and plans e.g., by event-driven process chains [89] or workflow management systems [90-94], particularly with business process model and notation [95]. The latter publication mainly emphasizes the need for domain-specific adaptation e.g., different types of resources, their usage, states, spatial allocation, and interdependencies. [96, 97] pursue an activity-centric approach to coordinate disaster response activities and develop a collaborative disaster response process management system. The authors specifically state that business process management technology is not suitable for disaster response processes mainly focusing on event-driven process chains. They essentially argue that "Disaster response processes do not have information dependencies between the activities, but temporal dependencies, which need a different kind of treatment."([96] p. 62). The authors' focus differ from ours and concentrate on an ad-hoc activity management system for different parties involved, specifically on the intra- and inter-organizational levels. We aim at a generic strategy model to be applied to different kinds of disasters, especially for storing strategies in the case base to be reused in the course of a new event. Hence, besides storing a strategy in a structured and unambiguous manner, an automatized further use is demanded. High-level Petri nets are regarded as being suitable to meet these requirements due to their mathematical representation and great expressiveness. Furthermore, they have analysis capabilities of structure and dynamic behavior and allow for analyses of effectiveness parameters. The latter is particularly interesting if two strategies are available for selection.

The model and merging mechanism presented are generic since they are neither linked to a specific event nor measure type. So far, the model takes into account two decisive factors for measure selection i.e., the objects endangered and the resources needed for implementation. Note that further decisive factors such as the area affected as well as relevant information in respect of release, are considered in the similarity calculation. For reuse, we oriented towards the key steps in constructing a strategy (e.g. [57]). A missing factor would be the radionuclides involved. However, the model can be extended according to more decisive factors by including more types. Note that the key steps in selecting and combining measures include the consideration of effectiveness parameters as well, which is partly covered by the degree of endangerment. However, waste produced or costs contribute to the effectiveness of a strategy also. This might be modeled through the post-mappings of the measures, for example.

In general, Petri nets offer various possibilities for enhancement such as the duration of implementing a measure or the probability of the occurrence of an event. The duration of implementing a measure might be uncertain and endowed with a probability distribution as well. Note that the merging step may result in a choice of several strategies making a subsequent strategy assessment necessary. In respect of the latter, multi-criteria assessment according to certain effectiveness parameters such as reduction of contamination, cost, and waste are possible. In addition, performance analyses related to the duration of a whole strategy as well as resource utilization may be used in the assessment as well providing the user a wide decision basis.

Furthermore, performance analyses offer possibilities to improve strategies according to resources and the implementation order of measures. Assume concurrently implemented measures of different durations resulting in waiting resources because both measures need to be finished before another measure can be implemented. A change in the distribution of resources or timely change in the implementation of measures may improve the performance of the entire strategy.

Acknowledgements

The research leading to these results has received funding from the European Atomic Energy Community Seventh Framework Programme FP7/2012-2013 under grant agreement 323287. Research is particularly conducted in the frame of the European project PREPARE (Innovative integrated tools and platforms for radiological emergency preparedness and post-accident response in Europe) where the results are applied and adapted in the project HARMONE (Harmonising Modelling Strategies of European Decision Support Systems for Nuclear Emergencies). The Center for Disaster Management and Risk Reduction Technology (CEDIM) has particularly supported research in the field of natural disasters.

The authors would like to thank all project partners for the great collaboration and data exchange. We owe thanks to all the experts from different European institutions for their insightful contributions and dedicated support.

References

[1]. UNISDR, UNISDR Terminology – Disaster
https://www.unisdr.org/we/inform/terminology
[2]. UNISDR, UNISDR Terminology – Disaster management
https://www.unisdr.org/we/inform/terminology
[3]. S. Asghar, D. Alahakoon, L. Churilov, A comprehensive conceptual model for disaster management existing approaches to disaster management, *Journal of Humanitarian Assistance*, Vol. 1360, Issue 0222, 2006, pp. 1-15.
[4]. ISCRAM, www.iscram.org
[5]. M. Dorasamy, M. Raman, M. Kaliannan, Knowledge management systems in support of disasters management: A two decade review, *Technological Forecasting and Social Change*, Vol. 80, Issue 9, 2013, pp. 1834-1853.
[6]. E. Rolland, R. A. Patterson, K. Ward, B. Dodin, Decision support for disaster management, *Operations Management Research*, Vol. 3, Issue 1-2, 2010, pp. 68-79.
[7]. J. Park, R. Cullen, T. Smith-Jackson, Designing a decision support system for disaster management and recovery, in *Proceedings of the Human Factors and Ergonomics Society 58th Annual Meeting (HFES'14)*, Vol. 17, 2014, pp. 1993-1997.

[8]. P. Currion, C. De Silva, B. Van de Walle, Open source software for disaster management, *Communications of the ACM*, Vol. 50, Issue 3, 2007, pp. 61-65.

[9]. M. Cioca, L.-I. Cioca, Decision support systems used in disaster management, in Decision Support Systems (C. S. Jao, Ed.), *IntechOpen*, 2010, pp. 371-390.

[10]. Z. Liao, B. Wang, X. Xia, P. M. Hannam, Environmental emergency decision support system based on Artificial Neural Network, *Safety Science*, Vol. 50, Issue 1, 2012, pp. 150-163.

[11]. A. M. Gadomski, S. Bologna, G. DiConstanzo, A. Perini, M. Schaerf, Towards intelligent decision support systems for emergency managers: The IDA approach, *International Journal of Risk Assessment and Management*, Vol. 2, Issue 3-4, 2001, pp. 224-242.

[12]. J. Ehrhardt, A. Weis (Eds.), RODOS : Decision support system for off-site nuclear emergency management in Europe, Final report of the RODOS project, Report EUR 19144, *European Commission*, Brussels, 2000.

[13]. S. Hoe, P. McGinnity, T. Charnock, F. Gering, L. H. Schou Jacobsen, J. Havskov Sørensen, K. Andersson, P. Astrup, ARGOS decision support system for emergency management, in *Proceedings of the 12th International Congress of the International Radiation Protection Association (IRPA'09)*, 2009.

[14]. M. M. Bradley, NARAC: An emergency response resource for predicting the atmospheric dispersion and assessing the consequences of airborne radionuclides, *Journal of Environmental Radioactivity*, Vol. 96, Issue 1-3, 2007, pp. 116-121.

[15]. The Fukushima Daiichi Accident: Technical Report 3/5, Emergency Preparedness and Response, 24/7, STI/PUB/1710, *International Atomic Energy Agency (IAEA)*, 2015.

[16]. Executive Summary of the Final Report, *Investigation Committee on the Accident at Fukushima Nuclear Power Stations of Tokyo Electric Power Company*, 2012.

[17]. The National Diet of Japan, *The Fukushima Nuclear Accident Independent Investigation Commission*, 2012.

[18]. K. N. Papamichail, S. French, 25 Years of MCDA in nuclear emergency management, *IMA Journal of Management Mathematics*, Vol. 24, Issue 4, 2013, pp. 481-503.

[19]. A. Aamodt, E. Plaza, Case-based reasoning: Foundational issues, methodological variations, and system approaches, *AI Communications*, Vol. 7, Issue 1, 1994, pp. 39-59.

[20]. D. W. Aha, J. Lieber, Case-based reasoning research and development, in *Proceedings of the 25th International Conference on Case-Based Reasoning (ICCBR'17)*, Trondheim, Norway, 2017.

[21]. D. Greene, J. Freyne, B. Smyth, P. Cunningham, An analysis of current trends in CBR research using multiview clustering, *AI Magazine*, Vol. 31, 2010, pp. 45-62.

[22]. S. Montani, L. C. Jain (Eds.), Successful Case-based Reasoning Applications 2, Studies in Computational Intelligence, Vol. 494, *Springer*, 2014.

[23]. G. Müller, Workflow Modeling Assistance by Case-based Reasoning, *Springer Vieweg*, 2018.

[24]. K. Amailef, J. Lu, Ontology-supported case-based reasoning approach for intelligent m-Government emergency response services, *Decision Support Systems*, Vol. 55, Issue 1, 2013, pp. 79-97.

[25]. B. Chakraborty, D. Ghosh, R. K. Maji, S. Garnaik, N. Debnath, Knowledge management with case-based reasoning applied on fire emergency handling, in *Proceedings of the 8th IEEE International Conference on Industrial Informatics (INDIN'10)*, Osaka, Japan, 2010, pp. 708-713.

[26]. Z.-P. Fan, Y.-H. Li, X. Wang, Y. Liu, Hybrid similarity measure for case retrieval in CBR and its application to emergency response towards gas explosion, *Expert Systems with Applications*, Vol. 41, Issue 5, 2014, pp. 2526-2534.

[27]. D. B. Leake, A. Kinley, D. Wilson, Case-based similarity assessment: estimating adaptability from experience, in *Proceedings of the Fourteenth National Conference on Artificial Intelligence (AAAI'97)*, 1997, pp. 674-679.

[28]. Z. Liao, X. Mao, P. M. Hannam, T. Zhao, Adaptation methodology of CBR for environmental emergency preparedness system based on an Improved Genetic Algorithm, *Expert Systems with Applications*, Vol. 39, Issue 8, 2012, pp. 7029-7040.

[29]. Z. Liao, X. Mao, Y. Liu, Z. Xu, P. M. Hannam, CBR respond and preparedness system development for environmental emergency, *Civil Engineering and Environmental Systems*, Vol. 28, Issue 4, 2011, pp. 301-323.

[30]. W. Liu, G. Hu, J. Li, Emergency resources demand prediction using case-based reasoning, *Safety Science*, Vol. 50, Issue 3, 2012, pp. 530-534.

[31]. J. L. Kolodner, An introduction to case-based reasoning, *Artificial Intelligence Review*, Vol. 6, Issue 1, 1992, pp. 3-34.

[32]. S. Moehrle, W. Raskob, Structuring and reusing knowledge from historical events for supporting nuclear emergency and remediation management, *Engineering Applications of Artificial Intelligence*, Vol. 46, 2015, pp. 303-311.

[33]. W. Raskob, S. Möhrle, S. Bai, Knowledge database and case-based reasoning, *Radioprotection*, Vol. 51, Issue HS2, 2016, pp. S185-S186.

[34]. S. Moehrle, Modeling of countermeasures for large-scale disasters using high-level petri nets, in *Proceedings of the 10th International Conference on Information Systems for Crisis Response and Management (ISCRAM'13)*, Baden-Baden, Germany, 2013, pp. 284-289.

[35]. S. Moehrle, Towards a decision support system for disaster management, in *Proceedings of the Safety, European Safety and Reliability Conference (ESREL'13)*, Amsterdam, The Netherlands, 2013, pp. 239-246.

[36]. T. Murata, Petri nets : properties, analysis and applications, *Proceedings of the IEEE*, Vol. 77, Issue 4, 1989, pp. 541-580.

[37]. C. A. Petri, Kommunikation mit Automaten, PhD Thesis, *Mathematisches Institut der Universität*, Bonn, 1962.

[38]. K. Jensen, G. Rozenberg (Eds.), High-level Petri Nets: Theory and Application, *Springer-Verlag*, Berlin, Heidelberg, 1991.

[39]. W. M. P. van der Aalst, The application of Petri nets to workflow management, *Journal of Circuits, Systems and Computers*, Vol. 8, Issue 1, 1998, pp. 21-66.

[40]. A. Oberweis, P. Sander, Information system behavior specification by high level Petri nets, *ACM Transactions on Information Systems*, Vol. 14, Issue 4, 1996, pp. 380-420.

[41]. Y. Ju, A. Wang, H. Che, Modeling and analysis of traffic accident rescue process using GSPN, in *Proceedings of the International Conference on Wireless Communications, Networking and Mobile Computing (WiCOM'07)*, Shanghai, China, 2007, pp. 6601-6604.

[42]. L. Ma, S. Li, L. Chen, Research on process of coal mine emergency plan based on stochastic Petri net, in *Proceedings of the International Conference on Information Management, Innovation Management and Industrial Engineering (ICIII'11)*, Shenzhen, China, 2011, pp. 535-538.

[43]. S. Shan, L. Wang, L. Li, Modeling of emergency response decision-making process using stochastic Petri net: an e-service perspective, *Information Technology and Management*, Vol. 13, Issue 4, 2012, pp. 363-376.

[44]. M. Zhong, C. Shi, T. Fu, L. He, J. Shi, Study in performance analysis of China Urban Emergency Response System based on Petri net, *Safety Science*, Vol. 48, Issue 6, 2010, pp. 755-762.

[45]. W. Huang, Z. Tong, Research on emergency plan business process modeling based on colored Petri nets, in *Proceedings of the 8th International Conference on Fuzzy Systems and Knowledge Discovery (FSKD'11)*, Vol. 4, Shanghai, China, 2011, pp. 2086-2089.

[46]. J. Zhou, Petri net modeling for the emergency response to chemical accidents, *Journal of Loss Prevention in the Process Industries*, Vol. 26, Issue 4, 2013, pp. 766-770.

[47]. J. Zhou, G. Reniers, Petri-net based modeling and queuing analysis for resource-oriented cooperation of emergency response actions, *Process Safety and Environmental Protection*, Vol. 102, 2016, pp. 567-576.

[48]. M. Cheminod, I. C. Bertolotti, L. Durante, A. Valenzano, Modeling Emergency Response Plans with Coloured Petri Nets, in *Proceedings of the International Workshop on Critical Information Infrastructures Security (CRITIS'12)*, 2013, pp. 106-117.

[49]. R. B. Dilmaghani, R. R. Rao, A systematic approach to improve communication for emergency response, in *Proceedings of the 42nd Hawaii International Conference on System Sciences (HICSS'09)*, 2009, pp. 1-8.

[50]. S. Karmakar, R. Dasgupta, A Petri net representation of a web-service-based emergency management system in railway station, *World Academy of Science, Engineering and Technology, International Scholarly and Scientific Research of Innovation*, Vol. 5, Issue 11, 2011, pp. 1417-1423.

[51]. P. Bammidi, K. L. Moore, Emergency management systems: A systems approach, in *Proceedings of IEEE International Conference on Systems, Man, and Cybernetics (SMC'94)*, Vol. 2, 1994, pp. 1565-1570.

[52]. O. Nývlt, S. Haugen, L. Ferkl, Complex accident scenarios modelled and analysed by stochastic Petri nets, *Reliability Engineering and System Safety*, Vol. 142, 2015, pp. 539-555.

[53]. J. C. Hill, P. C. Wright, From text to Petri nets: The difficulties of describing accident scenarios formally, in *Proceedings of the International Workshop on Design, Specification and Verification of Interactive Systems (DSVIS'97)*, 1997, pp. 161-176.

[54]. D. Vernez, D. Buchs, G. Pierrehumbert, Perspectives in the use of coloured Petri nets for risk analysis and accident modelling, *Safety Science*, Vol. 41, Issue 5, 2003, pp. 445-463.

[55]. M. Tavana, Dynamic process modelling using Petri nets with applications to nuclear power plant emergency management, *International Journal of Simulation and Process Modeling*, Vol. 4, Issue 2, 2008, pp. 130-138.

[56]. PREPARE, https://prepare-eu.org/

[57]. A. Nisbet, J. Brown, T. Cabianca, A. L. Jones, K. G. Andersson, R. Hänninen, T. Ikäheimonen, G. Kirchner, V. Bertsch, M. Hiete, Generic handbook for assisting in the management of contaminated inhabited areas in Europe following a radiological emergency, Version 2, https://euranos.iket.kit.edu/index.php?action = euranos&title = products

[58]. Arbeitsgruppe Hochwasser, Hochwasser 2002 im Land Sachsen-Anhalt Auswertung des Katastrophenschutzmanagements, *Abschlussbericht*, 2002.

[59]. Bericht der Unabhängigen Kommission der Sächsischen Staatsregierung Flutkatastrophe 2002, *Unabhängige Kommission der Sächsischen Staatsregierung*, 2002.

[60]. FwDV 100, https://www.bbk.bund.de/SharedDocs/Downloads/BBK/DE/FIS/DownloadsRechtundVorschriften/Volltext_Fw_Dv/FwDV%20100.pdf?__blob= publicationFile

[61]. J. L. Peterson, Petri Net Theory and the Modeling of Systems, *Prentice-Hall Inc.*, Englewood Cliffs, N. J., 1981.

[62]. J. Lim, M.-J. Chae, Y. Yang, I.-B. Park, J. Lee, J. H. Park, Fast scheduling of semiconductor manufacturing facilities using case-based reasoning, *IEEE Transactions on Semiconductor Manufacturing*, Vol. 29, Issue 1, 2016, pp. 22-32.

[63]. B. Dharani, T. V. Geetha, Adaptive learning path generation using colored petri nets based on behavioral aspects, in *Proceedings of the International Conference on Recent Trends in Information Technology (ICRTIT'13)*, 2013, pp. 459-465.

[64]. B.-S. Yang, S. Kwon Jeong, Y.-M. Oh, A. C. C. Tan, Case-based reasoning system with Petri nets for induction motor fault diagnosis, *Expert Systems with Applications*, Vol. 27, Issue 2, 2004, pp. 301-311.

[65]. B. G. Weber, S. Ontanón, Using automated replay annotation for case-based planning in games, in *Proceedings of the 18th International Conference on Case-Based Reasoning (ICCBR'10)*, Alessandria, Italy, 2010, pp. 15-24.

[66]. W. Raskob, S. Möhrle, Nuclear emergency response and Big Data technologies, Invited talk at *the 3rd BDE SC5 Workshop on Big Data in Climate Action, Environment, Resource Efficiency and Raw Materials*, Brussels, Belgium, 2017.

[67]. S. Moehrle, S. Bai, T. Mueller, E. Munz, D. Trybushnyi, W. Raskob, Triggering events and distributed responsibilities capabilities of web-based decision support in nuclear emergency management, in *Proceedings of the 4th NERIS Workshop*, Dublin, Ireland, 2018.

[68]. S. Moehrle, S. Bai, T. Mueller, E. Munz, W. Trybushnyi, Dmytro Raskob, Web-based decision support system for emergency management - System architecture and enhancement possibilities, Poster presented at *the 4th NERIS Workshop*, Ireland, 2018.

[69]. High-level Petri Nets – Concepts, Definitions and Graphical Notation Final Draft, ISO/IEC 15909, Version 4.7.1, *International Organization for Standardization*, 2000.

[70]. Systems and Software Engineering – High-level Petri Nets – Part 1: Concepts, Definitions and Graphical Notation, ISO/IEC 15909-1:2004, *International Organization for Standardization*, 2004.

[71]. S. Sun, A. Kumar, J. Yen, Merging workflows: A new perspective on connecting business processes, *Decision Support Systems*, Vol. 42, Issue 2, 2006, pp. 844-858.

[72]. M. D. Jeng, F. DiCesare, A review of synthesis techniques for Petri nets, in *Proceedings of the Rensselaer Second International Conference on Computer Integrated Manufacturing*, 1990, pp. 348-355.

[73] J. Cortadella, M. Kishinevsky, L. Lavagnot, A. Yakovlev, Synthesizing Petri nets from state-based models, in *Proceedings of the IEEE International Conference on Computer-Aided Design (ICCAD'95)*, 1995, pp. 164-171.

[74]. T. Agerwala, Y.-C. Choed-Amphai, A synthesis rule for concurrent systems, in *Proceedings of the 15th Design Automation Conference (DAC'78)*, 1978, pp. 305-311.

[75]. Y. Narahari, N. Viswanadham, A petri net approach to the modelling and analysis of flexible manufacturing systems, *Annals of Operations Research*, Vol. 3, Issue 8, 1985, pp. 449-472.

[76]. Z.-J. Ding, J.-L. Wang, C.-J. Jiang, An approach for synthesis Petri nets for modeling and verifying composite web service, *Journal of Information Science and Engineering*, Vol. 24, Issue 5, 2008, pp. 1309-1328.

[77]. M. D. Jeng, Modular synthesis of Petri nets for modeling flexible manufacturing systems, *International Journal of Flexible Manufacturing Systems*, Vol. 7, Issue 3, 1995, pp. 287-310.

[78]. E. Arjona, G. Bueno, E. López-Mellado, Synthesis of coloured Petri nets from natural-like language descriptions, in Advances in Petri Net Theory and Applications (T. Aized, Ed.), *InTech*, 2010, pp. 21-42.

[79]. I. Koh, F. DiCesare, Modular transformation methods for generalized Petri nets and their application to automated manufacturing systems, *IEEE Transactions on Systems, Man and Cybernetics*, Vol. 21, Issue 6, 1991, pp. 1512-1522.

[80]. S. Mauser, Synthese von Petrinetzen aus halbgeordneten Abläufen, PhD Thesis, *FernUniversität in Hagen*, 2010.

[81]. D. Fahland, H. Woith, Towards process models for disaster response, in *Proceedings of the International Conference on Business Process Management (BPM'08)*, 2008, pp. 254-265.

[82]. D. Fahland, Oclets – Scenario-based modeling with Petri nets, in *Proceedings of the International Conference on Application and Theory of Petri Nets (PETRI NETS'09)*, 2009, pp. 223-243.

[83]. I. Peťko, Š. Hudák, General composition for high level Petri nets and its properties, *Central European Journal of Computer Science*, Vol. 2, Issue 3, 2012, pp. 222-235.

[84]. F. Peres, B. Berthomieu, F. Vernadat, On the composition of time Petri nets, *Discrete Event Dynamic Systems*, Vol. 21, Issue 3, 2011, pp. 395-424.

[85]. F.-S. Hsieh, C. Y. Chiang, Collaborative composition of processes in holonic manufacturing systems, *Computers in Industry*, Vol. 62, Issue 1, 2011, pp. 51-64.

[86]. J. Guillen-Scholten, F. Arbab, F. de Boer, M. Bonsangue, Modeling the exogenous coordination of mobile channel-based systems with Petri nets, *Electronic Notes in Theoretical Computer Science*, Vol. 154, Issue 1, 2006, pp. 121-138.

[87]. K. Jensen, L. M. Kristensen, Coloured Petri Nets Modelling and Validation of Concurrent Systems, *Springer-Verlag*, Berlin, Heidelberg, 2009.

[88]. M. Hofmann, H. Betke, S. Sackmann, Process-oriented disaster response management: A structured literature review, *Business Process Management Journal*, Vol. 21, Issue 5, 2015, pp. 966-987.

[89]. M. La Rosa, J. Mendling, Domain-driven process adaptation in emergency scenarios, in *Proceedings of the International Conference on Business Process Management (BPM'08)*, 2008, pp. 290-297.

[90]. J. M. Jansen, B. Lijnse, R. Plasmeijer, Towards dynamic workflow support for crisis management, in *Proceedings of the 7th International Conference on Information Systems for Crisis Response and Management (ISCRAM'10)*, Seattle, USA, 2010, pp. 1-5.

[91]. U. Rueppel, A. Wagenknecht, Improving emergency management by formal dynamic process-modelling, in *Proceedings of the 24th Conference on Information Technology in Construction*, Maribvor, Slovenia, 2007.

[92]. S. Sackmann, H. Betke, M Hofmann, Towards a model-based analysis of place-related information in disaster response workflows, in *Proceedings of the 10th International Conference on Information Systems for Crisis Response and Management (ISCRAM'13)*, Baden-Baden, Germany, 2013, pp. 78-83.

[93]. C. Sell, I. Braun, Using a workflow management system to manage emergency plans, in *Proceedings of the 6th International Conference on Information Systems for Crisis Response and Management (ISCRAM'09)*, Gothenburg, Sweden, 2009, pp. 43-49.

[94]. J. Wang, W. Tepfenhart, D. Rosca, Emergency response workflow resource requirements modeling and analysis, *IEEE Transactions on Systems, Man, and Cybernetics. Part C (Applications and Reviews)*, Vol. 39, Issue 3, 2009, pp. 270-283.

[95]. H. Betke, M. Seifert, BPMN for disaster response processes – A methodical extension, *Proceedings of Lecture Notes in Informatics*, Chemnitz, Germany, Vol. P-275, 2017, pp. 1311-1324.

[96]. J. Franke, F. Charoy, C. Ulmer, A Model for temporal coordination of disaster response activities, in *Proceedings of the 7th International ISCRAM Conference*, Seattle, USA, 2010.

[97]. J. Franke, F. Charoy, Design of a collaborative disaster response process management system, in *Proceedings of the 9th International Conference on the Design of Cooperative Systems (COOP'10)*, Aix-en-Provence, France, 2010, pp. 57-77.

Chapter 4

Towards Human-like Behavior Generation Through Understating of the Complex Interplay Between Verbal and Non-verbal Signals in Multiparty and Informal Interactions by Utilizing Information Fusion Approach

Matej Rojc, Izidor Mlakar

4.1. Introduction

In the human co-verbal, behavior generation process exists a highly complex information fusion that establishes proper relationship between gestures, gaze and facial expressions, and speech. In a sense, such co-verbal behavior orchestrates speech [1]. Further, natural human like interaction may take different forms – including complex time synchronous fusion of the linguistic, para-linguistic, and non-verbal signals. Thus, sharing of information or exchange of information in human social interactions is far more complex than just sharing of words. It is multi-layered, including attitude and affect, and utilizes all bodily resources (embodiment) as well as physical environment in which humans operate [2, 3]. Hence, in human social interactions, the verbal signals carry symbolic/semantic interpretation of information through linguistic and paralinguistic properties of language, while the co-verbal signals serve as an orchestrator of the communication [4]. When analyzing these complex and time synchronized relationships between co-verbal behavior and speech, one can observe that the co-verbal

Matej Rojc
Faculty of Electrical Engineering and Computer Science, University of Maribor,
Slovenia

behavior effectively retains semantics of the information, helps in providing suggestive influences, and gives a certain degree of clarity in the overall human-human discourse [5-7].

Building on the notion that the co-verbal alignment and time synchronization processes are the conductor behind any affective and human-like social interaction, this chapter provides novel concepts to investigate, to fuse and to describe how complex related linguistic and paralinguistic signals interact with embodiments, and non-verbal signals as parts of a common process, during spontaneous and complex multi-party human interactions, and provides a novel methodology to realize the complex information fusion present in human like co-verbal behavior. The objective of the presented work is to utilize demanding conversational knowledge in order to automatically generate advanced natural and human-like conversational expressions in nowadays-immersive environments, by involving gestures, facial expressions, attitude, and emotion, properly synchronized with speech. Namely, these responses have then a potential to evoke attitude (positive or negative) in human users.

Most researches (in several scientific domains) agree that the co-verbal behavior (i.e. gestures, facial expressions, and emotions) is an essential component of human-human interaction, and that verbal and non-verbal behavior together form composite communicative signals that boost the understandability, naturalness, and effectiveness of complex interpersonal communications. Only when these signals are properly utilized in human-machine interaction (HMI) interfaces, it would be possible to further increase the successfulness in evoking the attitude and to establish even stronger personalization between machines (services), and users. In HMI and user-centered design tasks, the affective computing and social awareness represent nowadays those key directions in how a machine should respond to various user-generated stimuli in order to evoke attitude and response [8]. For instance, automatically machine generated information from a set of evidence, are in general still far from perfect or natural, and human intervention is often required to achieve the desired result or goal [9]. Namely, the uni-modal information, although semantically correct, may not be explicit enough for the machine, and due to the complexity of systems in the environment, in some cases even misleading. The end of the human-human interaction cycle is an active response generated by the user, and not the signals and human-human interaction itself [10].

In everyday lives the non-verbal concepts, such as: gestures, emotions, sentiment and prosody, aid us in decision-making and further elaborate situation awareness [11]. These concepts represent the basis of the human cognitive capabilities, which would enable the machine to recognize, interpret, and even express ideas and thoughts in a highly affective and human-like ways. Moreover, visual input/output signals are multi-functional, and operate on psychological, sociological and biological levels, in all time frames; e.g. moment-to-moment, ontogenetic, evolutionary in time, and in various discourse settings [12]. Furthermore, as [13] observed, during language perception and generation, the multimodal fusion of auditory and visual input/output signals facilitates understanding.

However, greater demands closely correlate with the multi-channel experiences and the human-like design [8, 11]. Namely, the more human-like the machine response, the greater and more intense the negative affect it will cause, when time dis-synchrony is present (e.g. less natural voice and animation). In immersive environments and human-machine (HMI) interfaces, however, text information is in general the main resource available as information source for the machine, or service. In some systems, text may be linked to a limited set of audio-visual signals generated by the users. Thus, text-to-speech synthesis (TTS) systems in general (with or without supportive embodied conversational avatar (ECA)) are drivers and generators of machine responses, generated automatically online, that process un-annotated text, and interpret them with some limited and in front specified situational context. Un-annotated text (e.g. orthographic text), as a dynamical response, is generally generated online and contain limited information regarding corresponding intent, or shape of verbal or co-verbal components. Clearly, the major source of possible dis-cohesion (negative perception) in the response is the lack of conversational knowledge. Therefore, in order to predict all involved communicative signals (linguistic, paralinguistic, and even social) and fuse them into a real human like responses, several knowledge sources originating from verbal domain and represented as linguistic signals (e.g. semantics, syntax, sentiment, morphology), semantic and syntactic data (e. g. linguistic information from verbal domain), and prosody (e.g. paralinguistic) are required. Similar, as in most human-behavior related research fields (e.g. sentiment and opinion mining, human action detection and recognition) trying to understand human communicative intents from available knowledge sources, in order to synthesize more natural communicative behavior, two key issues can be recognized: a) what knowledge sources are involved in the process of making some concept, and b) how these knowledge sources can be related with each other (e.g. all involved fusion functions, through which knowledge sources are utilized). To tackle the last issue, new ways of defining, extracting, and describing all involved knowledge sources and situational awareness, are required for automatic generation of advanced natural conversational responses, which have to involve non-verbal behavior as the essence of the natural use of language.

In order to attack these issues, a comprehensive multimodal knowledge source is used that is based on video data of spontaneous multi-party conversations, together with its utilization and information signals extraction through EVA annotation scheme [14], which has been defined, based on several theories in corpus linguistics, psycholinguistics, and cognitive linguistics. Based on this annotation scheme, the following conversational signals as realizations of linguistic theories and the basis of our conversational knowledge can be established: a) from purely linguistic domain we have information sources, such as: segmentation (word, sentence, statement, paragraph), sentence type, sentiment, morphology (POS tags), syntax and discourse markers, b) from the paralinguistic domain we have information sources, such as: semiotics (communicative intent), emotion, prosodic phrase, and accentuation, c) from the social domain, we have information sources, such as: person/relation, dialog acts, dialog role, dialog functions, dialog dimension, and d) from the representational domain, we have information sources, such as: pitch, duration (verbal and co-verbal), physical configuration, body part (e.g. gesture, head movement, facial expression), abstract pose, trajectory and propagation of co-verbal expression via movement phases. The novel comprehensive and multi signal based annotation scheme has to be applied to audio/video knowledge source e.g. by using ELAN and WebAnno annotation[1] tools. The created multimodal knowledge source, e.g. EVA Corpus as proposed in [15], in this way represents a rich conversational knowledge source, with those information signals that are used in human-human interactions. Based on recent advances in linguistics and human behavior, the multimodal knowledge source contains information signals, where all these signals can be transformed into action items.

---

[1] https://tla.mpi.nl/tools/tla-tools/elan/, https://webanno.github.io/webanno/

4.2. Embodied Language Processing (ELU)

There is still too little known about the cognitive interplay, when correlating gestures and speech. Most researches (in any given domain), however, agree that gesticulation is an essential component of natural and spontaneous human-human interaction. In human-machine interaction and user-centered design, such interplay represents a key direction in how a machine should respond to user-generated stimuli in order to evoke attitude and response. It is realized as a multi-channel representation of an 'idea' incorporating affect and social/situational awareness. Thus, automatically machine generated information from a set of evidence are in general still far from perfect, and human intervention is often required to improve that [9]. Further, the uni-modal information, although semantically correct, may not be explicit enough and due to the complexity of systems, and in some cases even misleading. The end of an interaction cycle is an active response generated by the user and not the signals and interaction itself [10]. In this highly multimodal process of information exchange, the non-verbal concepts such as: gestures, emotions, sentiment, and prosody play a crucial role. Since audio/visual representation of information is most effective, the most natural realization is by utilizing embodied conversational agents (ECA); e.g. virtual entities with human-like bodies and human-like motoric skills.

The representational framework SAIBA [16] was proposed in order to realize audio/visual interplay in the process of 'idea sharing' as part of an automatic multimodal conversational behavior generation platform. The SAIBA standard decouples the process of simulating how ideas are shared into the following phases (a) intent planning- in charge of defining the communicative intentions of the agent (e.g. formulation of an idea), (b) a behavior planning phase, in charge of selecting the different physical modalities (verbal and co-verbal signals) to be used to shape the intentions (e.g. to shape the idea), and (c) a behavior realization phase that produces the final animations and represents them to a user. Based on the SAIBA standard various non-verbal behavior generation engines were proposed, which has to transform conversational knowledge (some limited number of information signals) into human-like response via fusion of these signal. For instance, ARIA framework [17] is one realization of this SAIBA standard. In this case the signal fusion is mainly performed in the 'input' block, which gathers multimodal audio-visual user data, and the text uttered by the user interprets in order to define user's emotional state, in terms of valence and arousal. The dialog manager (DM) then decides what kind of 'predefined' response to generate to the user based on a template-based approach, in which the Intent Planner utilizes pre-condition rules that are activated when matching with the user's communicative function and topic of interest. Another example of the exploitation of conversational knowledge via fusion is SARA, a Socially-Aware Robot Assistant [18]. By utilizing fusion on user's visual (head and face movement), vocal (acoustic features) and verbal (conversational strategies) behavior, SARA estimates its rapport level with the user and utilizes in achieving tasks and social goals. Again, the fusion is performed primarily on the input part, whereas the output generator is based on a predefined template approach, which selects syntactic templates associated with the selected conversational strategy. In [19] the authors utilize fusion of social signals (such as prosody, head movements, and facial muscles activation) and dialogic events in order to generate relevant stance for an ECA.

Moreover, most of the related researches into these highly complex phenomena focus themselves to a narrow 'discourse' concepts, and utilize, therefore, much more dense multimodal data. Such set-ups utilize 'laboratory' conditions with targeted narration, and/or artificially constructed settings and discourse concepts between collocutors. Furthermore, the material is often subject to certain restrictions, such as: time restriction, agenda, and technical features (camera direction and focus, editing). As a result, the data source used may clearly reveal the specific phenomena, however, hinder several other signals that would appear in less restricted (more causal) settings [20, 21]. Since the settings are quite restricted, 'other' signals actually tend to be left out by the collocutors. As a result, such material provides no possibilities for exploring and fusing verbal and non-verbal signals of discourse cohesively, and as they interplay with each in the era of 'big data' and 'deep learning', the complexity and diversity of 'conversational noise' may outline those hidden relationships, which make co-verbal behavior so natural. Further, regarding the video content, the TV interviews and theatrical plays have shown themselves to be very appropriate resource of spontaneous conversational expressions that appears to be significantly more suitable for research in wider 'discourse concepts', attitudes, and emotions used during conversations [22, 23]. Generally, 'public' discussions with a completely unrelated goal to the research, represent a good mixture of institutional discourse, semi-institutional discourse, and casual conversation.

The major issue with 'public' material, which is not recorded for the specific goal, however, is the 'noise' usually obscuring (to a degree) a specific context being observed. In our opinion the 'noise', actually maintains the input information (e.g. the meta information) that can at least partially define the complex interplay (f^{C}) of various action items of conversational expressions [4]. The main focus in this work is to provide a path towards identifying and modeling of complex function f^{C}, via information fusion and 'big' data analytics approach. Thus, we propose to combine natural language processing (NLP) and embodied language processing (ELP) into embodied language understanding (ELU), as shown in Fig. 4.1.

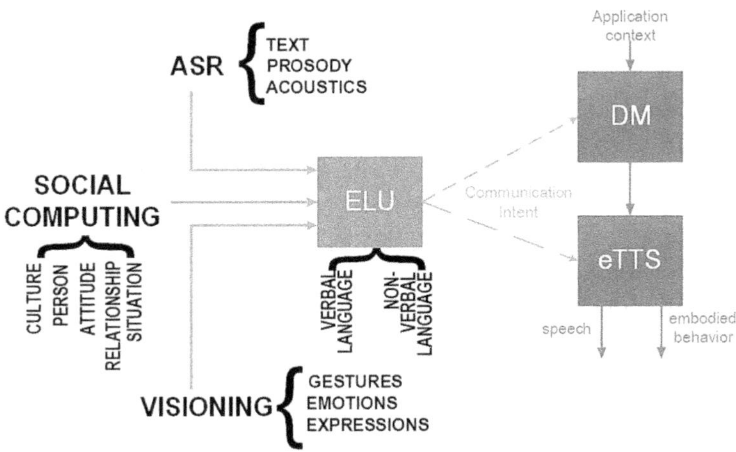

Fig. 4.1. Embodied Language Processing (ELU) as fusion of language, speech, embodiment, and social human nature.

As outlined in Fig. 4.1, and as a contrast to most of the related approaches in social computing, (cognitive) linguistics and embodied cognition, we adopt the information fusion approach of conversational signals at their foundation rather than interlinking them as a block-chain process. In the approach presented in this chapter, we propose that any theory existing or even new one, should represent an inference with a defined set of inputs e.g. action items. Each action item is actually a disparate feature that is annotated in the selected material by utilizing a novel EVA annotation scheme. Each inference may then utilize existing action items, exploit existing inferences, or define new. As a result, any new generated knowledge will always take into account the whole context and can also be quickly modeled against some context (e.g. new action items), when it arises. Main focus in the presented work is to propose and to provide a better path towards identifying and modeling of comprehensive and complex fusion functions to be established via data mining and 'big' data analytics methods. Moreover, most of the related researches into these highly complex phenomena focus themselves to a narrow 'discourse' concepts, and utilize, therefore, much more dense multimodal material. Such set-ups utilize 'laboratory' conditions with targeted narration and/or artificially constructed settings and discourse concepts between collocutors.

Furthermore, the material is often subject to some restrictions, such as: time restriction, agenda, and technical features (camera direction and focus, editing). As a result, the data source used may clearly reveal the specific phenomena, however, hinder several other signals that would appear in less restricted (more causal) settings [20, 21]. In many cases a wider scope of signals is not even taken into account. Since the observed phenomena are quite restricted, 'other' signals actually tend to be intentionally left out by the collocutors. As a result, such material provides less possibilities for exploring verbal and non-verbal features of discourse cohesively, and as they interplay with each in the era of 'big data' and 'deep learning', the complexity and diversity of 'conversational noise' may outline those hidden relationships, which make use of co-verbal behavior so natural. Regarding the video content, the TV interviews and theatrical plays have shown themselves to be very appropriate resource of spontaneous conversational expressions that appears to be significantly more suitable for research in wider 'discourse concepts', attitudes, and emotions used during conversations [22, 23]. Generally, 'public' discussions with a completely unrelated goal to the research represent a good mixture of institutional discourse, semi-institutional discourse, and casual conversation. The major issue with 'public' material, which is not recorded for the specific goal, however, is the 'noise' usually obscuring (to a degree) a specific context being observed. In our opinion the 'noise', actually maintains the input information (e.g. the meta information) that can at least partially define the complex interplay of various action items of conversational expressions [4].

4.3. Fusion-based Co-verbal Behavior Generation Model

In general, there is still little known regarding the cognitive interplay correlating gestures and speech into a synchronous interaction. Most researches, however, agree that gesticulation is essential component of natural and spontaneous human-human interactions. Namely, from a cognitive perspective one can argue that the dynamics of multi-modal human behavior are crucial for its interpretation. Moreover, there is constant interplay between linguistic and paralinguistic signals in formulation of an idea (e.g. intent planning) and in modeling its representation (e.g. behavior planning). Most of the existing methods in knowledge generation, however, tackle isolated signals in generated highly managed (narrow) contexts. Moreover, most of the components in the production of coverbal behavior are isolated and do not utilize the same data-sources to generate interlinks on symbolic (e.g. intent planning) and physical layers (e.g. behavior planning). As a result, mismatches and less-natural interpretations between verbal and co-verbal behavior are of relevance. Thus, the realized multimodal representation of an idea, especially over previously unseen contexts (e.g. unmarked text), may often appear less viable. In contrast we first define a conversational expression as an abstract and dynamical concept which is applied to both knowledge generation as well as its utilization on an ECA via generated conversational resources.

The proposed EVA model is outlined in Fig. 4.2. As can be seen, it is built around the concept that a 'multichannel' representation of an idea via audio and visual channels is first formulated on a cognitive level through symbolic fusion of various verbal and non-verbal signals. Thus, a conversational expression is proposed to be symbolically represented as

$$CE^s = f(L, P, S), \qquad (4.1)$$

where f represents the 'global' fusion function which shapes an idea without any reference to actual physical behavior. Thus, the f establishes an overall symbolic link among various signals, which are represented in various domains of cognitive linguistics, such as core linguistics L, para-linguistics P, and social context S. Further, each individual domain consists of various signals denoted by various relevant theories in the field of cognitive linguistics and communicative behavior. For instance, from a linguistic perspective a person utilizes concepts, such as: segmentation, syntax, morphology (POS), sentence type, sentiment, and discourse markers in order to formulate an idea via 'sentence'. Going beyond text, one also modulates the linguistic nature of an idea (expressed via e.g. sentence) by 'enhancing' it with paralinguistic concepts, such as: prosody, accentuation, attitude, emotion, and semiotic/communicative intent for which the conversational expression is generated. Finally, in each conversation modeling, an idea also involves a broader context expressed through social signals such as personality traits, social relation between collocutors, culture, collocutors role in the dialog, dialog function, and dimension of the act, etc. Thus, a conversational expression is described as a complex interplay of various verbal, non-verbal, and situational contexts represented as *L*, *P*, and *S*, and can be utilized like "sensors", where each one individually and as part of convergence (e.g. function *f*) contributing the comprehensive process of shaping some conversational expression.

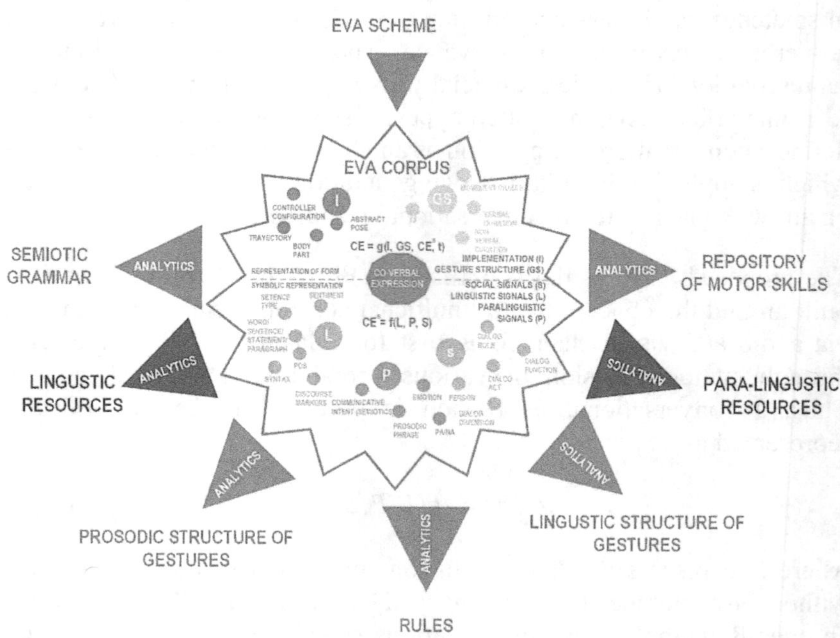

Fig. 4.2. The proposed co-verbal behavior model as a complex system of disparate time consistent conversational signals (linguistic, acoustic, paralinguistic, and non-verbal information sources).

The nature of individual signals and their individual contribution is in many cases already well described via the modern theories in cognitive linguistics and communicative behavior. However, we cannot simply 'glue' the narrower knowledge into a common strategy. Hence, we envisage that all conversational theories are relevant and contribute to the 'cohesive' generation of the human co-verbal behavior. Thus, any individual contributions must be observed under a common context and any generated knowledge must reflect this complexity induced due to convergence of signals. Moreover, as outlined in Fig. 4.2, this complexity must also be reflected in the physical realization of the conversational expression (e.g. behavior generation stage). Namely, the physical realization of the conversational expression adapts the visualization of the idea to the nature of the idea (e.g. CE^S), to the physical capacitates of the targeted realization entity I, and to the defined structure and temporal synchronization between verbal and co-verbal channels (GS) deployed via a common timeline (t). Thus, the form of the conversational expression is proposed to be defined as follows:

$$CE^F = g(CE^S, I, GS, t), \tag{4.2}$$

where g represents the fusion function for defining the physical nature of the 'multi-channel' representation of the idea with a clear reference to the actual physical preferences of the targeted realization entity. Thus, the Equation (4.2) not only denotes the shape of expressions, but also the propagation of how the shapes are formed (e.g. movement phases) in relation to the formulation of verbal counterparts (e.g. local pitches, prosody, and prosodic phrases). In the proposed model we envisage that all conversational theories are relevant and contribute to the cohesive generation of human co-verbal behavior. As a contrast to most of the related models in cognitive linguistics and communicative behavior, we propose information fusion approach in Equations (4.1) and (4.2), where existing and new theories (e.g. L, P, S, I, GS), represent an inference with a defined set of inputs e.g. signals. The inference converges (fuses) all these signals in a common knowledge base (e.g. grammar, rules, repositories, etc.). The convergence is performed via provided mechanisms for visual analytics. Each signal is, in this case, a disparate feature that is annotated by utilizing the multi-layer annotation scheme [14]. Each inference may also utilize any signal from any domain or even utilize existing inferences. Since all signals are annotated over a common context (e.g. same interactive situations and sequences), any new knowledge generated will always take into account the whole context and can also be quickly modeled against new context (e.g. new signals), when it arises. Moreover, the material used as a source, contains a good mixture of institutional discourse, semi-institutional discourse and casual conversation. By utilizing the fusion model in Fig. 4.1, the particular fusion functions in the local domains (L, P, S, I, GS) have to be derived and evaluated, as well as discovering the role of global fusion functions f and g interlinking conversational signals.

4.3.1. A Co-verbal Behavior Model's Data Source – EVA Corpus

In the research, the EVA corpus [15] as a data source has been used, in order to deploy and evaluate the proposed model. It is very crucial in the light of Fig. 4.1 that the data source maintains a mixture of institutional discourse, semi-institutional discourse, and casual conversations. Moreover, such material contains a lot of conversational noise. When the noise is properly analyzed and incorporated via e.g. the model, a lot of features and contexts that model the natural multimodal conversational expressions can be unraveled. For instance, emphasis commonly involves raising or lowering of the eyebrows, adjusting pitch and prosody, and exaggerated arm movement [26]. Thus, these conversational signals can give us insight into how informal communication really works, what stimuli triggers specific conversational phenomena, and how do these impulses interact, and even reflect on each other. Such relations can then provide synthetic agents with the basis for the multimodal literacy. Namely, the capacity to construct meaning through understanding of situation and responding to some not pre-defined situation.

The conversational setting in the EVA corpus as outlined in Fig. 4.3 is relaxed and unrestricted, and built around a talk-show that follows a general script/scenario. Further, topics discussed are highly unpredictable, informal, interchangeable, and full of humor and emotional responses. Although sequencing exists, it is performed highly unorderly, as also other functions related to the discourse structuring (e.g. role exchange, topic opening, grounding, etc.). This constant overlapping guarantees a causal and highly irregular progress of the discourse, with lots of overlapping statements and roles, vivid emotional responses, and facial expressions, with a lot of room for improvisation and without any fixed scenario. The EVA corpus is built based on GoS corpus [24] that consists of video and audio recordings and corresponding orthographic transcriptions of approximately 120 hours of speech. It is focused on conversations that we are exposed to daily and in various situations e.g.: radio and TV shows, school lessons and lectures, private conversations between friends, or within the family, meetings at work, consultations, conversations in buying, and selling situations, etc. The primary goal of the EVA corpus is to be able to discover in detail the multimodality of communicative intent as the driving force for the generation of the co-verbal and communicative behavior. The communicative intent is a concept that is used in order to try to define the nature and the intent of the generated co-verbal behavior. Currently, the EVA Corpus consists of four video recordings, or approximately four hours of video material with annotations. Each selected video contains around 57 minutes of transcribed highly informal and affective multiparty conversation, with 3-4 collocutors exchanging information in a highly unordered and dynamical manor. The conversational setting is in all video recordings relaxed and free and built around a talk-show that follows some general script/scenario, however, the topics discussed are highly changeable, informal and full of humor and emotions. Language used by the collocutors is very colloquial incorporating dialects and many grammatical irregularities.

Fig. 4.3. Conversational setting in the EVA corpus.

4.3.2. Segmentation and Quantification of Conversational Noise into Conversational signals – the EVA Annotation Scheme

To be able to study the nature and the intent of the generated co-verbal behavior, we deploy EVA annotation scheme for the EVA corpus material. In this way we segmented, classified and quantified several conversational signals originating from theories in corpus analytics, cognitive linguistics and communicative behavior. These signals then represent the input for the definition of the domain-specific fusion functions, as well as the global fusion functions f and g. Further, in order to transform the conversational noise into useful data, we utilize the so-called multimodal annotation approach as used in conversational analysis. This is generally achieved by applying specific annotation scheme over a conversational dataset. The annotation scheme specifies then conversational concepts as speaker independent features and normalizes them into conversational signal. The EVA annotation scheme applies two layered analysis of the conversational phenomena. The first layer – symbolics, analyzes the interpretation of a body language at a symbolic level, while interlinking linguistic and paralinguistic signals (e.g. Kinesics [25]). Thus, its goal is to find patterns and tendencies in how people communicate through joint use of language, prosody, gaze, gesture, facial expressions and other articulation of body. The second layer – gesture form, is then concerned with how a gesture, as abstract concept of co-speech body movement with some communicative intent, is physically realized; e.g. the form of gesture. This provides a detailed description, closest possible to the physical reality and the entity that will realize it (an ECA). How, the articulators are being moved is generally the basis for inferring gesture meaning, where the interpretation also depends on a wider conversational context, clarified at symbolics. In this way, the main goal of this layer is to describe how a gesture is formed from the use of bodily articulators (e.g. how hands propagate from one configuration to another). Thus, the layer is completely agnostic to the meaning. Or, the phenomena at symbolics utilize the repertoire of forms declared at the gesture form. The EVA annotation scheme is also extendable and defines all aspects of the coverbal expressions and its resented forms. Its rationale originates from multimodal conversational analysis and grounds the Equations (4.1) and (4.2) onto real-life situations.

The objective of the EVA annotation scheme is, therefore, a) to identify inferred meanings of co-verbal expressions as a function of linguistic, paralinguistic and social signals (e.g. where and when to gesture), and b) to identify the physical nature (e.g. articulation of body language) and use of the available imaginary forms (e.g. how to gesture). Thus, we start with a conversational act and define it as a set of *CEs* with mandatory verbal signals and optional co-verbal signals. We assume that the stimuli for the co-verbal behavior is verbal in nature and it may originate as a reflection of attitude/emotion, or even be a supportive artefact in the implementation of the communicative function (e.g. feedback, turn taking, turn accepting, sequencing, etc.). Similarly, the verbal behavior is primarily used for the representation of information, but may also reflect attitude/emotion, or be adjusted to serve as a part of the implementation of a communicative function. All artefacts are inter-connected through the temporal domain, and can be related among each other in numerous ways and combinations. Thus, the basis for the existence of a conversational act is statement. Further, we only observe the co-speech sequences, where each statement is described with orthographic transcription and sentiment. Since the material incorporates informal speech, also a lot of colloquialism exists. Thus, a standardized form is also annotated. Each statement is segmented into sentences, and each sentence is described with several linguistic signals it carries, such as: orthographic transcription and sentiment, standardized form, sentence type and syntax, and via the paralinguistic signals, e.g. prosodic phrase and pitch contour. Next, each sentence is segmented into words. Each word is described with the linguistic signals, such as: orthographic transcription, standardized form, and part-of-speech tag (POS), and its paralinguistic signals, e.g. prosodic token and prominence. Finally, words are used to define the boundaries of the following linguistic, paralinguistic, and social signals: discourse markers, emotions and dialog acts.

The optional co-verbal component is segmented into gesture units. As outlined by Kendon in [27] through conceptual motorics, a gesture unit denotes for, all hand and arm movement between rest states; namely, from the beginning a hand/arm starts moving away from a rest position until it returns to the same or new rest position. Since, natural embodiment involves more than use of hands we extend the definition of a gesture unit to any observable part, including facial expressions, head movement, and posture. At the same time, however, we still limit the observable movement to have to include some purpose. Thus, each gesture unit is observed completely independent of linguistic and other paralinguistic signals. However, to be co-verbal, it must occur in close vicinity of words. As a result, we further indicate the span of a gesture unit regarding the words indexes. Next, each gesture unit is further segmented into gesture phrases. This is actually the concept, which is referred to as 'gesture'. Thus, each phrase represents a conversational expression with a completed intent (semiotic class), e.g. what is conveyed with the body and language and does not necessarily meet the linguist's definition of language.

Through gesture phrase interpreted as a conversational signal, we also try to initiate the basic symbolic link between verbal and non-verbal language (e.g. CE^S parameter in Equation (4.2)). This signal does not concern with the form (or implementation) of a gesture. It is only described via the purpose of the co-verbal movement classified as semiotic intent, body parts, which were used as articulators and start/end word, which are used to symbolically ground the 'gesture' to language. The other parameters of the Equation (4.2), (e.g. I, GS) are defined through the annotation of gesture form. As proposed in [15], we also describe the gesture form as a function of structure and implementation. Body-parts are in this case the core objects of the observation in the annotation of the form. We adopt the idea of embodied cognition, in which one's motor capacities (ability of the body to respond to its senses with movement), body and environment play an important role in thinking. Further, the symbolic relations and concepts are established on the functional/symbolic level and realized via hand gestures (left, right arm and hands), facial expression, head movement, and gaze.

The EVA annotation scheme separates between hands, arms, head, and face. The structure (e.g. GS parameter in Equation (4.2)) is, therefore, addressed via the propagation and intensity of the observed movement in the form of movement phases, where each movement phrase (as symbolical concept) can, in line with Kita [28], be described via five consecutive movement phases, a mandatory stroke and optional preparation, hold (pre- and post-), and retraction phases. Finally, we address the physical realization of a gesture, e.g. parameter I in Equation (4.2) on an end-pose based approach. Each movement-phase identifies a pose (e.g. configuration of an articulator) at the beginning (start pose Ps) and a pose at the end (end pose Pe). Both poses are 'interconnected' with a trajectory T that identifies the path over which the observed body parts propagate from the start pose to the end pose. The trajectory T represents a parametric description of a propagation, which includes the partitioning of the trajectory T into movement primes (simple patterns), such as: linear and arc, each defined through the intermediate poses. A movement trajectory can reach various complexities, and outline complex forms, such as: spiral, roof, chair, etc. To properly animate it on the ECA, it is suggested to be splitted into simpler forms (primes), e.g. chair is partitioned into 2 linear elements, or 2 linear + 1 arcs. Further, each prime is segmented into 2 (or 3 for arc) key points, each identifying a transitional hand/arm pose. Mathematically, this relationship movement may be represented as a function of pose and trajectory (e.g. $M = f(Ps, Pe, T)$). In this way, the data generated for each signal is a noiseless as possible and follows the theory behind the signal as explicitly as possible.

4.4. A Framework for Analytics of Verbal and Non-verbal Behavior Signals

In Fig. 4.4 the framework for analytics on presented co-verbal behavior signals is presented. As can be seen, the EVA corpus annotated data are converted into JSON format. This format presents signals at the level of items, with full information regarding annotator, time, value etc. JSON (JavaScript Object Notation) is a lightweight data-interchange format. It is easy for humans to read and write, and it is also easy for machines to parse and generate. Further, it is also a text format that is completely language independent but uses conventions that are familiar to programmers of the C-family of languages, including C, C++, C#, Java, JavaScript, Perl, Python, and many others. These properties make JSON an ideal data-interchange language. At this stage, items within ELAN tracks are not directly related with each other (between tracks). Nevertheless, since JSON format is general standard, these data can be imported in various tools for performing analytics, although it is not easy to analyze inter-relations, or to analyze more complex cross-speaker relations and dependences for several linguistic in non-verbal phenomena in the data yet. These possibilities are then provided then in the next step, when data in JSON format are transformed into uniform heterogeneous relation graph (HRG) structure as presented in Fig. 4.5.

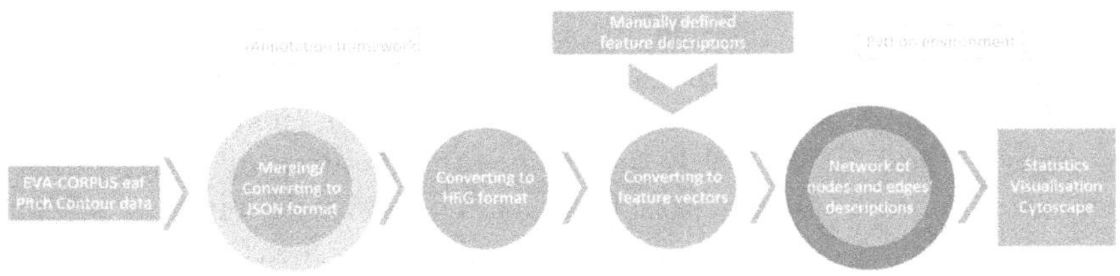

Fig. 4.4. A framework for comprehensive EVA corpus data analytics.

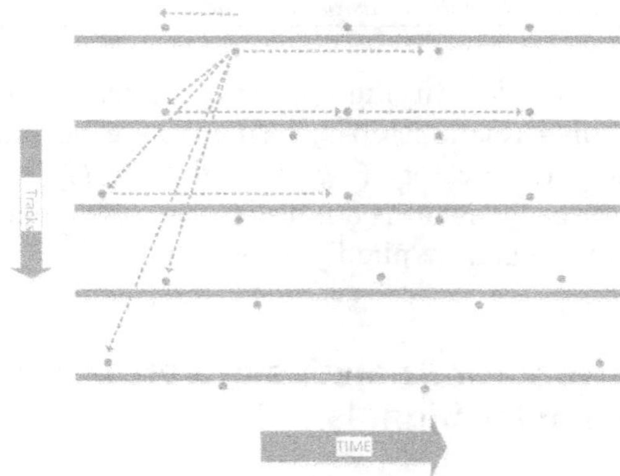

Fig. 4.5. HRG structure for comprehensive EVA corpus time-related analytics.

HRG structure provides clean general-purpose mechanisms for storing and representing all the information contained in the JSON tracks. Further, one HRG structure is created per each speaker in the multi-party dialogue and relates with each other all corresponding tracks. The HRG structure demonstrates the use of two different relation-structures for storing EVA corpus information, linear lists and trees. The objects within the relation-structures are e.g. words, phrase breaks, gesture phrases, facial expressions, head gestures, gaze etc. Linear lists are used here to specify the relation between objects within specific relation or track. In addition forward and backward traversals are possible within such structure. Additional tree relation-structures creates vertical relations between those objects included in linear lists. In this way, complex features for analytics, and then machine learning can easily be performed, by only utilizing the next step and by providing desired feature description file.

The last step then represents the utilization of features for analytics, and visualization, as presented in Fig. 4.6, where e.g. individual gesture phrase of speaker *S1* is represented in great detail. All information is stored in several tracks (high and low annotation part) that are positioned in outer circles. Whole circle determines the duration of the complete gesture. Further, these presentations and visualizations can be time-aligned with other representations of other co-speakers involved in the multi-speaker communication, and in this way we are also able to study cross-speaker signal fusion regarding the co-verbal behavior.

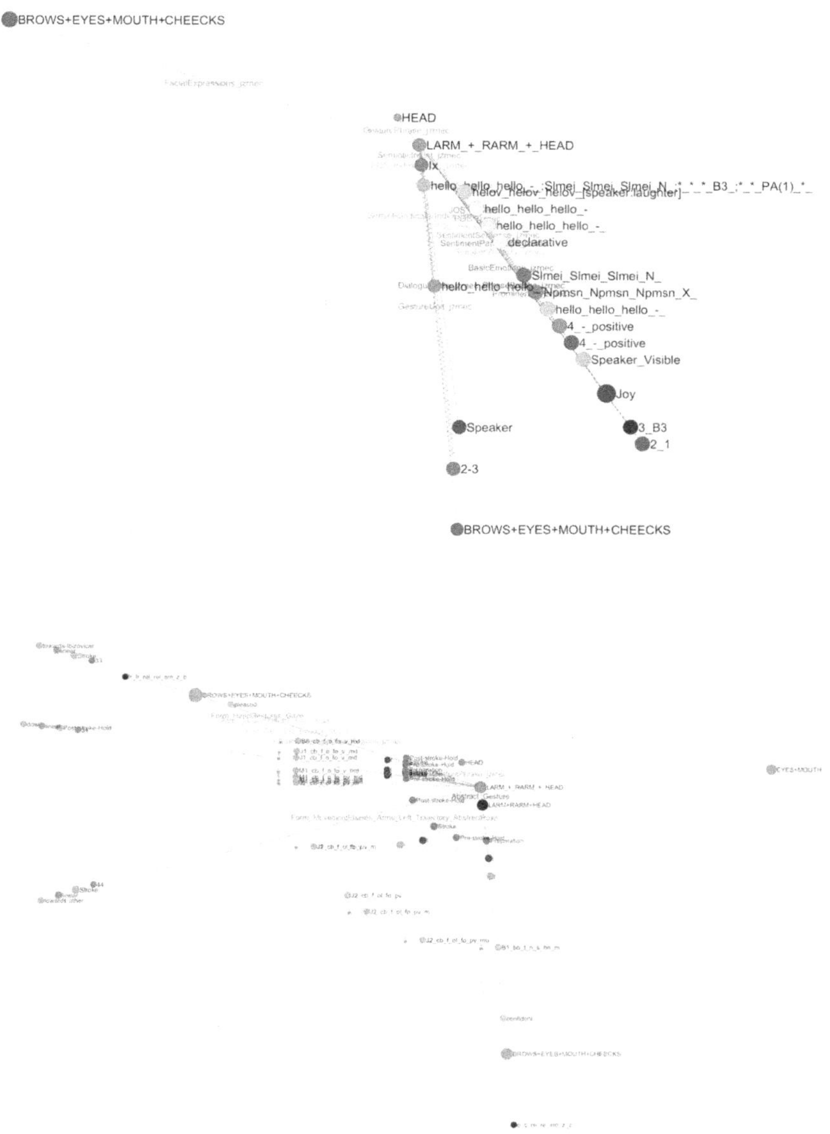

Fig. 4.6. Visualisation of the individual gesture phrase, together with relations to other information sources, including time-related information: (a) high level, and (b) low level annotation.

4.5. A Signal-fusion System for Automatic Co-verbal Behavior Generation

The main motivation for the proprietary EVA model is to provide and fuse conversational signals in order to automatically plan, generate, and realize human-like conversational expressions by using unannotated (unmarked) text. The key problems in the process of generating co-verbal behavior, especially when general and unannotated text is used, arise mostly in the intent planning and behavior planning level. Namely, the co-verbal behavior does not comply with underlying uniform grammar, and gestures in spontaneous dialogues are rarely deliberate, or done for a purpose. Nevertheless, gestures are non-accidental but rather actual components of speech. Therefore, no finite set of rules for deterministic planning can be defined, nor is there a definite (1-to-1) correlation between verbal and co-verbal behavior. Nevertheless, humans have tendencies to use similar behavior along with certain expressions, words, and actions, while participating in face-to-face communication. Several studies and annotations support this statement by showing the existence of a high semantic and functional correlation between verbal and co-verbal behavior, along with some degree of prosodic coherence.

Another issue in intent planning and behavior planning is the enormousness of semantic space in which gestures are related with different intents and interpretations of verbal content. As a result, the intent planning and behavior planning are often divided into sub-problems. In the intent planning level, concepts such as communicative functions (e.g. feed-back and turn-taking) and syntactic analysis are taken into account. The behavior planning level incorporates speech prosody and domain-restricted semantic grammar, or the limited semiotic classes generated through parameterization of the semantic space and subspaces (e.g. generation of iconic outlines, generation of deictic signals). These approaches define smaller and more manageable sub-sets, in which the specific semantic/syntactic and prosodic relationships can be established between the co-verbal and verbal behavior.

The idea behind the expressive conversational behavior generation model, or EVA model proposed for generating the co-verbal behavior, is to convert text (phrase, sentence, or statement) into corresponding communicative act – that is, into a human-like exchange of information – and convey it through highly synchronized verbal and non-verbal communication signals. Such interaction affects both the cognitive process of the listener, as well as the cognitive processes of the speaker. Furthermore, the information presented in the form of synchronous signals, where the co-verbal behavior is properly intertwined with the verbal one, is not only more understandable, but establishes social relationships among interlocutors. Therefore, in order to achieve an acceptable level of naturalness, a consistent relationship between verbal and co-verbal behavior must be established. Such a relationship must reflect the intent of the information presented, as well as the interlocutors' abilities to understand the physical realization of it. The main problems that the model deals with are, therefore, cognitive and pragmatic in nature, since in the communication between people the co-verbal behavior does not follow the same rules as language does.

Further, the represented shapes and their propagation throughout the interaction are not subordinated to some well-defined grammatical rules. In addition, general unannotated text does not contain a lot of context in terms of the intent/meaning identification, nor does it contain any deterministic markers. Such input, therefore, does not allow for direct and deterministic conclusions about the shapes of gestures to be used, and about their propagation or synchronization with the verbal parts. The EVA-model, therefore, covers a wide variety of concepts that include: analysis of data of conversational behavior, context-independent prediction of shapes, context-independent prediction of movements (the motor skills), design of semiotic grammar, and context-dependent co-verbal behavior lexicon (gesticon), algorithm for generating the co-verbal behavior, space- and time-efficient architectures for the integration of linguistically dependent and independent conversational signals, and a framework for the realization of the co-verbal behavior, which also includes the design of procedural description language, named EVA-Script. EVA expressive model for generating the co-verbal behavior is modular and can be used for different purposes and in different domains.

The EVA-model has the ability to re-use shapes and movements that are maintained in the co-verbal behavior lexicon. This lexicon contains context-independent repository of motor skills, which are best to be based on the analysis and annotation of spontaneous dialogue. The context of their use and the verbal context can then be introduced via semiotic classes that depend on the morphology. This can allow for the conversational agent to express a wide range of communicative concepts, such as: diversity, motivation, relevance, relation to theme, etc., and to incorporate emotional states and emotions, both simple and complex, into ECA co-verbal behavior. Since EVA-model can formulate various forms of co-verbal behavior with respect to general unannotated text, and since it can adjust the co-verbal behavior to different contexts, the use of an ECA can be flexibly extended to a variety of HMI concepts, ranging from virtual web readers to story tellers, intelligent virtual sellers, IPTV managers, virtual companions, listeners, therapists, etc.

In order to attack efficiently and comprehensively the problem of co-verbal behavior generation on unannotated texts, the fusion-based concept presented in Fig. 4.7 is proposed, where EVA annotation scheme provides conversational signals, obtained through the analysis and classification of the co-verbal behavior as proposed in previous section. This scheme combines the concepts of functional and descriptive annotation schemes, and allows identification of the functional characteristics of verbal behavior; identification of the intent of linguistic expressions; description of individual configurations, shapes and poses in high resolution as abstract concepts, or in the form of detailed 3D configuration of movement controllers. Next, a multimodal audio-visual data that contain natural spontaneous communication between several active interlocutors is used, in order to enable definition, design and utilization of language-independent conversational signals, to be used in the algorithm for generating the co-verbal behavior as proposed in [29].

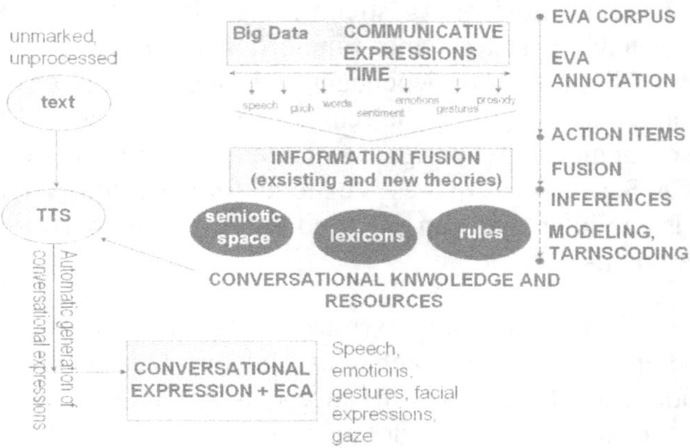

Fig. 4.7. The information fusion – from unannotated text to the human-like audio-visual conversational response.

The main language-independent information source is the repository of motor skills, maintained as part of the *co-verbal behavior lexicon*. This repository maintains its functional and contextual independence from speech or dialogue itself. As such, the source maintains the following three concepts: poses, shapes, and movements. The pose and shape constitute a functional and time-independent physical appearance. The movement is then represented as a sequential concatenation of shapes/poses over a spatial trajectory. Movement is time-independent; however, by itself (without any context) it does not add relevant meaning to the conversation. On the other hand, a gesture is understood as co-verbal movement; a movement, which is a result of semiotic intents and prosodic features of speech. Further, audio-visual are used for the definition, design, and implementation of language-dependent source, such as *gesticon*, (maintained within the co-verbal behavior lexicon) and *semiotic grammar*. The *gesticon* maintains gestures and is based on morpho-syntactic features, and serves as a contextual link between intent and co-verbal behavior. Gestures are sequences of shapes, poses, and movements with a given context or with specific semiotic intent. The *semiotic grammar* represents a set of morphological rules, which can be used for the definition of several intents in the text. These intents can be identified by using semiotic classification. Further, the proposed concept incorporates information sources provided through the omni-comprehensive TTS architecture that represents a multimodal core, able to convert general and unannotated text into speech, accompanied with corresponding gesticulation and lip movements, which are suitably aligned in order to look natural. The reasons for the design of the TTS architecture as proposed in [29] are several, but they are mainly arising from the theory behind the correlation of verbal and co-verbal behavior, which says: part of the thinking processes, which relates to the co-verbal behavior generation is based on lexica and lexical relations. Based on these processes some shapes of co-verbal behavior can be directly related to words, phrases, morpho-syntactic sequences, or sequences of even minor linguistic units, such as syllables [30, 31]. The second part of the thinking processes, which relates to the co-verbal behavior generation, is based on paralinguistic and non-verbal information, which is passed by gestures and speech [32, 33]. Therefore, the intent can also be introduced in the form of those expressions that represent communication concepts, such as speaker exchange, feedback, finding and planning communicative sequence. Such expressions and behavior are formed by using complex communicative mechanisms (functions) that people use during interaction [30, 33]. The relationship between verbal and co-verbal behavior is established through features, such as: pauses, nasal sounds, speech corrections, interrogative sentences, and linguistic fillers (e.g. hmm..., ehhh..., ufff, aaaa etc.) [34]. This omni-comprehensive architecture can then be used for complex and advanced co-verbal behavior generation on general un-annotated text. Namely, it is able to exploit the knowledge attained in the TTS-related modules. Nevertheless, in order to align gestures and speech at both symbolic and temporal levels, the algorithm and co-verbal behavior generation-related modules have to be fused, able to share data, language-dependent and independent information sources. Therefore, the omni-comprehensive architecture of the TTS system additionally integrates the following modules: tagger of movement phrases and phases, behavior-planning module, and procedure-generation module. Therefore, the engine's architecture extracts and fuses information sources about the meaning, intent, shape, and synchronization of the co-verbal behavior, automatically from general text, where modules for generating a co-verbal behavior (the visual communication channel) are based on prosodic and linguistic information sources, which are provided by the core TTS modules. The fusion of all information sources can then result in better efficiency and better interactive system responsiveness. Further, the proposed architecture also inherits and retains the modular structure, whereby the common processing flow supports the effective use and sharing of information sources between algorithms, fast and complex feature sets (as soon as proper data are available), and the optimization of individual processes. Unlike other similar systems, which consider TTS engine and co-verbal behavior generation as two independent processes, in this architecture the fusion of speech and co-verbal behavior are generated through one common processing stream.

4.6. Conclusion

We have presented EVA corpus, as generated by EVA annotation scheme, from data fusion point of view. The EVA annotation scheme is a result of research regarding recreation of spontaneous co-verbal behavior. This scheme is based on findings presented in [25, 26] and incorporates and correlates linguistic and paralinguistic, verbal and non-verbal features of multiparty informal conversations. The topology, the formal and functional part of the scheme were outlined in more detail, in order to demonstrate how the EVA corpus can be used for investigating several complex conversational phenomena and relations that are result of fusion of many conversational signals. The EVA corpus annotation is based on an on-going effort in searching and investigating those features and relations of conversational signals that may be used as stimuli in the synthesis of co-verbal emotions as well as how emotion may influence complete co-verbal behavior. The EVA annotation schema goes well beyond similar efforts, and efforts of the authors in the field of co-verbal synthetic behavior, and adds a linguistic and paralinguistic signals to the traditional verbal/co-verbal signals. Namely, it is designed in such a way that all phenomena regarding form, e.g. posture, gesture, gaze and facial expressions and higher-level phenomena regarding function, e.g. lemma & structure, POS tagging, semiotics, prosody and dialog, are described within a single session, and related via a common time-line. Thus, several relations in either track or between the tracks may be established and investigated. Additionally, the level of casualness detected in the EVA corpus material, and the level of spontaneous detected in the intrapersonal responses among interlocutors, goes well beyond laboratory settings, plays, and interviews. Namely, it incorporates a high degree of informality with overlapping, sarcasm, disorder, and spontaneous reactions. It also contains a colorful variety of conversational emotions incorporated into highly dynamical responses.

Multimodal conversational behavior and its stimuli beyond semantics is relatively new. Thus, ideas, concepts and corpora are still evolving. At this point the annotation of EVA corpus is largely a result of manual work, performed by skilled annotators. Although the EVA corpus incorporates already many perspectives, future development will focus on even deeper prosodic and linguistic analysis as well as detailed analysis from dialog point of view, and well beyond the collocutors role. The development of corpora is, therefore, still ongoing process. Further, the standardization of available annotation methods and approaches are still developing. The annotated data in the EVA corpus are generated mostly manually. Since this is very time-consuming process, tools and methods to at least partially automate the annotation process are highly demanded. Therefore, in the future we should develop new algorithms and procedures, which could at least partially automatize some of the annotation processes, e.g. gesture form and dynamics classification, sentiment classification, word segmentation, etc.

Acknowledgements

This work is partially funded by the European Regional Development Fund and the Ministry of Education, Science and Sport of Slovenia; project SAIAL.

References

[1]. D. McNeill, Why We Gesture: The Surprising Role of Hand Movements in Communication, *Cambridge University Press*, 2015.

[2]. D. Wardak, Gestures orchestrating the multimodal development of ideas in educational design team meetings, *Design Studies*, Vol. 47, 2016, pp. 1-22.

[3]. E. Davitti, S. Pasquandrea, Embodied participation: What multimodal analysis can tell us about interpreter-mediated encounters in pedagogical settings, *Journal of Pragmatics*, Vol. 107, 2017, pp. 105-128.

[4]. V. Bonsignori, B. C. Camiciottoli (Eds.), Multimodality Across Communicative Settings, Discourse Domains and Genres, *Cambridge Scholars Publishing*, 2017.

[5]. J. M. Colletta, M. Guidetti, O. Capirci, C. Cristilli, O. E. Demir, R. N. Kunene-Nicolas, S. Levine, Effects of age and language on co-speech gesture production: an investigation of French, American, and Italian children's narratives, *Journal of Child Language*, Vol. 42, Issue 1, 2015, pp. 122-145.

[6]. A. Esposito, J. Vassallo, A. M. Esposito, N. Bourbakis, On the amount of semantic information conveyed by gestures, in *Proceedings of the IEEE 27th International Conference on Tools with Artificial Intelligence (ICTAI'15)*, 2015, pp. 660-667.

[7]. Y. L. Lin, Co-occurrence of speech and gestures: A multimodal corpus linguistic approach to intercultural interaction, *Journal of Pragmatics*, Vol. 117, 2017, pp. 155-167.

[8]. L. Ciechanowski, A. Przegalinska, M. Magnuski, P. Gloor, In the shades of the uncanny valley: An experimental study of human-chatbot interaction, *Future Generation Computer Systems*, Vol. 92, 2019, pp. 539-548.

[9]. J. R. Navarro-Cerdan, R. Llobet, J. Arlandis, J. C. Perez-Cortes, Composition of constraint, hypothesis and error models to improve interaction in human-machine interfaces, *Information Fusion*, Vol. 29, 2016, pp. 1-13.

[10]. D. S. Opel, J. Rhodes, Beyond Student as User: Rhetoric, Multimodality, and user-centered design, *Computers and Composition*, Vol. 49, 2018, pp. 71-81.

[11]. S. Poria, E. Cambria, R. Bajpai, A. Hussain, A review of affective computing: From unimodal analysis to multimodal fusion, *Information Fusion*, Vol. 37, 2017, pp. 98-125.

[12]. R. B. Church, S. Goldin-Meadow, So how does gesture function in speaking, communication, and thinking?, Chapter 18, in Why Gesture (R. B. Church, M. W. Alibali, S. D. Kelly, Eds.), 2017, *John Benjamins*, pp. 397-412.

[13]. P. Wagner, Z. Malisz, S. Kopp, Gesture and speech in interaction: An overview, *Speech Communication*, Vol. 57, 2014, pp. 209-232.

[14]. I. Mlakar, Z. Kačič, M. Rojc, Form-Oriented annotation for building a functionally independent dictionary of synthetic movement, in Cognitive Behavioural Systems, *Springer*, Berlin, Heidelberg, 2012, pp. 251-265.

[15]. I. Mlakar, Z. Kačič, M. Rojc, A corpus for analyzing linguistic and paralinguistic features in multi-speaker spontaneous conversations – EVA corpus, in *Proceedings of the 17th International Conference on Applied Computer Science (ACS'17)*, 2017.

[16]. D. Heylen, S. Kopp, S. C. Marsella, C. Pelachaud, H. Vilhjálmsson, The next step towards a function markup language, in *Proceedings of the International Workshop on Intelligent Virtual Agents (IVA'08)*, 2008, pp. 270-280.

[17]. A. Cafaro, M. Bruijnes, J. van Waterschoot, C. Pelachaud, M. Theune, D. Heylen, Selecting and expressing communicative functions in a saiba-compliant agent framework, in *Proceedings of the International Conference on Intelligent Virtual Agents (IVA'17)*, 2017, pp. 73-82.

[18]. Y. Matsuyama, A. Bhardwaj, R. Zhao, O. Romeo, S. Akoju, J. Cassell, Socially-aware animated intelligent personal assistant agent, in *Proceedings of the 17th Annual Meeting of the Special Interest Group on Discourse and Dialogue (SIGDIAL'16)*, 2016, pp. 224-227.

[19] T. Janssoone, C. Clavel, K. Bailly, G. Richard, Using temporal association rules for the synthesis of embodied conversational agents with a specific stance, in *Proceedings of the International Conference on Intelligent Virtual Agents (IVA'16)*, 2016, pp. 175-189.

[20]. E. Fitzpatrick (Ed.), Corpus Linguistics Beyond the Word: Corpus Research from Phrase to Discourse, *Brill*, 2007.

[21]. D. Knight, Multimodality and Active Listenership: A Corpus Approach, *Bloomsbury*, London, 2011.

[22]. J. C. Martin, G. Caridakis, L. Devillers, K. Karpouzis, S. Abrilian, Manual annotation and automatic image processing of multimodal emotional behaviors: Validating the annotation of TV interviews, *Personal and Ubiquitous Computing*, Vol. 13, Issue 1, 2009, pp. 69-76.

[23]. Y. Li, J. Tao, L. Chao, W. Bao, Y. Liu, CHEAVD: A Chinese natural emotional audio-visual database, *Journal of Ambient Intelligence and Humanized Computing*, Vol. 8, Issue 6, 2017, pp. 913-924.

[24]. D. Verdonik, I. Kosem, A. Z. Vitez, S. Krek, M. Stabej, Compilation, transcription and usage of a reference speech corpus: The case of the Slovene corpus GOS, *Language Resources and Evaluation*, Vol. 47, Issue 4, 2013, pp. 1031-1048.

[25]. R. L. Birdwhistell, Kinesics and Context: Essays on Body Motion Communication, *University of Pennsylvania Press*, 2010.

[26]. G. Ambrazaitis, D. House, Multimodal prominences: exploring the patterning and usage of focal pitch accents, head beats and eyebrow beats in Swedish television news readings, *Speech Communication*, Vol. 95, 2017, pp. 100-113.

[27]. A. Kendon, Do gestures communicate? A review, *Research on Language and Social Interaction*, Vol. 27, Issue 3, 1994, pp. 175-200.

[28]. S. Kita, I. Van Gijn, H. Van der Hulst, Movement phases in signs and co-speech gestures, and their transcription by human coders, in *Proceedings of the International Gesture Workshop (GW'97)*, 1997, pp. 23-35.

[29]. M. Rojc, I. Mlakar, Z. Kačič, The TTS-driven affective embodied conversational agent EVA, based on a novel conversational-behavior generation algorithm, *Engineering Applications of Artificial Intelligence*, Vol. 57, 2017, pp. 80-104.

[30]. D. McNeill, Gesture and Thought, *University of Chicago Press*, 2005.

[31]. A. Esposito, A. M. Esposito, On speech and gestures synchrony, in *Proceedings of the Proceedings of the International Conference on Analysis of Verbal and Nonverbal Communication and Enactment (COST'10)*, 2010, pp. 252-272.

[32]. B. De Carolis, I. Mazzotta, N. Novielli, S. Pizzutilo, User modeling in social interaction with a caring agent, in User Modeling and Adaptation for Daily Routines (Martín, Estefanía, Haya, A. Pablo, Carro, M. Rosa, Eds.), *Springer-Verlag*, London, 2013. pp. 89-116.

[33]. J. Allwood, Dialog Coding – Function and Grammar, *Gothenburg Papers in Theoretical Linguistics*, Vol. 85, 2001.
http://sskkii.gu.se/jens/publications/docs076-100/093.pdf

[34]. A. Kendon, Gesture: Visible Action as Utterance, *Cambridge University Press*, 2004.

Chapter 5

A Survey of Temporal Extensions to Resource Description Framework (RDF)[1]

Di Wu, Abdullah Uz Tansel

5.1. Introduction

The "Semantic Web", introduced by Tim Berners-Lee et al. in their 2001 article, is defined as "an extension of the current one [WWW], in which information is given well-defined meaning, better enabling computers and people to work in cooperation" [1]. Along with the wide spread expansion of the Internet, Semantic Web is adopted by major search engines, governments, and big companies.

The Semantic Web has been proposed two decades ago; and its methodologies such as Resource Description Framework (RDF) being implemented in many domains, albeit slowly. Semantic Web allows sharing data and knowledge that are dispersed on servers connected via the Internet not only by human users but also by computers. It enriches the web pages by semantic information that can be automatically processed by computers. The semantic information in RDF is represented by only binary predicates, i.e., triples in the form of ⟨subject, predicate, object⟩. This simple representation scheme is the basis of an elaborate layers of methodologies, called Semantic Web Layer Cake, to include more semantics that allow inferencing of new triples from the given ones. Though this simple representation is very powerful for

Di Wu
Department of Computer Science, Graduate Center, CUNY, USA
[1] An earlier version of the chapter appears in the *Proceedings of the ICENTE 2018*, October 26-28, 2018, Konya, Turkey

modeling data and basic knowledge, it is very limited in representing their temporal variation. Reification is the method proposed in RDF for modeling temporal changes in data and knowledge. However, reification is cumbersome since it requires at least four more triples to represent just one temporal fact. By their very nature, RDF repositories are large in general and reification causes them to explode in size. In this paper, we review various representative Semantic Web techniques that are proposed for representing temporal data in RDF, in an effort to lay the foundation for developing a better solution for representing temporal knowledge in RDF.

The Semantic Web Layer Cake introduces conceptual structures and richness for enhanced semantic. The stack of conceptual tools in the Semantic Web Layer Cake are downward compatible. The bottom layer, Universal Resource Identifier (URI), provides a unique Id for every subject, object, and relationship thus makes linkage and integration among different knowledge bases possible [1]. Extensible Markup Language (XML) and XML Schema provide a standard for writing structured web documents with a user-defined vocabulary. RDF is a basic data model that includes a set of statements which are triples. RDF Schema (RDFs) is based on RDF but provides modeling primitives for building hierarchy of objects. On top of RDF and RDFs, ontology vocabularies add more power for representing more complex relationships among objects. Web Ontology Language (OWL) is a logic-based language which allows more inferencing, so machine agents are able to exploit knowledge expressed in OWL. OWL 2 as the most current version includes structures as classes, properties, individuals, and data values. RDF/XML is the only mandatory syntax for RDF, RDFs, and OWL 2. Other notations are proposed for ease of use, such as OWL/XML, Functional Syntax, Manchester Syntax, and Turtle, etc. [8, 12]. The upper layer of Semantic Web Layer Cake includes logic and proof, to derive information from the knowledge base represented by the bottom layers.

A temporal database has temporal data and is able to deal with insertion, deletion, and query of temporal data. There are two major types of time: valid time and transaction time. Valid Time is a time period during which the data is true (valid) in the real world. Transaction Time is a time period during which the data is recorded in the database. Bitemporal Time covers both valid and transaction time. Based on the type of time support, temporal databases have three forms: historical databases that support only valid time, rollback databases that support only transaction time, and bitemporal databases that support both. Naturally, previous research in temporal databases provides a solid basis for adding temporality to the Semantic Web.

RDF triples are statements without temporal attributes and they are assumed to be true at present. However, many applications need temporal knowledge and data. To build a temporal extension for the Semantic Web, researchers proposed extending RDF with a temporal component. There are various proposals that extend RDF to express temporal knowledge. In this study, we review the major extensions to RDF to handle temporal knowledge. It is not comprehensive, however, we believe it is a satisfactory examination of the literature that would provide the reader sufficient background to understand temporal aspects of Semantic Web.

In the remaining of this chapter, we first briefly explain the basic RDF model. Then we examine the proposals that add a time dimension to RDF in detail. We summaries these proposals with a taxonomy that classifies these proposals to provide further insight into representing temporal knowledge.

5.2. RDF

RDF is a framework for expressing information about resources, which include documents, people, physical objects, and abstract concepts. RDF is designed for applications to process information that are included in the web pages by providing a common framework by which applications can exchange information without loss of meaning. The subject and object in an RDF triple represent two resources and the predicate represents the relationship between the subject and the object. This relationship is directional from the subject to the object and is also called an RDF property. RDF triples can be represented as a directional graph that has nodes for subjects and objects and directed edges for predicates. These three elements in a triple can be Internationalized Resource Identifier (IRI), blank nodes, and literals.

An IRI is a Unicode string that can be used instead of Universal Resource Identifier (URI) to identify resources [4, 5]. For example, an IRI "http://example.com" denotes a website, another IRI "http://example.com/data" denotes a sub-category of the website, and another IRI "http://example.com/data/list.html" denotes a particular web page. IRIs have global scope and IRIs are absolute and may additionally have a fragment identifier (#). Two IRIs are equivalent only when they are equivalent strings. Thus, two IRIs may be not equivalent but refer to the same resource. For simplicity, namespaces are introduced to the syntax to represent repeated the portion of the IRIs. In this paper, for convenience, we use the namespace "ex:" for "http://example.com/" and another useful namespace "rdf:" as "http://www.w3.org/1999/02/22-rdf-syntax-ns#".

A blank node represents any resource that does not have an IRI but has meanings in triples if represents existential quantification. For example, if "a person has something to do", although we cannot express that "something" with an IRI, we can use a blank node as a placeholder. Blank nodes have some unique characteristics: 1) Blank nodes have local scope and cannot be externally referenced; 2) Blank nodes are used to represent some resources that do not need or cannot be assigned with IRIs, i.e. existential quantifications; 3) Blank nodes have blank node identifiers that are local. In RDF, literals can appear only as object and predicate can only be an IRI [3, 12].

Consider the RDF triple:

ex:William ex:livesIn ex:NYC

The subject is the IRI referring to a person "William", and the predicate is the IRI that refers to a relation "livesIn", and the object is the IRI that refers to a city, NYC. This simple triple is represented in an RDF graph as Fig. 5.1 below.

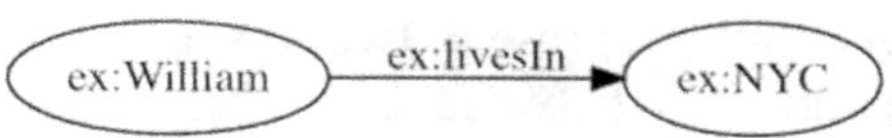

Fig. 5.1. An example RDF triple.

Note that this triple simply represents a true binary predicate: "William lives in NYC", *livesIn(William, NYC)*. There is no temporal information at all. We don't have information about when this statement is recorded, nor when the statement becomes valid and expired. It is usually assumed to represent current (present) knowledge.

5.3. Temporal Extensions to RDF

In the RDF model, the three elements of the RDF triple are IRIs, Blank Nodes, or Literals. To embed temporal information to the RDF model, some part (or the whole) of the triple need to be converted into meta units. Following proposals take different approaches by converting various part of the RDF model into meta unites. We explain these proposals in detail then summarize them by which part is converted. We use a running example "William lives in NYC in 2004" throughout this chapter and use each proposal to express this statement.

5.3.1. Reification

Reification is a logic construct and is W3C working group recommendation [8, 12]. The RDF vocabulary, rdf:Statement, rdf:subject, rdf:predicate, and rdf:object, are used for reification purpose as shown in Fig. 5.2.

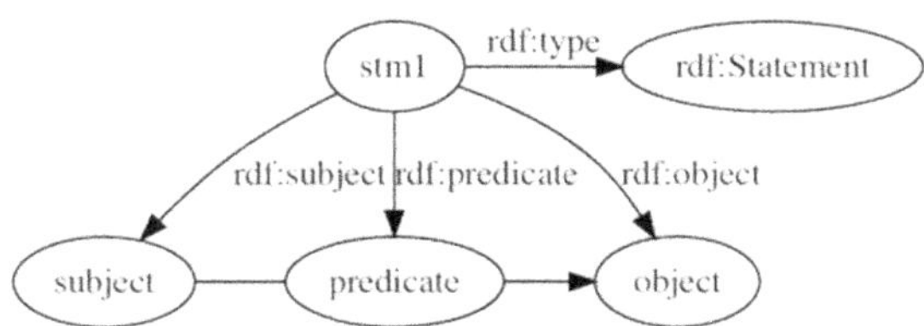

Fig. 5.2. RDF reification.

For example, In order to introduce the temporal information, that the triple ⟨ex:William, ex:livesIn, ex:NYC⟩ is valid in 2004, we need to create a blank node "_:x" representing a statement and 4 additional triples will be created to express the additional temporal information as shown in Fig. 5.3.

> _:x rdf:type rdf:Statement
>
> _:x rdf:subject ex:William
>
> _:x rdf:predicate ex:livesIn

_:x rdf:object ex:NYC

_:x ex:isValid 2004

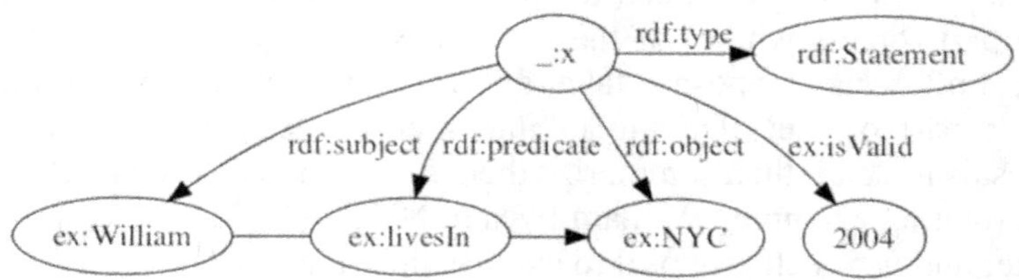

Fig. 5.3. RDF reification for the running example.

If there is another statement, "William lives in Boston in 2018", using Reification approach, another new resource ":y" has to be created and 4 additional triples have to be created as well. Although "William" in ":x" is the same "William" in ":y", we still have to create two triples. We can see from this example that the Reification approach has a significant data redundancy problem. Not only we need to use four triples to express one temporal information, but also the four triples are hard to be reused.

_:y rdf:type rdf:Statement

_:y rdf:subject ex:William

_:y rdf:predicate ex:livesIn

_:y rdf:object ex:Boston

_:y ex:isValid 2018

Furthermore, if we need to express a bitemporal information, a second layer of reification has to be introduced and many more triples have to be added. For example, if the statement ⟨ex:William, ex:livesIn, ex:Boston⟩ is valid in 2018 and is recorded in a database in the period 2018. Then we need to describe the bitemporal information as below:

_:s1 rdf:type rdf:Statement

_:s1 rdf:subject ex:William

    _:s1 rdf:predicate ex:livesIn

    _:s1 rdf:object ex:Boston

    _:s1 ex:isValid 2018

    _:s2 rdf:type rdf:Statement

    _:s2 rdf:subject _:s1

    _:s2 rdf:predicate ex:isValid

    _:s2 rdf:object 2018

    _:s2 ex:isRecorded 2018

5.3.2. Temporal RDF

Gutierrez et al. propose "temporal RDF" to add temporal information into standard RDF [6] as shown in Fig. 5.4. Temporal RDF adopts the labeling solution to handle evolving RDF data. The definition of Temporal RDF starts with a Temporal Triple: *(s, p, o): [t]*, where *(s, p, o)* is an RDF triple, and *t* is the temporal label. In this definition, *t* is a natural number that represents a time point. To represent a time interval, the temporal triple is expressed as *(s, p, o): [t$_1$,t$_2$]* as the union of all *(s, p, o): [t]* where $t_1 \leq t \leq t_2$. A Temporal Graph is a set of Temporal Triples. This definition has several advantages: 1) It avoids the complex format of time. A natural number is used to represent a time point, which is very simple and straightforward; 2) It integrates point-based and interval-based temporal information; 3) It combines an existing RDF triple with a temporal label so that modification is minimized; 4) The temporal label can be further extended for not only valid time, but also transaction time; 5) It is entirely within the standard definition of RDF.

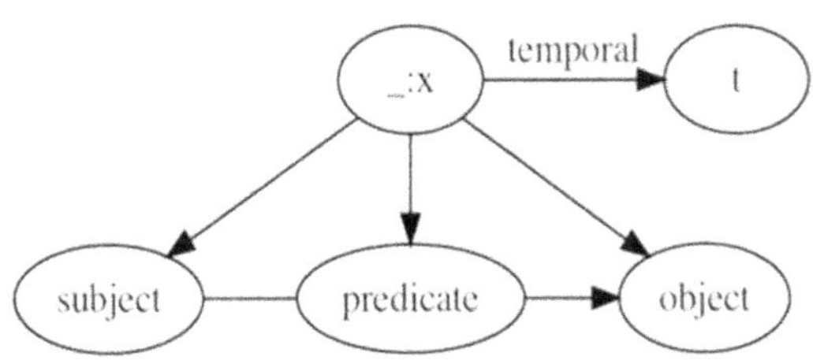

Fig. 5.4. Temporal RDF.

To express the running example, temporal RDF approach will attach a temporal label with a time instant to the triple as shown in Fig. 5.5.

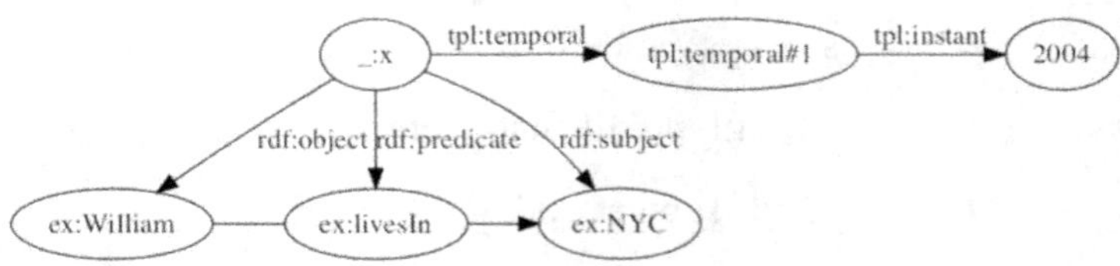

Fig. 5.5. Temporal RDF for the running example.

Gutierrez et al. further extend the temporal RDF model to include implicit temporal labels (anonymous time) [7]. In their original paper, a temporal label t associates with either a time point which is a natural number, or a time interval that composed by two time points [6]. The advantages of having anonymous time are: 1) In the case that triples lack precise temporal information, anonymous time can specify them naturally. With anonymous time, RDF triples can easily be converted to a temporal graph. 2) Anonymous time itself has many uses. For example, a triple A occurs at time t_1, and another triple B occurs at the same time as A does. Although we don't know the explicit time point of the "same time" that triple B occurs at, we can infer by both triples A and B that the "same time" is actually t_1.

5.3.3. Named Graph

The named graph approach is developed by Carroll et al. [2] and Tappolet and Bernstein [13] as shown in Fig. 5.6. Carroll et al. define a named graph as an RDF graph with a URIref. Let U be URIs, B be Blank Nodes, L be Literals, then all nodes in an RDF graph are $V = U \cup B \cup L$. The set $T = V \times U \times V$ is the set of all RDF triples (or an RDF graph). The set of all RDF graphs G is the power set of T. A named graph ng is a pair (n, g) with $n \in U$ and $g \in G$ [2].

Named graph is adopted by W3C Recommendations in the RDF dataset definition as a standard RDF feature: The dataset is a default RDF graph (with no name) and some (zero or more) named graphs may also be included. Or more formally: An RDF dataset is a set of $\{G, (u_1, G_1), (u_2, G_2),... (u_n, G_n)\}$ where G is the default graph, and (u_i, G_i) are named graphs where u_is are URIref and G_is are graphs. Each u_i is distinct [3].

For our running example, the statement "William lives in NYC" will be a named graph with an IRI, say, ng01, and the temporal information will be attached to this named graph as shown in Fig. 5.7.

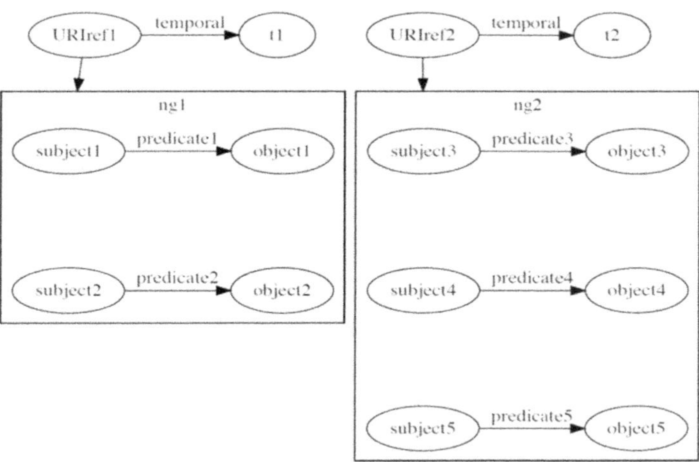

Fig. 5.6. Named graph.

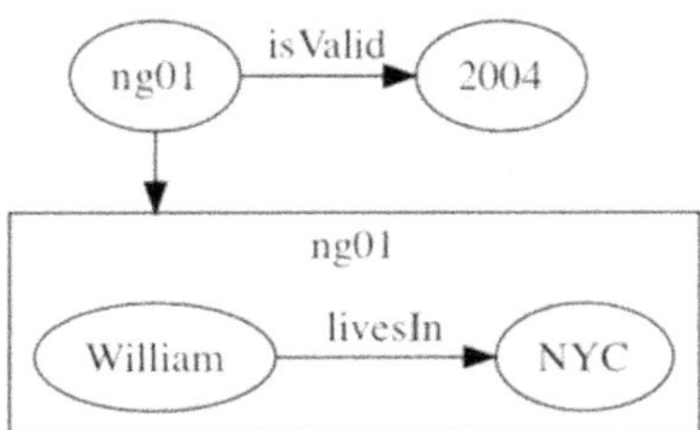

Fig. 5.7. Named graph for the running example.

Tappolet and Bernstein adopt the named graph approach for adding temporal interval into RDF triples [13]. Because named graph is adopted as part of the RDF dataset definition, the difficulty of using this approach for adding temporal information is minimal. Since each named graph *ng* has a name which is an URIref and has a set of triples, the temporal information *t* can be attached to the URIref so that all the triples of that named graph share the same temporal information *t*.

5.3.4. 4D Fluents

McCarthy and Hayes define a fluent as a function that maps from objects and situations to truth [9]. Thus, fluents are relations that hold within some time interval and not in others. Welty and Fikes further develop the 4D Fluents approach to describe information changes over time [15] as shown in Fig. 5.8. The basic problem is how to logically account for the fact that the "same" entity appears to be "different" at different times. 3D view distinguishes endurants that are wholly present at all times and perdurants that have temporal parts that only exist during the time the entities exist. 4D view (also called perdurantist view) maintains that all entities are perdurants. Thus, all entities have temporal parts and can be thought of intuitively as four dimensional.

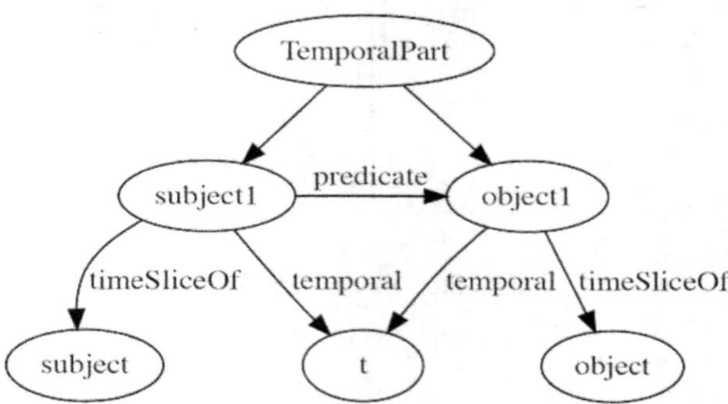

Fig. 5.8. 4D fluents.

One consequence of the 4D approach is that time is "bundled in" with the temporal parts themselves and binary fluents can be represented as a simple binary relation between them. The time interval of a temporal part is defined to be the duration when fluent holds. A single fluent in the 4D approach requires two extra objects, a temporal part and additional six triples, which is more than needed in reification. The most significant aspect of the 4D Fluents approach is that it benefits the defined capabilities of OWL, such as transitive, inversive etc.

For our running example, the relationship between "William" and "NYC" is considered between the temporal parts of them. The "William" in 2004 and "NYC" in 2004 have the relationship "livesIn". Thus, the running example is expressed in Fig. 5.9.

5.3.5. RDF*

RDF* differs from RDF by allowing a triple in place of subject and object resources in a triple: such triples are called RDF* triples. Thus, the definition of an RDF* triple allows nesting: an RDF* triple may have another RDF* triple as its subject or object. The depth of the nesting is denoted as k. Thus, if $k = 0$, the triple is an ordinary RDF triple; and if $k > 0$, it is a nested RDF* triple. Figs. 5.10 - 5.12 show the nested subject, nested object, and nested both subject and object RDF* triple, respectively.

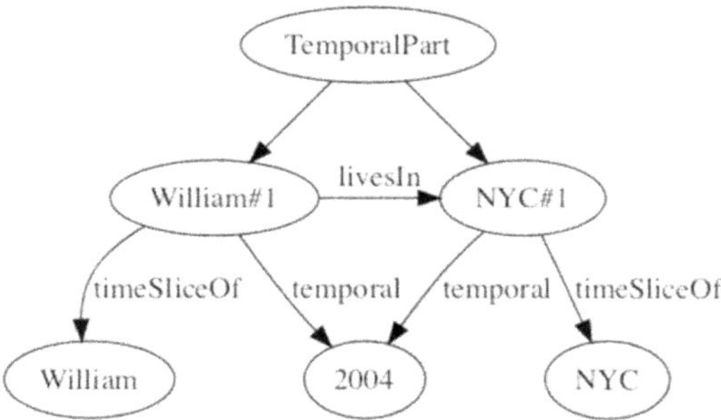

Fig. 5.9. 4D fluents for the running example.

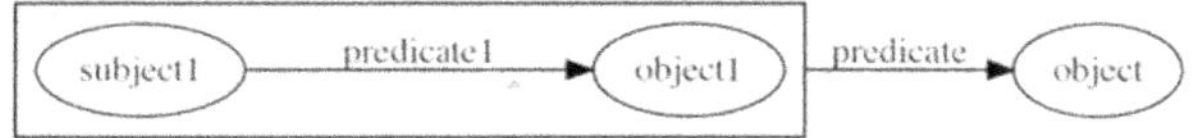

Fig. 5.10. RDF* (a) nested subject.

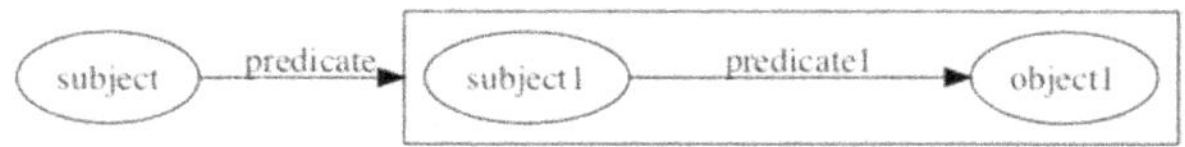

Fig. 5.11. RDF* (b) nested object.

Fig. 5.12. RDF* (c) nested subject and object.

Since the definition of RDF* allows nesting, the unfolding process is defined recursively: If the unfolded RDF graph contains RDF* triples, then the transformation process will continue until all triples are ordinary RDF triples. Turtle* is provided by adding three additional terms: tripleX for an RDF* triple, subjectX and objectX for referring the subject and object of a tripleX. Also, the standard Turtle grammar is updated to include the definition of subject and object in tripleX. SPARQL* is also developed as a metadata extension of SPARQL. This extension enables querying for RDF* graphs. The specification of SPARQL* grammar has an embedded triple pattern as a new syntax element.

The RDF* approach can express our running example simply using a nested subject (Fig 5.13).

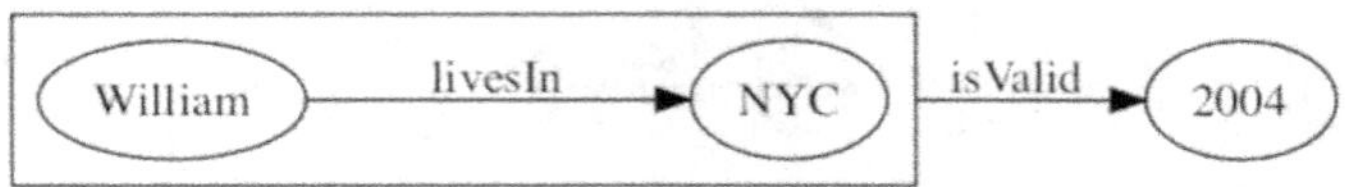

Fig. 5.13. RDF* for the running example.

5.3.6. Singleton Property

Nguyen et al. [10] make a general extension to RDF by introducing singleton property as shown in Fig. 5.14. Temporality is one special kind of singleton property in this approach. The singleton property is based on the notion that "the nature of every relationship is universally unique". A triple in RDF is considered as a relation that connects two entities. In every context, the relation is unique. There may be many relations between two entities, such as time, location, source, certainly, etc. The authors give examples to show how generic properties together with their sub-properties that represent different types of information about statements. For example, "isMarriedTo" relationship is considered as a generic property. All relevant information about "isMarriedTo" relationship is represented as its sub-properties. If there are two triples that have same "isMarriedTo" relationship between the same entities, then two sub-properties will be created, and each corresponding to its unique source. If there is temporal information, then it will be attached to the singleton property that represents the temporal relationship [10].

Thus, by definition, for a triple *(s, p, o)*, *p* is a generic property, and *p* has multiple sub-properties as singleton property, *p#i*. Consequently, the relationship that connects *s* and *o*, is not *p*, but *p#i* and it defines a unique context. Each *p#i* defines multiple relationships for instantiating different values for *i*. It is important to keep the singleton property unique to avoid inconsistencies. Universally Unique Identifier (UUID) can be used to address this problem. UUID is supported by SPARQL and programming languages.

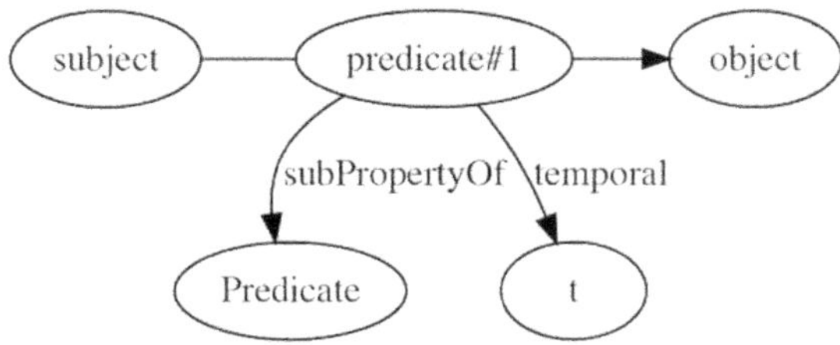

Fig. 5.14. Singleton property.

For our running example, the "livesIn" predicate will be considered as a general property. A sub-property "livesIn#1" will be created to embed the temporal information "2004" as shown in Fig. 5.15.

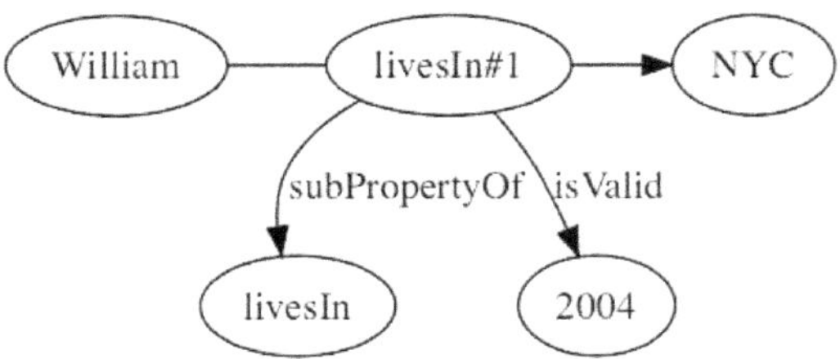

Fig. 5.15. Singleton property for the running example.

There are two types of queries: for data and for metadata that includes singleton properties. Querying for data basically follows standard RDF notation whereas querying metadata needs to include multiple triples in the query pattern. Nguyen et al. compare and evaluate five approaches: the Singleton Property, standard RDF reification, and three flavors of

Provenance Context Entity (PaCE) in an experiment. In the comparison, three factors are considered: number of triples, query length, and time for query execution. The result shows the Singleton Property approach has better performance [10].

5.3.7. N-ary Relations

N-ary Relations approach addresses three major issues in RDF/OWL binary representation of relationships. Since a binary relation can only relate two individuals, then there are three issues that need to be addressed: 1) How to describe the relation itself; 2) How to relate more than two individuals; and 3) How to state the linked individuals are ordered. The sample scenarios for each problem are: 1) A patient with a disease and its probability; 2) A transaction that has buyer, seller, price, purpose, etc., and 3) A flight that has multiple ordered airports on its route. The proposed solutions as n-ary relations for the three use cases are: 1) Introduce a new class of the particular relation, add the disease and probability as property of that class, then use an instance of that relation class to replace the old relation; 2) Introduce a new class of the product that has all other individuals as properties; 3) Use a list of arguments in a relation and use constraint on cardinality for arguments to represent city-on-the-road and destination [11]. The n-ary relations is shown in Fig. 5.16.

Noy et al. distinguish n-ary relations and reification in RDF [11]. The most significant difference between these two is: reification focuses on the statement which has 3 parts *(s, p, o)*; while n-ary relations focuses on the property, which is one part of the statement.

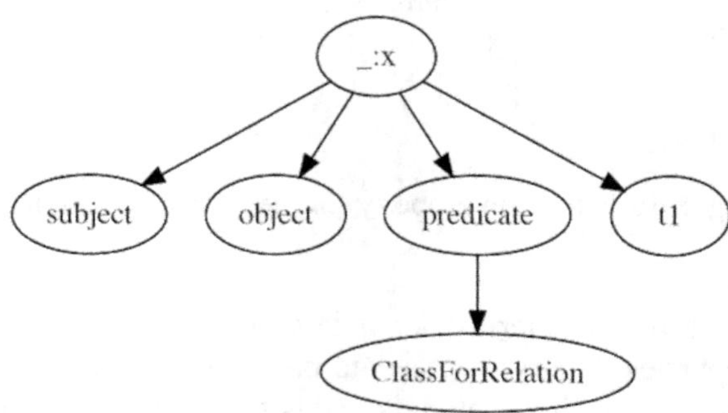

Fig. 5.16. N-ary relations.

For our running example, we can create a new class of residence information, say "Residence". Two properties of the class can be the name of the city and the year of the residence. Thus, an instance of the class can be the object of the relation and cover both the location and valid time as shown in Fig. 5.17.

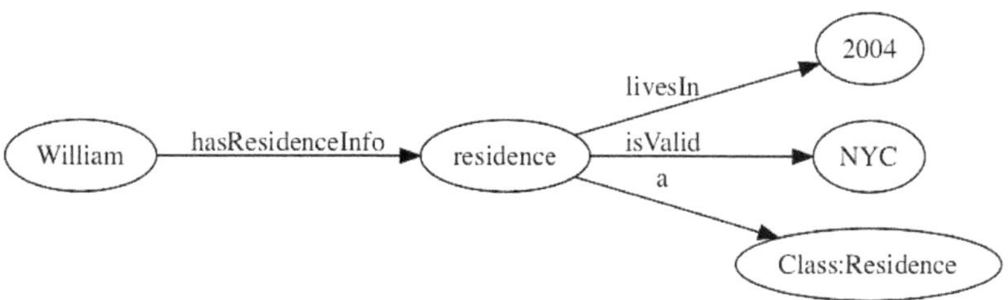

Fig. 5.17. N-ary relations for the running example.

5.3.8. Annotated RDF

Udrea et al. develop the Annotated RDF (aRDF) as a generic extension to the standard RDF model as shown in Fig. 5.18. This approach uses aRDF as a single uniform framework to support various extensions, such as uncertainty, pedigree, time, etc. [14].

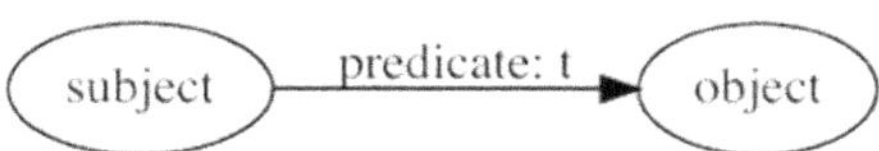

Fig. 5.18. Annotated RDF.

Annotated RDF, short for aRDF, has two parts. The first part is an ordinary RDF triple, *(s, p, o)*; and the second part is an annotation *a* from a partially ordered set *A*. An annotated RDF triple thus, is in the form of *(s, p:a, o)*. For a temporal extension, *A* can be a set of non-negative integers representing time instants. *A* can also be a pair of ordered integers *x, y* as time intervals [14]. In addition, the annotation is attached to the predicate *p*, not the entire triple *(s, p, o)*. Also, aRDF is similar to temporal RDF. In fact, we can consider temporal RDF as a variation of aRDF. However, temporal RDF uses arbitrary labeling t on ordinary

RDF triples as *(s, p, o)[t]* while aRDF uses annotations from a partially ordered set on predicates as *(s, p:a, o)*.

For our running example, Annotated RDF simply adds an annotation to the relationship (Fig. 5.19).

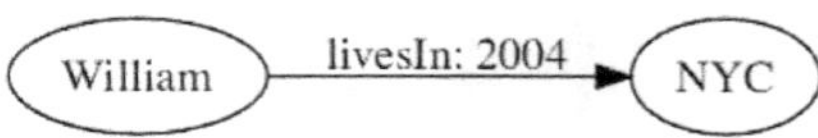

Fig. 5.19. Annotated RDF for the running example.

5.4. Taxonomy of Temporal Extensions to RDF

We examine various approaches that extend standard RDF for temporal information. Since all of them extend the standard RDF model and they are developed with the goal of minimizing the needed modifications they have common aspects and also differences. These approaches convert one or more element of the triples into a meta resource to carry extra information. Depending on the element converted, we can categorize these approaches: graph, triple, or element level.

Graph level. As an RDF dataset contains one or more RDF graphs, named graph approach uses the URIref of the named graph to carry temporal information. A named graph attaches the same time reference on all of its triples.

Triple level. Triple level extensions treat an RDF triple as metadata and convert the triple into a resource to carry temporal information. Reification explicitly converts an RDF triple to a statement; and temporal RDF implicitly attaches a temporal label to an RDF triple.

Element level. 4D fluents converts the subject and object in a triple to be a timeslice of a fluent object to carry temporal information. Singleton Property converts the predicate in a triple and defines a unique sub-property that only exists in a temporal context. N-ary Relations creates a new class for the relation to carry temporal information. Annotated RDF attaches a partially ordered annotation to an RDF triple, and in terms of its syntax, the annotation is attached to the predicate. RDF* allows the subject and object in a triple to be metadata to form nested triples.

5.5. Conclusion

Standard RDF model is built upon the simple *(s, p, o)* triple structure and thus is limited in expressing only binary relationships. Along with the need to embed temporal information to standard RDF, scholars have developed various approaches. We examine these temporal extensions to RDF; and categorize them into three groups depends on how they extend the standard RDF model. Graph level extensions have Named Graph; Triple level extensions have Reification and temporal RDF; Element level includes 4D fluent, Singleton Property, Annotated RDF, RDF* and N-ary Relations approaches. Naturally, each extension has performance differences in space and computation time. A detailed performance comparison of these extensions would be a beneficial study. We plan to explore this direction and also search for a better approach for handling temporal knowledge.

Acknowledgements

The research of the second author is partially supported by the PSC CUNY Award, 60342-00-48.

References

[1]. T. Berners-Lee, O. Lassila, J. Hendler, The semantic web, *Scientific American Magazine*, May 2001, pp. 29-37.

[2]. J. J. Carroll, C. Bizer, P. Hayes, P. Stickler, Named graphs, *Web Semant.*, Vol. 3, Issue 4, December 2005, pp. 247-267.

[3]. R. Cyganiak, D. Wood, M. Lanthaler, RDF 1.1 Concepts and Abstract Syntax, *W3C Recommendation*, Feb. 2014.

[4]. M. Duerst, M. Suignard, Internationalized resource identifiers (IRIS) https://tools.ietf.org/html/rfc3987

[5]. M. Dürst, M. Suignard, Internationalized Resource Identifiers (IRIS), *RFC*, 2005, pp. 832-843.

[6]. C. Gutierrez, C. A. Hurtado, A. Vaisman, Temporal RDF, in *Proceedings of the Second European Semantic Web Conference (ESWC'05)*, 2005, pp. 93-107.

[7]. C. Gutierrez, C. A. Hurtado, A. Vaisman, Introducing time into RDF, *IEEE Trans. on Knowledge and Data Engineering*, Vol. 19, February 2007, pp. 207-218.

[8]. F. Manola, E. Miller, RDF 1.0 Primer, *W3C Recommendation*, 2004.

[9]. J. McCarthy, P. J. Hayes, Some philosophical problems from the standpoint of artificial intelligence, in Machine Intelligence (B. Meltzer, D. Michie, Eds.), Vol. 4, *Edinburgh University Press*, 1969, pp. 463-502.

[10]. V. Nguyen, O. Bodenreider, A. Sheth, Don't like rdf reification?: Making statements about statements using singleton property, in *Proceedings of the 23rd International Conference on World Wide Web (WWW'14)*, New York, NY, USA, 2014, pp. 759-770.

[11]. N. Noy, A. Rector, P. Hayes, C. Welty, Defining N-ary relations on the semantic web, *W3C Working Group Note*, Vol. 12, Issue 4, 2006.

[12]. G. Schreiber, Y. Raimond, RDF 1.1 Primer, *W3C Working Group Note*, 2014.

[13]. J. Tappolet, A. Bernstein, Applied temporal RDF: Efficient temporal querying of RDF data with sparq, in The Semantic Web: Research and Applications (L. Aroyo, P. Traverso, F. Ciravegna, P. Cimiano, T. Heath, E. Hyvönen, R. Mizoguchi, E. Oren, M. Sabou, E. Simper, Eds.), *Springer*, Berlin, Heidelberg, 2009, pp. 308-322.

[14]. O. Udrea, D. Reforgiato Recupero, V. S. Subrahmanian, Annotated RDF, *ACM Trans. Comput. Logic*, Vol. 11, Issue 2, January 2010, pp. 10:1-10:41.

[15]. C. Welty, R. Fikes, S. Makarios, A reusable ontology for fluents in OWL, in *Proceedings of the International Conference on Formal Ontology in Information Systems (FOIS'06)*, 2006, pp. 226-236.

Chapter 6

Bee Algorithms

Mina Salim

6.1. A Review of the Bee Algorithms

Evolutionary algorithms can obtain suboptimal solutions for very difficult problems for which no other method can find a good solution in a reasonable time. These solutions are called suboptimal since usually there is no way to proof their optimality. Among evolutionary algorithms are bee algorithms. The bee algorithms have been used in a vast range of optimization problems such as multivariable problems [1-3], parallel optimization [4], Image contrast enhancement [5], model predictive control design [6], optimal back stepping controller design [7], nonlinear constraint problems [8], and training of feed-forward neural networks [9], data clustering [10, 11], ANFIS training [12], designing controllers for robots [13], and navigation [14]. Bee algorithms can also be hybridized with other intelligent algorithms such as particle swarm optimization (PSO) [15, 16].

6.1.1. The Queen Bee Algorithm (QB)

The QB algorithm is a relatively new method in the class of collective search algorithms [17]. It has some common concepts with the genetic algorithms as genes, population, selection, crossover, mutation, and reproduction.

Mina Salim
Assistant Professor, Faculty of Electrical and Computer Engineering,
University of Tabriz, Tabriz, Iran

It has two main differences with standard genetic algorithms:

(a) Fixing the best member of the population as one of the parents (called queen);

(b) Having two different mutation rates, i.e. normal mutation rate and strong mutation rate;

Before performing mutation, the population is sorted based on ascending cost function.

The better members of population (ζ %) are mutated with normal mutation rate (pm probability), and to prevent premature convergence of the algorithm the remaining members, i.e. $(1-\zeta)$ % of the population, are mutated with strong mutation rate (p'm probability), (pm < p'm, $0.4 \leq \zeta \leq 0.8$).

Remarks:

1. Selection of the second parent is performed based on the roulette wheel selection method.

2. In this chapter, we have used blending crossover. This operator works on two selected members of population (parents) to produce two offspring. To this end, a gene position is selected randomly, and the values of genes located before the selected point are swapped between the parents, and the values of genes located in the selected position and hereafter are replaced with two new values, i.e.

$$x_1 = x_m - \beta(x_m - x_d), \qquad (6.1)$$

$$x_2 = x_d + \beta(x_m - x_d), \qquad (6.2)$$

where x_m, x_d are the initial values, and β is the random value $(0 < \beta < 1)$.

6.1.2. The Artificial Bee Colony Algorithm (ABC)

This algorithm is based on the natural behavior of honey bees in finding food resource [18]. In the following, we briefly describe this algorithm.

In an artificial hive the population of bees is divided into three groups: onlookers, scouts, and workers. In the beginning, the hive has only onlooker and worker bees, and the number of onlooker and worker bees are equal. Algorithm start with a population of solutions (for worker bees) seeking food resources. Each worker bee search around the solution to find the food resource with some additional nectar. Completion of send by all of the employed bees, they share their earned information with onlooker bees in the dancing hall to introduce a new solution depending on the probability associated for each solution

$$p_i = \frac{cost_i}{\sum_{n=1}^{SN} cost_n} \tag{6.3}$$

This process is continued until all onlooker bees find a solution. If one solution isn't improved for a predetermined number of iterations (limit), it would be called an abounded solution and the corresponding bee is called a scout bee. This solution is replaced with another random solution. The value of limit is a parameter for controlling the algorithm The ABC algorithm is given below.

The ABC Algorithm

1. Initialize the population of solutions and evaluate them

$$x = var\ l + (var\ h - var\ l) \times rand(SN, D) \tag{6.4}$$

2. Introduce new solutions from x by

$$v_{ij} = x_{ij} + \emptyset_{ij}(x_{ij} - x_{kj}), \tag{6.5}$$

   and evaluate them, where $\varphi \in [-1,\ 1]$, $k \in \{1,\ 2,...,\ SN\}$, $j \in \{1, 2,..., D\}$.

3. Replace each member of population with corresponding member of v if its fitness is improved. For all members repeat stages 4-6.

4. Assume a probability p for each member of population (using Eq. (6.3)).

5. Introduce new solution v2 from selected solution similar to stage 2(x_{ij} selected with p probability).

6. Replace each member of population with the member of v2 if the fitness is improved.

7. Determine the abandoned solution and replace it with a random solution.

8. Save the best solution so far.

9. While stopping criteria are not satisfied repeat stages 2-8.

6.1.3. The Discrete Artificial Bee Colony Algorithm (DABC)

In this section, a discretized version of the artificial bee colony algorithm introduced by Karaboga and Basturk (2007) is presented. The discrete artificial bee colony algorithm (DABC), is first introduced by Salim and Vakil-Baghmisheh [19]. Logical XOR, OR, and operators are used instead of subtraction, addition, and multiplication operators, respectively.

The Discrete Artificial Bee Colony Algorithm (DABC)

1. Initialize a population of solutions

$$X_1 = \text{round}(\text{rand}(SN, Nt)), \tag{6.6}$$

   where SN denotes population size, and $Nt = D \times nbits$, D is the dimension of the search space, nbits the number of bits used for encoding each variable in binary format.

2. Decode population into continuous variables according to the range of variables and evaluate them.

3. Sort population according to increasing cost function.

   While stopping criteria is not satisfied repeat the following stages:

4. Produce new solutions V_1 from X_1 according to the following stages:

   For all members of population repeat:

   a. Choose a member of population randomly and name it k.

   b. Define a random vector with binary arrays:

$$\emptyset = \text{round}(\text{rand}(1, Nt)) \tag{6.7}$$

c. Produce

$$V_{1i} = X_{1i} \vee (\emptyset \wedge (X_{1i} \oplus k)) \tag{6.8}$$

5. Decode V_1.

6. Replace each member of population with the corresponding new solution if the fitness improves.

7. Calculate the probabilities p_i for solutions X_1(using Eq. (6.3)).

8. Produce new solutions V_2 from the solutions X_1 selected randomly depending on p_i and evaluate them (similar to stage 4).The easiest way to format text and save a time is to use the proposed styles.

9. Replace each member of population with new solutions if the fitness improves.

10. Determine the abandoned solution and replace it with the best solution.

11. Save the best solution achieved so far.

6.1.4. The Fast Marriage in Honey Bee Optimization Algorithm (FMBO)

This algorithm was inspired by the mating process of honey bees [20]. The algorithm is presented in the following.

The FMBO Algorithm

1. Initialize the population of queens and workers with random solutions.

2. Improve the fitness of queens using worker bees.

3. For each queen generate a drone randomly.

4. Apply single point crossover between selected queen and drone and generate a brood.

5. Mutate the brood.

6. Improve the fitness of the brood using worker bees and improve the fitness of workers.

7. Replace the worst queen with the brood if the brood's fitness is better than worst queen's fitness.

6.1.5. The Discrete Fast Marriage in Honey Bee Optimization

Here are three versions of the discrete fast marriage in honey bee optimization algorithm, i.e. DFMBO1, and DFMBO2, and DFMBO3, which were first introduced by Salim and Vakil-Baghmisheh [19].

The DFMBO1 Algorithm

1. Initialize the population of queens and workers with random solutions.

2. Repeat stages 3–7 for all queens.

3. Select a worker from the worker's population randomly, choose a bit of queen randomly and replace it with the result of applying the logic AND operator between this bit and the selected worker's bit. (If the queen's fitness improves).

4. Select a drone randomly.

5. Apply crossover between the drone and the queen and generate a brood.

6. Mutate the brood.

7. Replace the worst queen with the brood if the brood's fitness is better than queen's fitness.

The DFMBO2 Algorithm

The algorithm of DFMBO2 is similar to DFMBO1 with the following differences:

1. Using logic OR ($\vee$) operator instead of AND ($\wedge$) operator.

2. Using $\vee$ operator on the entire chromosome instead of only on one bit.

The DFMBO3 Algorithm

1. Initialize two populations of queens and workers with random solutions

$$qpop = round(rand(Q, Nt), \qquad (6.9)$$

$$wpop = round(rand(w, Nt), \qquad (6.10)$$

Q is the number of queens, w is the number of workers, $Nt = npar \times nbits$, npar is the dimension of the search space, nbits is the number of bits used for encoding each variable in binary format).

2. Decode qpop into continuous variables according to the range of variables and evaluate them.

3. Repeat following stages for all queens:

   a. Select a worker from wpop and name it k.

   b. Define a random vector with binary arrays (using Eq. (6.7)).

   c. Generate a chromosome according to

$$x_i = qpop_i \vee (\emptyset \wedge (qpop_i \oplus k)) \qquad (6.11)$$

   d. Replace each member of qpop with the corresponding member of x if the fitness improves.

   e. Generate a drone randomly.

   f. Repeat following stages M times ($M \geq 1$).

     i. Apply single point crossover between generated drone and the selected queen and generate a brood.

     ii. Mutate the brood.

     iii. Apply the selected worker for improving the fitness of brood according to the following stages

$$b = brood \vee (\emptyset \wedge (brood \oplus k)) \qquad (6.12)$$

Replace the brood with b if the fitness improves.

iv. Apply the brood for improving the fitness of the selected worker according to the following stages

$$k' = k' \vee (\emptyset \wedge (\text{brood} \oplus k')) \tag{6.13}$$

Replace k with k' if the fitness improves.

4. Replace the worst queen with the brood if the brood's fitness is better than the fitness of worst queen.

5. While stopping criteria are not satisfied repeat stages 2-4.

6.1.6. Modified Fast Marriage in Honey Bee Optimization Algorithm

The algorithm of marriage in honey bee optimization (MBO) was introduced by Abbass [21]. Later on Yang et al. [22] introduced a faster version of this algorithm (FMBO) by eliminating the randomness of mating between queens and the encountered drones. But, seemingly there is a shortcoming in the FMBO algorithm introduced by Yang et al., and that is replacing the worst queen by any new-born brood (in the case of cost improvement), before finishing the processing cycle for the current queen and all remaining queens. This replacement may cause the processing cycle for the current queen to get aborted, also may drive the algorithm to leave behind or eliminate some queens without processing them, and altogether it downgrades the performance of algorithm. In the modified versin of FMBO which is first introduced by Vakil-Baghmisheh, M. Salim (2010), this matter is addressed and the replacement of queens is postponed with broods until the end of reproduction process for all queens. Also some changes in modifying the fitness of queens, broods, and workers are made as explained in Remarks 1 to 5. The main stages of modified FMBO algorithm are as follows [23]:

A. Initialization.

B. Production of $B = M \times Q$ broods.

C. Selection of Q new queens.

D.   If stopping criteria are not met go to step 2 and repeat the algorithm.

The detailed modified FMBO (MFMBO) algorithm is presented below.

The MFBOM Algorithm

A. Initialize a random population of Q queens and W workers.

B. Produce M broods for each queen.

for q = 1, ..., Q.

1. Select a worker and name it k, and improve the queen's fitness using the selected worker (see Remark 2).

for m = 1,...M.

2. Generate a drone randomly (A drone is a random solution which is generated to be used as the mate of a queen for reproduction).

3. Apply the crossover operator between the queen and the drone to produce an offspring, which is called a brood (see Remark 5).

4. Mutate the brood.

5. Improve the brood's fitness using k (selected worker in step B-1), also improve the worker (see Remarks 3 and 4).

   (In later steps the modified worker is used, when necessary).

   end for.

   end for.

C. Sort the unified list of queens and broods, and select the Q best individuals as the new queens for the next iteration.

D. If stopping criteria are not met, go to step B and repeat the algorithm.

Remarks:

1. Initially we select two random chromosomes as the workers, which are modified through algorithm.

2. Improve the fitness of queens by using the selected worker

$$\text{queen}_1 \; = \; \text{queen} + \emptyset(\text{queen} - \text{k}) \qquad (6.14)$$

Replace queen with queen$_1$ if fitness improves.

3. Improve the fitness of brood by using the selected worker

$$\text{brood}_1 \; = \; \text{brood} + \emptyset(\text{brood} - \text{k}) \qquad (6.15)$$

Replace brood with brood$_1$ if fitness improves.

4. Improve the fitness of worker using Eq. (6.16)

$$\text{k}' \; = \; \text{k} + \emptyset(\text{brood} - \text{k}) \qquad (6.16)$$

Replace k with k' if fitness improves.

5. To mutate a brood, select a gene randomly and change its value as follows

$$\text{New}_{\text{value}} \; = \; \text{old}_{\text{valu}} + (2 \times \text{rand} - 1) \times \text{rate}, \qquad (6.17)$$

$$\text{rate} \; = \; (\text{H}_\text{j} - \text{L}_\text{j})/3,$$

where rand is a random number in the range [0, 1], and H_j and L_j are respectively the upper and lower bounds of the selected gene (j^{th} variable). In the case of crossing the upper or lower bound, its value is limited to the boundary value.

6.2. The Benchmark Functions

All bee algorithms ae tested on four benchmark functions. These functions are described in the following.

6.2.1. Sphere Function

$$f(x) \; = \; \sum_{i=1}^{n} x_i^2 \,, x_i \in [-100, 100], i \; = \; 1, \cdots, n \qquad (6.18)$$

The sphere function is smooth, strongly convex, continuous, and symmetric. The global minimum $f(x) = 0$ is obtainable for $x_i = 0$, $i = 1,\ldots,n$.

6.2.2. Schwefel Function

$$f(x) = \sum_{i=1}^{n} -x_i \sin \sqrt{|x_i|}, x_i \in [-500, 500], i = 1, \cdots, n \quad (6.19)$$

This function is highly multimodal and non-linear. The surface of Schwefel function is composed of a large number of peaks and valleys. The global minimum $f(x) = 0$ is obtainable for $x_i = 420.9867$, $i = 1,\ldots,n$.

6.2.3. Rastrigin Function

$$f(x) = \sum_{i=1}^{n} [x_i^2 - 10 \cos 2\pi x_i + 10],$$

$$x_i \in [-5.12, 5.12], i = 1, \cdots, n \quad (6.20)$$

This function is highly multimodal and non-linear. It contains millions of local minima. The locations of the minima are regularly distributed. The difficulty about this function is that an optimization algorithm easily could be trapped in a local minimum. The global minimum $f(x) = 0$ is obtainable for $x_i = 0$, $i = 1,\ldots,n$.

6.2.4. Griewank Function

$$f(x) = \frac{1}{4000} \sum_{i=1}^{n} x_i^2 - \prod_{i=1}^{n} \cos \left(\frac{x_i}{\sqrt{i}} \right) + 1, x_i \in [-600, 600],$$

$$i = 1, \cdots, n \quad (6.21)$$

This function is non-linear. Since the number of local minima increases with the dimensionality it is strongly multimodal. The global minimum $f(x) = 0$ is obtainable for $x_i = 0$, $i = 1,\ldots, n$.

6.3. The Simulation Results and Analysis

The simulation results are given in Tables 6.1-6.4. In these tables the success rate and the average number of function evaluations obtained in successful runs (over 30 runs) are given.

In these tables * illustrates that obtaining success rates are computationally too time consuming, so we gave up computing them.

The results obtained on Sphere function are presented in Table 6.1. We see that by increasing the number of variables up to 10, when the tolerance of answer is equal or less than 10^{-2}, the MFMBO is faster than the FMBO in all cases, but when the tolerance of answer is 10^{-3} the FMBO is faster than the MFMBO, but the MFMBO achieves a success rate of 100 % on all these cases. For 50 and 100 variables, when the tolerance of answer becomes smaller than 10^{-2}, the FMBO performs better than the MFMBO in terms of speed and success rate. The MFMBO algorithm performs better than QB in all cases and only when the tolerance of answer is 10^{-3} and the number of variables is 100 the ABC algorithm performs better than the MFMBO algorithm. When number of variables grows, and the tolerance of answer becomes small enough, i.e. equal or less than 10^{-3}, the speed of the continuous algorithms, i.e. QB, ABC, and FMBO algorithms become prohibitively slow and their success rates decrease. On the other hand by increasing number of variables up to 100, and decreasing the tolerance of answer as small as 10^{-3}, the discrete algorithms are still fast and number of function evaluations is still manageable. The DFMBO3 algorithm is the fastest one and number of function evaluations doesn't grow beyond 1010.

By analyzing the results presented in Table 6.2, we see all discrete counterparts of the FMBO and the MFMBO are faster than the FMBO on all cases; especially when number of variables is too large the differences between their speeds are clear. The DABC is too faster than the ABC on all cases. The DFMBO1, the DFMBO2, the DFMBO3 are faster than the DABC on all cases. For 2, 5, 10 and 20 variables the QB, and for more variables the DFMBO3 are the fastest algorithms.

The results obtained on Rastrigin function are presented in Table 6.3. We see that for 2 variables the MFMBO is faster than the FMBO and the ABC and the QB. For other cases other algorithms perform better than the MFMBO in terms of speed and success rate, but the MFMBO is competitive with them. The DFMBO3 performs better than the FMBO in terms of both success rate and speed in all cases. Also, in all cases the DABC is faster than the ABC. In Table 6.3, the DFMBO3 is the strongest algorithm.

From Table 6.4, we see all discrete counterparts of the FMBO algorithm work better than the FMBO in terms of both success rate and speed. The speed of DABC is better than the ABC. The DFMBO3 is the strongest and the FMBO is the weakest algorithm among all methods.

The MFBMO performs better than the FMBO in all cases, also it performs better than the QB and the ABC algorithm for the 2, 5, 10 and 20 variables in terms of both success rate and speed. The computation of the FMBO for n = 100 is too time consuming, so we abandoned the computations, but the MFMBO is still fast and number of function evaluations is manageable.

In general the success rates of the DABC and the DFMBO3 in all cases are 100 %. Also the average function evaluations for the DFMBO3 are less than all continuous algorithms. All discrete algorithms have less average function evaluations than their continuous counterparts.

Table 6.1. Simulation results for Sphere function.

Algorithm	Tolerance	No. of Variables					
		2	**5**	**10**	**20**	**50**	**100**
QB	0.5	100(1406)	100(6579)	100(8836)	100(42315)	100(18936)	100(148610)
	0.1	100(3126)	90(10933)	90(22056)	70(60801)	90(42036)	80(148610)
	0.01	100(9903)	80(23220)	60(18523)	30(80200)	70(59686)	40(202140)
	0.001	100(10470)	60(28288)	40(18735)	20(73185)	20(89860)	20(193177)
ABC	0.5	100(148)	100(869)	100(2647)	100(34820)	100(422490)	100(5893100)
	0.1	100(247)	100(1277)	100(3251)	100(42900)	100(505290)	100(6947800)
	0.01	100(444)	100(1796)	100(4177)	100(56408)	100(619960)	100(8396910)
	0.001	100(649)	100(2273)	100(5124)	100(67035)	100(742520)	100(9808800)
DABC	0.5	100(333)	100(793)	100(1075)	100(1178)	100(3001)	100(9337)
	0.1	100(368)	100(872)	100(1163)	100(1296)	100(3257)	100(9337)
	0.01	100(577)	100(978)	100(1295)	100(1469)	100(3498)	100(9709)
	0.001	100(687)	100(1106)	100(1442)	100(1593)	100(3739)	100(10441)
FMBO	0.5	100(2721)	100(7526)	100(14651)	100(22592)	100(210328)	100(421030)
	0.1	100(2721)	100(7526)	100(14651)	100(22592)	100(210328)	100(421030)
	0.01	100(2721)	100(7526)	100(14651)	100(22592)	100(210328)	100(421030)
	0.001	100(2721)	100(7526)	100(14651)	100(22592)	100(210328)	100(421030)
DFMBO1	0.5	100(73)	100(185)	100(397)	100(5663)	100(14696)	100(72696)
	0.1	100(95)	100(240)	100(511)	100(7004)	100 (18635)	100(87785)
	0.01	100(119)	100(302)	100(655)	100(8893)	100(24217)	100(109910)
	0.001	100(147)	100(366)	100(797)	100(10771)	100(29699)	100(131480)
DFMBO2	0.5	100(60)	100(105)	100(458)	100(1870)	100(6189)	93.3(26716)
	0.1	100(67)	100(124)	100(614)	100(2400)	100(7687)	93.3(32561)

	Tolerance	2	5	10	20	50	100
	0.01	100(74)	100(159)	100(846)	100(3152)	100(9832)	93.3(40939)
	0.001	100(86)	100(188)	100(1097)	100(3911)	100(11994)	93.3(49350)
DFMBO3	0.5	100(305)	100(406)	100(439)	100(538)	100(671)	100(742)
DFMBO3	0.1	100(349)	100(455)	100(501)	100(599)	100(784)	100(808)
DFMBO3	0.01	100(414)	100(545)	100(585)	100(681)	100(867)	100(942)
DFMBO3	0.001	100(476)	100(628)	100(677)	100(765)	100(999)	100(1010)
MFMBO	0.5	100(259)	100(774)	100(2355)	100(6899)	100(24357)	100(16200)
MFMBO	0.1	100(364)	100(1320)	100(4163)	100(20658)	100(64251)	100(44267)
MFMBO	0.01	100(620)	100(3962)	100(10650)	100(66905)	100(215855)	100(169730)
MFMBO	0.001	100(1103)	100(10637)	100(51630)	100(147040)	20(462645)	0

Table 6.2. Simulation results for Schwefel function.

Algorithm	Tolerance	No. of Variables					
		2	5	10	20	50	100
QB	0.5	100(12)	100(20)	100(30)	100(60)	100(80)	100 (120)
QB	0.1	100(12)	100(20)	100(30)	100(60)	100(80)	100 (120)
QB	0.01	100(12)	100(20)	100(30)	100(60)	100(80)	100 (120)
QB	0.001	100(12)	100(20)	100(30)	100(60)	100(80)	100 (120)
ABC	0.5	100(147)	100(151)	100(157)	100(612)	100(3758)	100(15060)
ABC	0.1	100(147)	100(151)	100(157)	100(612)	100(3758)	100(15060)
ABC	0.01	100(147)	100(151)	100(157)	100(612)	100(3758)	100(15060)
ABC	0.001	100(147)	100(151)	100(157)	100(612)	100(3758)	100(15060)
DABC	0.5	100(41)	100(147)	100(328)	100(329)	100(562)	100(1323)
DABC	0.1	100(41)	100(147)	100(328)	100(329)	100(562)	100(1323)
DABC	0.01	100(41)	100(147)	100(328)	100(329)	100(562)	100(1323)
DABC	0.001	100(41)	100(147)	100(328)	100(329)	100(562)	100(1323)
FMBO	0.5	100(4886)	100(4495)	100(10200)	100(43753)	100(67101)	100(328620)
FMBO	0.1	100(4886)	100(4495)	100(10200)	100(43753)	100(67101)	100(328620)
FMBO	0.01	100(4886)	100(4495)	100(10200)	100(43753)	100(67101)	100(328620)
FMBO	0.001	100(4886)	100(4495)	100(10200)	100(43753)	100(67101)	100(328620)
DFMBO1	0.5	100(9)	100(34)	100(122)	100(270)	100(463)	100(469)
DFMBO1	0.1	100(10)	100(34)	100(122)	100(270)	100(463)	100(469)
DFMBO1	0.01	100(10)	100(34)	100(122)	100(270)	100(463)	100(469)
DFMBO1	0.001	100(10)	100(34)	100(122)	100(270)	100(463)	100(469)
DFMBO2	0.5	100(34)	100(38)	100(40)	100(118)	100(253)	100(437)

	0.1	100(34)	100(38)	100(40)	100(118)	100(253)	100(437)
	0.01	100(34)	100(38)	100(40)	100(118)	100(253)	100(437)
	0.001	100(34)	100(38)	100(40)	100(118)	100(253)	100(437)
DFMBO3	0.5	100(17)	100(19)	100(42)	100(48)	100(62)	100(80)
	0.1	100(17)	100(19)	100(42)	100(48)	100(62)	100(80)
	0.01	100(17)	100(19)	100(42)	100(48)	100(62)	100(80)
	0.001	100(17)	100(19)	100(42)	100(48)	100(62)	100(80)
MFMBO	0.5	100(35)	100(38)	100(75)	100(95)	100(115)	100(130)
	0.1	100(35)	100(38)	100(75)	100(95)	100(115)	100(130)
	0.01	100(35)	100(38)	100(75)	100(95)	100(115)	100(130)
	0.001	100(35)	100(38)	100(75)	100(95)	100(115)	100(130)

Table 6.3. Simulation results for Rastrigin function.

Algorithm	Tolerance	No. of Variables					
		2	5	10	20	50	100
QB	0.5	100(1450)	100(2357)	100(5190)	100(36486)	100(55392)	80 (35133)
	0.1	100(2298)	100(13534)	100(22122)	100(44469)	80(95115)	60(69222)
	0.01	100(7044)	100(43464)	60 (31150)	60(78270)	80 (99235)	50 (71162)
	0.001	100(12880)	70(35639)	50 (39368)	30 (73080)	30 (89640)	40 (158332)
ABC	0.5	100(839)	100(10681))	100(35735)	100(208631)	100(2167000)	100(5399925)
	0.1	100(1074)	100(12541)	100(38647)	100(221901)	100(2275100)	100(5618400)
	0.01	100(1405)	100(15952)	100(43395)	100(251126)	100(2388300)	100(5827800)
	0.001	100(1593)	100(18963)	100(49237)	100(276042)	100(2536245)	100(5941800)
DABC	0.5	100(237)	100(734)	100(887)	100(2791)	100(5027)	100(7802)
	0.1	100(292)	100(842)	100(968)	100(2860)	100(5399)	100(8111)
	0.01	100(386)	100(949)	100(1090)	100(3261)	100(5841)	100(8439)
	0.001	100(472)	100(1056)	100(1219)	100(3427)	100(6051)	100(8732)
FMBO	0.5	100(6110)	100(10886)	100(22966)	100(45072)	100(215150)	100(631824)
	0.1	100(6110)	100(10886)	100(22966)	100(45072)	100(215150)	100(631824)
	0.01	100(6110)	100(10886)	100(22966)	100(45072)	100(215150)	100(631824)
	0.001	100(6110)	100(10886)	100(22966)	100(45072)	100(215150)	100(631824)
DFMBO1	0.5	100(203)	100(472)	100(19096)	96.6(43852)	76.6(402860)	40(1813600)
	0.1	100(227)	100(528)	100(21239)	96.6(47023)	76.6(437010)	40(1916300)
	0.01	100(260)	100(604)	100(24256)	96.6(51494)	76.6(485620)	40(2062700)
	0.001	100(295)	100(682)	100(27193)	96.6(55775)	76.6(533930)	36.6(1864200)

Algorithm	Tolerance	2	5	10	20	50	100
DFMBO2	0.5	100(373)	100(910)	100(2204)	96.6(8450)	80(65110)	46.6(129630)
	0.1	100(413)	100(1002)	100(2418)	96.6(9345)	80(73030)	46.6(137420)
	0.01	100(421)	100(1099)	100(2790)	96.6(10603)	80(84359)	46.6(148610)
	0.001	100(456)	100(1195)	100(3123)	96.6(11777)	80(95634)	46.6(158990)
DFMBO3	0.5	100(109)	100(120)	100(217)	100(348)	100(472)	100(658)
	0.1	100(126)	100(135)	100(244)	100(385)	100(534)	100(714)
	0.01	100(153)	100(161)	100(286)	100(440)	100(588)	100(826)
	0.001	100(178)	100(187)	100(332)	100(497)	100(672)	100(887)
MFMBO	0.5	100(473)	100(22852)	90(5942)	90(7851)	60(68770)	40(495080)
	0.1	100(661)	100(33929)	90(10717)	90(24369)	60(91751)	40(137600)
	0.01	100(1180)	100(40236)	90(20850)	90(50002)	60(185955)	40(401695)
	0.001	100(1568)	100(53575)	90(58675)	90(147400)	30(533100)	0

Table 6.4. Simulation results for Greiwank function.

Algorithm	Tolerance	No. of Variables					
		2	5	10	20	50	100
QB	0.5	100(364)	100(605)	100(2210)	100(8577)	100(10994)	100(35921)
	0.1	100(2947)	100(2405)	90(30198)	90(5678)	80(21724)	60(53214)
	0.01	80(18258)	90(31323)	40(36730)	40(45195)	40(60230)	40(80443)
	0.001	60(20268)	80(41402)	40(41290)	30(118340)	30(123450)	30(303094)
ABC	0.5	100(662)	100(9980)	100(26909)	100(66063)	100(183710)	100(104010)
	0.1	100(1031)	100(13405)	100(35007)	100(80313)	100(216720)	100(122632)
	0.01	100(1069)	100(29653)	86.6(61248)	100(108070)	100(268192)	96.6(141470)
	0.001	100(2688)	76.6(42542)	66.6(63718)	93.3(122230)	96.6(311210)	96.6(166830)
DABC	0.5	100(308)	100(967)	100(1069)	100(2431)	100(4874)	100(5560)
	0.1	100(650)	100(1002)	100(1111)	100(2529)	100(5170)	100(5917)
	0.01	100(807)	100(1098)	100(1257)	100(2861)	100(5609)	100(6402)
	0.001	100(1121)	100(1234)	100(1445)	100(3179)	100(5985)	100(6938)
FMBO	0.5	100(10415)	100(80051)	100(277724)	100(2712132)	100(352050)	*
	0.1	100(10415)	100(80051)	86.6(275820)	83.3(2702300)	56.6(3538800)	*
	0.01	100(10415)	26.6(83563)	10(279970)	6.6(2811120)	13.3(3645390)	*
	0.001	63.3(10591)	10(91000)	3.3(283960)	6.6(2811120)	6.6(3645300)	*
DFMBO1	0.5	100(134)	100(537)	100(1150)	100(9414)	96.6(150390)	83.3(410890)
	0.1	100(226)	100(639)	100(1369)	100(11023)	96.6(174260)	83.3(504730)
	0.01	100(262)	100(694)	96.6(1630)	100(13085)	96.6(203340)	83.3(620504)

	0.001	100(282)	100(754)	96.6(1876)	100(15201)	96.6(231120)	83.3(733000)
DFMBO2	0.5	100(146)	100(295)	100(2293)	100(4115)	96.6(53298)	86.6(51297)
	0.1	100(189)	100(327)	100(3048)	100(4868)	96.6(59758)	86.6(61465)
	0.01	100(233)	100(378)	100(3936)	100(5858)	96.6(67890)	86.6(73140)
	0.001	100(247)	100(422)	100(4887)	100(6830)	96.6(75948)	86.6(84221)
DFMBO3	0.5	100(44)	100(71)	100(89)	100(180)	100(189)	100(308)
	0.1	100(65)	100(81)	100(100)	100(206)	100(213)	100(350)
	0.01	100(87)	100(96)	100(116)	100(236)	100(247)	100(405)
	0.001	100(97)	100(109)	100(132)	100(269)	100(282)	100(451)
MFMBO	0.5	100(123)	100(1000)	100(4760)	100(9281)	100(4737)	100(49818)
	0.1	100(469)	100(33600)	100(85850)	100(50294)	100(14403)	100(204723)
	0.01	100(3668)	33.3(102600)	100(199070)	80(179810)	66.66(229970)	20(501860)
	0.001	100(17199)	33.3(172680)	0	33.33(79380)	33.33(109330)	0

6.4. Designing of the PID Controllers

In this section, PID controllers for two benchmark transfer functions are designed using the ABC, the QB, the FMBO algorithms. Then the performance of these controllers are compared. The two transfer functions are

$$G_1(s) = \frac{1}{s^2-1}, G_2(s) = \frac{1}{(s+1)^2} \qquad (6.22)$$

The transfer function of a PID controller is defined as:

$$H(s) = K_p + K_d s + \frac{K_i}{s}, \qquad (6.23)$$

where K_p, K_d, K_i are the proportional, derivative, and integral gain, respectively. The characteristics of the step response like overshoot M_P, settling time t_s, rise time t_r and steady state error E_{ss} could be used as performance measures for the PID controllers, but in this way the design problem would be a multi-objective optimization problem. To convert the multi-objective problem to a single-objective problem, a single cost function is defined using afore-said measures [24]

$$f(k) = \left(1 - e^{-\beta}\right)\left(M_p + E_{ss}\right) + e^{-\beta}(t_s - t_r), \qquad (6.24)$$

where β is the weighting factor. For $\beta < 0.7$ t_r and ts are more affected, but for $\beta > 0.7$ MP and Ess are affected more than t_r and t_s. If $\beta = 0.7$ emphasis on all of four measures will be equal. To evaluate each chromosome, its genes inserted in the controller transfer function H(s), and the step response of the system is calculated. By obtaining E_{ss}, M_P, t_r and t_s, the cost function is evaluated. We set an upper and a lower bound for K_p, K_d, K_i as 350 and 0, respectively. The value of β is set equal to 0.7. Parameters setting for algorithms has been given in Tables 6.5-6.7.

Table 6.5. The values of parameters in the QB algorithm.

	Population size	Normal mutation rate	Strong mutation rate	ζ	Iteration
G1(s)	10	0.01	0.6	0.7	100
G2(s)	10	0.1	0.6	0.7	200

Table 6.6. The values of parameters in the ABC algorithm.

	Population size	Iteration	Limit
$G_1(s)$	10	500	400
$G_2(s)$	10	100	80

Table 6.7. The values of parameters in the FMBO algorithm.

	Q	W	Iteration
$G_1(s)$	10	5	100
$G_2(s)$	8	3	40

The simulation results are presented in Figs. 6.1, 6.2 and Tables 6.8, 6.9. The step responses of transfer functions are presented in Figs. 6.1, 6.2. In Tables 6.8, 6.9, the PID factors and the step response specifications for each transfer function have been presented.

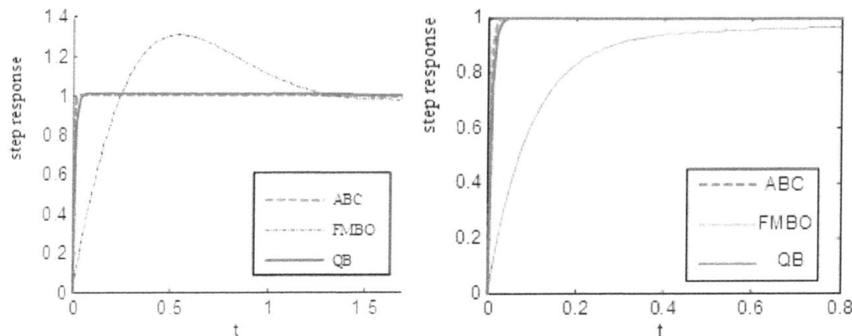

Fig. 6.1. The step response of $G_1(s)$.

Fig. 6.2. The step response of $G_2(s)$.

Table 6.8. The obtained results for $G_1(s)$.

Algorithm	k_d	k_d	k_i	M_p	E_{ss}	t_s	t_r	Mincost	t (s)
ABC	225.59	319.28	203.87	0.006	0.043	0.02	0	0.0287	590.8
FMBO	5.91	20	13.58	0.31	0.61	2.5	0	1.71	346.9
QB	95.24	98.68	98.73	0.014	0.091	0.06	0	0.0826	130.3

Table 6.9. The obtained results for G2(s).

Algorithm	k_d	k_d	k_i	M_p	E_{ss}	t_s	t_r	Mincost	t (s)
ABC	221.16	259.27	171.79	0	0.03	0.02	0	0.0197	118.2
FMBO	10.11	13.71	7.43	0.004	0.32	2.38	0	1.348	35.86
QB	144.51	197.9	111.06	0	0.034	0.04	0	0.0373	298.5

From the results we see that for each transfer function the ABC algorithm achieves minimum cost function. For G1(s) the QB algorithm and for G2(s) the FMBO algorithm require minimum calculation times. But since designing PID controller is an off-line process calculation time is not the most important factor.

6.5. Conclusion

In this chapter eight honey bee algorithms are reviewed i.e. QB, ABC, DABC, FMBO, DFMBO1, DFMBO2, DFMBO3, and MFMBO. These algorithms are tested on four multivariable benchmarks for various numbers of variables up to 100. Success rates and the average function evaluations are reported to find optimum point in thirty runs and for four predefined threshold values.

In general, when the precision of answer and number of variables are small, all above mentioned algorithms are performing well. However, by increasing the precision of answer and number of variables, the average function evaluations in the continuous algorithms will be increase beyond manageable amounts, and as a result the success rates will be decrease. Simulation results show that DFMBO3 is the most efficient algorithm among all tested algorithms in terms of both success rate and speed. DFMBO1 and DFMBO2 perform better than FMBO in most cases. In general, DABC performs better than the ABC in all cases. DFMBO3 algorithm is suggested to be called as the DFMBO algorithm in future works.

In addition, in this chapter PID controllers for two benchmark transfer functions are designed using three bee algorithms, i.e. ABC, QB, and FMBO. To this end, four features of the step response, i.e. E_{ss}, M_p, t_r and t_s are adopted and a cost function is introduced including these features and then the introduced cost function, is minimized. In this way a multi-objective function optimization problem is converted into a single-objective function optimization problem. In general, one algorithm could not be preferred to another one. The results show that the ABC algorithm is the most proper algorithm for this case.

References

[1]. D. Karaboga, B. Basturk, A powerful and efficient algorithm for numerical function optimization: Artificial Bee Colony, *Glob. Optim.*, Vol. 39, Issue 3, 2007, pp. 459-471.

[2]. J. Luo, Q. Liu, Y. Yang, X. Lia, M.-R. Chena, W. Caoa, An Artificial Bee Colony algorithm for multi-objective optimization, *Applied Soft Computing*, Vol. 50, 2017, pp. 235-251.

[3]. A. Saad, S. A. Khan, A. Mahmood, A multi-objective evolutionary Artificial Bee Colony algorithm for optimizing network topology design, *Swarm and Evolutionary Computation*, Vol. 38, 2018, pp. 187-201.

[4]. H. Wang, J. Wei, S. Wen, Y. Hou, Research on parallel optimization of Artificial Bee Colony algorithm, in *Proceedings of the International Conference on Advanced Mechatronic Systems (ICAMechS'18)*, Zhengzhou, China, Aug. 30 – Sep. 2, 2018.

[5]. J. Chena, W. Yua, J. Tianb, L. Chen, Z. Zhoud, Image contrast enhancement using an Artificial Bee Colony algorithm, *Swarm and Evolutionary Computation*, Vol. 38, 2018, pp. 287-294.

[6]. M. Sarailoo, Z. Rahmani, B. Rezaie, A novel model predictive control scheme based on bees algorithm in a class of nonlinear systems: Application to a three tank system, *Neurocomputing*, Vol. 152, 2015, pp. 294-304.

[7]. R. Gholipour, A. Khosravi, H. Mojallali, Multi-objective optimal backstepping controller design for chaos control in a rod-type plasma torch system using Bees algorithm, *Applied Mathematical Modelling*, Vol. 39, 2015, pp. 4432-4444.

[8]. L. D. Qin, Q. Y. Jiang, Z. Y. Zou, Y. J. Cao, A queen-bee evolution based on genetic algorithm for economic power dispatch, in *Proceedings of the 39th International Universities Power Engineering Conference (UPEC'04)*, Bristol, UK, 2004, pp. 453-456.

[9]. D. Karaboga, B. Akay, C. Ozturk, Artificial Bee Colony (ABC) optimization algorithm for training feedforward neural networks, in *Proceedings of the 4th International Conference on Modeling Decisions for Artificial Intelligence*, 2007, pp. 318-329.

[10]. F. Zabihi, B. Nasiri, A novel history-driven artificial bee colony algorithm for data clustering, *Applied Soft Computing*, Vol. 71, 2018, pp. 226-241.

[11]. P. Das, D. K. Das, S. Dey, A modified Bee Colony Optimization (MBCO) and its hybridization with k-means for an application to data clustering, *Applied Soft Computing*, Vol. 70, 2018, pp. 590-603.

[12]. D. Karabogaa, E. Kayab, An adaptive and hybrid Artificial Bee Colony algorithm (aABC) for ANFIS training, *Applied Soft Computing*, Vol. 49, 2016, pp. 423-436.

[13]. M. T. Vakil-Baghmisheh, M. Salim, The design of PID controllers for a Gryphon robot using four evolutionary algorithms: a comparative study, *Artificial Intelligence Review*, Vol. 34, Issue 2, 2010, pp. 121-132.

[14]. G. Sandini, J. Santos-Victor, F. Curtto, S. Garibaldi, Robotic bees, in *Proceedings of the IEEE/RSJ International Conference on Intelligent Robots and System (IROS'93)*, Vol. 1, Yokohama, Japan, 1993, pp. 629-635.

[15]. G. Yuxi, An improved hybrid group intelligent algorithm based on artificial bee colony and particle swarm optimization, in *Proceedings of the International Conference on Virtual Reality and Intelligent Systems (ICVRIS'18)*, 2018, pp. 160-163.

[16]. H. Zarea, F. M. Kashkooli, M. Soltani, M. Rezaeian, A novel single and multi-objective optimization approach based on Bees Algorithm Hybrid with Particle Swarm Optimization (BAHPSO): Application to thermal-

economic design of plate fin heat exchangers, *International Journal of Thermal Sciences*, Vol. 129, 2018, pp. 552-564.

[17]. S. H. Jung, Queen-bee evolution for genetic algorithms, *Electron. Lett.*, Vol. 39, Issue 6, 2003, pp. 575-576.

[18]. B. Basturk, D. Karaboga, An artificial bee colony (ABC) algorithm for numeric function optimization, in *Proceedings of the IEEE Swarm Intelligence Symposium (SIS'06)*, Indianapolis, Indiana, USA, 2006, pp. 459-471.

[19]. M. Salim, M. T. Vakil-Baghmisheh, Discrete bee algorithms and their application in multivariable function optimization, *Artif. Intell. Rev.*, Vol. 35, 2011, pp. 73-84.

[20]. C. Yang, J. Chen, T. Xuyan, Algorithm of fast marriage in honey bees optimization and convergence analysis, in *Proceedings of the IEEE International Conference on Automation and Logistics (ICAL'07)*, China, 2007, pp. 1794-1799.

[21]. H. A. Abbass, Marriage in Honey Bees Optimization (MBO): A haplometrosis polygynous swarming approach, in *Proceedings of the IEEE Congress on Evolutionary Computation (CEC'01)*, Korea, 2001, pp. 207-214.

[22]. C. Yang, J. Chen, T. Xuyan, Algorithm of fast marriage in honey bees optimization and convergence analysis, in *Proceedings of the IEEE International Conference on Automation and Logistics ((ICAL'07)*, China, 2007, pp. 1794-1799.

[23]. M. T. Vakil-Baghmisheh, M. Salim, A modified fast marriage in honey bee optimization algorithm, in *Proceedings of the 5th International Symposium on Telecommunications (IST'10)*, Tehran, Iran, 2010, pp. 950-955.

[24]. L. Gaing, A particle swarm optimization approach for optimum design of PID controller in AVR system, *IEEE Transactions on Energy Conversion*, Vol. 19, Issue 2, 2004, pp. 384-391.

Chapter 7

AI-based Tools for Performance and Monitoring of Sustainable Built and Natural Environments, and the Climate

Rafaat Hussein

7.1. Overall Background

The AI field has gone through decades of developments starting with the idea of solving problems by searching for possible solutions and apply various techniques to search efficiently, the use of application-data, or information, to the consolidation and a combining of different types of problem-solving methods in order to deal with the complexity of problems. The AI has different descriptions including symbolic computation, tools that generate descriptions of an image, the understanding of actual written or spoken language, etc. The AI could also be described in terms of the types of processing and the information.

The AI has spawned subfields that are concerned with practical applications including knowledge-based systems (building systems and models for specific tasks), natural language & vision and understanding (building sensors and effectors for performing intelligent action), and hardware & software environments (for building systems that manipulate and reason about symbolic information). The knowledge engineering is one of the risen fields from the decades of AI developments. Without distinction among its various descriptions, it is concerned with the acquisition and representation of knowledge to imitate expert human reasoning and advice, and solve problems that

Rafaat Hussein
State University of New York, New York, USA

normally require human attention. These sub-systems assist in diagnosis, trouble-shooting and solving issues either on its own or in a support role to a human agent. One may see them as hitting upon the same or similar results as the human experts. In other words, transferring the expertise of problem-solving human experts into a program that could take in the same data and come to the same conclusion but faster and with providing more choices.

This chapter groups the knowledge-based systems members of the AI's shell under knowledge engineering. They obtain solutions for specific problems and exhibit expert-level performance in their respective application domains, are easy to modify, and their behavior are understandable. The main idea is that AI-based knowledge engineering can assist non-experts in dealing with complex problems, and can save times and money in dealing with volumes of documentations.

The chapter introduces a fresh look at engineering applications that benefit from integrating human experts with factual and experiential procedural and systematic processing associated with the problem or task at hand. The users can realize benefits in consistency, accuracy, and reliability in problem-solving and decision support activities.

The following three AI-based tools illustrate how the AI could solve real-world challenges such as the ailing built infrastructure construction systems; the unprecedented global natural environmental vulnerability, risks, threats, and pollutions; and the indisputable climate change impacts. They are tools that reasonably solve complex problems in their respective applications for diagnosing, interpreting, predicting, and instructing. Human experts could interact with the tools to integrate the human and machine expertise to enhance their own intelligent abilities. Again, these specific applications aim at the following challenges:

1. The built infrastructure construction;

2. The natural environmental protection;

3. The global climate change.

Each of these challenges are inherently complex and probably beyond the abilities of humans to entirely comprehend. Each of the described AI-based tools harnesses on one hand the collection of provided inputs and applications of focused algorithms to be utilized for best results and on the other hand the use of data or information representation to reason and extract specific results. The tools maintained two essential characteristics: modular and justification. By applying the formalism, the modular component provides a set of stand-alone algorithms with own outputs which the human expert may consider as a justified and reasonable advice or recommendation. Human expert system could choose which advice or recommendation is an appropriate answer to the specific problem at hand.

From a bird's eye view of the real big picture, no one could nowadays dispute that our planet is under unprecedented stress. Sustainability is an overarching umbrella that covers almost all challenges. The list of sustainability challenges includes the man-made built environment, the natural environment, the climate, and natural resources. The AI technologies have already played significant roles in meeting most challenges because they can, like humans, think, learn, and act. This is a game changer for a sustainable future. It revolves around the AI proven positive impacts and the boundless potentials for urgently needed solutions. One could see the emerging game changers for the built and natural environments, the natural resources, and climate. The applications of AI technologies are needed now more than ever before for the design, operation, monitoring, and remediation of the vulnerable and under high risks of each of these systems. The AI introduces to each day practice in these sectors predictability, renewability, and the integration of reliable intelligent assistance in the decision making processes. A new era for AI applications in these sectors is steadily blossoming harnessing the AI to each of application and need because humans already have large amounts of data and so many lessons learned from generations of modeling some of which were unsuccessful.

Last but not least, this chapter is a seed sowed for future AI blossoming that farther mimicking human expertise and intelligence. Such a seed is a catalyst for mapping human engineering specific expertise. This perspective is reasonable based on the emerging developments with no end in sight.

7.2. The Built Infrastructure Construction

7.2.1. Literature Review

Infrastructure is globally the backbone of the national economy and vital to every nation's prosperity. Report after report reinforces the prevailing critical disrepair state of the built infrastructure that must be replaced, and governments around the world are grappling with the costly problems of the inevitable aging and degrading infrastructure [1-3]. If ignored, those conditions could lead to catastrophic failures with probable human loss. Also, the deteriorating infrastructure affects businesses and households in various ways leading to reductions in efficiencies and increasing costs. In its 2017 report card, the American Society of Civil Engineers concluded that the overall grade average for the national infrastructure is D+. This situation brings serious economic consequences by 2025 including $3.0 trillion in losses to the GDP and $7 trillion in lost business sales. The cumulative investment needs for the infrastructure is $4,590 billion.

Retrofitting and rehabilitation [4-8] are means to reduce the vulnerability and risks of the built systems. There are many benefits from retrofitting and rehabilitation such as reduced loss of lives and damage to facilities, and the continuity of the society daily functioning. Thus, the retrofitting is an essential component of long term infrastructure sustainability. The decision of whether rehabilitation or retrofitting is needed or not requires data about in order to perform calculations. Nonetheless, the true condition of any system is challenging in many situations because of the complexity of geometry, framing, detailing of connections, workmanship, etc. This situation calls for reliable AI-based knowledge engineering tools to smartly probe the existing condition of infrastructure components.

Using AI-based health monitoring tools can accommodate the modern challenges because innovative developments continue expanding the envelope of conventional practice. The primary goal of the AI-based tools described next is to extend the service life and/or strengthen them for higher loads capacity. The objectives of these AI-based tools include:

1. Vulnerability, safety, and risk intelligent assessment;

2. Identification, prioritization, and protection reasonable protocols;

3. Conditions and performance monitoring;

4. Assist human experts to move the outcomes from the tools to deployment.

The process of AI-based implementing a condition identification and performance monitoring strategy is referred to as health monitoring. It involves the observation over a period of time, the identification of features, and their thoughtful consideration to provide reliable information about the performance level of the system. This AI-based tool comes with benefits as:

1. Increasing the life span;

2. Reducing the cost of in-situ maintenance routines;

3. Converting schedule based into condition based practices;

4. Increasing the safety and performance.

7.2.2. Description of the Systems

In general, the AI-based monitoring process can be categorized into five stages:

1. Identification of fault presence;

2. Localization of fault;

3. Identification of the fault type;

4. Quantification of fault severity;

5. Prediction of the service life.

Customarily, the approach for monitoring can be depicted as a four-part process:

1. Operational;

2. Experimental;

3. Data extraction;

4. Reasonable examination.

Operational step defines why the monitoring is to be done, tailors the monitoring to unique aspects and unique features that are to be identified. It answers three main questions regarding the implementation of a monitoring system:

1. How is fault defined?

2. What are the conditions under which the system functions?

3. What are the limitations on data in the operational environment?

Current experimental techniques require that the vicinity of the system being monitored is readily accessible. The basic premise of these methods is that fault alter the system properties, which, in turn, alter the response. To date, some of the drawbacks of these methodologies include:

1. The use of expensive data processing hardware;

2. Varying environmental and operational conditions.

The drawbacks place serious limitations on the practical use of existing methodologies. This AI-based tool is based on a fresh look at the overall picture taking into consideration the drawbacks. This new concept emerges from an open-end modular approach that can be adapted and is not limited to a particular detection or identification techniques. The tool equally performs supervised and unsupervised learning. Supervised learning refers to situations where data are available. Unsupervised learning refers to situations where data is sometime available. At the core, the algorithm answers the following queries:

1. The existence of an issue;

2. Its type;

3. Its extent;

4. Its prediction.

This AI-based tool integrates a number of unmatched sub-tools for various applications. Advanced materials like biobased, biodegradable, and renewable materials represent a new generation of sustainable class of materials that have revolutionized the sustainable infrastructure industry in recent years and open the door to alternative approaches. This AI-based tool accounts for all possible properties of the constituents including:

1. Different boundary conditions;

2. Different loads;

3. Instability conditions;

4. Bonding.

For utility grids, the objectives of the AI-based tool include intelligently probing for:

1. Existence of faults;

2. Location of faults;

3. Extent of faults;

4. Prediction of service life.

This AI-based tool avoids the drawbacks of existing technologies such as:

1. Guessing;

2. Induced damages;

3. Disruptive services;

4. Limited constraints and materials;

5. Costly operation.

The underlying principle of this novel AI-based tool is that dynamic signatures are sensitive indicators of integrity. This reasoning is based on the fact that conditions change the dynamic characteristics, and therefore, fundamental signal can be used for identification and monitoring. This smart approach is very attractive for the development of this AI-based monitoring system for the utilities. The performance monitoring considered for the AI-based development is also based on an inverse engineering in which the objective is to find the properties using minimum response information and data. Because the sought source of indicators and their locations are not known beforehand, the tool reverse its customary process to overcome the difficulties associated with the large number of possible scenarios, and to reduce the domain by eliminating the unaffected regions. This approach represents an intelligent facet of the entire AI-based tool.

Another application of the AI for sustainable infrastructure is in the connections [9]. They are integral parts of any system. The connections are commonly assumed either pined or rigid. In reality, they fall somewhere between these two extreme cases. Flexible connections are thus suitable to represent actual connections. For elements with flexible connections at its ends, the explicit mathematic forms for characteristics are easily available in many references. The dynamic signals can also be measured using portable and affordable signal conditioners. Each signal can then be analyzed using FFT from which the fundamental characteristic is determined. The governing equation can then be invoked using smart reverse engineering techniques, i.e. conducted backward to obtain an input that would result in the given data. Given the state and objective of the solution scenario, a search is provoked to on the initial state to produce a new state, and the process is recursively applied to this new state and the new objective. This is another example of the usefulness of an applied AI.

7.3. Environmental Protection

7.3.1. Literature Review

The agricultural wastes and agriculture pollution, as embodied in livestock for example, have been proven and reported by the EPA (US Environmental Protection Agency), USDA (US Department of Agriculture), USAID, UN, and others as a source of significant degradation [18]. The pertinent multifold big picture of environmental hazardous wastes and pollution can be revealed via an isometric projection that conceptualizes the complexity of the pervasive multi-dimensions in the picture, and facilitates making the case for the application to forge a holistic monitoring and control, i.e. protection framework.

The EPA, USDA, USAID, UN consensually agreed on the massive scale of the agriculture wastes' adverse effects on the natural resources. The FAO (Food and Agriculture Organization of the United Nations) reported that [13] "With increased prosperity, people are consuming more meat and dairy products every year. Global meat production is projected to more than double from 229 million tons in 1999/2001 to 465 million tons in 2050." The FAO reported that [12, 13, 16, 23] "production is one of the major causes of the world's most pressing environmental problems, including global warming, land degradation, air and water pollution, and loss of biodiversity", "This sector emerges as one of the top two or three most significant contributors to the most serious environmental problems, at every scale from local to global", its contribution to environmental problems is on a massive scale and its potential contribution to their solution is equally large. These impacts are so significant that it needs to be addressed with urgency".

The relevance and significance of this wastes and pollution alarming situation can be clarified further in light of what constitutes the impacts on the natural resources. In this regard, the pertinent usage is represented in 3.4 billion hectares of land, more than 67 % of the planet's surface and

33 % of its total land area, are used to cultivate at least 320 million hectares of land, and are the sole source of livelihood for at least 20 million families. According to the USDA, for instance, the US 2010 meat statistics reveal [28] 90,774 million pounds, 206 pound per capita, $430 market price per hundredweight, 8,502,161 million pounds in trade, 243 million pounds in imports, and 1,184 pounds in exports. From a different angle of view, the EPA [26] reported its inability to document manure statistics [29] whereas the World Bank [33] thoroughly disputed the published pollution records including underestimation, overlooking, and omission of data. In addition, the USDA [29] indicated that there is more manure produced than human sewage in US (more than 5 tons for every citizen), 64 % of it could not be absorbed by the natural resources such as soil, more than 50 % of its storage areas leak to drinking water streams, and the cost of transporting is exorbitant, let alone the emission of fossil-based pollution. Yet, there are no effective techniques to tackle the broad scope of wastes and pollution overall adverse ramifications.

The aforementioned metrics reflect the implications of hazardous wastes and pollution because as the human population and prosperity increase, their adverse impacts can't be ignored. This understanding calls for an urgent need of holistic monitoring and control, i.e. protection, frameworks [14, 15, 20, 23, 24, 28]. Thus, the AI technologies became one of the biggest game-changer in the environmental sustainability. To clarify, the 2017 UN AI Summit held in Geneva identified that AI has the potential to accelerate progress towards a dignified human life, in peace and prosperity and suggested the use of its technologies for protecting the environment and conserve natural resources.

Furthermore, organizations such as the EPA, USDA, UN, PETA and SPAR provided evidences indicating that the practices in the livestock sector, which again represent one of the key sources of wastes and pollution of the natural environment and resources, incorporate sustained substandard protocols such as the habitual working style and attitudes, animals' treatment and welfare, conditions of the built environment; carcass protection; evisceration, slaughter equipment, and the marketing of unrefrigerated meat. These practices incubate and hatch serious health threats to humans. To elaborate, the borne syndromes which appeared in three regions and rapidly affected the world including salmonellae, foot mouth disease, bovine spongiform encephalopathy, H1N1, etc. [10, 17, 16, 22, 31, 32]. The number of borne disease outbreaks and epidemics has notably increased in recent years including bovine spongiform encephalopathy, avian influenza, and H1N1. There are 176 countries or 74 % of the world presently confirmed with cases of H1N1 [30]. The threats are not confined to particular regions nor do they discriminate between underdeveloped and developed countries. In fact, once contaminated, the natural surface and underground waters become vehicles to spread these threats.

In addition, an estimated 51 % of the world's annual green gas emission, 9 % of anthropogenic carbon dioxide, 37 % of anthropogenic methane, 65 % of anthropogenic nitrous oxide [11, 13, 33], 70 % of anthropogenic ammonia (which contributes significantly to acid rain and acidification of the ecosystems), untold estimate of hazardous wastes (such as condemned meat, undigested ingesta, bones, horns, hairs, aborted fetuses, hides, and manure), untold estimate of various compounds (such as fat, oil, protein, carbohydrates, salt, hydrogen sulfide, lime, chromium tannin, antibiotics, and hormones), and untold estimate of liquid wastes (such as blood and urine) are annually produced. These substances deoxygenate the surface and ground waters, affect fisheries [19, 21] and irrigating lands, deteriorate or destroy the aquatic ecosystems, and choke the sewer [11] to name a few adverse effects. They pose a threat to the biodiversity [13], account for about 20 % of the total terrestrial animal biomass, now occupy lands that were the habitat for wildlife, are identified as "a current threat" in the 37 % terrestrial eco-regions identified by the Worldwide Fund for Nature, are responsible for serious levels of habitat loss in 65 % of the "global hotspots for biodiversity".

Taken as a whole, the alarming environmental issues call for technologies to tackle the causes and extent of hazardous wastes and pollution; provide means for their prevention, reduction and elimination before entering the natural resources. The application of AI-based technologies came to the forefront lines of defense against these challenges. They provide the needed robust monitoring and control tools that help the human experts to contain the threats from wastes and pollution and minimize the risks before infiltration to the natural resources.

7.3.2. Description of the Systems

The novel AI-based tool described here aims directly at environmental protection frameworks to enhance the positive and mitigate the negative inherited potentials. In the livestock sector, this technology creates incalculable benefits because the world has an estimated 1.3 billion heads (10 % of which are in the US) and at least one billion poor people who depend solely on them for their livelihood. By smartly diagnosticating the related wastes and pollution (almost two trillion pounds per year in the US), this AI-based tool paves the way to unleash promising opportunities. The primary objective of this AI-based tool is to tackle the aforementioned environmental challenges via a proactive intervention-based approach for controlling and monitoring the problems at their roots; i.e. before they emerge and spread. The main output is a framework to tackle the causalities of hazardous wastes and pollution, and provide solid basis for best practices. Its scope spans over several critical environmentally viable issues regarding the way in which the sector is designed, maintained, and operated. It's a useful tool to quantify the key environmental parameters that are very essential for the planning, design, and management of agriculture facilities including water, energy, electricity, recovery, rendering for wastes or beneficial utilization, by products including the hazardous ones, and the performance metrics of facilities. The conceptualization of this AI-tool encompasses the following tasks:

1. Sizing wastes and pollution at the source;

2. Probing the different data on wastes and environmental pollution;

3. Conceptualize the various scenarios on wastes and environmental pollution;

4. Determine the trade-offs involved the various performance and operation scenarios;

5. Define best management and practice techniques;

Its methodological steps are described in the following five stages:

1. Identification of the existence of problems and the sources;

2. Identification of the type;

3. Quantification of severity;

4. Identification of the adverse impacts.

These stages route the process of the AI-based tool by addressing key questions such as:

1. Are there hazards?

2. What kind of hazard is present?

3. How severe are the hazards?

In each stage, the hazards and pollution can be captured via the following procedure:

1. Evaluation. This steps defines the hazards being captured and the conditions;

2. Data extraction and limitations;

3. Computational investigation.

Once the existence, type, and extent are captured, the following components start:

1. Characterization of wastes and pollution. This component generates the size and composition of each type;

2. Wastes and pollution extent. This component assists in benchmarking the extent and characteristics of wastes and pollution.

3. Needed utilities. This component quantifies the utilities usage;

4. Expert recommendation(s). This component includes recommendations for best available techniques for wastes and pollution control and monitoring.

Environmental health and safety (EH&S) is another field for the applications of AI-based technologies. All too often, things fall through the cracks, allowing chronic problems to continue. This can allow the unsafe conditions to persist until eventually a release of a hazardous chemical or waste occurs. This AI-based tool relies on multi-page environmental rules that control and monitor data in key areas that EH&S personnel normally struggle with in their customarily practices. The tool is intelligent to trend the performance in key target areas and then apply data to identify the aspects that require greater attention and improvement. The tool has nine categorical areas. Within each of these categories are multiple subcategories which enable specific functions that have an impact on the performance. The existing main categories are: environmental (air emission, waste water, ground water, hazardous and solid waste, and spill prevention), safety, protection, storage, distribution, and documentation. The outputs from this AI-based tool intelligently monitor and control the effectiveness of the provided expert' measures via six different metric. The index-based (for multi-times, one facility, and one category), rate-based comparison (for multi facilities, one category, and one time), radar and histogram chart (for rate/frequency, one facility, one category, and one time). The performance rating is based on 1 to 10 scale; 1-3 (low meaning an immediate corrective action is needed), 4-7 (average meaning a room for improvement and corrective actions are needed), and 8-10 (high meaning a minor corrective actions are required). The smartness of this tool is further enhanced using two databases. The first one includes a 400-hazardous substances and is easy to search for vital information. The second creates a central depository using nine different types of information.

The tool also includes a vulnerability assessment database that is necessary for incorporating control and monitoring measures to improve the performance.

7.4. Climate Change

7.4.1. Literature Review

The adverse impacts of climate change [34, 38, 39, 47] are glowing and will not go away in the foreseeable future. In addition, humans can no longer deny or ignore these changes in each day scientific and technological practices [36, 41, 43-46]. To elaborate, the earth's average temperature rose to its highest level in the past four centuries with the fastest rise in a thousand years [35, 37, 40, 42]. In fact, 2015 was the warmest year ever on record. The sea level has risen between four and eight inches in the past century and is projected to continue rising. Globally, 100 million people live within three feet of sea level, thus are exposed to future displacement. Hurricanes and tropical storms became more intense, are occurring more frequent and lasting longer than before, unleashing extreme winds, and causing irreversible damages to coastal ecosystems. Furthermore, the climate change is intensifying the circulation of fresh water above and below the surface of the earth causing drought and floods to occur more frequent with devastating blows to agriculture, water supply and human health. This particular change increases the likelihood of forest fires, causes early snowmelts, long summers, and prolonged spring and summer temperatures. The statistics indicate that the US fire frequency was increased by 400 percent and the amount of land burned was increased by 650 percent since 1970. From a different perspective, at least one-fourth of Earth's species are expected to extinct in less than two decades. The list of species includes polar bears, Baltimore oriole, black-capped chickadee of Massachusetts, and the American goldfinch of Iowa to name some examples. Vegetation shifts are also on the rise forcing trees and plants around the world to move toward Polar Regions and up mountain slopes. Climate change is one of the areas that benefitted significantly from AI technologies. the new field of climate informatics is harnessing AI to weather forecasting including prediction of extreme events and to better understanding of the of climate change. The availability of supercomputing machines increased the accuracy of climate simulations outcomes and reliable forecasts. The world is witnessing the gains imparted by the AI technologies to climate informatics.

7.4.2. Description of the System

This AI-based tool uses data and information to reason with it. Some of the climate change data is adopted for the development of the concept of an AI-based tool that emulates the experienced scientists. By using this AI approach, one could make decisions or provoke an array of climate change problems using a long list of attributes such as:

1. Data and information domains;

2. Adaptability for heuristic approach;

3. Modular platforms for scientific education;

4. Search abilities and scenarios.

This AI-based tool rests on a number of modules for the understanding of how to address the complex and interconnected challenges of climate change. The main modules are: basics, impacts, and resources. The basics module uses actual climate data according to the given the user-chosen time length for the output. It can be used to examine past climate variations, the factors that influence climate, and various prediction scenarios. The impacts module is useful as audio-visual smart approach about global climate change and its adverse impacts. It covers the CO_2, GHG, temperature, arctic ice, sea level rise, plants, wild-life, ice melt, flooding, drought, and lakes in various regions in the world. It is also an approach to capture to develop scenarios or models to predict future climate. The resources module is designed to effectively find the technical and scientific data necessary for investigative tasks. This is essential for the development of accurate forecast models, the assessment of climate scenarios, and even learning the data.

7.5. Conclusions

Today's world realizes the beneficial impacts of AI on human life. In general, the AI imitates human reasoning and advice, and solve problems that normally require human attention. A number of subfields relate to the AI and are applied in practical engineering. The AI-based knowledge engineering is one of the risen fields. One may see it as hitting upon the same or similar results as the human experts. In other words, transferring the reasonable expertise of problem-solving human experts into a program that could take in the same data and come to same conclusion.

The AI-based technologies provide myriads of game changers for a better future sustainability on our planet. Without a doubt, the intelligence imparted by the AI can unlock new solutions to the most pressing built and natural environments, and climate challenges. This chapter introduced three AI-based tools that rest on smart systematic processing of data associated with the problem at hand. Three real-world is inherently complex challenges were used to illustrate the advantages of using the AI:

1. The ailing built infrastructure construction systems;

2. The unprecedented global natural environmental vulnerability, risks, threats, and pollutions;

3. The indisputable climate change impacts. Human experts could interact with the tools for diagnosing, interpreting, predicting, and instructing.

This chapter is a seed sowed for future blossoming that closely mimic human expertise and intelligence. One may see how such a seed catalyst could mean for mapping human expertise. This perspective is reasonable based on the so many decade of developments with no end in sight.

References

[1]. Infrastructure Report Card, Report, *American Society of Civil Engineers*, 2017, pp. 4-11.

[2]. Manual for Restoration and Retrofitting of Rural Structures, Report, *United Nations Educational, Scientific and Cultural Organization*, 2007, pp. 45-53.

[3]. M. Raiser, Close Infrastructure Gap in Time of Austerity, Report, *World Bank Group*, pp. 1-8.

[4]. S. Chandar, Rehabilitation of Buildings, *International Journal of Civil Engineering Research*, Vol. 5, Issue 4, 2014, pp. 333-338.

[5]. Different Strengthening Techniques, https://repositorium.sdum.uminho.pt/

[6]. J. Branco, Experimental evaluation of different strengthening techniques, *Journal Engineering Structures*, Vol. 33, Issue 8, 2014, pp. 2259-2270.

[7]. Dina D'Ayala, Jorge Branco, Mariapaola Riggio, *at al.*, Assessment, reinforcement and monitoring of timber structures: FPS Cost Action FP1101, in *Proceedings of the World Conference on Timber Engineering (WCTE'14)*, Quebec City, Canada, 2014, pp. 2753-2758.

[8]. J. Branco and T. Descamps, Reinforcement of Timber Structures, Report, COST, *European Cooperation in Science and Technology*, 2015, pp. 55-76.

[9]. W. Chen, Handbook of Structural Engineering, *CRC Press*, 2015, pp 143-175.

[10]. A. Adesemoye, Microbial content of abattoir wastewater and its contaminated soil, *Journal of African Journal of Biotechnology*, Vol. 5, Issue 20, 2016, pp. 1968-1968.

[11]. C. De-Haan, Livestock & the Environment, WRENmedia, Report, *European Commission Directorate*, 2016, pp. 86-87.

[12]. Livestock a Major Threat to Environment, Report, *Food and Agriculture Organization, United Nations*, 2006, pp. 1-3.

[13]. Livestock Impacts on the Environment, *Report, Food and Agriculture Organization, United Nations*, 2014, pp. 1-4.

[14]. D. Hallam, A quantitative framework for livestock development planning, *Journal of Agricultural Systems*, Vol. 14, Issue 3, 1984, pp. 123-142.

[15]. G. Heinz, Abattoir Development Options and Designs, Report, *Food and Agriculture Organization*, 2008, p. 14.

[16]. International Monetary Fund and the CIA World Factbook, Top 10 Poorest Countries in the World, https://www.pulse.ng/lifestyle/food-travel-arts-culture/10-poorest-countries-in-the-world-id7928912.html

[17]. T. Kupusovic, Cleaner production measures in small-scale slaughterhouse industry – Case study in Bosnia and Herzegovina, *Journal of Cleaner Production*, Vol. 15, Issue 4, 2017, pp. 378-383.

[18]. H. H. Li Pun, Global Consultation on Balancing Livestock, Environment and human needs, in *Proceedings of the International Conference on Livestock and the Environment*, 1998, pp. 1-7.

[19] Y. Michelle, Workers trying to contain effects of big spill upstate, *New York Times*, 2015, pp. 1-3.

[20]. T. Morris, Alternative Health Practices for Livestock, *John Wiley*, 2006, pp. 14-22.

[21]. Issues Violations for Manure Spill and Fish Kill, *New York Department of Environmental Conservation*, 2013, pp. 2-5.

[22]. M. Saad, Possible avian influenza from migratory bird, Egypt, *Emerging Infectious Diseases*, Vol. 13, 2017, pp. 1120-1121.

[23]. H. Steinfeld, Livestock's Long Shadow, Report, *United Nations*, 2016, pp. 5-20.

[24]. The World's Women, Report, *United Nations*, 2010, pp. 1-17.

[25]. Composition of Macro Geographical Continental Regions, Geographical Sub-regions, and Selected Economic and Other Groupings, Report, *United Nations*, 2011.

[26]. Background Document for Final CPG V, Report, Report, *Environmental Protection Agency*, 2007, pp. 5-8.

[27]. Methane Sub-model for the US EPA MARKAL Model, Report, *Environmental Protection Agency*, 2004, pp. 2-9.

[28]. Livestock, Dairy, and Poultry Outlook, LDP-M-293, *US Department of Agriculture*, 2018, pp. 1-27.

[29]. Annual Report Manure and Byproduct Utilization, *US Department of Agriculture*, 2015, pp. 3-9.

[30]. J. Wiemers, Analysis of the National Animal Identification System, Animal and Plant Health Inspection Service, Report, *APHIS-USDA*, 2009, pp. 355-361.

[31]. G. I. Woke, Influence of abattoir wastes on the physico-chemical parameters, *African Journal of Applied Zoology & Environmental Biology*, Vol. 9, 2017, pp. 5-7.

[32]. World Health Organization, http://www.emro.who.int/egy/programmes/influenza.html

[33]. Livestock and Climate Change, Report, *World Watch*, 2009, pp. 11-15.

[34]. Global Climate Change, http://climate.nasa.gov/

[35]. Climate Change Indicators, https://www3.epa.gov/climatechange/

[36]. Climate Science Special Report, http://www.globalchange.gov/

[37]. Global Climate Dashboard, https://www.climate.gov/

[38]. Climate Change, http://www.state.gov/e/oes/climate/

[39]. Climate Change, http://ers.usda.gov/topics/

[40]. Climate and Land Use, https://www.usgs.gov/faq/climate-and-land-use-change

[41]. Implications of Climate Related Risks, http://archive.defense.gov/pubs/150724-congressional-report-on-national-implications-of-climate-change.pdf?source = govdelivery

[42]. Using Data to Better Understand Climate Change, https://www.nsf.gov/discoveries/disc_summ.jsp?cntn_id = 189519

[43]. Climate Summit, http://www.un.org/climatechange/

[44]. Climate Change Synthesis Report, http://www.ipcc.ch/

[45]. Helping Countries Tackle Climate Change,
  https://www.unenvironment.org/
[46]. The Changing Earth, http://www.esa.int/
[47]. Climate Change, https://en.wikipedia.org/wiki/Climate_change

Chapter 8

Fuzzy Circle and AI

Janani Bharatraj, M. Clement Joe Anand

8.1. Artificial Intelligence

> *"By far, the greatest danger of Artificial Intelligence is that people conclude too early that they understand it".* ***Eliezer Yudkowsky***

Artificial Intelligence (AI) is an area of computer science that emphasizes the creation of intelligent machines that work and react like humans. Some of the activities computers with AI are designed for include speech recognition, learning, planning and problem solving. The core problems of artificial intelligence include programming computers for certain traits such as knowledge, learning, reasoning, planning, problem solving, perception and ability to manipulate and move objects.

Knowledge engineering is a core part of AI. Machines can often act and react like humans only if they have abundant information regarding/ relating to the world. Artificial intelligence must have access to objects categories, properties and relations between all of them to implement knowledge engineering. Initiating common sense, reasoning and problem-solving power in machines is a difficult and tedious task.

Robotics is also a major field related to AI. Robots require intelligence to handle tasks such as object manipulation and navigation along with sub-problems of localization, motion planning and mapping.

Human intelligence is not characterized by just one trait but by the combination of many diverse abilities.

Janani Bharatraj
Hindustan Institute of Technology and Science, Chennai, Tamil Nadu, India

The following components of intelligence have been the focus with regard to AI; learning, reasoning, problem-solving, perception and language usage:

1. **Learning:** There are several different learning forms about artificial intelligence, of which, the trial and error method of learning is the simplest. The technique of rote learning is relatively easy to implement on a computer, but generalization technique is a challenging task. The generalization technique involves application of experience and intuition to work on new situations. For example, a human being can, to certain extent, predict the outcome of a task using his experience by performing the task based on trial and error method.

2. **Reasoning:** Reasoning plays a vital role in critical thinking. By reasoning, human beings draw inferences and sometimes conclusions/decisions to a particular situation. There are two classifications under reasoning – inductive reasoning and deductive reasoning.

Inductive reasoning is used in science where tentative models are developed to describe and predict the future behavior of the collected data set. The anomalies, if found in the data set, will only lead to revision of the model.

Deductive reasoning, on the other hand, involves construction of elaborate theorems built from a small set of basic axioms or rules. Thus, one of the hardest problems with AI is deriving true influence using simple logic for a task or situation:

1. **Problem solving:** Human beings are naturally gifted to think and act according to the given situation. We analyse a range of possible solutions and in many cases, develop a new solution to arrive at the conclusion. Machines on the other hand, must be fed with programs and data to solve a given problem. They can systematically search through a range of possible actions to reach some predefined destination. Problem-solving methods can be broadly classified into two categories; general purpose and special purpose. A special purpose method is usually tailor-made for a problem. This often fails to address certain features of the task in which the problem rests. A general-purpose technique is more useful in a wide variety of problems. A common general-purpose technique used in AI is the

"incremental" technique where in actions are performed step-by-step based on the difference between the current state and the final goal. An example of AI using problem-solving technique is the solution to Rubik's cube. Researchers developed an algorithm which let an AI solve Rubik's cube in 44 hours, with 30 moves or less. Solving Rubik's cube unlike board games is very hard to evaluate the next move. In such cases, a deep learning machine is given the rules of the game and is rewarded at each step to differentiate good move from a bad move. In order to achieve this success, autodidactic iteration is used, where in the system configures a finished cube and works backward to find a configuration similar to the proposed move. This process of machine learning doesn't work in real-world situations since rewards are often hard to determine. So AI in this regard has 'algebraically manipulated previously acquired knowledge to answer a new question'.

2. **Perception:** The ability of a human being depends a lot on the way he perceives real world and uncertainties. It is a process of acquiring, interpreting, choosing and organizing sensory information.

Various types of sensors are used to capture, assemble data and to make some meaning out of them. This is achieved by the perception mechanism. The inputs are basically sensory data and the outputs are categorical decisions and conceptual relations.

The difficulty in case of AI arises when the task requires multiple levels of abstraction with uncertainties changing over a period of time. Also, every individual sees things from his own "perspective". Thus, it becomes difficult for machines to perceive notions and analyze them, without human assistance. In AI, it is a bigger challenge to replicate aural and visual signals just like the way we humans perceive.

Aural perception plays a vital role in perception. Speech recognition is a forefront runner in this regard. The voice command interface should understand various syllables and styles of a native language speaker. For example, a person in Ecuador speaks a different style of Spanish when compared to a native Spanish speaker. This perception of pronunciation is a challenging task while tuning an AI machine. Also, a major problem lies in naturalness, especially context and meaning related adjustments which includes factors like tone, emotion and stress.

Visual perception goes hand-in-hand with aural and sensory perception. Vision is not a pure input process. The movement of eyes has an impact on human visual perception. An active vision system is one which is able to interact with the environment by varying its viewpoint rather than observing it passively on a single frame instead of operating on a sequence of images.

An AI's computational vision consists of three primary stages:

i.   Early representations which capture location, contrast and sharpness of intensity or edges in the image, which are static in nature. For a dynamically changing scenario, the representations involve the measurement of parameters like direction and speed of movement.

ii. Intermediate representations provide information regarding 3D shape of an object.

iii. Higher level representation of objects describes the 3D structure and orientation relative to a coordinate frame in which the object is located.

Tasks involving object recognition, manipulation and navigation operate in the intermediate or higher-level representations.

At present, thanks to Google and tesla, artificial perception is quite advanced to enable identification of individuals and other nearby moving objects to enable autonomous vehicles to drive in a restricted path at moderate speeds.

3. **Language:** The term language can be defined in many ways. For some, it is "an expression of ideas by means of speech-sounds combined into words". For a few, it "is a system of arbitrary vocal symbols by means of which a social group cooperates". Typically, people acquire a single language initially which usually is their native tongue. Thus, language is specific to human beings. Other members of the animal kingdom communicate through vocal noise. A philosopher would interpret an animal's eyes to have power to speak a great language. Some claim music to be the world's most popular language. Many consider a warm smile to be the language of kindness. These hidden meaning of language again depends on how we interpret it.

The question now arises whether an AI can interpret such natural occurrences. Can such data which are natural to living beings be programmed into an AI?

The answer is AI can only be programmed. Humans are capable of "programming" an AI using commands and codes through various platforms, but will we be successful in bringing natural language instincts is the big question.

Having spoken about AI, we now shift our focus to a more abstract concept related to natural occurrences. What appears in nature is bizarre. It is perfect at times and imperfect at many occasions. One of the bizarre brainchild of AI is robotics. The field of robotics has seen a boom in its achievements over the past few years. It is a fast-growing field where robots are outperforming their predecessors. The new generation robots can perform complicated moves with elegance. The proof of such an advancement is Sophia, a robot child of Hanson robotics. Sophia has a human-like appearance with complex ability to express emotions. She can represent several emotional states and read emotional expressions on a human face. Sophia must clearly integrate three distinctive traits of humans: creativity, empathy and compassion.

The purpose of a humanoid is to solve problems in medical healthcare, decision-making scenarios where complex calculations are required for a large amount of data. A lot of this data encompasses the three magical terms of nature: *uncertainty, imprecision* and *vagueness*. Will a humanoid be able to calm a crying child with its intelligence and intuition is a next question? The key lies in differentiating precision from significance which comes from intuition and perception. AI can provide precise date which may not be required at all circumstances. The need of the hour is to program the "significance" of the situation. There exists too many "fuzziness" in nature. Human thinking and emotions can be associated with fuzziness. Humans can give acceptable answers which are usually apt whereas machines at times fail miserably. Here again the question of precision and significance comes into picture. As an example, given a cup of coffee, an AI can provide precise information about temperature and quantity. Where as a human can "precisely" explain it is drinkable. This attribute can to some extent be modelled using fuzzy logic. The answers in real world just don't lie in 0 and 1. To obtain complete information in terms of giving opinions fuzzy sets play a major role. Here again, fuzziness is being perceived in different ways. In a narrow sense, it is a logical system which is an extension of multivalued logic. However, in a wider sense, fuzzy logic relates to "classes of objects with unsharp boundaries in which the degree of membership matters a lot". The underlying concept in FL is the linguistic variable i.e. a variable whose values are words rather than numbers. Therefore, FL can be viewed as a methodology for computing with words, which even though is less precise than numbers, their usage is much closer to human intuition.

Another concept in FL, which plays a central role in wide variety of applications is the fuzzy 'if-then' rule. Even though rule-based systems have a long history of applications in artificial intelligence, a 'mechanism to deal with fuzzy antecedents and consequents' is essential. This mechanism is provided by the calculus of fuzzy rules, which serve as a foundation for fuzzy dependency and command language (FDCL). In most of the applications of fuzzy logic, the solution is 'a translation of a human solution into FDCL'. In this sense, fuzzy logic is both old and new because, although the modern and methodical science of fuzzy logic is still young, the concepts of fuzzy logic relies on age-old skills of human reasoning.

8.2. Need for Fuzzy Logic

The next question which arises is, do we really need fuzzy logic and how beneficial is it to mankind and machines. Some of the observations on use of fuzzy logic are given below.

1. FL has a more intuitive approach and the idea behind reasoning is very simple.

2. FL is flexible and can be trained to add more functionality without redoing the work.

3. FL can handle imprecision. One of the highlights of FL is its ability to build the imprecision into the process rather than pulling it till the end.

4. A fuzzy system can be created to match any set of input-output data.

5. FL can be built on the experience of experts. It allows you to rely on the experience of people who already understand the system.

6. Fuzzy logic systems can be easily blended with other systems.

7. The basis for fuzzy logic is human communication. It is built on the structures of qualitative description used in everyday language.

So, is fuzzy logic chicken soup for the soul? The answer is No. FL is not a cure-all remedy. FL doesn't have to overrule other systems. If a simpler solution exists, then the wise advice would be to stick to it rather than complicating things. Many controllers do a fine job without FL however, FL can be a powerful tool for dealing with imprecision and non-linearity in a quick and efficient way.

The larger picture that needs to be painted is automation. To achieve efficiency in automation, fuzzy control and advanced technologies are integrated to provide an approach that can replicate human thinking. The concept provides a great help in dealing with most complex situations and has great potential in transforming systems.

8.3. Fuzzy Architecture

The foundation on which the edifice of fuzzy logic stands mainly consist of the following parts:

1. Fuzzification module;

2. Knowledge base;

3. Inference engine;

4. Defuzzification module.

Further enhancements to fuzzy logic such as fuzzy set theory, fuzzy modellings, fuzzy control system have contributed to advancements in the field.

8.4. Fuzzy Logic in AI

Fuzzy logic, since its inception has faced criticism for being inconsistent meaningless. Japanese were the first people to experiment on fuzzy logic and bring them into application. They used fuzzy logic to launch their electric trains and various other gadgets. This also saw a boom in its usage from other parts of the world. Researchers started working on various aspects of fuzzy logic and developed on fuzzy sets and systems. Although fuzzy set theory to this date has an extensive literature, the core meaning of fuzziness has been defined in different ways. The term "fuzzy" is itself fuzzy which depends on the perception of an individual.

In the seminal paper, Zadeh [49] called for a "mathematics of cloudy or fuzzy quantities which are not describable in terms of probability distributions". The reason supporting the representation of inexact concept was given by Goguen. This inexactness was convincingly brought up in the representation theorem, which states that "any system satisfying certain uncertainty axioms is equivalent to a system of fuzzy sets". Essentially fuzziness is a type of imprecision that arises from a grouping or class which doesn't have "sharply defined boundaries".

Fuzzy logic has long been used in medical diagnosis, pattern recognition, probabilistic controllers, computer mode of speech, knowledge-based systems, expert systems, automata and decision theories, system analysis and so on. In this chapter we concentrate mainly on fuzzy trigonometry and qualitative analysis which are used in spatial reasoning and robotics.

8.5. Space, Orientation and Distance: Spatial Reasoning

Like time, space is one of the fundamental categories of human cognition, which structures our activities and connections with reality; structures our reasoning capabilities. Space has given rise to mathematics itself in which geometry is one of the first formal system. Space is more complex than time due to its multidimensionality. Many knowledge sources contribute to establish mental representation of space: vision, touch, hearing and kinesthesis. Language can also be added to the list of representation.

Modeling spatial knowledge is a crucial domain of AI but reducing a macrocosm to microcosm is more challenging. Areas like robotics, computer vision, natural language processing, computer-aided design, geographic information systems have largely contributed to the spatial knowledge representation and reasoning.

Spatial relations are grouped into three domains: topology, orientation and distance. Studies have proved that these three domains are acquired by a child successively in the same order. Likewise, an AI is a child. A complete AI machine should successively understand the topology, orientation and distance of objects in its vicinity.

Orientation can be distinguished into two levels which arise out of geometry. The first level consists of concepts of elementary geometry related to straight lines; incidence of a point, parallelism of lines, orthogonality between lines.

The second level consists of vectorial geometry concepts which establishes an order throughout the space. Orientation can be broadly classified into three types; absolute orientation, intrinsic orientation and contextual extrinsic and deictic orientation.

Researchers in AI generally model either physical space or commonsense space. Physical space is applicable in robotics whereas commonsense space is used for natural language processing. Hence orientation in a space combines qualitative analysis with Euclidean geometry consisting of points, lines and planes. Speaking in terms of mathematics and computation in AI, we must choose between a coordinate space like cartesian geometry and an "axiomatic theory of space" like Euclidean geometry.

The former involves spatial properties which are implicitly given by the algebraic properties of numerical orders on several coordinate axes. Thus, analytical geometry keeps us committed to the goal from the beginning to standard analysis, as well to the higher-order language, since a set of coordinate points define a geometric figure. The latter is generally called elementary geometry where axioms state fundamental properties of space.

8.5.1. Fuzzy Circle – A Literature Review

A circle is a simple closed space described as a set of all points in a plane which are at a fixed distance from a given point called the Centre. In other words, a circle is a simple closed curve which divides a plane into two regions; an interior and an exterior. In strict technical usage, the circle is only the boundary and the whole figure is called a disc. Circles form a major part of study in geometry which led to researchers in mathematics and physics extend classical concepts to fuzzy. The attempts made in reducing the imprecision in measurements have been described below.

Rosenfeld and Haber [44] proposed a definition of perimeter for fuzzy subsets of the plane, which plays a key role in pattern recognition. In their research, a fuzzy disk was defined as a collection of membership functions whose value depended purely on its distance from the centre. This was an extension of the definition of circle from classical geometry.

Buckley and Eslami [11] used the sup-min composition of fuzzy sets directly to define fuzzy lines and fuzzy circles. But the fuzzy circle defined did not agree to the conventional geometrical idea that a circle is the locus of the point which moves at a fixed distance from a fixed point. The membership function corresponding to the definitions of fuzzy circles were also very difficult to depict and could rarely find its closed form. This study is the pioneer study on fuzzy geometry which has been used in various applications.

Yuan and Shen [48] assigned membership functions to fuzzy distances, lines, area, and circumference of a fuzzy circle, which were initially proposed by Buckley and Eslami [11]. The concept of fuzzy circle was first introduced using Zadeh's extension principle. The inclusion of membership functions using maxima-minima principle helped in shaping the fuzzy circle and provided slightly sharper boundaries to the vagueness prevailing in trigonometric functions.

Liu and Coghill [36] proposed fuzzy qualitative representation of trigonometry. This bridged the gap between qualitative and quantitative representation of physical systems using trigonometric functions. The conventional unit circle was replaced using fuzzy qualitative circle and the cartesian orientation and translation were replaced by their membership functions. Identities, rules, and extensions of classical trigonometry were transformed into their fuzzy qualitative counterparts. The characteristics of FQT were tested using X-Trig tool box for MATLAB with 4-tuple or trapezoidal fuzzy numbers.

Qiu and Zhang [39] introduced a space geometry by laying a foundation for research in fuzzy geometry. Fuzzy cone was pictured as a crisp cone with noisy boundary. The geometry of fuzzy circles was obtained by intersecting a double-mapped fuzzy right circular cone with a crisp cone. The geometrical figure of fuzzy circle was obtained by intersecting a double-mapped fuzzy right circular cone with a crisp plane and not with a fuzzy plane, perpendicular to the axis of the cone.

Li and Guo [37] investigated and developed techniques for modelling fuzzy objects based on fuzzy sets. Fuzzy conics were defined by blurring the boundaries using a smooth unit step function and implicit functions.

Liu *et al.* [36] with an aim to bridge symbolic cognitive functions with numerical sensing and control tasks in the physical systems domain, presented a fuzzy qualitative representation of the conventional trigonometry. They provided an extension of their previous research findings and gave a representation transformation interface from an artificial intelligence perspective. The examples focused on robot kinematics and described how FQT contributed to the intelligent connection of low-level sensing and control tasks to higher level cognitive tasks. The study introduced fuzzy qualitative circle in which the conventional unit circle was modified by introducing qualitative spaces for orientation and translation. The fuzzy qualitative representation of conventional trigonometry bridged the gap between symbolic cognitive functions and numerical sensing and control tasks in the domain of physical systems. Conventional trigonometric functions, rules, and the extensions to triangles in Euclidean plane were converted to their counterparts in fuzzy qualitative coordinates using fuzzy logic and qualitative reasoning techniques.

Zadeh [53] described that a fuzzy circle is a counterpart of a crisp unit circle C in Euclidean geometry. A fuzzy circle can be obtained using the fuzzy transform of C, which is a prototype for the fuzzy circle. The fuzzy circle can be viewed as a fuzzy transformation of C drawn with a spray pen.

Savoj and Monadjemi [45] defined a fuzzy circle as a collection of several concentric circles with continuous radius.

Ghosh and Chakraborty [26] presented two approaches to define fuzzy circle. The first approach used the basic definition of a circle and the second considered three fuzzy points on the plane and formulated a fuzzy circle based on those three points. The concept of fuzzy circle described is like Zadeh's idea of fuzzy circle. They constructed fuzzy circles in a fuzzy plane, by formulating the circles using the conventional definitions of crisp circles. It was proved that the centre of the fuzzy circle need not be a fuzzy point, and the radius of the fuzzy circle was also a fuzzy number. Detailed methodologies of constructing fuzzy circle were given and the equivalence between the two methods were proved.

8.5.2. Fuzzy Trigonometric Functions – A Literature Review

Trigonometry has long been a widely used branch of mathematics. Trigonometry though was little known till 16th century, the need driven by the demands of navigation and the growing needs for accurate maps of large geographical areas boomed into a major branch of mathematics. The numerical imprecision arising during measurements and calculations led to the development of fuzzy trigonometry. The following review gives a bird's eye view of research development on trigonometric functions in fuzzy.

Dong and Shah [16] introduced the vertex method for computing functions of fuzzy variables, which could avoid abnormality due to the discretization technique on the domain of variables. The method is based on the alpha-cut concept and interval analysis, which is a more refined method developed for fuzzy weighted averages. The functions were defined as $Y = [\min(f(a), f(b)), \max(f(a), f(b))]$ in the interval variable $X = [a, b]$ to find $Y = f(X)$. The expression works for any function f which is continuous and monotonic over the interval defined by X. The major drawback of this algorithm is that the support of x must be checked for each alpha-cut for the presence of extreme points, and then, these points are to be included if they exist.

Dong *et al.* [17] developed an algorithm which utilizes alpha cuts and interval operations to create a four-step procedure for solving the algebraic relation $Z = X * Y$.

The algorithm involves the following steps;

1. Select an alpha-value where $0 \leq \alpha \leq 1$.

2. Find the intervals in X and Y which correspond to this value of alpha.

3. Using the binary interval operations, compute the interval in Z corresponding to those of X and Y.

4. Repeat the above steps for different values of alpha to complete an alpha-cut representation of the solution.

The DSW algorithm works well on the trigonometric functions if their approximation equations are used. Thus, Maclaurin's series for trigonometric functions are used while implementing the algorithm.

Givens and Tahani [22] proposed a special case of the DSW algorithm called restricted DSW algorithm. This algorithm is restricted to the special case where intervals X and Y are defined only on R^{+0}, where all interval endpoints must be greater than or equal to zero, and no subtraction is involved with the interval variables.

Kaufman and Gupta [29] presented a comprehensive explanation of fuzzy arithmetic which covers everything from algebraic operations to random fuzzy numbers to derivatives of functions of fuzzy numbers. They developed specific algorithms for fuzzy cosine, sine, and tangent functions. Three approaches were presented; the first two were based upon exponential approximations and involved the imaginary number, $j = \sqrt{-1}$ which led to difficulty in evaluating the functions on a real time basis. The third approach was based on the concept of fuzzy angle θ, and alpha cuts of this angle. The approach starts with the restriction that $\forall \alpha \in [0,1]$ of the fuzzy angle $\tilde{\theta} = [a_\alpha, b_\alpha]$, the domain must conform to

$$0 \le b_\alpha - a_\alpha \le \frac{\pi}{2}$$ which implies that the fuzzy angle is restricted to a

spread no greater than 90 degrees. This algorithm is based on where the endpoints of the alpha-cut falls with respect to certain boundary points.

Ress [41] developed fuzzy trigonometric and fuzzy inverse trigonometric functions necessary to carry out engineering design. The concept of a fuzzy vertical asymptote was defined and supported by the firm mathematical foundations of discontinuous interval arithmetic. The fuzzy vertical asymptotes clearly represent a region where the fuzzy trigonometric functions cannot be evaluated. Further fuzzy trigonometric functions and fuzzy inverse trigonometric functions were discussed, and fuzzy identities were evaluated in fuzzy realm.

8.5.3. Fuzzy Particle Swarm Optimization – A Literature Review

Kennedy and Eberhart [30] were the pioneers in introducing PSO which is one of the widely used heuristic optimization techniques. The approach to artificial intelligence (AI) includes traditional statistical method, symbolic AI, and Computational Intelligence (CI). CI comprises of computational techniques which are inspired by nature. This inspiration addresses complex real-world problems for which certain traditional methodologies are not effective and feasible. Artificial neural network, fuzzy logic, and evolutionary computation (EC) form integral parts of CI, of which Swarm Intelligence (SI) under EC forms a major area of research. SI looks for the collective behavior of natural and artificial systems which are self-organized and decentralized. The inspiration is sought from nature. There are two famous SI based optimization algorithms. Ant Colony optimization proposed by Dorigo [15] and PSO proposed by Kennedy and Eberhart [30] based on bird flocking. Certain limitations of PSO in terms of accuracy and rate of convergence lead to the development of FPSO which made PSO more powerful. In the following review, a report on the advances in FPSO has been given.

Abdelbar *et al.* [1] proposed Fuzzy PSO (FPSO) which generalized standard PSO. The charisma was defined to be a fuzzy variable, and more than one particle in each neighbourhood could have a non-zero degree of charisma. Therefore, the charisma can influence others to a degree that depends on its charisma. The model was evaluated on max-sat problem and the performance was compared with standard PSO and Walk-Sat platforms.

Juang *et al.* [27] developed an adaptive FPSO (AFPSO) algorithm which used the benefit of fuzzy sets to adjust the acceleration coefficients adaptively. This inclusion improved the accuracy and efficiency of searches. Further, a new variant called AFPSO-Q1, was developed which combined AFPSO with quadratic interpolation and crossover operator.

A novel Improved FPSO (IFPSO) was developed by Alfi and Fateh [4]. The algorithm optimally evaluated the system's parameters and controller by minimizing the average of squared errors. An intelligent enhancement for PSO was obtained which utilized fuzzy inertia weight to rationally balance the global and local exploitation abilities. The inertia weight of the particles was adjusted dynamically based on the best memories of particles using a non-linear fuzzy model.

Yang *et al.* [47] developed a novel FPSO algorithm based on fuzzy velocity updating strategy which optimized the machining parameters. The algorithm achieved some good results on certain benchmark problems and was able to achieve notable improvements on two case studies of multi-pass face milling.

Norouzzadeh *et al.* [38] suggested a light adaptive FPSO, which used two adjunct operators along with the fuzzy system to improvise the base algorithm.

Robati *et al.* [42] discussed balanced FPSO algorithm which was used to solve the classic travelling salesman problem to find the optimum path.

Khan and Engelbrecht [31] incorporated fuzzy logic in PSO to handle the multi-objective nature of the distributed local area networks (DLAN) topology design problem. Unified "AND-OR" logical operators were used for aggregating the objectives. The results suggested that FPSO is a favourable algorithm for solving such multi-objective optimization problems.

A path breaking development was made by Aminian and Teshnehlab [5] who introduced a novel FPSO method where in the inertia weight and the socio-cognitive coefficients were modified for each particle separately corresponding to the input data sent by the fuzzy logic controller.

Abdelbar *et al.* [2] gave a comparative study between the use of the Gaussian and Cauchy membership function as the membership function of the charisma fuzzy variable. The performance of the membership functions was evaluated using the weighted max-sat problem. It was found that the Gaussian MF does not perform as well as the Cauchy MF. The difference is more when the number of charismatic particles is larger, because of the relatively narrower tail of the Gaussian function, which makes it more conservative in allocating charisma. The Cauchy membership function was found to be relatively better at promoting diversity and search space exploration.

Anantathanavit and Munlin [6] proposed the R-PSO by regrouping the particles within a given radius and determining the best particle for each local optimum. The R-PSO was able to maintain appropriate swarm diversity, jump out of the local optimum using the agent particle to achieve the global optimum.

8.6. Gaussian Membership Function with Fuzzy Qualitative Trigonometry

Fuzzy qualitative trigonometry has its application in robotics. But, the idea of having generalized membership functions as circle partitions helps in understanding the properties and behaviour of fuzzy circles from the point of view of geometry and trigonometry. The standard trigonometric functions developed from a crisp circle and the trigonometric functions developed using a fuzzy circle should match to avoid conflict of interest. By developing this theory, an effort has been made to retain the essence of standard trigonometric functions. The fuzzy Gaussian qualitative coordinates are proposed to give a clear idea of geometrical interpretation of Gaussian Qualitative Trigonometric functions. To achieve this, we first defined a fuzzy circle obtained using Gaussian membership function.

8.6.1. Gaussian Qualitative Coordinates

The X and the Y-axis are defined for a unit circle. For the sake of simplicity and ease of use, the abscissa and ordinate are first considered as a real line. The circumference of the fuzzy unit circle is obtained by partitioning the circumference into Gaussian membership functions. The crisp centre of the circle has a neighbourhood, which is formed by extending the core area of every Gaussian membership function and converging them to the crisp centre of the circle. Thus, the centre of the derived fuzzy circle will have infinitely many sides depending on the number of partitions of the GMF. We can henceforth generalize the centre to be an infinitesimal circle with an infinitesimal radius, say l. (Fig. 8.1).

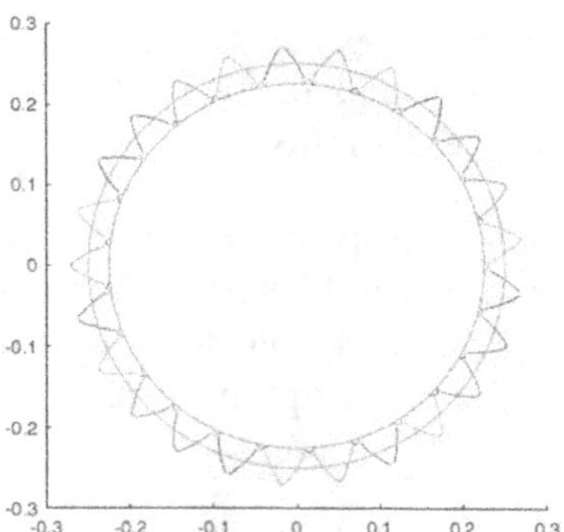

Fig. 8.1. Fuzzy circle with Gaussian membership function.

8.6.2. The Fuzzy Centre and Position of a Point

The values of a and b obtained on the circumference of the fuzzy circle are now extended towards the core of the circle. Without loss of generality, a point on the proposed fuzzy circle can be assumed to be the centre of some Gaussian membership function. The position of a point can be mapped as shown in Fig. 8.2.

The graphs of fuzzy sine, fuzzy cosine and fuzzy tangent curves were obtained using Geometer's Sketchpad v.5 (Figs. 8.3-8.8).

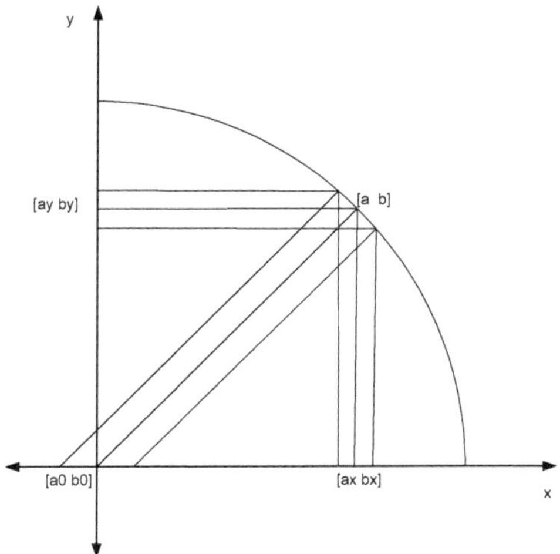

Fig. 8.2. Coordinates of a point on the Gaussian Fuzzy Qualitative Circle.

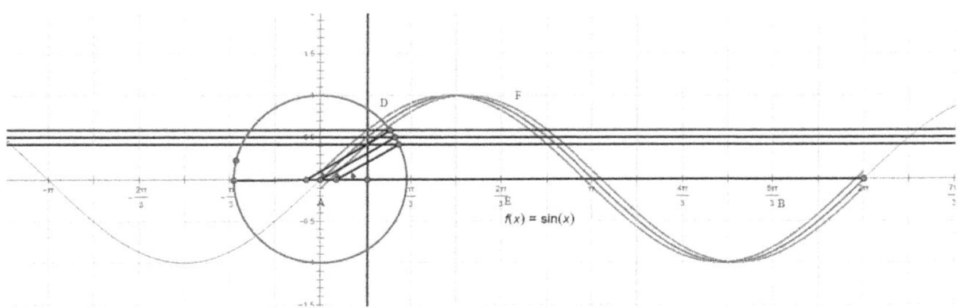

Fig. 8.3. Fuzzy Sine wave generated from Gaussian Fuzzy Qualitative Circle at 45^0.

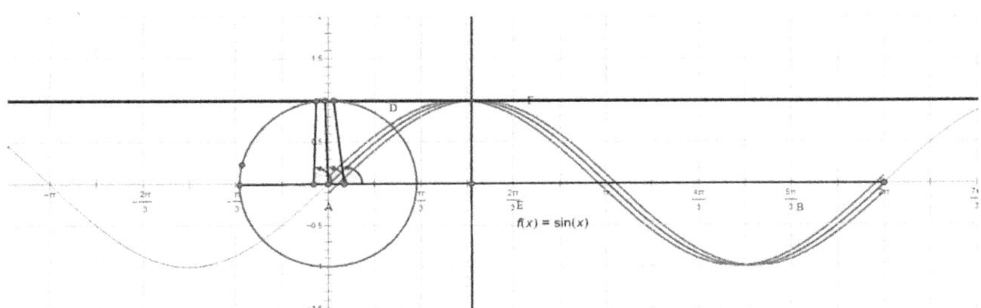

Fig. 8.4. Fuzzy Sine wave generated from Gaussian Fuzzy Qualitative Circle at 90^0.

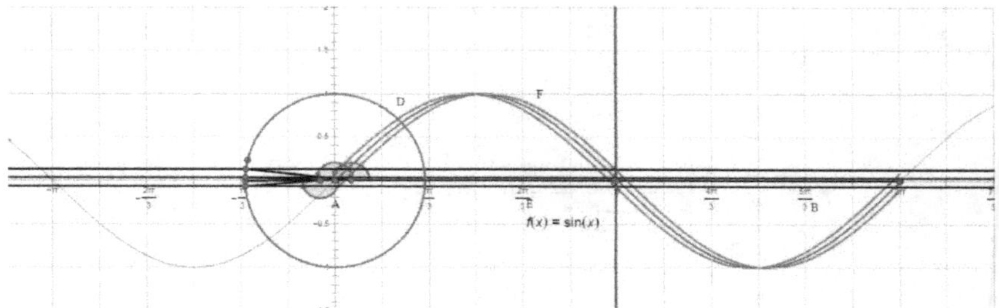

Fig. 8.5. Fuzzy Sine wave generated from Gaussian Fuzzy Qualitative Circle at 180⁰.

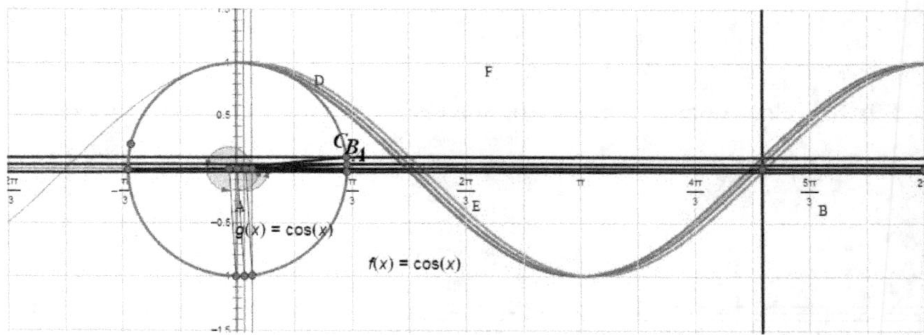

Fig. 8.6. Fuzzy Cosine wave generated from Gaussian Fuzzy Qualitative Circle at 270⁰.

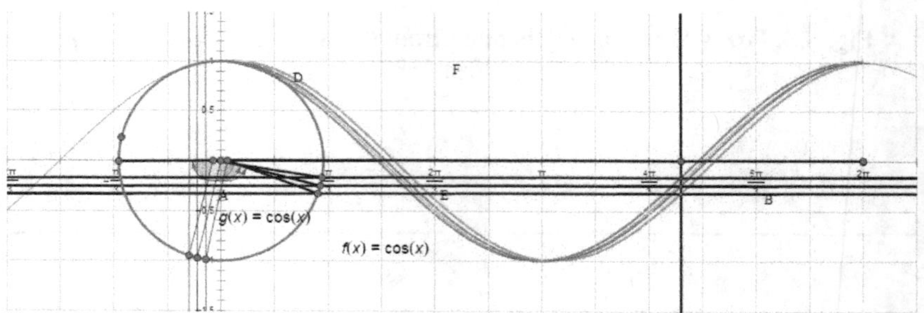

Fig. 8.7. Fuzzy Cosine wave generated from Gaussian Fuzzy Qualitative Circle around 275⁰.

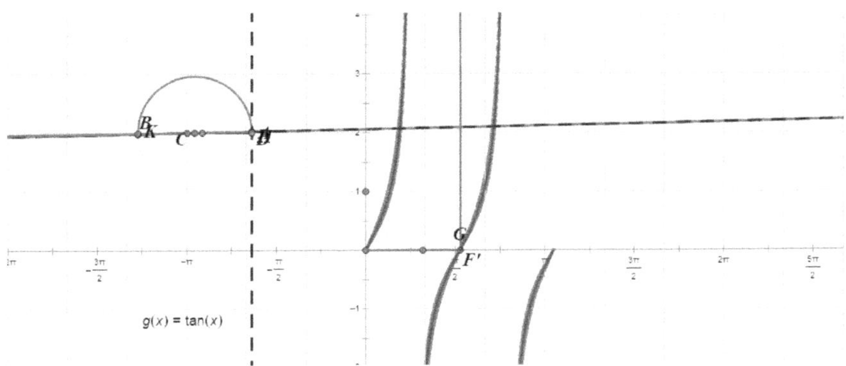

Fig. 8.8. Fuzzy Tangent wave generated from Gaussian Fuzzy Qualitative Circle.

Result 1: Ratio identities.

i. $\sin(G_{mf}[-\delta\ \delta]) = \dfrac{G_{mf}[a_y\ b_y]}{G_{mf}\left[\sqrt{(a_x - a_0)^2 + a_y^2}\ \sqrt{(b_x - b_0)^2 + b_y^2}\right]}$,

ii. $\cos(G_{mf}[-\delta\ \delta]) = \dfrac{G_{mf}[a_0 - b_x\ b_0 - a_x]}{G_{mf}\left[\sqrt{(a_x - a_0)^2 + a_y^2}\ \sqrt{(b_x - b_0)^2 + b_y^2}\right]}$,

iii. $\tan(G_{mf}[-\delta\ \delta]) = \dfrac{G_{mf}[a_y\ b_y]}{G_{mf}[a_0 - b_x\ b_0 - a_x]}$

Result 2: Pythagorean identities.

i. $\sin^2\left(G_{mf}[-\delta\ \delta]\right) + \cos^2\left(G_{mf}[-\delta\ \delta]\right) = support <1,1,0,0>$,

ii. $\sec^2\left(G_{mf}[-\delta\ \delta]\right) - \tan^2\left(G_{mf}[-\delta\ \delta]\right) = support <1,1,0,0>$,

iii. $\operatorname{cosec}^2\left(G_{mf}[-\delta\ \delta]\right) - \cot^2\left(G_{mf}[-\delta\ \delta]\right) = support <1,1,0,0>$

Result 3: Laws to obtain solutions to triangle.

i. Law of Sines:

This law gives the relationship between the sine of the angles of the triangle and the length of the sides of the triangle.

$$\frac{\sin\left(G_{mf}[\theta_y - \delta_f \ \theta_y + \delta_f]\right)}{G_{mf}[a_y \ b_y]} = \frac{\sin\left(G_{mf}[\theta_x - \delta_f \ \theta_x + \delta_f]\right)}{G_{mf}[a_x \ b_x]} =$$

$$= \frac{\sin\left(G_{mf}[\theta_z - \delta_f \ \theta_z + \delta_f]\right)}{G_{mf}[a_z \ b_z]}$$

ii.　Law of Cosines:

This law relates the sides of the triangle with the cosine of the angle in the triangle.

a.
$$G_{mf}[a_x - b_y \ a_y - b_x]^2 =$$
$$= G_{mf}[c_x - b_y \ c_y - b_x]^2 + G_{mf}[a_x - c_y \ a_y - c_x]^2 -$$
$$-2G_{mf}[c_x - b_y \ c_y - b_x] \times$$
$$\times G_{mf}[a_x - c_y \ a_y - c_x] \times \cos(G_{mf}[C - \delta \ C + \delta]),$$

b.
$$G_{mf}[c_x - b_y \ c_y - b_x]^2 =$$
$$= G_{mf}[a_x - c_y \ a_y - c_x]^2 + G_{mf}[a_x - b_y \ a_y - b_x]^2 -$$
$$-2 \times G_{mf}[a_x - c_y \ a_y - c_x] \times G_{mf}[a_x - b_y \ a_y - b_x] \times$$
$$\times \cos(G_{mf}[A - \delta \ A + \delta]),$$

c.
$$G_{mf}[a_x - c_y \ a_y - c_x]^2 =$$
$$= G_{mf}[b_x - c_y \ b_y - c_x]^2 + G_{mf}[a_x - b_y \ a_y - b_x]^2 -$$
$$-2 \times G_{mf}[b_x - c_y \ b_y - c_x] \times G_{mf}[a_x - b_y \ a_y - b_x] \times$$
$$\times \cos(G_{mf}[B - \delta \ B + \delta])$$

iii.　The law of tangents:

This law gives the relationship between the sides and tangent of the angles of the triangle.

$$\frac{G_{mf}[b_x + c_x - (a_y + c_y) \quad b_y + c_y - (a_x + c_x)}{G_{mf}[b_x + a_x - 2c_y) \quad b_y + a_y - 2c_x)]} =$$

$$= \frac{\tan\left(\dfrac{1}{2}G_{mf}[A - B - 2\delta \quad A - B + 2\delta\right)}{\tan\left(\dfrac{1}{2}G_{mf}[A + B - 2\delta \quad A + B + 2\delta\right)}$$

iv.   Mollweide's identity:

This identity is a tool to check solutions of triangles. It uses all sides and angles of the triangle.

$$\frac{G_{mf}[a_x + b_x - 2c_y \quad a_y + b_y - 2c_x]}{G_{mf}[a_x - b_y \quad a_y - b_x)]} =$$

$$= \frac{\cos\left(\dfrac{1}{2}G_{mf}[A - B - 2\delta \quad A - B + 2\delta]\right)}{\sin\left(\dfrac{1}{2}G_{mf}[C - \delta \quad C + \delta]\right)}$$

Result 4: Expansions of Trigonometric functions using Taylor's series.

The Taylor's series expansions of the trigonometric functions are evaluated as follows:

a.

$$\cos\left(G_{mf}[x_{mf} - \delta_{mf} \quad x_{mf} + \delta_{mf}]\right) = 1 - \frac{\left(G_{mf}[x_{mf} - \delta_{mf} \quad x_{mf} + \delta_{mf}]\right)^2}{2!} +$$

$$+ \frac{\left(G_{mf}[x_{mf} - \delta_{mf} \quad x_{mf} + \delta_{mf}]\right)^4}{4!} - \ldots$$

Thus

$$\cos\left(G_{mf}[x_{mf} - \delta_{mf} \quad x_{mf} + \delta_{mf}]\right) =$$

$$= G_{mf}[\cos(x_{mf} - \delta_{mf}) - \Delta_{mf} \quad \cos(x_{mf} - \delta_{mf}) + \Delta_{mf}],$$

where $\Delta_{mf} = 2 \sum\limits_{n=2,4,6,\ldots}^{\infty} \dfrac{(x_{mf} + \delta_{mf})^n + (x_{mf} - \delta_{mf})^n}{n!}$.

$$\sin\left(G_{mf}[x_{mf} - \delta_{mf} \, x_{mf} + \delta_{mf}]\right) =$$

b. $= G_{mf}[x_{mf} - \delta_{mf} \, x_{mf} + \delta_{mf}] - \dfrac{\left(G_{mf}[x_{mf} - \delta_{mf} \, x_{mf} + \delta_{mf}]\right)^3}{3!} +$

$\qquad + \dfrac{\left(G_{mf}[x_{mf} - \delta_{mf} \, x_{mf} + \delta_{mf}]\right)^5}{5!} - + \ldots$

Thus

$$\sin\left(G_{mf}[x_{mf} - \delta_{mf} \ x_{mf} + \delta_{mf}]\right) =$$
$$= G_{mf}[\sin(x_{mf} - \delta_{mf}) - \Delta_1 \ \sin(x_{mf} - \delta_{mf}) + \Delta_1],$$

where $\Delta_1 = 2 \sum\limits_{n=1,3,5,\ldots}^{\infty} \dfrac{(x_{mf} + \delta_{mf})^n + (x_{mf} - \delta_{mf})^n}{n!}$

$$\tan\left(G_{mf}[x_{mf} - \delta_{mf} \ x_{mf} + \delta_{mf}]\right) = G_{mf}[x_{mf} - \delta_{mf} \ x_{mf} + \delta_{mf}] +$$

c. $+ \dfrac{1}{3} G_{mf}[(x_{mf} - \delta_{mf})^3 \ (x_{mf} + \delta_{mf})^3] +$

$\qquad + \dfrac{2}{5} G_{mf}[(x_{mf} - \delta_{mf})^5 \ (x_{mf} + \delta_{mf})^5] + \ldots$

Thus

$$\tan\left(G_{mf}[x_{mf} - \delta_{mf} \ x_{mf} + \delta_{mf}]\right) =$$
$$= G_{mf}[\tan(x_{mf} - \delta_{mf}) \ \tan(x_{mf} + \delta_{mf})]$$

Result 5: Differentiation of the Gaussian trigonometric functions.

The trigonometric functions thus obtained are also fuzzy differentiable. Suppose that $F(x) = f(G_{mf}[c \ \sigma])$ is a Gaussian fuzzy trigonometric function then the derivatives of the function are given as follows:

First derivative: $F'(x) = f'(G_{mf}[c \ \sigma]) \times \exp\left(-\dfrac{x^2}{2\sigma^2}\right) \times \left(-\dfrac{x}{\sigma^2}\right)$

The concept of intersecting fuzzy circles is introduced and study of the structure and properties of the intersecting fuzzy circles is given and is compared with the regular intersecting circles.

Result 6: Circles touching at exactly one point.

a. Consider two circles of equal number of partitions. This implies the radius of both circles are equal. The following diagram shows the fuzzified point of intersection. It is observed that the Centre of both the curves intersect at a point which is crisp (Fig. 8.9). The fuzzified area of intersection are congruent triangles. The area of the triangle is given by, $F_{ta} = \dfrac{1}{2} \times (2r) \times \sigma = r \times \sigma$ square units. Thus, the fuzzy area is $2r\sigma$ square units.

b. Suppose that the number of partitions on the intersecting circles are unequal, as shown in Fig. 8.10.

It is observed that the crisp point of intersection is obtained where the centres of both the Gaussian curves meet. The point of intersection is bounded by triangles whose areas are given by

$$Area\ of\ \Delta_1 = \frac{1}{2} \times \sigma_1 \times (r_1 + \sigma_1) = \frac{\sigma_1(r_1 + \sigma_1)}{2},$$

$$Area\ of\ \Delta_2 = \frac{1}{2} \times \sigma_1 \times (r_1 - \sigma_1) = \frac{\sigma_1(r_1 - \sigma_1)}{2},$$

$$Area\ of\ \Delta_3 = \frac{1}{2} \times \sigma_2 \times (r_2 + \sigma_2) = \frac{\sigma_2(r_2 + \sigma_2)}{2},$$

$$Area\ of\ \Delta_4 = \frac{1}{2} \times \sigma_2 \times (r_2 - \sigma_2) = \frac{\sigma_2(r_2 - \sigma_2)}{2}$$

Hence, the total area $= r_1\sigma_1 + r_2\sigma_2$ sq. units.

The area obtained is in coherence with the traditional way of determining area of intersection. The intersection of circles becomes interesting when we consider circles intersecting at two points. In such a case, the area of intersection can be symmetric or dominated by a single circle with small portion of the second circle as a common area.

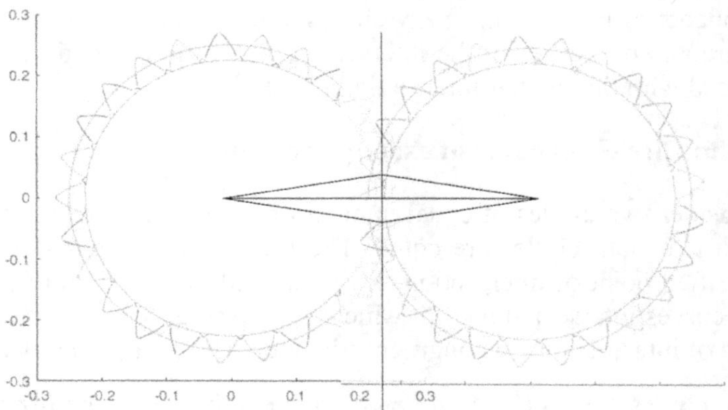

Fig. 8.9. Gaussian Fuzzy Qualitative Circles of equal radii touching at a point.

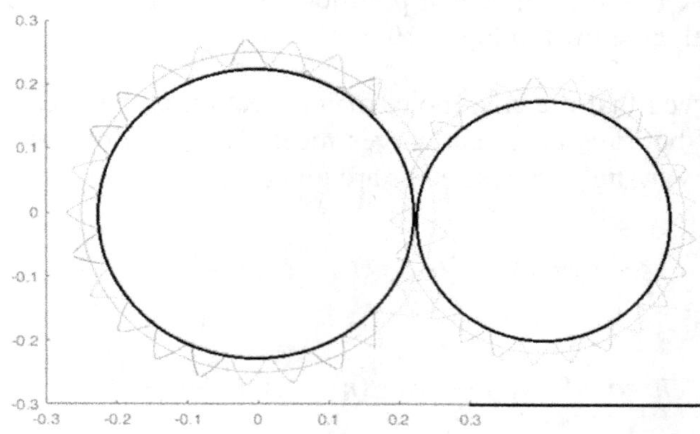

Fig. 8.10. Gaussian Fuzzy Qualitative Circles of unequal radii touching at a point.

Result 7: Fuzzy Circles intersecting at two points.

a. Consider two circles with equal number of partitions. Fig. 8.11 shows the intersecting fuzzy circles. It is observed that the crisp points of intersection and the common chord are obtained during the fuzzification process. Congruent triangles in the fuzzy area of intersection are obtained. The centres of the Gaussian curve meet to produce the crisp point of intersection. The two points when joined produces the crisp common chord for the intersecting circles.

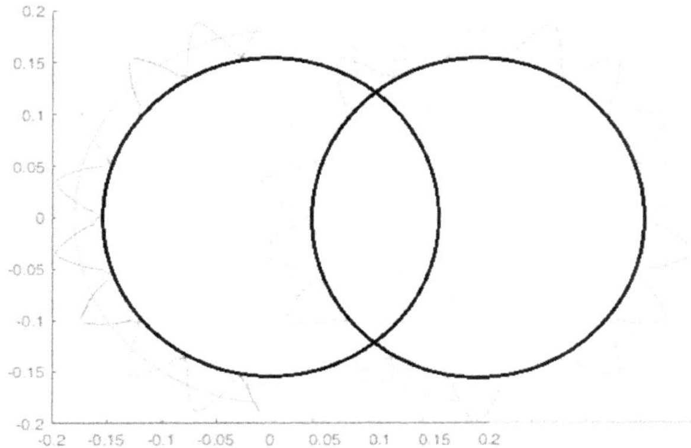

Fig. 8.11. Gaussian Fuzzy Qualitative Circles of equal radii intersecting at two points.

Area of the overlapping region is calculated as follows:

i. Calculate the areas of the sectors encompassing the overlapping area of the circles.

ii. The area of a sector is $x = r_1\sigma_1 + r_2\sigma_2$.

iii. The length of the arc of the sector is given by $r \times \theta$.

iv. Thus, the area of the fuzzified sector is $\dfrac{r_1^2 \times \theta}{2}$.

v. The area of the smaller sector is $\dfrac{r_2^2 \times \theta}{2}$. Here, $r_1 = r + \sigma$ and $r_2 = r - \sigma$.

vi. Suppose the line r_1 cuts the smaller radius in the ratio $m : n$ then $m = \dfrac{r_1}{2}$. Thus the area $= \dfrac{r_1^2 \times \theta_1}{4}$ and hence the total area $= \dfrac{r_1^2}{2} \times (2\theta + \theta_1)$ sq. units.

b. Consider two circles with unequal number of partitions, which implies that the radii of both circles are different. The area of the bigger fuzzy sector is $A = \dfrac{r^2 \times \theta}{2} + \dfrac{r^2 \times \theta_1}{4} = \dfrac{r^2}{4}(2\theta + \theta_1)$ sq. units.

Similarly, the area of the smaller fuzzy sector $= \dfrac{r_1^2}{4}(2\delta + \delta_1)$ sq. units.

Thus, in both cases, a fuzzy diagram bounded by 10 points it is obtained. The area of the overlapping section is obtained using the formula

$$Area_{fuzzy} = \frac{1}{Dis}\sqrt{C \times J \times A \times M},$$

$$C = (-Dis + rad_1 + rad_2), \quad J = (Dis - rad_1 + rad_2),$$

$$A = (Dis + rad_1 - rad_2), \quad M = (Dis + rad_1 + rad_2)$$

$Dis = [O_1 - O_2 - (\sigma_1 + \sigma_2) \; O_1 - O_2 + (\sigma_1 + \sigma_2)]$ is the distance between the centres.

$$rad_1 = [r_1 - \sigma_1 \; r_1 + \sigma_1] \text{ and } rad_2 = [r_2 - \sigma_2 \; r_2 + \sigma_2]$$

are the Gaussian radii of the fuzzy circles.

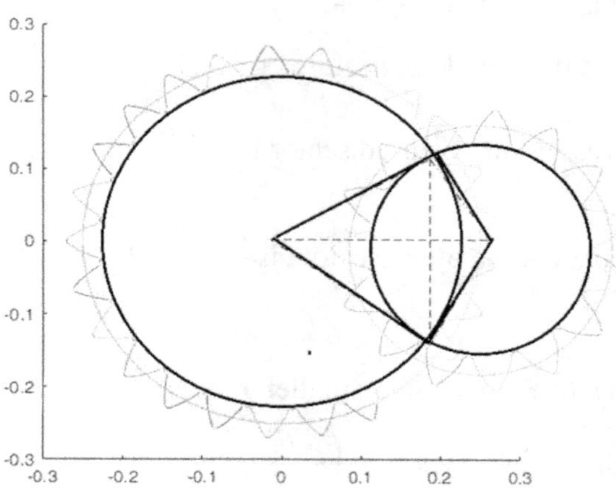

Fig. 8.12. Gaussian Fuzzy Qualitative Circles of unequal radii intersecting at two points.

Result 8.

Three circles can intersect in many ways, but we consider two cases where in we obtain circular triangle and irregular convex quadrilateral.

But, it is required to check whether the overlapping area exists between the considered circles.

To verify, we check if the following conditions are satisfied:

i.   The point of intersection of two circles should be a point inside the third circle.

ii. One of the circles should be engulfed completely inside another circle.

iii. Suppose that three fuzzy circles with equal number of partitions are considered.

This implies, the radius of all the three circles are equal. The overlapping area formed by the three segments and an inner triangle whose sides are the chords of the three circles is called a circular triangle (Fig. 8.13).

The area of the triangle is calculated using Heron's formula

$$Area_{abc} = \sqrt{S(S-A)(S-B)(S-C)}$$

Here

$$S = \frac{1}{2}(A+B+C), \quad A = G_{mf}[a_x \ a_y],$$

$$B = G_{mf}[b_x \ b_y], \quad C = G_{mf}[c_x \ c_y]$$

The area of the combined overlap is given by

$$Area_{seg} = \sum_{n=1}^{3} R_n^2 \sin^{-1}\left(\frac{A_n}{2R_n}\right) -$$

$$- \sum_{n=1}^{3} \frac{A_n}{4}\sqrt{4 \times R_n^2 - A_n^2} + \sqrt{S(S-A)(S-B)(S-C)}$$

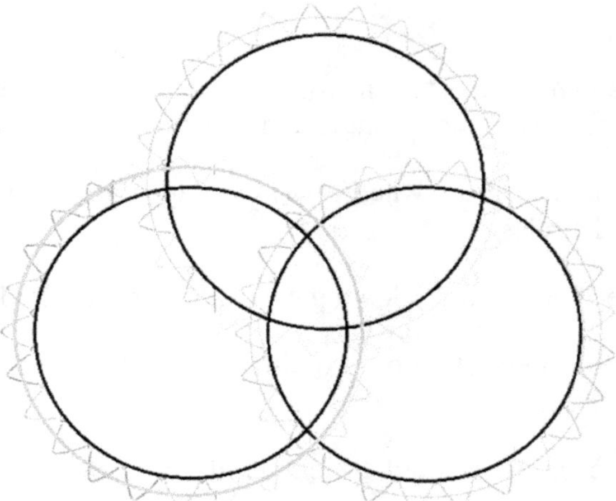

Fig. 8.13. Three Intersecting Gaussian Qualitative Fuzzy Circles of equal radii.

Suppose three fuzzy circles with unequal number of partitions are considered, then the radii of the circles are different (Fig. 8.14). In this case, the overlapping segment area using the area of the bigger circle will be calculated.

Step 1: Find the mid-point of the chord in the segment. The mid-point is given by $x_{mid} = \dfrac{x_{i12} + x_{i13}}{2}$ and $y_{mid} = \dfrac{y_{i12} + y_{i13}}{2}$.

Step 2: Find the equation of the line joining mid-point and the centre of the circle. The equation of the line is given by

$$y = \frac{B_1 - y_{mid}}{A_1 - x_{mid}} \times x - \frac{x_{m23}(B_1 - y_{mid})}{A_1 - x_{mid}} + y_{mid}$$

Step 3: Next, determine the points of intersection of the above line and circle. The point of intersection is given by

$$X_{ic1,ic2} = \frac{a_1 + b_1 \times m - m \times n \pm \sqrt{\delta}}{1 + m^2},$$

$$Y_{ic1,ic2} = \frac{n + a_1 \times m + b_1 \times m^2 \pm m \times \sqrt{\delta}}{1 + m^2}$$

Here $m = \dfrac{B_1 - Y_{mid}}{A_1 - X_{mid}}, \quad n = \dfrac{-X_{mid} \times (B_1 - Y_{mid})}{A_1 - X_{mid}} + Y_{mid}$.

Step 4: Finally, check whether the other two radii of the circles are greater than or smaller than the distance between the centre and the midpoint. Thus, the area of the bigger segment completely encompassed by the bigger circle is $\dfrac{R_1^2}{2}(\theta_1 - sin\theta_1)$.

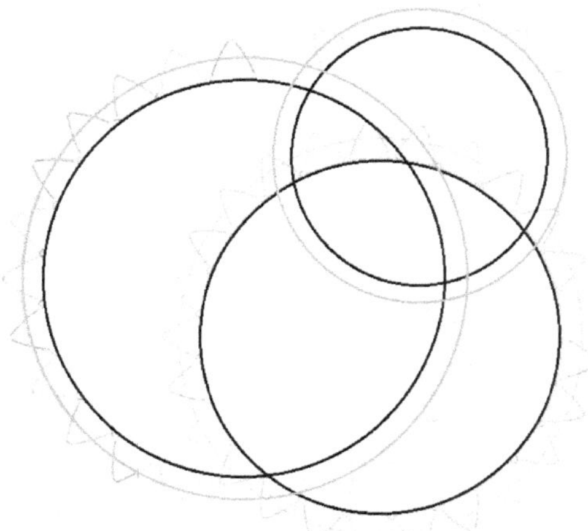

Fig. 8.14. Three Intersecting Gaussian Qualitative Fuzzy Circles of unequal radii.

a. The most complex case is the study of overlapping area which is obtained when the circular segments form the boundary of the diagram. In the process, an irregular convex quadrilateral is obtained (Fig. 8.15). The area of the quadrilateral which is irregular and convex, is given by, $Area_{quad} = \dfrac{1}{2} P \times Q \times sin\phi$ where ϕ is the angle between the diagonals P and Q. Hence the combined area of the segments will be given by

$$Area = \sum_{n=1} 4R_n^2 sin^{-1}\left(\frac{A_n}{2 \times R_n}\right) - \sum_{n=1}^{4} \frac{A_n}{4}\sqrt{4 \times R_n^2 - A_n^2}$$

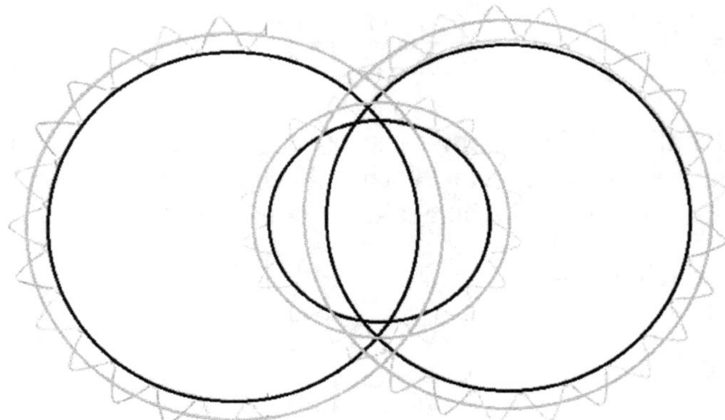

Fig. 8.15. Three Intersecting Gaussian Qualitative Fuzzy Circles of unequal radii forming a convex quadrilateral.

The literature review of fuzzy PSO shows that FPSO are mostly applied in automation control systems, operation research, medicine, chemistry, and biology to name a few. FPSO has also been used in solving TSP and various modifications of the algorithm have been proposed. In the following section, a new variant of FPSO has been defined using fuzzy qualitative circle with Gaussian membership function as the charisma of the algorithm.

8.6.3. Fuzzy PSO with Fuzzy Matrices and Gaussian Membership Function

In PSO, a finite number of particles define a swarm. The particles move in the n-dimensional space with certain velocity. The particle's velocity and position are updated using the formula given by

$$V_i^{k+1} = w \otimes V_i^k \oplus (c_1 \otimes r(.)) \otimes (P_i^k \ominus X_i^k) \oplus$$

$$\oplus \sum_{h \in \eta(i,k)} c_2 \otimes r(.) \otimes \psi(p_h)(P_g^k \ominus X_i^k)$$

Here $\eta(i,k)$ denotes k-best particles in the neighbourhood of the particle and $\psi(p_h)$ denotes the matrix containing the corresponding membership degrees of the particles defined using Gaussian membership function.

8.6.3.1. Radial Fuzzy PSO with Gaussian Membership Function

Step 1: Initialization of position of the particles.

The position of the particles is initialized and represented in the form of a fuzzy matrix. The position matrix is given by

$$
P_{rij} = \begin{bmatrix} p_{r11} & p_{r12} & \cdots & p_{r1n} \\ \vdots & \ddots & & \vdots \\ p_{rn1} & p_{rn2} & \cdots & p_{rnn} \end{bmatrix}
$$

The position of the particles for the fuzzy matrix is generated randomly and satisfy the following conditions:

$$
\sum_{j=1}^{n} p_{rij} = 1, \ P_{rij} \in [0,1], \ i = 1,2,\ldots,n
$$

Step 2: Initialization of the velocity of the particles.

The velocity matrix is given by

$$
V_{rij} = \begin{bmatrix} v_{r11} & v_{r12} & \cdots & v_{r1n} \\ \vdots & \ddots & & \vdots \\ v_{rn1} & v_{rn2} & \cdots & v_{rnn} \end{bmatrix},
$$

where the velocities of the particles are generated according to the randomly generated position of the particles with condition

$$
\sum_{j=1}^{n} v_{rij} = 0, i = 1,2,\ldots,n
$$

Step 3: Normalization of the particle position matrix.

The particle position matrix generated based on random positions may sometimes not adhere to the constraint $P_{rij} \in [0,1]$. Hence, we need to normalize the particle position matrix.

The first step in normalization involves replacing all negative values in the matrix with zero. Then the matrix is transformed into

$$P_{rij} = \begin{bmatrix} \dfrac{p_{r11}}{\sum\limits_{i=1}^{n} p_{r1i}} & \dfrac{p_{r12}}{\sum\limits_{i=1}^{n} p_{r1i}} & \cdots & \dfrac{p_{r1n}}{\sum\limits_{i=1}^{n} p_{r1i}} \\ \vdots & \ddots & & \vdots \\ \dfrac{p_{rn1}}{\sum\limits_{i=1}^{n} p_{rni}} & \dfrac{p_{rn2}}{\sum\limits_{i=1}^{n} p_{rni}} & \cdots & \dfrac{p_{rnn}}{\sum\limits_{i=1}^{n} p_{rni}} \end{bmatrix}$$

Step 4: Choosing the best agents with α-levels.

The agent particles are now selected based on the value of α, where α is a real number in the interval $[0,1]$. Once the agent particles are selected, they are placed on the circumference of the circle of radius α units. Further, the global best position of the particle was calculated using the distance formula

$$d(p_{rij}, p_{rwj}) = \sqrt{\sum_{i=1}^{m}(p_{rij} - p_{rwj})^2} \; ; d \le 2\alpha$$

8.6.3.2. Algorithm for the Radial Fuzzy PSO with Gaussian Membership Function

Step 1: Start.

Step 2: Initialize: maximum number of particles in the target neighbourhood = max_p, maximum number of iterations = max_n.

Step 3: Assign random position and velocity matrices for the particles.

For $i = 0$ to max_p calculate position and velocities of the particles.

Step 4: Normalize the particle position matrix.

Step 5: Fix the α-level for the normalized particle position matrix.

If particle's position in the normalized matrix is $\leq \alpha$, then update the first neighbourhood circle.

Step 6: Calculate the distance between the particles and locate global best position.

Step 7: Stop.

The method describes FPSO contained in a Gaussian fuzzy qualitative circle.

Further, Gaussian fuzzy qualitative circle was used to develop a fuzzy PSO algorithm where in thresholds were fixed to obtain global best within a circle whose radius was fixed using the threshold. The movement of the particles in search of the *gbest* position is shown (Figs. 8.16-8.20). The threshold value helps in searching the best particle at a faster rate as compared to the standard PSO algorithm.

The Gaussian Fuzzy Qualitative Circle and alpha cuts were used to describe Fuzzy PSO. The figure clearly shows that the universe of search elements is greatly reduced with the introduction of alpha-cut and the global best position of the particle is obtained at a faster rate.

The rate of convergence of the FPSO algorithm using random variables and a benchmark function namely Schwefel function are shown (Figs. 8.21 and 8.22).

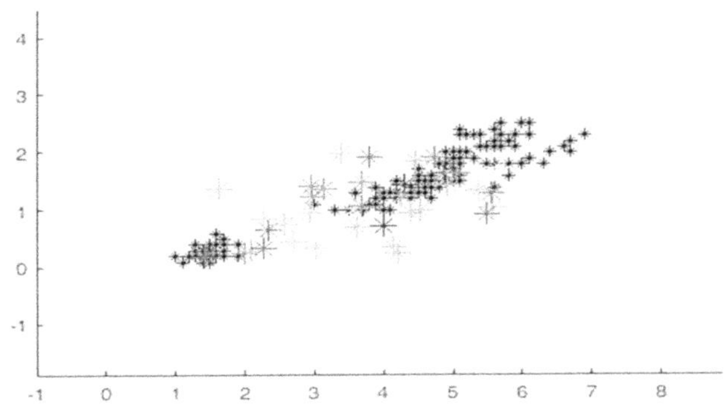

Fig. 8.16. Particles in radial fuzzy particle swarm optimization.

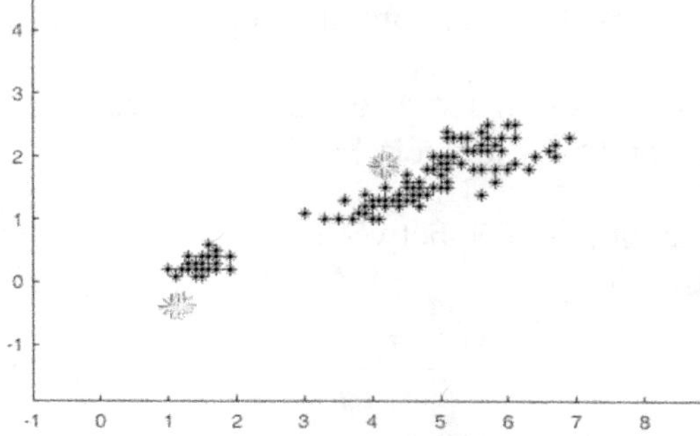

Fig. 8.17. Particles moving towards the threshold in search of global best.

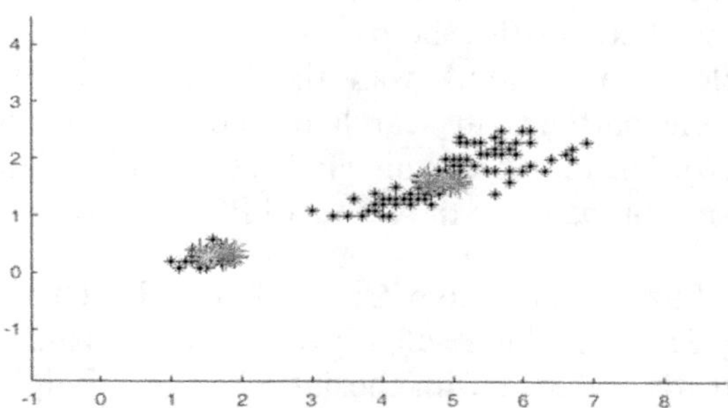

Fig. 8.18. Particles finding the global best position.

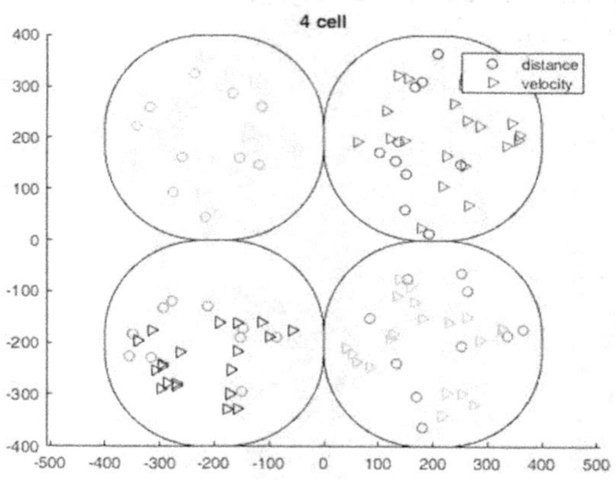

Fig. 8.19. Particles aligned inside the Circle whose radius
is the fixed threshold.

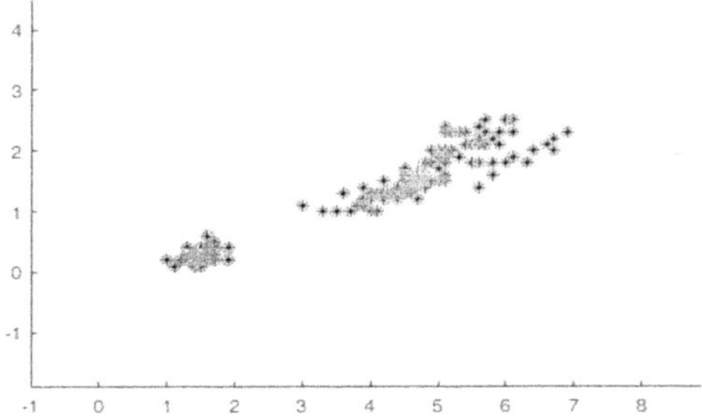

Fig. 8.20. Particles inside the radial Gaussian fuzzy qualitative circle.

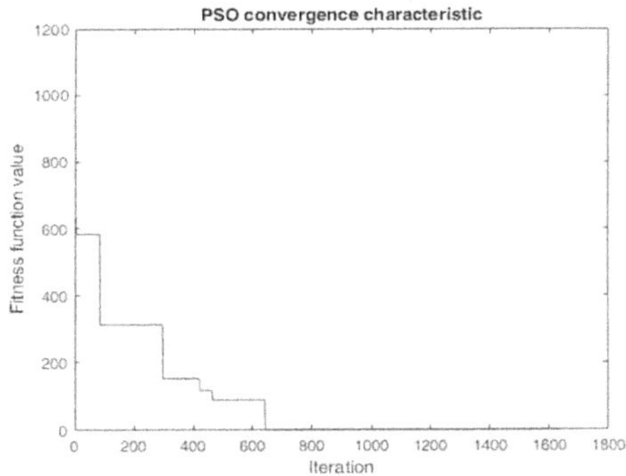

Fig. 8.21. Rate of convergence using random variables.

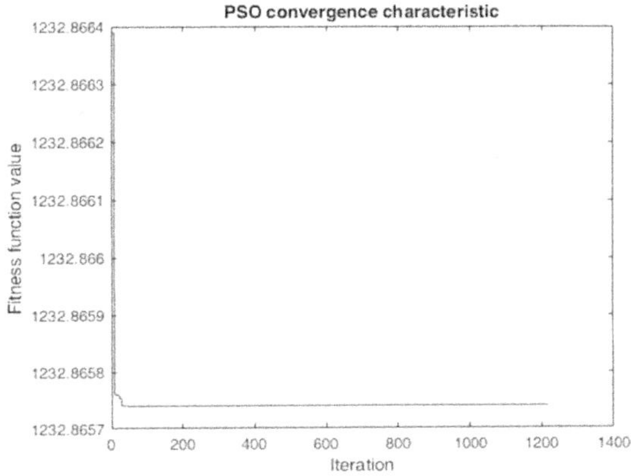

Fig. 8.22. Rate of convergence using Schwefel functions.

8.7. Conclusion

The following conclusion can be drawn in comparison to the existing methods:

i.   The core of the fuzzy unit circle is a crisp unit circle.

ii. The core of the sine, cosine and tangent graphs obtained obeys the rule of classical trigonometric curves.

iii. The curves are continuous and are well defined in the interval $[0, 2\pi]$

iv. The fuzziness at the points of inflection are also nullified with max-curve and min-curve falling well inside the interval $[-1,1]$.

v.   The centre and the radius are real lines partitioned into Fuzzy numbers.

Thus, the results obtained from the Gaussian fuzzy qualitative circle clearly extends all the existing theories and provides a wholesome approach to fuzzy trigonometry.

Further, the intersecting fuzzy circles, which has been developed for the first time, has been found to be coherent to the properties and theorems of intersecting circles in classical geometry.

Even though the algorithm seems to converge at a faster rate, the algorithm was developed with the aim of implementing it to small radars for easy navigation of visually impaired people. The alpha cut or the threshold helps in fixing the radius of the neighbourhood falling near the moving particle. If the velocity and position of the obstacle is within the fixed threshold, an alert can be generated to avoid hitting the obstacle.

Fuzzy qualitative circle can be refined by partitioning the circle into parts using type-2 fuzzy sets. The graphs of the functions and the orientations obtained can be easily applied in robotics which forms a major chunk in AI.

Acknowledgements

We sincerely thank Prof. Sergey Y. Yurish for giving me an opportunity to contribute a chapter towards this prestigious book.

References

[1]. A. M. Abdelbar, S. Abdelshahid, D. C. Wunsch, Fuzzy PSO: A generalization of PSO, in *Proceedings of the IEEE International Joint Conference on Neural Networks (IJCNN'05)*, Vol. 2, December 2005, Montreal, Canada, pp. 1086-1091.

[2]. A.M. Abdelbar, S. Abdelshahid, D.C. Wunsch, Gaussian vs. Cauchy membership functions in Fuzzy PSO, *International Joint Conference on Neural Networks,* 2007, pp. 2902-2907.

[3]. A. K. Adak, M. Bhoumik, M. Pal Interval cut set of generalized interval-valued IFSs, *International Journal of Fuzzy System Applications,* Vol. 2, Issue 3, 2012, pp. 35-50.

[4]. A. Alfi, M. M. Fateh, Intelligent information and control using improved fuzzy particle swarm optimization, *Expert Systems with Applications,* Vol. 38, Issue 10, 2011, pp. 12312-12317.

[5]. E. Aminian, M. Teshnehlab, A novel fuzzy particle swarm optimization, in *Proceedings of the 13th Iranian Conference on Fuzzy Systems (IFSC'13),* 2013, pp. 1-6.

[6]. M. Anatathanavit, M. A. Munlin, Radius particle swarm optimization, in *Proceedings of the International Computer Science and Engineering Conference (ICSEC'13),* 2013, pp. 126-130.

[7]. S. R. Barbhuiya, Quasi-cut of fuzzy sets and quasi-cut of intuitionistic fuzzy sets, *International Journal of Computer Applications,* Vol. 122, Issue 22, 2015, pp. 1-8.

[8]. H. K. Baruah, Construction of the membership function of a fuzzy number, *ICIC Express Letters,* Vol. 5, Issue 2, 2010, pp. 545-549.

[9]. H. K. Baruah, The Mathematics of Fuzziness: Myths and Realities, *Lambert Academic Publishing,* Germany, 2010.

[10]. S. Bodjanova, Median alpha-levels of a fuzzy number, *Fuzzy Sets and Systems,* Vol. 157, Issue 1, 2006, pp. 879-891.

[11]. J. J. Buckley, E. Eslami, An Introduction to Fuzzy Logic and Fuzzy Sets, *Physica-Verlag,* Heidelberg, New York, 2002, pp. 1-94.

[12]. J. J. Buckley, E. Eslami, Fuzzy trigonometry, in An Introduction to Fuzzy Logic and Fuzzy Sets, *Springer,* 2002, pp. 185-194.

[13]. C. S. Chan, H. Liu, Fuzzy qualitative human motion analysis, *IEEE Transactions on Fuzzy Systems,* Vol. 17, 2009, pp. 851-862.

[14]. C.-C. Chou, The square roots of triangular fuzzy number, *ICIC Express Letters,* Vol. 3, Issue 2, 2010, pp. 207-212.

[15]. M. Dorigo, Optimization, learning and natural algorithm, PhD Thesis, *Politecnico di Milano,* Italy, 1992.

[16]. W. Dong, H. C. Shah, Vertex method for computing functions of fuzzy variables, *Fuzzy Sets and Systems*, Vol. 24, 1987, pp. 65-78.

[17]. W. M. Dong, H. C. Shah, F. S. Wong, Fuzzy computations in risk and decision analysis, *Civil Engineering Systems*, Vol. 2, 1985, pp. 201-208.

[18]. D. Dubois, H. Prade, Fuzzy Sets and Systems: Theory and Applications, *Academic Press,* New York, 1980, pp. 5-30.

[19]. D. Dubois, H. Prade, Operations on fuzzy numbers, *International Journal of Systems Science,* Vol. 9, Issue 6, 1978, pp. 613-626.

[20]. P. Dutta, H. Boruah, T. Ali, Fuzzy arithmetic with and without using alpha-cut method: A comparative study, *International Journal of Latest Trends in Computing,* Vol. 2, Issue 1, 2011, pp. 99-107.

[21]. I. Eyoh, R. John, G. D. Maere, Interval type-2 intuitionistic fuzzy logic system for non-linear system prediction, in *Proceedings of the IEEE International Conference on Systems, Man, and Cybernetics (SMC'16),* 2016, pp. 001063-001068.

[22]. I. Givens, H. Tahani, An improved method of performing fuzzy arithmetic for computer vision, Proceedings of NAFIPS, Purdue University, 1987, pp. 275-280.

[23]. M. M. Gupta, Fuzzy set theory and its applications: A survey, *IFAC Proceedings Volume*, Vol. 10, Issue 6, 1977, pp. 247-259.

[24]. D. Ghosh, D. Chakraborty, Analytical fuzzy plane geometry I, *Fuzzy Sets and Systems,* Vol. 209, 2012, pp. 66-83.

[25]. D. Ghosh, D. Chakraborty, Analytical fuzzy plane geometry II, *Fuzzy Sets and Systems*, Vol. 243, 2014, pp. 84-104.

[26]. D. Ghosh, D. Chakraborty, Analytical fuzzy plane geometry III, *Fuzzy Sets and Systems,* Vol. 283, 2016, pp. 83-107.

[27]. Y. T. Juang, S. L. Tung, H. C. Chiu, Adaptive fuzzy particle swarm optimization for global optimization of multimodal functions, *Information Sciences*, Vol. 181, Issue 20, 2011, pp. 4539-4549.

[28]. K. Kankar, R. P. Singh, Design of spur gear and its tooth profile on MATLAB, *Asia Pacific Journal of Research*, Vol. 1, 2015, pp. 39-44.

[29]. A. Kaufman, M. M. Gupta, Introduction to Fuzzy Arithmetic, *Van Nostrand Reinhold,* New York, 1985, pp. 242-249.

[30]. J. Kennedy, R. Eberhart, Particle swarm optimization, *IEEE Neural Networks,* Vol. 4, 1995, pp. 1942-1948.

[31]. S. A. Khan, A. P. Engelbrecht, A fuzzy particle swarm optimization algorithm for computer communication network topology design, *Applied Intelligence,* Vol. 36, Issue 1, 2012, pp. 161-177.

[32]. G. J. Klir, B. Yuan, Fuzzy Sets and Fuzzy Logic: Theory and Applications, *Prentice Hall,* Upper Saddle River, 1995.

[33]. J. Li, H. Li, The cut sets, Decomposition theorems and representation theorems on fuzzy sets, *International Journal of Information and Systems Sciences*, Vol. 6, Issue 1, 2010, pp. 61-71.

[34]. Q. Li, S. Guo, Fuzzy geometric object modelling, *Fuzzy Inf. Eng.*, Vol. 40, 2007, pp. 551-563.

[35]. X. S. Li, X. H. Yuan, E. S. Lee, The three-dimensional fuzzy sets and their cut sets, *Computers and Mathematics with Applications*, Vol. 58, Issue 7, 2009, pp. 1349-1359.

[36]. H. Liu, G. M. Coghill, D. P. Barnes, Fuzzy qualitative trigonometry, *International Journal of Approximate Reasoning*, Vol. 51, Issue 1, 2005, pp. 71-88.

[37]. Q. Li, S. Guo, Fuzzy geometric object modelling, *Fuzzy Inf. Eng.*, Vol. 40, 2007, pp. 551-563.

[38]. M. S. Norouzzadeh, M. R. Ahmadzadeh, M. Palhang, LADPSO using fuzzy logic to conduct PSO algorithm, *Applied Intelligence*, Vol. 37, Issue 2, 2012, pp. 290-304.

[39]. J. Q. Qiu, M. Zhang, Fuzzy space analytic geometry, in *Proceedings of the International Conference on Machine Learning and Cybernetics (ICMLC'06)*, 2006, pp. 1751-1755.

[40]. S. Rahman, On cuts of Atanassov's intuitionistic fuzzy sets with respect to fuzzy connectives, *Information Sciences*, Vol. 340, 2016, pp. 262-278.

[41]. D. A. Ress, Development of fuzzy trigonometric functions to support design and manufacturing, PhD Thesis, *North Carolina University*, 1999, pp. 1-10.

[42]. A. Robati, G. A. Barani, *et al.*, Balanced fuzzy particle swarm optimization, *Applied Mathematical Modelling*, Vol. 36, Issue 5, 2012, pp. 2169-2177.

[43]. A. Rosenfeld, The diameter of a fuzzy set, *Fuzzy Sets and Systems*, Vol. 13, 1984, pp. 241-246.

[44]. A. Rosenfeld, S. Haber, The Perimeter of a fuzzy set, *Pattern Recognition*, Vol. 18, Issue 2, 1985, pp.125-130.

[45]. M. Savoj, S. A. Monadjemi, Iris localization using circle and fuzzy circle detection method, *World Acad. Sci., Eng. Technol.*, Vol. 61, 2012, pp. 848-850.

[46]. Y. Shi, R. Eberhart, Fuzzy adaptive particle swarm optimization, in *Proceedings of the Congress on Evolutionary Computation*, 2001, pp. 101-106.

[47]. W. A. Yang, Y. Guo, W. H. Liao, Optimization of multipass face milling using a fuzzy particle swarm optimization algorithm, *International Journal of Advanced Manufacturing Technology*, Vol. 54, 2011, pp. 45-57.

[48]. X. Yuan, Z. Shen, Notes on fuzzy plane geometry I, II, *Fuzzy Sets and Systems*, Vol. 121, 2001, pp. 545-547.

[49]. L. A. Zadeh, Fuzzy sets, *Information and Control*, Vol. 8, 1965, pp. 338-353.

[50]. L. A. Zadeh, The concept of linguistic variable and its application to approximate reasoning – Part I, *Information Sciences*, Vol. 8, Issue 1, 1975, pp. 199-249.

[51]. L. A. Zadeh, The concept of linguistic variable and its application to approximate reasoning – Part II, *Information Sciences*, Vol. 8, Issue 1, 1975. pp. 301-357.

[52]. L. A. Zadeh, The concept of linguistic variable and its application to approximate reasoning – Part III, *Information Sciences*, Vol. 9, Issue 1, 1975, pp. 43-80.

[53]. L. A. Zadeh, Toward extended fuzzy logic – A first step, *Fuzzy Sets Syst.*, Vol. 160, 2009, pp. 3175-3181.

Chapter 9

Intelligent Methods and Models for Big Data Analysis. Application for Smart Quality Control in Steel Plant

Salah Bouhouche

9.1. Overview of Big Data Analysis for Smart Quality Control

The world of today is characterized by a huge data generated by the unfolding of the different processes, the latter are often interconnected and sometimes generate redundant data. Based on the importance of data size, an area of R&D has been developed and various processing tools for making reliable decisions have been developed.

Classical methods based on the processing of statistical data seem to be limited by the intelligence generated in the data themselves: The notions of Big data, data mining and others techniques have been also developed. Indeed, most of the data comes from the sensors associated with connected objects, which are the basic elements generating the big data, this is known often as the smart process. As the field of Big Data is very large, we will propose in this chapter of book some theoretical and practice elements, a particular importance will be given to typical applications for smart industrial processes.

The principle of data processing is illustrated in the diagram of Fig. 9.1.

Intelligent methods and models are a soft computing approaches based on complex algorithms with a relative easy implementation in a

Salah Bouhouche
Research Center in Industrial Technologies CRTI, Algiers, Algeria

numerical form. The intelligence is introduced via inferential reasoning, the learning tools are then introduced, some practical algorithms such as SVR and ANN will be considered and applied to process data from real word.

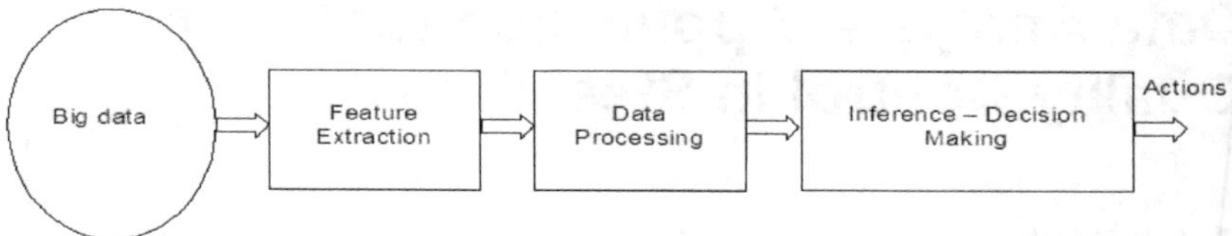

Fig. 9.1. Principe of decision based data mining.

Feature Extraction

As given by Fig. 9.1, the procedure of big data processing begins by the feature extraction, in this step it is extracted the useful information's, in some way data are firstly filtered. The PCA and its allied algorithms are the most recommended tools.

Data Processing

This is a large field where several algorithms and methods can be chosen according to the nature of data type and their interactions. In this step, we are interested to find correlations and relationships between all data or between sub domains. We are asked to give an answer to how we explore data? Do any relations between data exist? If yes how we can extract a reasonable number of variables for decision making? We know that the data generation processes is complex. A black box input output model is built: The followings tools can be used:

- Clustering followed by PCA and its allied methods,

- Dynamic operators such as signal processing tools.

Inference and decision making

Decision making is generally obtained by an automatic classification after data processing step. Logical and numerical information's are processed and intelligent algorithms are used.

Specific applications for one line quality control

Today, industrial processes are heavy instrumented and therefore
smarter; this dominance of measurements generates big data, it is
important to exploit them to make quality control in real time.
For simple systems, the quality of the finished product is measured in a
direct and online way using the associated sensors, a routine check in the
laboratory is carried out periodically to adjust any drifts.
For complex systems which are generally characterized by phase
changes between the beginning and the end of the process, the problem
of quality control is complex because it cannot be done by a simple
analysis of data directly or indirectly: Such systems achieve large
dimension of acquired data, so complex algorithms are needed for a good
processing. The development of complex soft sensors based big data
analysis could be a solution requiring validations. Fig. 9.2 shows the
principle.

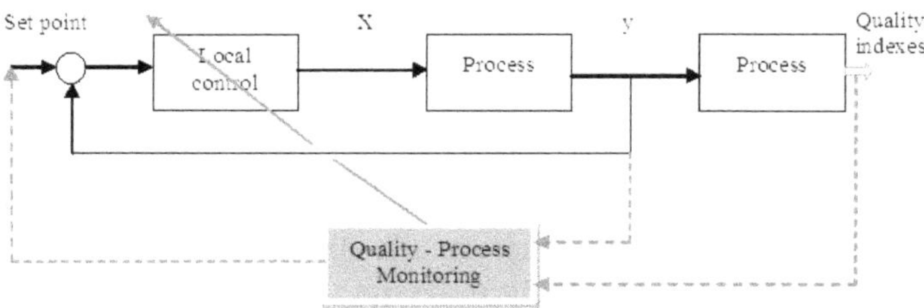

Fig. 9.2. Principle of quality – process monitoring.

Quality – Process Monitoring and Control

Industrial processes is characterized by complex interactions between
different influencing factors, this pose challenging problems due to the
increasing complexities of system structures and parameters. Control
systems are generally designed to achieve the target quality by exploring
all measurements data which are accurately acquired.

Today big processes and systems are heavily instrumented and huge data
are generated and need to be processed using the required methods and
algorithms. By such instrumentation, the process becomes smart and
intelligent algorithms are strongly recommended to use, particularly for
that used to decision making. In many complex industrial processes, key

variables defining the quality of products are not measured online; they are obtained by laboratory testing and analysis, which sometimes leads to a delay in production.

The use of measurement data on different scales of production is a promising solution; they must be associated with algorithms and methods with a high level of intelligence. In this part we will study the main approaches used for data processing, they are based on the big data analysis such as data driven, modeling and identification methods [1-6]. Linear time-invariant systems, the parametric uncertainties and the unmodeled dynamics associated with the data-driven scheme are irrelevant with sources of uncertainty of the measurement process.

We present modeling cases for the prediction of process quality using different measurements; a particular importance will be attached to the practical aspects connected to the proposed algorithms and methods.

In the fields of big data analysis for quality control such as quality prediction and quality assurance; a particular importance is given to the relationships between process data and the final product quality. The process data can be changed by activating the control; but the final product is generally observed i.e. measured at the end of the production by a feedback from the laboratory tests and analysis.

There are two different approaches; one is about the classification of the product quality by logical indicators as good, bed, very good etc. The second is a quantitative prediction of different measured indexes. Generally when the model output is continuous values, it is regression, and when the model output is class values, it is classification.

The statistical process control models connect information on the process variables including the control inputs with their corresponding indexes of the product quality; it is possible to estimate the quality indexes – values of new operating conditions, without experiments, by inputting their process variables values into the models. This has applications in virtual screening and quality prediction [1-10]. Supervised learning is a method to learn the relationships between explanatory variables (X) and objective variables (y).

In industrial context, quantitative information on process variables corresponds to (X), and the quality indexes of the corresponding samples are the y-values. Supervised learning can be classified into two forms:

classification, in which (y) consists of categories, and regression, in which (y) consists of continuous values. Linear classification methods include linear discriminant analysis, and support vector machine (SVM) [11-18], while nonlinear classification methods include the k-nearest neighbor algorithm [11-18]. Regression analysis includes both linear methods, such as principal component regression (PCR), partial least squares (PLS and support vector regression (SVR) [19-21].

There also exist numerous variables and virtual process structures without (y)-values, i.e., for which the product quality has not been measured. For these, only information on the X-variables is available. Given a database of process variables without (y) values, the essential structure hidden behind the dataset must be learned by a process called unsupervised learning. This process is classified into two forms: dimensionality reduction (or data visualization), and clustering.

9.1.1. Principle of SVR Algorithm [19-21]

The principle of model identification based statistical learning is given by Fig. 9.3.

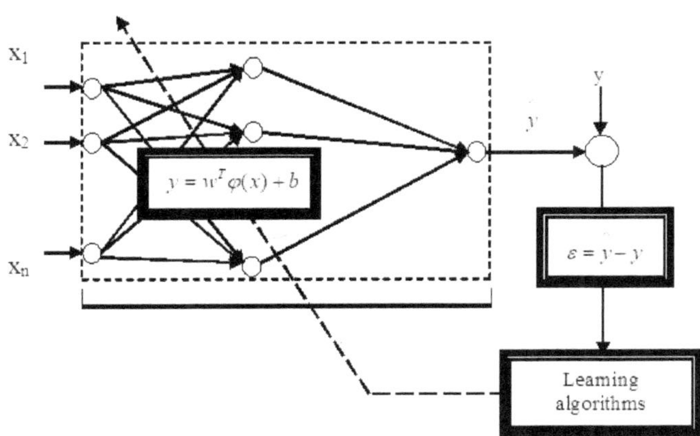

Fig. 9.3. Principle of model identification based learning algorithms.

Let a training set of data points $\{x_1(i), x_2(i)...x_n(i), y(i)\}_{i=1}^{m}$ with input $x(i) \in R^n$ and $y(i) \in R$, the SVR models can be written as.

$$y = w^T \phi(x) + b, \tag{9.1}$$

where the non linear function $\phi(.)$ maps the input data into higher dimension feature space, x is the inputs variables and y is the model output. w and b are the model identification parameters which are estimated using measurement data $\{x(i), y(i)\}$. The training objective is to estimate the optimal parameters $\langle w, b \rangle$ in the regression function (9.1). SVR is a method based on statistical learning theory, selects error ξ_i as the loss function. Therefore, the following optimization problem is considered as

$$\min J(w, \xi) = \min \frac{1}{2} w^T w + \frac{1}{2} \gamma \sum_{i=1}^{m} \xi_i^2 \tag{9.2}$$

Subject to the equality constraints

$$y(i) = w^T \phi(x(i)) + b + \xi, i = 1, 2, ... m, \tag{9.3}$$

ξ is a positive constant used to control the tradeoff between the training error and the model complexity. The larger ξ is, the less error of regression model will make. This is the only free parameter in SVR formulation.

w can be evaluated according to objective function (9.2) and constraints (9.3). This corresponds to a form of ridge regression and Lagrange function is given by

$$L(w, b, \xi, a) = \frac{1}{2} w^T w + \gamma \sum_{i=1}^{m} \xi_i^2 - \sum_{i=1}^{m} a_i (w^T \phi(x(i)) + b + \xi_i - y(i)), \tag{9.4}$$

$$a_i, i = 1, ..., m$$

The optimal $a = [a_1, ..., a_m]^T$ can be solved on KKT conditions [19-21], which is optimally computed as

$$\begin{cases} \dfrac{\partial L}{\partial W} \to \sum_{i=1}^{m} a_i \phi(x(i)) \\[2ex] \dfrac{\partial L}{\partial b} \to \sum_{i=1}^{m} a_i = 0 \\[2ex] \dfrac{\partial L}{\partial \xi_i} \to a_i = \gamma \xi_i \\[2ex] \dfrac{\partial L}{\partial a_i} \to w^T \phi(x(i)) + b + \xi_i - y(i) = 0 \end{cases} \tag{9.5}$$

After elimination of ξ_i, w, the solution is solved by the following set of linear equations

$$\begin{bmatrix} 0 & \theta^T \\ \theta & \Lambda + \gamma^{-1} I \end{bmatrix} \begin{bmatrix} b \\ a \end{bmatrix} = \begin{bmatrix} 0 \\ Y \end{bmatrix}, \tag{9.6}$$

I is the identity matrix: $\theta = [1,.....,1]^T$, $a = [a_1,.....,a_n]^T$ and the Mercer condition has been applied.

$$\Lambda_{ij} = \phi(x(i))^T \phi(x(j)) = \Psi(x(i), x(j)) \tag{9.7}$$

Lagrange multiplier a and the model bias could be solved in the Eq. (9.6), which could also be expanded as

$$\theta^T a = 0$$
$$b\theta + (\Lambda + \gamma^{-1} I) A = Y$$

Namely

$$\hat{a} = (\Lambda + \gamma^{-1} I)^{-1} (Y - b\theta) \tag{9.8}$$

The substitution of Eq. (9.8) into Eq. (9.6), and

$$\theta^T a = 0 \to \theta^T (\Lambda + \gamma^{-1} I)^{-1} (Y - b\theta) = 0$$
$$\to \hat{b} = \dfrac{\theta^T (\Lambda + \gamma^{-1} I)^{-1} Y}{\theta^T (\Lambda + \gamma^{-1} I)^{-1} \theta} \tag{9.9}$$

The final estimation of the model output is defined as

$$\hat{y} = \sum_{i=1}^{m} a_i (w^T \Psi(x, x(i)) + \hat{b} \tag{9.10}$$

The principle of statistical learning defined by Fig. 9.3 can be easily extended to the dynamic system by considering the following changes:

- The inputs x of the model contain dynamic changes and feedback of the model output,

- The model structure should be stable chosen.

Extension to dynamic systems:

- The model input is

$$x(k) = [y(k-1), ..., y(k-N_y), u_1(k-1), ..., u_1(k-N_{u1}), .., u_p(k-1),$$
$$..., u_p(k-N_{up})],$$

where u_i is the control inputs of the system, N_{up} and N_y are the maximum derivative order respectively for control inputs and the model output.

- The model output is $y(k) = w^T \phi(x(k)) + b, k = 1, 2, ...m$, is the sampling time.

9.1.2. ANN Algorithm

Advanced process – quality control and monitoring require accurate process models. The development of analytical models from the relevant physical and chemical knowledge, especially for complex systems with phase changes, can be too costly or even technically impossible. For such models, based mainly on the data production, operational data should be capitalized.

Many systems and processes are characterized by a non-linear dynamic behavior. Then, they need non-linear models. Indeed, Neural Networks have been shown to be able to approximate continuous non-linearities and have been applied in modeling of non-linear and complex processes of which the complexity is due to the large number of network weights.

In practice, many non-linear processes are approximated by reduced order and possibly linear models and which are clearly related to the underlying process characteristics.

The model identification principle using NN is given by Fig. 9.4. A model structure is chosen, the input and the output variables are defined, the modeling residual or error is computed and used as a tool to adapt the model parameters w_{ij}^t by means of the computing procedure which includes a recursive form, more details about this method can bed founded in different documents [23-25].

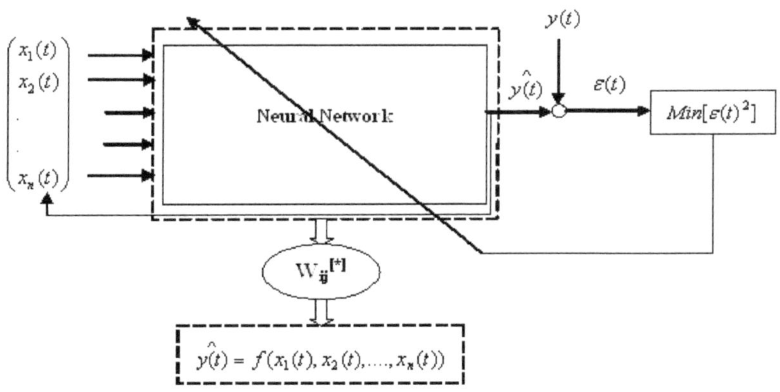

Fig. 9.4. Principle of model identification using NN.

The model output is defined by

$$y_t = f(X^t, w_{ij}^t), \qquad (9.11)$$

f is the model structure, X^t is the model input and w_{ij}^t are the ANN weights. The output is y_t is an estimate of the model output and X^t is formed by the past outputs, actual and past inputs and other dynamic of exogenous inputs if exist. ε is the modelling error which is minimized using the required algorithm such as Levenberg – Marquardt (LVM) [23-25].

They are estimated by the corresponding algorithm that minimizes the modelling error as shown in Fig. 9.4. The recursive form is given by the following equation

$$w_{ij}^t = w_{ij}^{t-1} - [H_{t-1} + \lambda_{t-1}.I]^{-1}.J_{t-1}^T.\varepsilon_{t-1},\qquad(9.12)$$

H_{t-1} and J_{t-1} are respectively the Hessian and Jacobian. λ_{t-1} and I are respectively a constant and the identity matrix. ε_{t-1} is the modelling error.

The computing procedure is described by the following steps:

Step1: Define the model structure: $f \to NN$.

Step2: Initialize the network weights $w_{ij}^0 = [-0.5 \text{ to } +0.5]$.

Step3: Acquisition of inputs/outputs (x^t, y_t).

Step4: Compute the model output $\hat{y}_t$.

Step 5: Compute the modeling error $\varepsilon(t) = y_t - \hat{y}_t$:

a) if $\varepsilon(t) \approx 0$, $w_{ij}^t = w_{ij}^{t-1} \to$ Stop: $w_{ij}^t = w_{ij}^{[*]}$;

b) Else, Adjust the NN Weights using the recursive Algorithm Eq.(9.12).

Step6: Go to Step3.

9.2. Proposed Regression Model Using Data Mining

9.2.1. General Formalism

A process model can be defined by a complex relation between its inputs and output variables. The complex relationship between the input space (χ) and the output space (γ) can be defined by an unknown ideal function Φ

$$\gamma = \Phi(\chi)\qquad(9.13)$$

This relation can be approximate by a model defining the dependency between the input data (X) and output data (y)

$$y = f(X) + \varepsilon, \tag{9.14}$$

$\varepsilon \in N(0, \sigma)$ is a residual error of the prediction which is normally distributed with mean value zero and a standard deviation σ.

Firstly the model f is developed and trained using historical data $D^{Hist} = (X^{Hist}, y^{Hist})$ where D^{Hist} is the historical domain containing the input /output data base, the estimated output at each time (t) is given by

$$\hat{y}_t = f(X_t^f), \tag{9.15}$$

where X_t^f is the input of the model depending on the model structure used, the input is composed by input data $[x_t, ..., x_{t-Nx}]$ the past values of the target data $[y_{t-1}, ..., y_{t-Ny-1}]$ and the prediction residual $[\varepsilon_{t-1}, ..., \varepsilon_{t-N\varepsilon-1}]$.

Using residual $[\varepsilon_{t-1}, ..., \varepsilon_{t-N\varepsilon-1}]$ as an input of the model can lead a problem with the stability.

To overcome the consequence of the model changes on the precision, stability and performance, adaptive form is necessary, the model needs to be equipped with adaptation mechanism (see Fig. 9.5) which allows them to accommodate feedback information and online data. Additionally to the model description given by Eq. (9.15), there is an adaptation function R, in the case of the adaptive system, this function changes i.e. adapts the model during runtime as

$$f_t = R(f_{t-1}, X_t^R) \tag{9.16}$$

Different technique can be applied such as moving windows technique, recursive method and its allied techniques.

The moving window and recursive technique can be formulated respectively by $f_t = R(X_t^R)$ with $X_t^R = [D^{MW} = (X_{t-i}, y_{t-i})]_{i=1}^{N-1}$, N is the moving window length $f_t = R(f_{t-1}, X_t^R)$ with $X_t^R = [X_{t-1}, y_{t-1}, f_{t-1}]$.

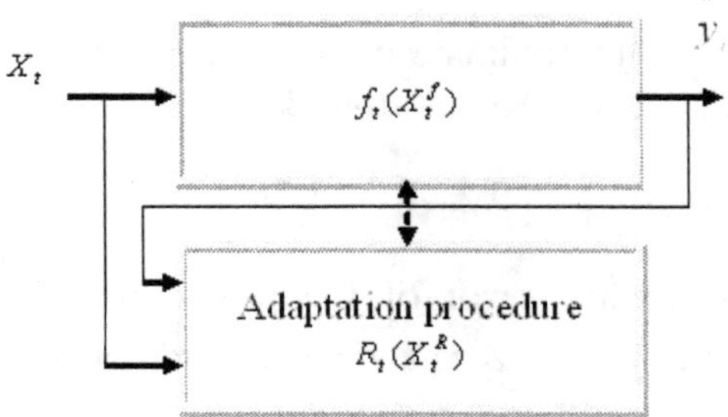

Fig. 9.5. Principle of the Adaptation mechanism.

9.2.2. Least Square PCA Based Prediction (LS – PCA)

Principal component analysis (PCA) is a mathematical procedure that uses an orthogonal transformation to convert a set of observations of possibly correlated variables into a set of values of uncorrelated variables called principal components. The number of principal components is less than or equal to the number of original variables. This transformation is defined in such a way that the first principal component has as high a variance as possible (that is, accounts for as much of the variability in the data as possible), and each succeeding component in turn has the highest variance possible under the constraint that it be orthogonal to (uncorrelated with) the preceding components. Principal components are guaranteed to be independent only if the data set is jointly normally distributed. PCA is sensitive to the relative scaling of the original variables. Generally a matrix of the input data X to be normalized to zero mean and unit variance, the scaling is obtained by the following formula

$$X_{scaled} = \frac{X_{real} - X_{min}}{X_{max} - X_{min}}, \tag{9.17}$$

where X_{scaled} is the scaled data, X_{min} is a minimum value of the real data, X_{max} is the amaximum value of the real data, X_{real} is the real value.

The scaling is applied in order to assume equal influence of the input variables in the model. The normalized data is then transformed to l-dimensional ($l \leq m$) scores matrix $T \in \Re^{nxl}$ using the following relation

$$X = TP^T + E, \tag{9.18}$$

X is the normalised form of the original data, $P \in \mathfrak{R}^{mxl}$ and $E \in \mathfrak{R}^{nxm}$ are the loading and residuals matrices respectively.

In the case of the covariance approach, the correlation matrix C of the input data X is calculated as

$$C = \frac{1}{n-1} X^T X \tag{9.19}$$

The eignevalues and eigenvectors of this matrix are derived by solving

$$V^{-1}CV = eig(C), \tag{9.20}$$

where $eig(C)$ is the diagonal eigenvalues matrix and V the eigenvector matrix. The eigenvalues λ_i are then stored in descending order such as $\lambda_1 > \lambda_2 > ..... > \lambda_m$, the columns of matrix P are then formed by the eigenvectors v_i corresponding to the highest eigenvalues ($l \leq m$), there is a truncation of the neglected eigenvalues that not have a significant contribution

$$P = [v_1, v_2, ...v_l] \text{ with } v_i \in \mathfrak{R}^{mxl} \tag{9.21}$$

The calculation of the eigenvalue decomposition the Singular Value Decomposition technique (SVD) can be used.

$$T = XP \tag{9.22}$$

Having the matrix T, one can build a regression model using the Least Square (LS) algorithm:

$$\hat{y} = T.B \tag{9.23}$$

Using LS algorithm, the estimated value of B can be obtained by:

$$B = [T^T T]^{-1} T^T . y = L^{-2} T^T . y, \text{ with } L \in \mathfrak{R}^{lxl} \tag{9.24}$$

As shown in Eq. (9.22), (9.23) the predicted value $\hat{y}$ depend on two variables T and B, it is developed in this section an adaptive approach based on the moving window. The combined use of PCA and regression is shown in Fig.9.6.

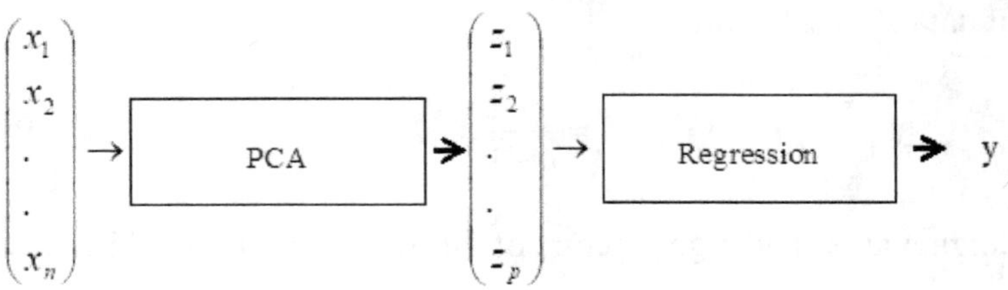

Fig. 9.6. Principle of the adaptive prediction using PCA.

The proposed computing procedure related to the prediction using the adaptive PCA is defined as follows:

1. Select an optimal moving window length ($N_x = N_y = N_\varepsilon$) and a target residual MSE (Mean Squared Error) of residual (MSEA).

2. Data acquisition: $X = [x_t...x_{t-Nx}, y_{t-1}...y_{t-Ny-1}, \varepsilon_{t-1}...\varepsilon_{t-N\varepsilon-1}]$, $y = [y_t...y_{t-Ny}]$.

3. Compute the eigenvalues λ.

4. Select the significant values of $\lambda = [\lambda_1, \lambda_2,...............\lambda_l]$, $l \leq m$.

5. Compute the matrices P and T using Eq. (9.21) and Eq. (9.22).

6. Compute the matrix B using Eq. (9.24).

7. Predict the output $\hat{y}$ using Eq. (9.25).

8. Compute residual $\varepsilon_t = y_t - \hat{y}_t$ and residual performance defined by Mean Squared Error (MSE) of residual.

9. If (MSE<MSEA), go to Step 7.

10. Else go to Step 1.

11. From Eq. (9.9) and Eq. (9.10), the predicted output can be written as:

$$\hat{y}_t = XPB = X\beta =$$
$$= [x_t...x_{t-Nx}, y_{t-1}...y_{t-Ny-1}, \varepsilon_{t-1}...\varepsilon_{t-N\varepsilon-1}][\beta_1.........\beta_{Nx+Ny+N\varepsilon}]^T$$

$$(9.25)$$

12. By extending Eq. (9.24) to the dynamic behaviour, the optimal values of the regression matrix β is given by the following Eq. (9.26).

$$\hat{\beta}_t = (XX^T)^{-1}X^T\hat{y}_t \qquad (9.26)$$

Details of the implementation of such model are given by Fig. 9.7.

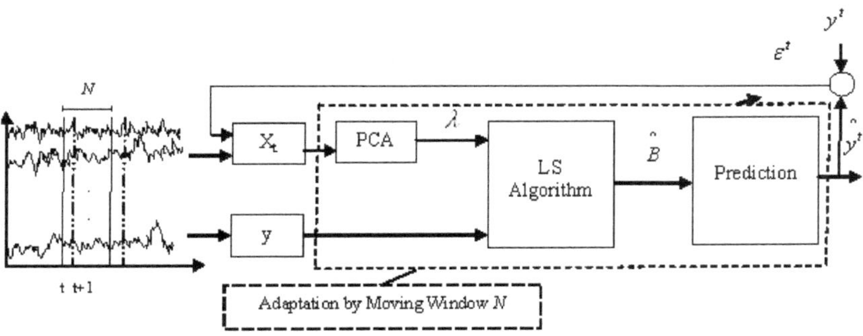

Fig. 9.7. Scheme of the LS – PCA regression model implementation.

9.3. Application

9.3.1. Process Description

The whole of LD converter is considered as a thermal chemical reactor at high temperature. The objective of the oxygen converter is to refine molten iron to crude steel through oxidization to achieve a specified temperature and chemical composition at the end blow. Failure to do this leads to the need to reblow. At the start of the refining process to molten metal along with cold scrap is charged to the steelmaking vessel. This is known as charging. There is usually 80 % hot metal, and 20 % scrap when charging, and the balance between these amounts is used to regulate the temperature of the steel in the furnace, and also the specification of the required steel. Lime is added and then an oxygen lance is lowered into the vessel to blow oxygen at supersonic velocities through specially designed nozzles at the tip. The principle of the process is shown in Fig. 9.8.

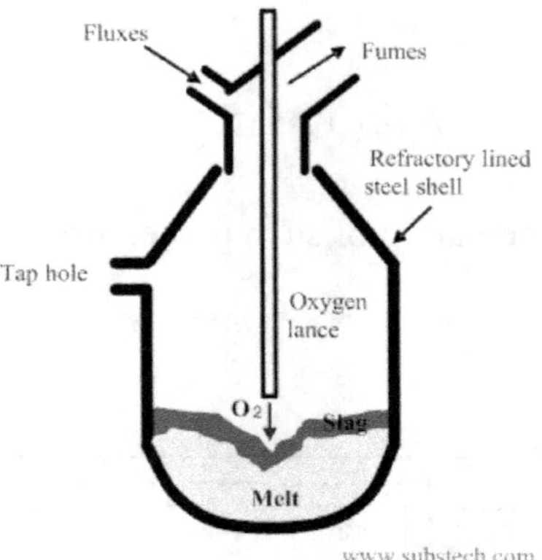

Fig. 9.8. Principle of steel refining in LD converter.

To define the charge conditions and oxygen blowing requirements to achieve the temperature and chemical composition, mathematical and thermodynamic models have been developed. The LD process is of course a very complex batch reaction, which can vary significantly from heat to heat, while many of variables involved are not accurately known. As a consequence, therefore, it is necessary to take into account of the uncertainty affecting the whole process reactions, in this case, we introduced in the models all process variables affecting the model output defined by the chemical composition and the temperature of liquid steel.

9.3.2. Metallurgical Reactions

The basic oxygen furnace uses no additional fuel. The pig iron impurities (carbon, silicon, manganese and phosphorous) serve as fuel. Iron and its impurities oxidize evolving heat necessary for the process. Oxidation of the molten metal and the slag is complicated process proceeding in several stages and occurring simultaneously on the boundaries between different phases (gas-metal, gas-slag, slag-metal). Finally the reactions may be presented as follows:

$$1/2\{O_2\} = [O],$$

$$[Fe] + 1/2\{O_2\} = (FeO),$$

$$[Si] + \{O_2\} = (SiO_2),$$

$$[Mn] + 1/2\{O_2\} = (MnO),$$

$$2[P] + 5/2\{O_2\} = (P_2O_5),$$

$$[C] + 1/2\{O_2\} = \{CO\},$$

$$\{CO\} + 1/2\{O_2\} = \{CO_2\}$$

Most oxides are absorbed by the slag. Gaseous products CO and CO_2 are transferred to the atmosphere and removed by the exhausting system. Oxidizing potential of the atmosphere is characterized by the post-combustion ratio: $\{CO_2\}/(\{CO_2\}+\{CO\})$.

1. Operation of a Basic Oxygen Furnace,

2. Charging steel scrap (25-30 % of the total charge weight),

3. Pouring molten pig iron from blast furnace,

4. Charging fluxes,

5. Starting oxygen blowing. Duration of the blowing is about 20 min,

6. Sampling. Temperature measurements (by disposable thermocouple) and taking samples for chemical analysis are made through the upper cone in tilted position of the furnace,

7. Tapping – pouring the steel to a ladle. Special devices (plugs, slag detectors) prevent penetration (carry-over) of the slag into the ladle,

8. De-slagging – pouring the residual slag into the slag pot. The furnace is turned upside down in the direction opposite to the tapping hole.

9.3.3. Model Input/Output

The following Table 9.1 defines the Process Parameters / inputs – outputs data:

Table 9.1. Nomenclature of inputs and outputs data.

Variable	Designation	Unit
Control inputs		
VO_2	Volume of Oxygen	Nm^3
QCaCo	Weight lime	ton
$QCaCo_3$	Weight limestone	ton
Initial sets		
QFR	Weight of scrap	ton
QFL	Weight cast iron	ton
ACFL	C% cast iron	Weight%
QSiFL	Si% cast iron	Weight%
ASFL	S% cast iron	Weight%
APFL	P% cast iron	Weight%
TFL	Temperature cast iron	°C
Age	wear of lining refractory	
Waiting	Wait between heats	Minute
Outputs		
ACACL	C% content of refined steel	Weight%
AMnACL	Mn% content of refined steel	Weight%
APACL	P% content of refined steel	Weight%
ASACL	S% content of refined steel	Weight%
TACL	End Temperature of refined steel	°C

The model structure describes the influence of input space on the outputs. Outputs are composed of several independents sub-models, the model acts in total input space where each output is constructed by several combinations of inputs.

9.3.4. Prediction and Result Analysis

Fig. 9.9 present typical example of input/output of the model. The application results of various presented algorithms are given in the following figures (Figs. 9.10-9.19). It is important to give the following details.

The curve in blue color is the non-adaptive version of the algorithm, the curve in green color is the adaptive version of the algorithm.

Curves shown by Figs. 9.10-9.19 give a global trend of different computed errors; the exact performances are evaluated by the MSE index as shown in Table 9.2.

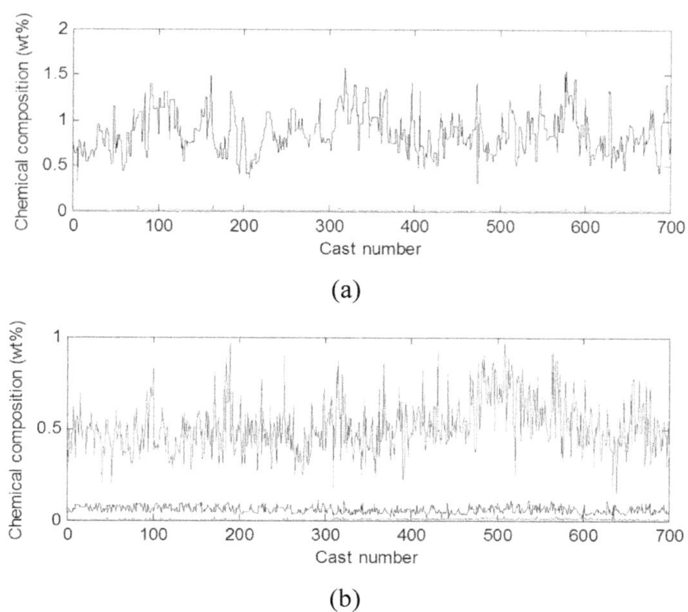

Fig. 9.9. (a) Typical inputs – chemical composition of cast iron;
(b) Typical soutputs – chemical composition of steel.

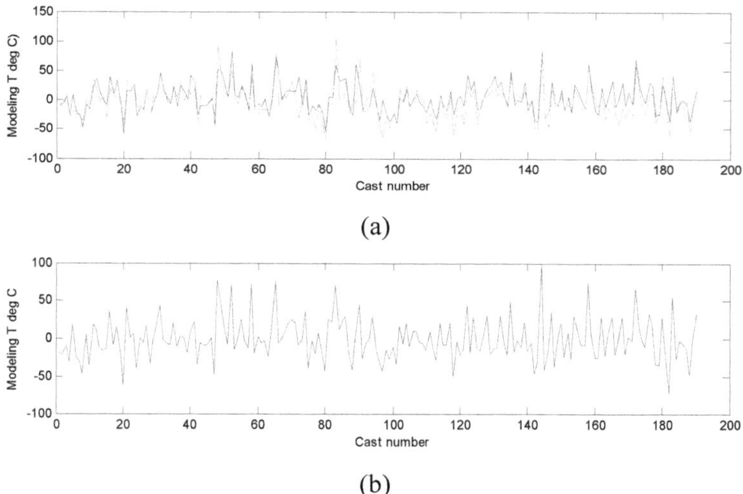

Fig. 9.10. (a) TACL – modelling errors using ANN and PCA-ANN models;
(b) TACL – modelling errors using LS-PCA models.

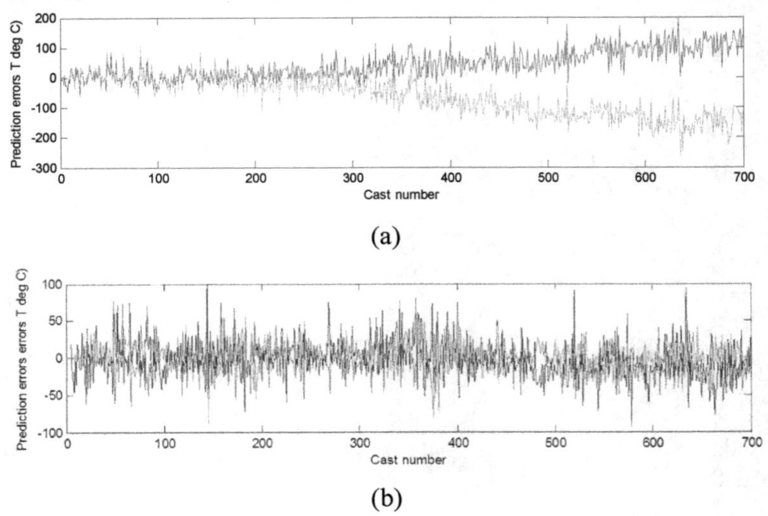

Fig. 9.11. (a) Prediction errors using ANN and PCA-ANN models;
(b) Prediction errors using LS-PCA and adaptive LS-PCA models.

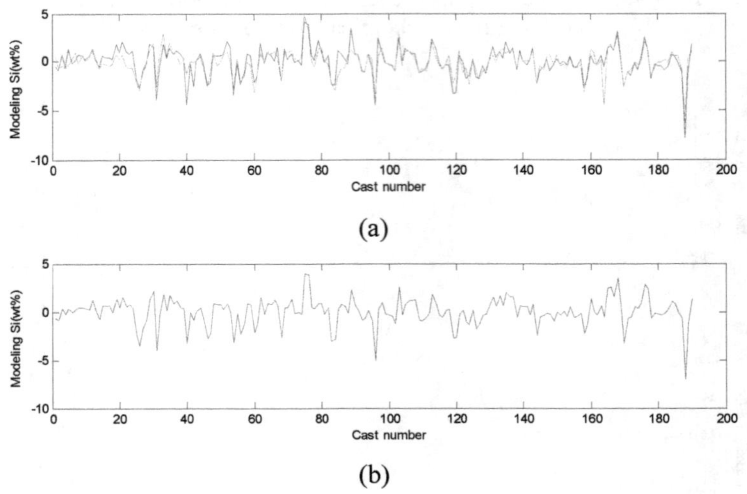

Fig. 9.12. (a) ASACL – modelling errors using ANN and PCA-ANN models;
(b) ASACL – modelling errors using LS-PCA models.

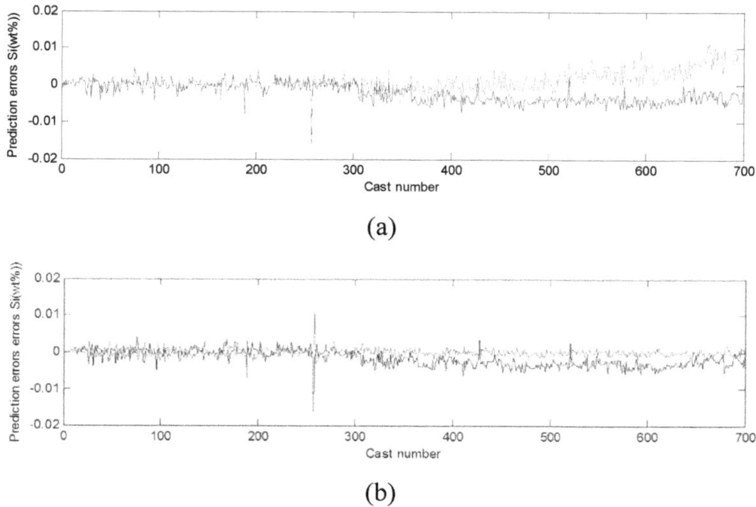

(a)

(b)

Fig. 9.13. (a) Prediction errors using ANN and PCA-ANN models; (b) Prediction errors using LS-PCA and adaptive LS-PCA models.

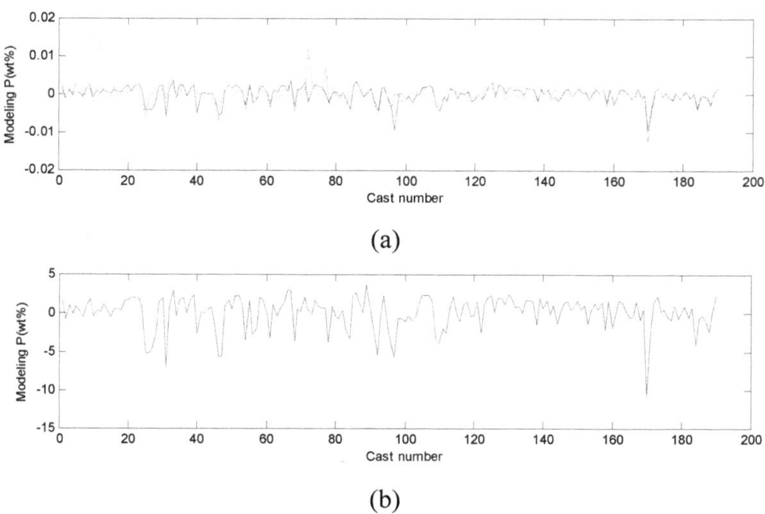

(a)

(b)

Fig. 9.14. (a) APACL – modelling errors using ANN and PCA-ANN models; (b) APACL – modelling errors using LS-PCA models.

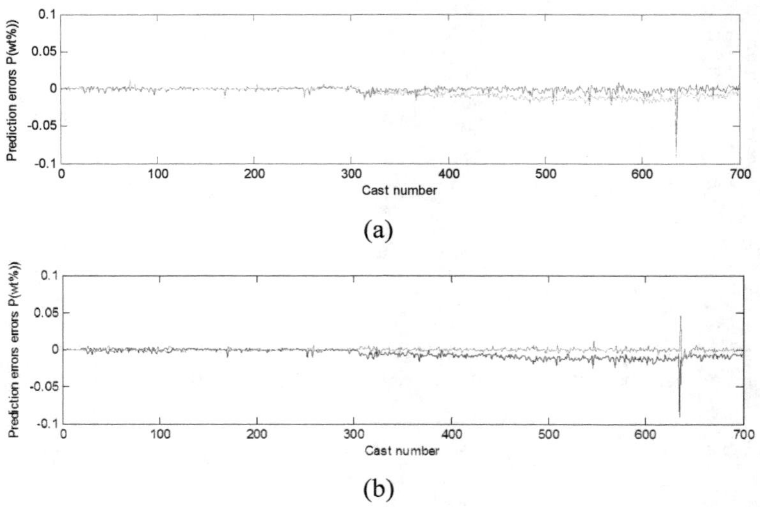

Fig. 9.15. (a) APACL – prediction errors using ANN and PCA-ANN models; (b) APACL – prediction errors using LS-PCA and adaptive LS-PCA models.

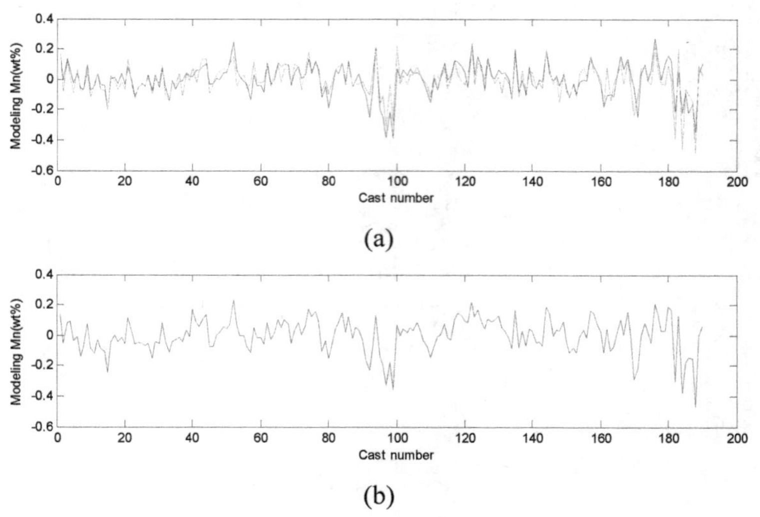

Fig. 9.16. (a) AMnCL – modelling errors using ANN and PCA-ANN models; (b) AMnCL – modelling errors using LS-PCA models.

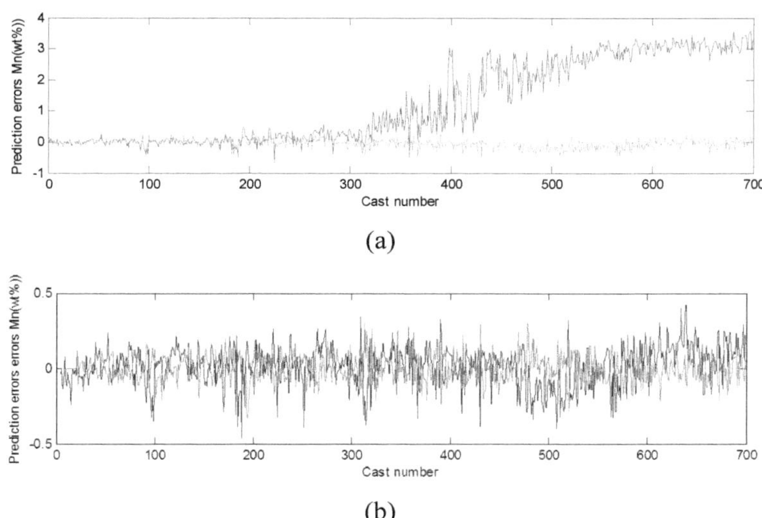

Fig. 9.17.(a) AMnCL – prediction errors using ANN and PCA-ANN models;
(b) AMnCL – prediction errors using LS-PCA and adaptive LS-PCA models.

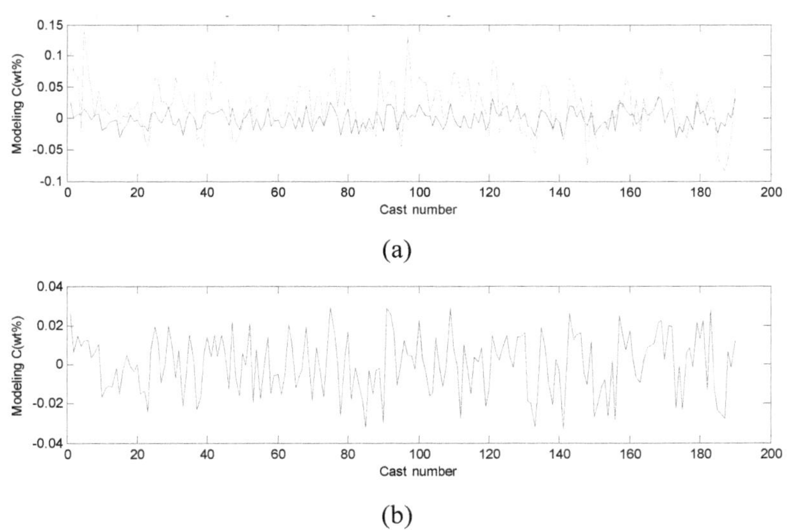

Fig. 9.18. (a) ACACL – modelling errors using ANN and PCA-ANN models;
(b) ACACL – modelling errors using LS-PCA models.

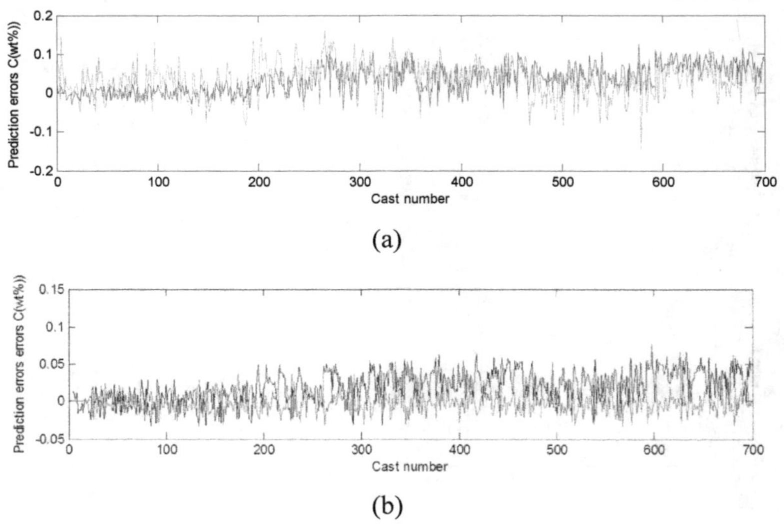

(a)

(b)

Fig. 9.19. (a) ACACL – prediction errors using ANN and PCA-ANN models; (b) ACACL – prediction errors using LS-PCA and adaptive LS-PCA models.

Table 9.2 summarizes the computational results of the predicted and modeled outputs. As mentioned above, 05 key elements were considered, these elements are the model output defined in the Table 9.1 (TACL, ASACL, APACL, AMnACL and ACACL). All these variables have been computed using different methods.

Table 9.2. Performance in modeling and prediction.

Method/Model	Output				
	TACL	ASACL	APACL	AMnACL	ACACL
MSE Modeling - ANN	701	23510	45590	0.0115	0.0002
MSE Modeling PCA-ANN	818	18870	44450	0.0116	0.0019
MSE Modeling LS-PCA	782	21240	44790	0.0130	0.0002
MSE Modeling LS-PCA Adaptive	33655	26230	44790	0.0168	0.0003
MSE Prediction - ANN	3952.6	1019	2036	3.2754	0.0024
MSE Prediction PCA-ANN	8253.5	897	8435	0.0207	0.0031
MSE Prediction LS-PCA	770.7	689	7155	0.0184	0.0008
MSE Prediction LS-PCA Adaptive	**396.4**	**109**	**833**	**0.0084**	**0.0002**

MSE: Mean Squared Error

For each element and for each method, the performances have been evaluated using MSE (Mean Squared Error) in modeling and in

prediction. The length of time series is about 190 samples in modeling
and about 700 samples in prediction. All data are collected from real
operating conditions of steel plant.

On the Table 9.2 are the MSE results for each method, the best
performance is attributed to the developed adaptive LS-PCA approach,
it gives a minimum MSE in prediction, this has been described by the
Eq. (26), other considered techniques such as SVR, ANN and their
combination with PCA remain less reliable.

9.4. Conclusion

Some intelligent methods based on big data analysis and regression
search have been considered, they have been carried out by data driven,
regression and its allied methods. Particular importance has been given
to adaptive LS-PCA based moving window algorithm. Existing methods
have been presented and an adaptive version has been obtained
and tested.

The combined use of PCA-ANN and PCA-SVR remains limited
compared to the proposed adaptive form, this is confirmed by the
obtained results and evaluated by the MSE.

This computed procedure can be easily implemented to conduct the
charge calculation program in steel refining process.

References

[1]. J. Fan, Online monitoring of nonlinear multivariate industrial processes
using filtering KICA-PCA, *Control Engineering Practice*, Vol. 22, 2014,
pp. 205-216.
[2]. L. Ma.et al., A novel data-based quality-related fault diagnosis scheme for
fault detection and root cause diagnosis with application to hot strip mill
process, *Control Engineering Practice*, Vol. 67, 2017, pp. 43-51.
[3]. B. Rashidia, et al., Data-driven root-cause fault diagnosis for multivariate
non-linear processes, *Control Engineering Practice*, 2018, Vol. 70,
pp. 134-147.
[4]. C. A. Escobar, et al.,Process-monitoring-for-quality – Applications,
Manufacturing Letters, Vol. 16, 2018, pp. 14-17.

[5]. Q. Zhu, Q. Liu, S. J. Qin, Concurrent quality and process monitoring with canonical correlation analysis, *Journal of Process Control*, Vol. 60, 2017, pp. 95-103.

[6]. K. Peng, et al., Quality-related process monitoring for dynamic non-Gaussian batch process with multi-phase using a new data-driven method, *Neurocomputing*, Vol. 214, 2016, pp. 317-328.

[7]. Q. P. He, J. Wang, Statistical process monitoring as a big data analytics tool for smart manufacturing, *Journal of Process Control*, Vol. 67, 2018, pp. 35-43.

[8]. S. Lee, S. B. Kim, Time-adaptive support vector data description for nonstationary process monitoring, *Engineering Applications of Artificial Intelligence*, Vol. 68, 2018, pp. 18-31.

[9]. G. Andonovski, et al., Evolving model identification for process monitoring and prediction of non-linear systems, *Engineering Applications of Artificial Intelligence*, Vol. 68, 2018, pp. 214-221.

[10]. C. A. Escobar, et al., Process-monitoring-for-quality — Big models, *Procedia Manufacturing*, Vol. 26, 2018, pp. 1167-1179.

[11]. W. Li, G. Lin, D. X. Zhang, An adaptive ANOVA-based PCKF for high-dimensional non linear inverse modeling, *Journal of Computational Physics*, Vol. 258, 2014, pp. 752-772.

[12]. I. Lira, Monte Carlo evaluation of the uncertainty associated with the construction and use of a fitted curve, *Measurement*, Vol. 44, 2011, pp. 2156-2164.

[13]. D. J.-R. Bouveresse, et al., Identification of significant factors by an extension of ANOVA–PCA based on multi-block analysis, *Chemometrics and Intelligent Laboratory Systems*, Vol. 106, 2011, pp. 173-182.

[14]. T. Kuti, A. Hegyi, S. Kemény, Analysis of sensory data of different food products by ANOVA, *Chemometrics and Intelligent Laboratory Systems*, Vol. 72, 2004, pp. 253-257.

[15]. T. Naes, et al., Multi-block regression based on combinations of orthogonalisation, PLS-regression and canonical correlation analysis, *Chemometrics and Intelligent Laboratory Systems*, Vol. 124, 2013, pp. 32-42.

[16]. G. Mazerolles, et al., Analysis of experimental design with multivariate response: A contribution using multiblock techniques, *Chemometrics and Intelligent Laboratory Systems*, Vol. 106, 2011, pp. 65-72.

[17]. K. Manabu, N. Yoshiaki, Data-based process monitoring, process control, and quality improvement: Recent development and applications in steel industry, *Computer. Chem. Eng.*, Vol. 32, 2008, pp. 12-24.

[18]. O. Marjanovic, et al., Real-time monitoring of an industrial batch process, *Computer. Chem. Eng.*, Vol. 30, 2006, pp. 1476-1481.

[19]. S. Ghosh, et al., Support vector regression based metamodeling for seismic reliability analysis of structures, *Applied Mathematical Modelling*, Vol. 64, 2018, pp. 584-602.

[20]. Y. Yu, Intelligent quality prediction using wighted least square support vector regression, *Physics Procedia*, Vol. 24, 2012, pp. 1392-1399.

[21]. M. Z. Li, W. Li, Study on least squares support vector machines algorithm and its application,in *Proceedings of the 17thIEEE Inter. Conference Tools with Artificial Intelligence(ICTAI'05)*, 2005,pp. 1082-3409.

[22]. Z. Ye, M. K. Kimb, Predicting electricity consumption in a building using an optimized backpropagation and Levenberg-Marquardt back-propagation neural network: Case study of a shopping mall in China, *Sustainable Cities and Society*, Vol. 42, 2018, pp. 176-183.

[23]. B. Xia, State of charge estimation of lithium-ion batteries using optimized Levenberg-Marquardt wavelet neural network, *Energy*, Vol. 153, 2018, pp. 694-705.

[24]. L. Daniel, et al., Dynamic economic load dispatch using Levenberg Marquardt algorithm,*Energy Procedia*, Vol. 144, 2018, pp. 95-103.

[25]. Estimation of FeO content in the steel slag using infrared imaging and artificial neural network, *Measurement*, Vol. 117, 2018, pp. 380-389.

Chapter 10

Aspects of Program Design for Electromagnetic Environment Visualization Near Cellular Antennas

*Marina Yu. Zvezdina, Yuliya A. Shokova, Hayder T. A. Al-Ali,
Ghassan H. A. Al-Farhan*

10.1. Rationale for Electromagnetic Environment Visualization

Technological advancement in wireless communication ensured high data rates; in its turn, it led to mobile web applications being embedded into the business significantly, which has given a start to the digital economy [1]. Since data transmission is carried out by cellular networks, a sharp increase in data traffic and compact location of mobile users have caused an essential strengthening of electromagnetic background in residential areas [2]. The results of medical trials [3-5] on the health effects of low-intensity electromagnetic fields excited by cell tower antennas were confirmed by statistical research data [6-8]. The fact that the electromagnetic field has a harmful influence on health along with the impossibility to eliminate this factor made it necessary to introduce electromagnetic monitoring in megalopolises. The type of monitoring depends on the information user. Since socially oriented monitoring is intended for the population; it should display the state of electromagnetic environment in residential areas [4, 5-8]. For this type of monitoring, visual form is the most straightforward to present the information about the electromagnetic environment. At the same time, a number of requirements must be met to plot the information; they are related to the aspects of socially oriented electromagnetic monitoring.

Marina Yu. Zvezdina
Don State Technical University, Rostov on Don, Russia

10.2. Requirements for Electromagnetic Environment Visualization for Socially Oriented Monitoring

Let us formulate and justify the plot requirements that visualize electromagnetic environment near cell tower antennas in the framework of socially oriented monitoring. In addition, let us assume that the research results were obtained by computational forecasting method. We do not consider the instrumental measurement method because it is applied when the antennas have been already mounted; moreover, it gives no explanation on the observed pattern of the energy flux density distribution [4, 5]. In our opinion, the main advantages of the computational forecasting method are the following. First, the electrodynamic theory is used both to simulate antenna field structure and to give physical interpretation of the results. Second, the "preventive principle" recommended by the World Health Organization [9] is implemented to assess the worst case scenario.

We suggest using the following three criteria to plot visualizations:

- Computational costs are minimal;

- Environment analysis can be carried out at ease;

- It is possible to give evidence-based recommendations for vital practical applications.

The first criterion doesn't impose any additional restrictions on computer hardware and allows carrying out calculations in real time. The second criterion imposes restrictions on the plot types. The third criterion ensures that the visual form of the results is in compliance with practical tasks. Typically, two tasks are relevant as the main problems: one is to assess the people safety to be on the roof when antenna is working (e.g. having rooftop greenfield recreation areas, swimming pools etc.), and another one is to do safety evaluation of the apartments in the surrounding buildings. It should be noted that all three criteria listed above should be applied together to solve the problem of assessing the electromagnetic environment; their segregation is purely theoretical. Let us give the case study.

10.3. Specification of the Presentation Requirements for the Electromagnetic Environment Assessment Results

Let us analyze the information that should be visualized according to several parameters:

- *Variables in question.* According to the recommendations [4, 5, 11, 12], the electromagnetic environment is assessed with energy flux density Π per unit area at specified points in space, which surrounds the antenna. In spherical coordinate system, the origin of which coincides with the antenna phase center, coordinates of an arbitrary point M are determined by the formulae [5, 11]

$$R = \sqrt{(H_A - H_T)^2 + \rho^2}, \tag{10.1}$$

$$\theta_m = \mathrm{acos}\left((\rho\cos\varphi\cos\alpha - (H_A - H_T)\sin\alpha)/R\right), \tag{10.2}$$

$$\varphi = \mathrm{atan}\left(x/y\right), \tag{10.3}$$

where H_A is the antenna suspension height above the ground [m]; α is the angle of deviation of the maximum antenna radiation direction from the horizon plane; H_T is the horizon plane height in which the energy flux density is calculated; (x, y) is the M point Cartesian coordinates. The above mentioned parameters are shown in Fig. 10.1.

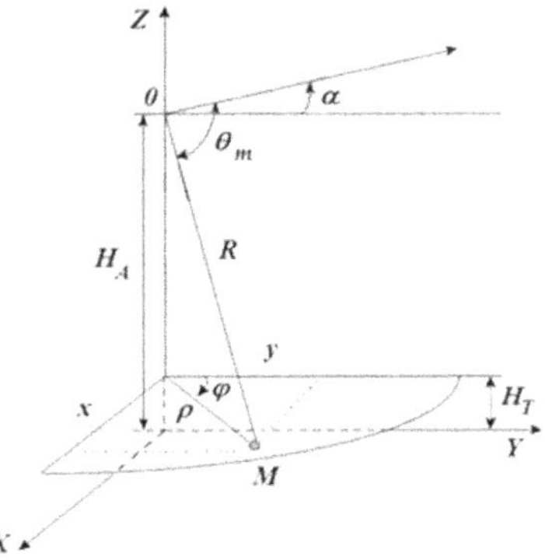

Fig. 10.1. Geometry of the energy flux density calculation at an arbitrary point.

- *Information volume.* The volume of the visualization information depends directly on the following aspects: the presentation form of the solution (3D or 2D); spatial layout of calculation points; plot type and the presentation aspects. When solving the problem, it is necessary to consider both the criteria formulated above and the physical meaning of the visualized variables.

Obtaining 3D solution to assess the electromagnetic environment is counterproductive. First and foremost, this is due to the fact that computational cost in 3D case is significantly higher than in 2D. Secondly, it is impossible to analyze electromagnetic environment at the obtained plot by energy flux density levels. This, in turn, does not allow formulating recommendations to solve practical problems of safety assessment described above. The 2D solution meets the above mentioned criteria; however, it requires specifying the calculation planes positions. These positions can be selected based on the third criterion. Thus, when solving the first practical problem, the calculation plane should be located 2 m above the ground or above the roof if we consider rooftop antenna; the height corresponds to the definition of the sanitary protection zone [5, 11]. For the worst-case scenario, additional calculations are carried out at the height of the antenna phase center, when the antenna radiation is at its maximum. To solve the second practical problem, the vertical plane must pass through the antenna phase center and the direction of antenna maximum radiation (or another direction of interest). Thus, the electromagnetic environment can be assessed either in one plane or in several.

Finally, computational costs essentially depend both on the calculated point layout within the calculation plane, and on plane dimensions. To obtain reliable results and take electrodynamic effects into an account, the spacing of plane grid nodes, where the calculated points are located, is to be about 0.25 λ (where $\lambda = c / f$ is the wavelength in free space; $c = 3 \cdot 10^8$ m/s is the speed of light; f is transmitter frequency [Hz]). The calculated plane dimensions of the antenna relative phase center, as shown in [13], should be $14 \times 14 \times 40$ of antenna linear size for near-omnidirectional antenna; $14 \times 14 \times 40$ of antenna linear size in the front half-space and $1 \times 1 \times 7$ in the back half-space for unidirectional antenna (e.g. dish antenna). The largest size of the plane corresponds to the direction of maximum radiation.

With this layout, the number of calculation points for cellular communication systems (where wavelength is about 0.1 m) will approach $2 \cdot 10^9$. The dimension of the problem can be significantly reduced by a combination of two techniques proposed by the authors [13]. First is to assess the electromagnetic environment in the front and back half-spaces (for dish antennas) separately. Second is selecting point coordinates with the adaptive algorithm, which takes into an account the overall structure of the generated electromagnetic field. It was shown in [13], that these measures can reduce computational costs by almost 20 % for dish antenna, while reducing the number of calculation points to $3.4 \cdot 10^4$ for each half-space.

- Aspects of plot presentation. To present the visual results, contour plot is the most convenient plot type for analysis. Its lines should correspond to displayed variable levels. This type of plot allows selecting sanitary protection zones corresponding to the maximum allowable level of energy flux density equal to 10 μW/cm^2 [11, 12].

Thus, the analysis of the aspects of solution presentation for electromagnetic environment assess problem allows us formulating the requirements towards the program implementation.

10.4. Dividing Calculation Space into Characteristic Regions with an Account to the Reflective Properties of the Roof

The computational forecasting method assumes that the further development of the algorithm is determined by electrodynamic models [5]. Models are complex; they depend on antenna structure and suspension height above the roof or above the ground and comprise a set of solutions to canonical problems. Each of these problems holds for a separate spatial region, the so-called characteristic region. In the general case, two model types are considered, which take into account either the influence of a flat reflecting surface (for example, a roof or the Earth), or diffraction phenomena on the antenna structure. In the second case, the influence of reflection from the underlying surface is neglected, since the directivity pattern of the antennas is considered to be unidirectional. In respect to this, let us consider the aspects of visualization algorithm design for each model type.

Let's start with a simpler antenna structure. Here it is necessary to consider the reflective properties of a finite size surface. In turn, this case can be divided into two options:

- The reflecting surface is horizontally oriented,

- The reflecting surface is at some angle to horizontal surface of the Earth (pitched roof).

Both options are considered when assessing the electromagnetic environment near rooftop cell tower antenna. Roof shape depends on the area climate; it can be either horizontally oriented surface or have a certain pitch angle to the horizon (pitched roof). Since the simulation for a pitched roof is carried out by upgrading the solution for a flat roof, let us start with the algorithm analysis in case of a horizontally oriented surface.

10.4.1. Horizontally Oriented Rooftop

In [5, 11, 14, 15] it was shown that three characteristic regions must be identified, as shown in Fig. 10.2(a) to assess the electromagnetic environment near cell tower antenna mounted on a flat rooftop. Characteristic regions are selected by solving the classical electrodynamic problem of wedge diffraction with the geometric theory of diffraction [16]. According to it, the following regions are distinguished: the region of the direct and reflected beam superposition (region I), the region where only the direct beam exists (region II) and the shadow region (region III). Point Φ on Fig. 10.2(a) corresponds to antenna phase center. Interference phenomena at the region boundaries ("light-shadow" borders) are not considered when assessing the electromagnetic environment.

It is necessary to consider the contribution of direct and reflected waves in region I, as it is clear from the analysis of the electrodynamic problem for the region. Hence, Fig. 10.1 is converted to Fig. 10.2 (b), and relations (10.1)-(10.3) are replaced by the following ones

$$r_1 = \sqrt{\rho^2 + (h_1 - h_2)^2}, \tag{10.4}$$

$$r_2 = \sqrt{\rho^2 + (h_1 + h_2)^2}, \tag{10.5}$$

$$\theta_1 = \text{asin}\left(\frac{h_1 - h_2}{r_1}\right), \tag{10.6}$$

$$\theta_2 = \theta_1 + \text{atan}\left(\frac{h_1 + h_2}{\rho}\right) - \text{atan}\left(\frac{h_1 - h_2}{\rho}\right), \tag{10.7}$$

$$\varphi_1 = \varphi_2 = \varphi = \text{atan}(y_M / x_M), \tag{10.8}$$

$$\rho = \sqrt{x_M^2 + y_M^2} \tag{10.9}$$

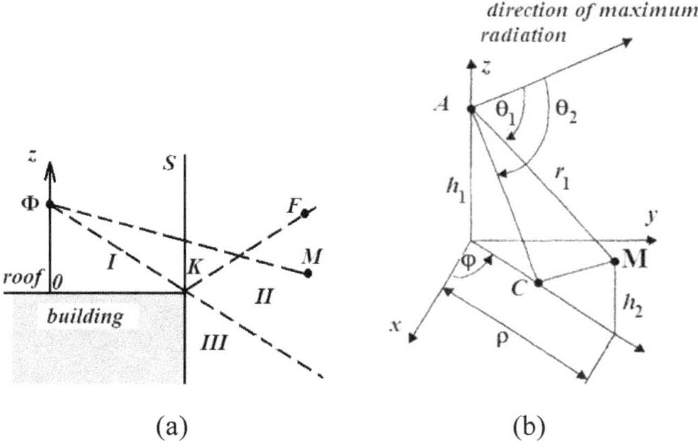

Fig. 10.2. *M* point position: (a) is the geometry of the problem in the vertical plane; (b) is the geometry of the problem in *I* region.

The meaning of the parameters in (10.4)-(10.9) is shown in Fig. 10.2(b).

Edge diffraction phenomenon is considered only for the edge closest to the antenna. In this regard, the position of K point is calculated at ij^{th} roof edge as a result of its intersection by the straight line between the antenna phase center Φ and the observation point M located at an angle of φ. The coordinates of K point are determined by the following relations

$$x_k = a_{ij} / (k_\varphi - k_{ij}), \tag{10.10}$$

$$y_k = k_\varphi x_k, \tag{10.11}$$

$$k_{ij} = (y_j - y_i)/(x_j - x_i), \tag{10.12}$$

$$a_{ij} = [y_i(x_j - x_i) - x_i(y_j - y_i)]/(x_j - x_i), \tag{10.13}$$

$$k_\varphi = \tan\varphi, \tag{10.14}$$

where k_{ij} is the slope factor of $ij^{\,\text{th}}$ edge and a_{ij} is the absolute term of an equation for $ij^{\,\text{th}}$ edge

$$y = k_{ij}x + a_{ij} \tag{10.15}$$

According to the calculated coordinates, the corresponding roof region is selected. An example of dividing into regions for the roof with the corner coordinates $A(x_a, y_a, z_a)$, $B(x_b, y_b, z_b)$, $C(x_c, y_c, z_c)$ and $D(x_d, y_d, z_d)$, is shown on Fig. 10.3.

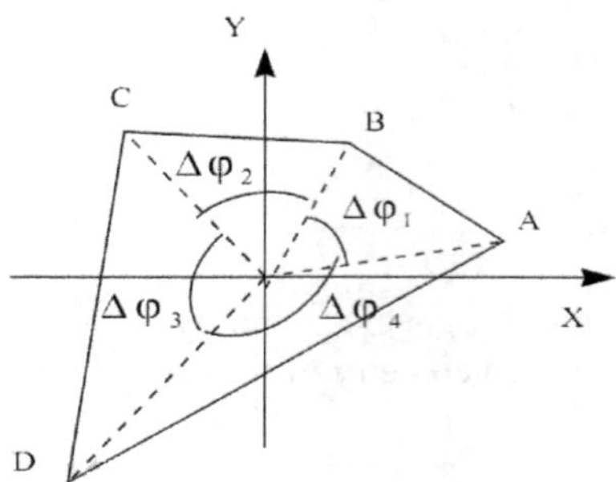

Fig. 10.3. Dividing the horizontal plane of a roof along the edges.

In the following, the selected edge is divided into regions I-III in the vertical plane, and we determine the characteristic region where the calculated point M (observation point) belongs to. The conditions of M point belonging can be written as

$$d_{\Phi M} = \sqrt{x_M^2 + y_M^2 + (h - z_M)^2}, \tag{10.16}$$

$$M \in \begin{cases} I, \ for \ (d_{\Phi M} > d_{\Phi S}) \cup (z_I \leq z_M \leq z_{II}), \\ II, \ for \ (d_{\Phi M} \leq d_{\Phi S}) \cup (z_M > 0), \\ III, \ for \ (d_{\Phi M} > d_{\Phi S}) \cup (\cos \Phi M < \cos \Phi K), \\ building, \ for \ (d_{\Phi M} \leq d_{\Phi S}) \cup (z_M \leq 0), \end{cases} \quad (10.17)$$

$$d_{\Phi S} = \sqrt{x_S^2 + y_S^2 + z_S^2}, \quad (10.18)$$

$$\cos_{\Phi M} = (z_M - h) / d_{\Phi M}, \quad (10.19)$$

$$\cos_{\Phi K} = (z_K - z_\Phi) / d_{\Phi K}, \quad (10.20)$$

$$z_I = x_M (z_K - h) / x_k + h, \quad (10.21)$$

$$z_{II} = (x_M - x_K)(h - z_K) / (x_\Phi - x_k) + z_K, \quad (10.22)$$

where h is phase center Φ height above the rooftop.

10.4.2. Pitched Rooftop

The relations for the pitched roof can be obtained by converting the expressions of Section 10.4.1 with the following transformations:

- by introducing Cartesian coordinate system *0xyz* with the plane *x0y* coincident to the roof surface *ABCD*. The geometry of the problem is shown in Fig. 10.4.

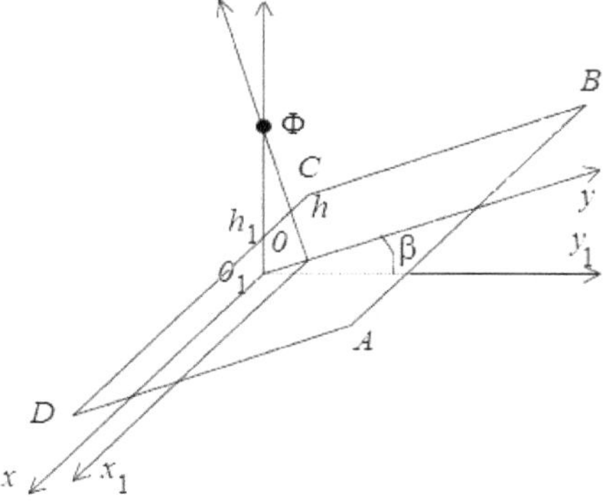

Fig. 10.4. The geometry of the pitched roof problem.

In this coordinate system, antenna phase center Φ will have height h_1 above the roof surface. The normally distance to the roof is still equal to h. These heights are linked by an expression that takes into an account the roof pitch angle β.

$$h = h_1 \cos\beta \tag{10.23}$$

- by introducing another Cartesian coordinate system $0x_1y_1z_1$, obtained from the given one with the following transformations: parallel translation of an origin point to point 0 (which is antenna phase center projection on a plane $x0y$) and plane rotation by angle α. The displacement value is determined by the relations [5, 11]

$$y_0 = h_1 \sin\beta \cos\beta, \tag{10.24}$$

$$z_0 = h_1 \sin^2\beta \tag{10.25}$$

The rotation matrix is the following

$$M_p = \begin{bmatrix} \cos\beta & 0 & \sin\beta \\ 0 & 0 & 0 \\ -\sin\beta & 0 & \cos\beta \end{bmatrix} \tag{10.26}$$

In the newly introduced coordinate system one of the planes ($0x_1y_1$) is parallel to the ground surface, which corresponds to the case of a flat roof. The further calculations of characteristic regions are carried out according to the flat roof algorithm (see Section 10.4.1).

10.5. Dividing Calculation Space into Characteristic Regions with an Account to Diffraction Phenomena on Antenna Structure

A more complicated electromagnetic field structure can be found near dish antennas. In the general case of axisymmetric structures, the space is divided into 5 characteristic regions (zones), whose boundaries depend on the mirror type: long-focus (half-aperture angle $\psi_0 < \pi/2$) and short-focus ($\psi_0 > \pi/2$). The boundaries of the characteristic regions for both cases are given in Figs. 10.5 and 10.6 respectively.

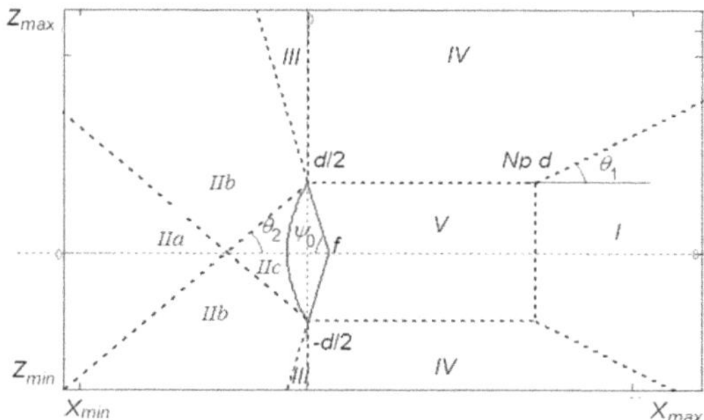

Fig. 10.5. Dividing the space into characteristic regions with an account to diffraction phenomena on long-focus dish antenna structure.

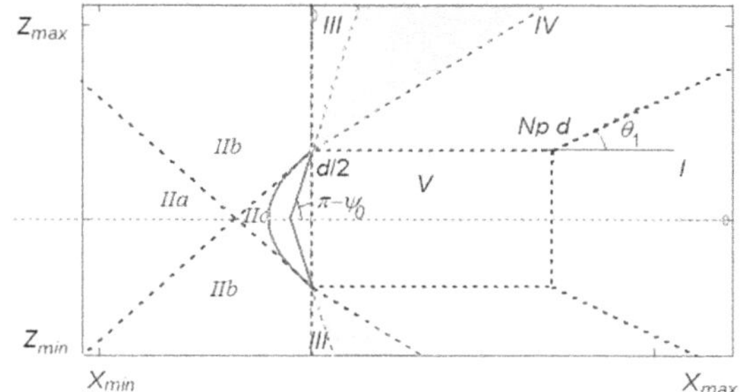

Fig. 10.6. Dividing the space into characteristic regions with an account to diffraction phenomena on short-focus dish antenna structure.

These areas correspond to the following solutions of electrodynamic problems. In region I (the region of the main lobe and the side lobes close to it), the aperture component of the field dominates, and in region II the diffraction components dominate. In turn, region II is divided into subregions: in the subregion IIa, the entire antenna edge is visible, in subregion IIb only part of the edge is visible, in subregion IIc, the mirror edge is invisible. Region IV consists of the space where the components of the electromagnetic field, emitted along the far side lobes of the directivity pattern, have the greatest influence. Region V (beam) characterizes the ultra-close radiation zone. Regions I, IV and V belong to the front half-space of the antenna, while region II is the back half-space. Region III is the boundary region between the front and back half-space.

$$-N \cdot d \leq x \leq NV \cdot d \,, \quad -H_A \leq z \leq NT \cdot d \,, \tag{10.27}$$

where NB, NV are $0x$ dimensions (number of antenna diameters d) of the half-spaces, front and back to antenna aperture, NT is $0z$ vertical size (number of antenna diameters d) in the upper half-space and H_A is antenna suspension height above the ground.

It should be noted that the consideration of diffraction phenomena on the antenna structure in the electromagnetic environment visualization process requires the imaging the antenna profile. In the coordinate system $x0z$, the origin of which coincides with antenna aperture center, antenna profile is defined by the following functions [17]:

- for long-focus antenna

$$\tilde{x}(\tilde{z}) = \tilde{z}^2 / 4f - 0.5d / \tan \psi_0 \tag{10.28}$$

- for short-focus antenna

$$\tilde{x}(\tilde{z}) = \tilde{z}^2 / 4f - 0.0625d^2 / f, \tag{10.29}$$

where ψ_0 if half-aperture angle, the $0z$ variable in the interval of $-0.5d \leq \tilde{z} \leq 0.5d$ and f is the focus distance defined with a formula:

$$f = 0.5d / \tan(0.5\psi_0) \tag{10.30}$$

The region II boundaries for the specified parameters are determined by the ratios:

- for long-focus dish

$$A = \{0; 0.5d\}, \quad B = \{X_{\max}; (f + X_{\max}) \tan(\pi - \psi_0)\} \tag{10.31}$$

is for short-focus dish

$$A = \{0; 0.5d\}, \quad B = \{X_{\min}; 0.5d + |X_{\min}| \tan \psi_0\}, \tag{10.32}$$

where $X_{\min}$ and $X_{\max}$ are the minimum and maximum coordinates of the studied region, which are determined from the inequalities (10.27).

The inner boundaries of region II, which divide it into subregions IIa, IIb, and IIc, are determined by the upper and lower tangents given by the coordinates of two points [18]:

- for long-focus dish

$$A = \{X_{max}; 4f(X_{max} - 2f)/d\}, \quad B = \{X_{max}; 4f(X_{max})/d\} \quad (10.33)$$

- for short-focus dish

$$A = \{-2f(1 + 2|Z_{max}|)/d; Z_{min}\}, \quad B = \{0; 0.5d\} \qquad (10.34)$$

The lower tangent is symmetric to the upper one.

The boundary of region III with regions II and IV passes along the line $x = 0$ at $Z_{min} \leq z \leq Z_{max}$, and the boundaries between areas I and IV are defined by a line with the following coordinates

$$A = \{Np \cdot d; 0.5d\}, \qquad B = \{X_{max}; 0.5d + (|X_{min}| - Np \cdot d)\tan\theta_1\},$$
$$(10.35)$$

where θ_1 is the angular half-aperture of region consisting of the main and near side lobes.

Region V is the antenna structure region; it is located inside a hypothetical cylinder with a base area equal to the area of the aperture and height of $(2..4)d$.

Relations (10.27)-(10.35) are given for the case when the antenna maximum radiation direction is inclined to the horizon by an angle of $\alpha = 0°$. When the angle is changed, the boundary coordinate matrices are multiplied by the rotation matrix

$$M_{pr} = \begin{pmatrix} \cos\alpha & -\sin\alpha \\ \sin\alpha & \cos\alpha \end{pmatrix} \qquad (10.36)$$

An example of dividing the space into characteristic regions for a deflected antenna is shown in Fig. 10.7.

10.6. Conventional Software Analysis

It should be noted that the standards for the electromagnetic environment assessment are valid only in some countries of the former Soviet Union.

In this regard, in these countries there is a large number of specialized software, which was developed to meet the requirements listed in [11, 12]. The examples include the software package for the electromagnetic environment analysis "PK AEMO" [19], as well as programs to calculate sanitary protection zones near radiating radio engineering objects like SanZone [20], CalcSZZ [21], RPS2 [22], "Software package POEMA" [23], "Antenna influence calculation" [24]. The main purpose of these programs is to create a sanitary-epidemiological certificate for a transmitting radio engineering object. So, if any of these programs is run, the result is drawing the object and sanitary protection zone boundaries. However, there are two main shortcomings of the above mentioned programs in terms of factors, which change the electromagnetic field structure. First, it is impossible to display the characteristic zones boundaries in the spatial region near the radiating object. Second, it is impossible to give scientifically based recommendations for carrying out the research on the calculation point layout and its spacing with the instrumental procedure. As a result, the number of calculation points can be overestimated, and hence, the computational cost will be increased.

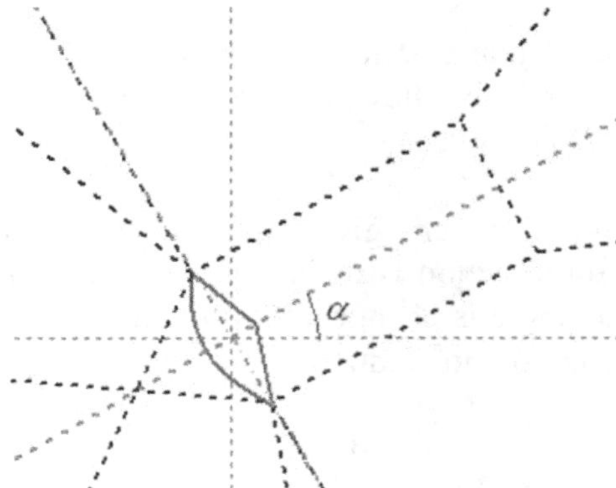

Fig. 10.7. Dividing the space into characteristic regions for a deflected long-focus dish antenna.

10.6.1. A Model Considering the Reflection from a Flat Surface

To confirm this, let us use the example from [25]. In this work, the authors estimated the data efficiency for a full-scale experiment from

[26], conducted by instrumental procedure. The research zone was considered to be a circle of 300 m radius around the cell tower radiating antenna. Fig. 10.8 shows the percentage base of location distribution for the measurements of the generated power level of the electromagnetic field. For these locations, the electromagnetic environment data, shown in Table 10.1, was obtained.

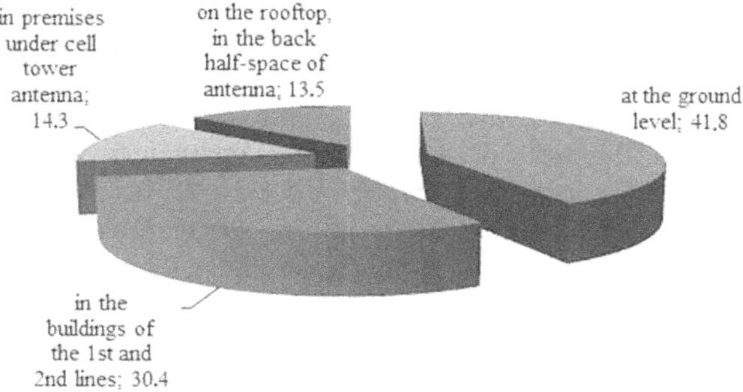

Fig. 10.8. Distribution of instrumental measurements locations without prior evaluation by computational forecast method.

Table 10.1. Electromagnetic environment data obtained by measuring [26].

Measurement location	Mean value of energy flux density, $\mu W/cm^2$	Maximum value of energy flux density, $\mu W/cm^2$
Roof	2-10	500
Premises under cell tower antenna	< 2	10
Adjacent residential area	0.2-0.7	5
1st and 2nd line of buildings	0.5-1	30

The cost effectiveness for the research in [26], which was carried out by instrumental procedure, was analyzed using the results of a computational experiment. The computational experiment was carried out with the programs developed by the authors [27, 28], which provide calculation and visualization of the electromagnetic environment for an arbitrary layout of calculation points. To assess the result reliability for the developed programs, the authors conducted studies of worst-case scenario from [26], which corresponds to the maximum power level and the location on the roof near the antenna. This choice was due to the lack of information available in [26] on the building height and the antenna location. A computational experiment was carried out for two types of antenna: an omnidirectional and a directional. In the latter case, the electromagnetic field was assumed to be excited by a GSM RAO-14GL-70 antenna with operating range 860..970 MHz, gain of 14 dB, the main lobe width of 15° in the H-plane, and 70° in the E-plane, transmitter power of 40 W. The obtained visualizations of the electromagnetic field structure in the vertical plane for the considered antennas from [15] are shown in Figs. 10.9 and 10.10 divided into characteristic regions with indicated levels of energy flux density. Figs. 10.9, 10.10 and Table 10.1 analysis shows that instrumental studies in [26] were carried out for an omnidirectional antenna, for in this case the energy flux density of 500 μW/cm^2 is created on the roof of a building. In case of directional antenna, the energy is radiated away from the roof. The calculated maximum power level on the roof coincides with the data from [26]; it confirms the correctness of the developed programs, therefore, they can be used to develop recommendations for conducting instrumental studies.

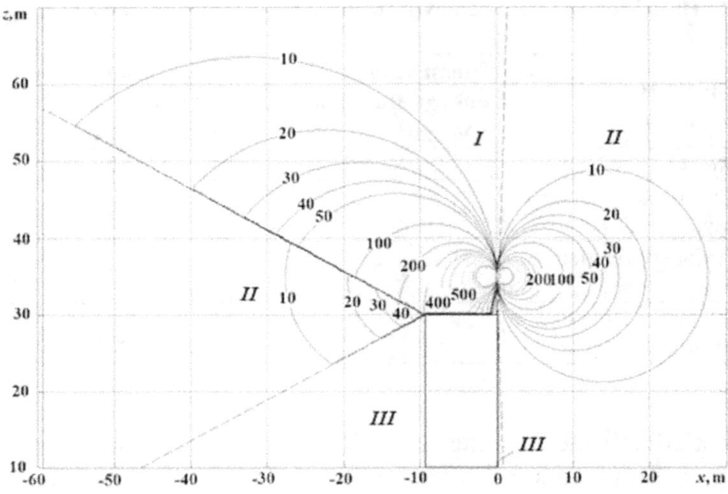

Fig. 10.9. Electromagnetic environment visualization in vertical plane near cell tower omnidirectional antenna.

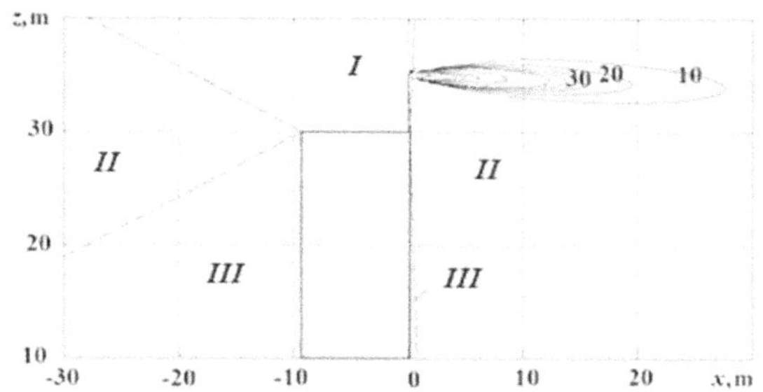

Fig. 10.10. Electromagnetic environment visualization in vertical plane near cell tower directional antenna.

The results of a computational experiment were compared with the data in [26]; the developed programs provide reliable results and, therefore, can be used to develop recommendations for conducting instrumental studies. In particular, for the experiment described in [26] the radius of the research zone could be reduced to 100 m without losing in accuracy. In the premises of the building with the cell tower antenna mounted on the roof (even on the roof edge), research could be performed in a smaller scope, since they are not illuminated by the directional antenna. Measurements should be performed without fail on the open areas of the upper floors of the building with the cell tower only and only in the case of their large dimensions.

10.6.2. A Model Considering Diffraction Phenomena on Antenna Structure

An example of the influence of measurement point spacing on the visualization accuracy of the electromagnetic environment for a dish antenna is shown in Figs. 10.11 and 10.12. They are the contour plots of electromagnetic field structure excited by a dish antenna of 1.44 m diameter with half-aperture equal to 89°, directional coefficient equal to 30 dB, the transmitter power is 100 W and the measurement points spacing is $d = 1.51$ m and $d = 0.1$ m, respectively.

An analysis of the results given above shows that, for dish antennas, inhomogeneities are observed in the structure of the excited electromagnetic field. The inhomogeneities are caused by diffraction phenomena on the mirror edge. As a consequence, increasing the calculated points spacing can lead to a significant roughening of the results. The field structure heterogeneity allows the use of the adaptive grid spacing selection algorithm described earlier [13]. According to that algorithm, in the antenna back half-space the grid spacing should be minimal, since in this direction the diffraction phenomena on the mirror edges appear at relatively small distances from the mirror. In the front half-space, a decrease in the grid spacing is impractical, since it leads only to small refinements.

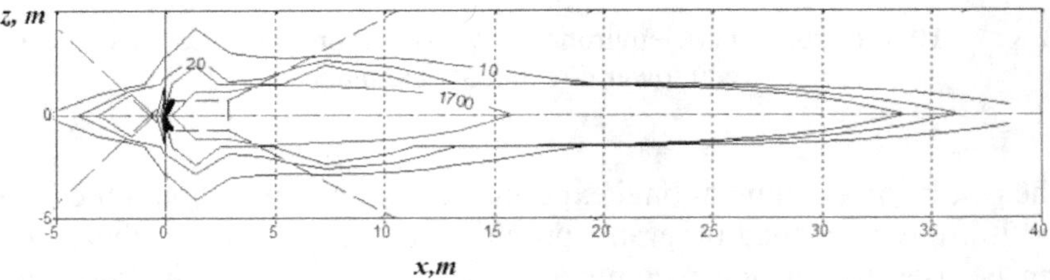

Fig. 10.11. Electromagnetic environment visualization near dish antenna (the spacing of measurement points is $d = 1.51$ m).

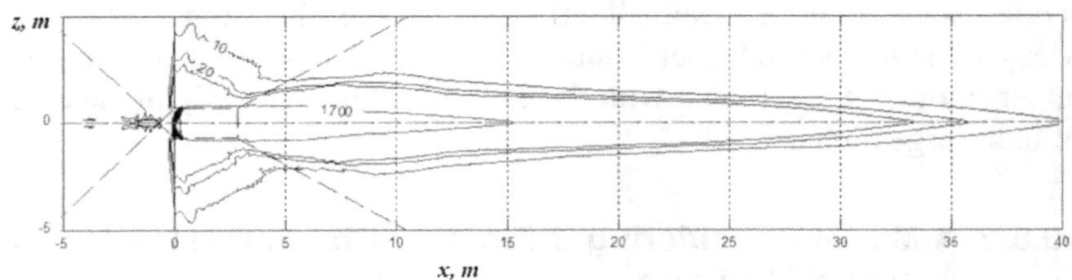

Fig. 10.12. Electromagnetic environment visualization near dish antenna (the spacing of measurement points is $d = 0.1$ m).

10.6.3. Notes on the Choice of Programming Language

When developing one's own programs for assessing the electromagnetic environment near cellular communication antennas within the framework of socially oriented electromagnetic monitoring, a profound interest is found in plotting the sanitary protection zones boundaries, i.e. isolines for the level of 10 μW/cm^2. This requirement has already been cited earlier in Section 10.3.

Let us analyze two conventional software packages that are commonly used to assess electromagnetic environment near radiating objects: MathCad and MATLAB language environments. Both software packages perform operations on complex numbers, which are essential to describe the electric and magnetic field strength vectors. Both environments have a tool to draw contour plots. However, in MathCad, the number of displayed levels and their values are automatically selected from the calculated ones. As a result, the required level of $10\ \mu W/cm^2$ may not be reflected in the plot. In the MATLAB package, these parameters are customizable.

Another MathCad disadvantage for developing programs for electromagnetic environment assessing is the complicated calculation algorithm, which results in large file size. Some operations are implemented as external procedures in MathCad; hence, it is more complicated than MATLAB package.

Summarizing, we can say that the MathCad language environment can be used to debug a program. It is advisable, however, to select MATLAB to build the final program. The MATLAB developed programs can be used only in the educational process, since it is necessary to have the language environment installed to run the calculation program. Executable programs can be obtained, for example, by converting MATLAB program to a C ++ based program [29].

10.7. Conclusions

The results of the research show that a negative consequence of a significant expansion of wireless communication technologies is the strengthening of electromagnetic background near cell tower antennas. The population living close to cell towers has serious concerns about the harmful health effects of the electromagnetic field excited by the antennas. Social tension can be eased by socially oriented electromagnetic monitoring with the electromagnetic environment displayed in a way that is easy to understand for non-professional user.

Visual form is the most straightforward type of displaying the electromagnetic environment state in the framework of socially oriented monitoring. A relatively narrow application field imposes special requirements on both the displayed results and the solution methodology.

It is shown that the results of computational experiments obtained with the programs based on computational forecast method are the most convenient for analyzing the electromagnetic environment and giving scientifically based recommendations to alter it. The materials of the chapter, which relate to the software implementation specifications for visualizing the electromagnetic environment assessment, show that conventional specialized software packages does not fully meet the specifications. As a consequence, independent program development is required.

Acknowledgements

All the authors express deepest appreciation to Professor Yu.M. Spodobaev for his goodwill towards this research.

References

[1]. K. Schvab, The Four Industrial Revolution, *Crown Business*, NY, 2017.
[2]. V. Mordachev, A. Svistunov, Reduction of the radiated power of cellular base station on urban area at high intrasystem EMC requirements, in *Proceedings of the Conference on Electromagnetic Compatibility (EMC'15)*, Dresden, Germany, 16-22 August 2015, pp. 1153-1158.
[3]. M. Markov, Electromagnetic Field in Biology and Medicine, *CRC Press*, NY, 2015.
[4]. M. Maslov, M. Spodobaev, Yu. Spodobaev, Modern problems of electromagnetic ecology, *Telecommunications*, Vol. 10, 2014, pp. 39-42.
[5]. Yu. Spodobayev, D. Kubanov, Electromagnetic Ecology Basics, *Radio i Svyaz'*, Moscow, 2000 (in Russian).
[6]. A. Suleiman, T. Gee, A. Krihnapillai, K. Khall, M. Hamid, M. Mustapa, Electromagnetic radiation health effects in exposed and non-exposed residents in Penang, *Journal of Geoscience and Environment Protection*, Vol. 2, 2014, pp. 77-83.
[7]. O. Pchjol'nik, On the possible cell tower influence on the incidence rates of malignant neoplasms of the oral cavity and pharynx, *International Journal of Experimental Education*, Vol. 3-2, 2017, pp. 178-179.
[8]. M. Zvezdina, Yu. Shokova, H. Al-Ali, G. Al-Farhan, Electromagnetic background strengthening as a negative result of digital economy and advance (Review), *International Journal Theoretical & Applied Science*, Vol. 59, Issue 3, 2018, pp. 29-42.
[9]. WHO Library Cataloguing-in-Publication Data 2004, Establishing a Dialogue on Risk from Electromagnetic Fields,
http://www.who.int/peh-emf/publications/en/russian_risk.pdf

[10]. V. Dovbish, V. Sivkov, Yu. Spodobaev, Visualization of an electromagnetic environment established by telecommunication means, located on major territories, *Antennas*, Vol. 10, Issue 113, pp. 58-62.

[11]. MG 4.3-1167-02, Methodological guidelines for energy flux density estimation for electromagnetic field for location of radio facilities with operating band of 300 MHz – 300 GHz, *Ministry of Health of the Russian Federation*, Moscow, 2002.

[12]. SanPin 2.1.8/2.2.4.1190-03 Hygienic requirements on land-based mobile communication location and operation, *Ministry of Health of the Russian Federation*, Moscow, 2003.

[13]. M. Zvezdina, Yu. Shokova, M. Krivtsova, T. Golovko, A. Cherskaya, Visualization characteristics of electromagnetic environment near communication system reflector antenna, in *Proceedings of the Conference on Radiation and Scattering of Electromagnetic Waves (RSEMW'17)*, Divnomorskoe, Russia, 26-30 June 2015, pp. 73-76.

[14]. M. Zvezdina, Yu. Shokova, A. Shokov, S. Gorbunov, Visual representation of energy flux density for mobile system serial in MATHCAD, *Modeling of Artificial Intelligence*, Vol. 1, Issue 5, 2015, pp. 42-48.

[15]. M. Zvezdina, Yu. Shokova, N. Kundryukova, V. Kutukova, A. Pozdnyakova, Visualization of electromagnetic environment near GSM antennae, *IOP Conference Series: Earth and Environmental Science*, Vol. 50, 2017, http://iopscience.iop.org/article/10.1088/1755-1315/50/1/012029/pdf

[16]. J. Kong, Electromagnetic Waves, *Jon Wiley & Sons*, NY, 1986.

[17]. C. Balanis, Antenna Theory. Analysis and Design, *Jon Wiley & Sons*, NY, 1997.

[18]. M. Zvezdina, Yu. Shokova, A. Shokov, Visual representation characteristics of calculation results in laboratory research on electromagnetic ecology, in *Proceedings of the Conference on Application of Information and Communication Technologies (AICT'15)*, Rostov-on-Don, Russia, 14-16 October 2015, pp. 399-403.

[19]. Electromagnetic environment analysis software package «PK AEMO», http://pkaemo.ru/

[20]. SanZone 5.1 - Sanitary protection zone calculation, https://www.ctt-group.ru/sanzone

[21]. CalcSZZ v18 – Calculation program for sanitary protection zones and zones of limited development for transmitting radio objects, http://texnosoft.wixsite.com/calcszz

[22]. RPS2: Radio Planning System 2, http://www.rps2.ru/

[23]. Software package POEMA, http://www.proincom.biz/index.html

[24]. Antenna influence calculation, http://www.rva.com.ua

[25]. Innovation Application in Radio System Development (M. Zvezdina, Ed.), *Publishing House of the Academy of Natural History*, Moscow, 2015.

[26]. O. Grigoriev, A. Merkulov, Hygienic studies of the electromagnetic environment around cell towers, *Bulletin of Medical Internet Conferences*, Vol. 2, Issue 6, 2012, pp. 458-460.

[27]. Electromagnetic environment visualization for a residential building roof with an antenna mounted, № 2015612312 (RU), http://www1.fips.ru/fips_servl/fips_servlet

[28]. Electromagnetic environment visualization in the vertical plane near the building with cell antenna, № 2015615602 (RU), http://www1.fips.ru/fips_servl/fips_servlet

[29]. B. Stroustrup, The C++ Programming Language, *Addison-Wesley Professional*, New Jersey, 2013.

Chapter 11

Artificial Intelligence Approaches Applied to Arabic Digits, Letters and Isolated Words Recognition

Lotfi Boussaid, Mohamed Hassine

11.1. Introduction

Speech is the predominant mode of human communication for every day interaction. It is also the preferred mode for human-machine interaction [1]. The design and implementation of voice interaction between man and machine requires the involvement of a wide spectrum of disciplines, namely linguistics (i.e., phonetics, phonology, prosody, and computational linguistics), computer science, ergonomics, and speech processing. The current advances in the microelectronic devices with the advent of digital signal processors (DSP) have facilitated the availability of complex commercial speech recognition systems. Hence, speech recognition is becoming a very important concept for any type of system requiring human interaction in today's high-tech pervasive services. Controlling a system with speech rather than using hardware e.g. keyboard or keypad definitely much more easy and appealing. Recognition should be accurate and quick.

On the other hand, feature extraction methods and classifiers have a direct influence on speech recognition systems [2].

Speech recognition systems falls into two classes: isolated word recognition and continuous speech recognition. Each class can be further

Lotfi Boussaid
EµE Lab, Ecole Nationale d'Ingénieurs de Monastir (ENIM), University of Monastir, Monastir, Tunisia

subdivided into two categories as speaker dependent and speaker independent.

Speaker dependent speech recognition systems operate only on the speech of a particular speaker for which the system is trained while the speaker independent systems can be operated on the speech of any speaker.

Nowadays, the automatic speech recognition attracts the attentions of researchers due to the development of communication tools (computers, mobiles, internet, etc.). Compared to other languages such as English, French, Japanese, Spanish, etc., the research in Arabic speech recognition is poor due to the complexity of such language in different levels: Phonetic, linguistic, semantic, contextual, morpho-syntactic, etc.

In Arabic language, there are three classes: Standard or Classical Arabic (CA), which is the language of the Quran, Modern standard Arabic (MSA), which is used in media and studied in schools, and finally the dialect which is the spoken language that varies from one country to another or even from one region to other in the same country.

In this chapter, we are particularly interested in recognizing Arabic digits, letters and isolated words. Words are a combination of phonemes, which represent the smallest contrastive unit in the sound system of a language. In a language or dialect, a phoneme is the smallest segmental unit of sound employed to form meaningful contrasts between utterances.

In Arabic, there are 34 phonemes, six of them are vowels and 28 are consonants [3]. We distinguish two classes of phonemes: pharyngeal and emphatic which characterize the Semitic language such as Arabic and Hebrew [4].

Arabic alphabets are used in many other languages beside Arabic such as Persian and Urdu. The allowed syllables in Arabic are: CV, CVC, and CVCC [5]. "C" represents a consonant and "V" represents a long or a short vowel [3].

In spoken Arabic, consonants are followed by four short vowels: "fatha", "dhamma", "kasra" and "soukoon". "Fatha" represents the /a/ sound and is an oblique dash over a letter. "Dhamma" represents the /u/ sound and has the shape of a comma over a letter. "Kasra" represents the /i/ sound and is an oblique dash under a letter. "Soukoon", which has the shape of a little circle over a letter [3].

In addition to these features that make speech recognition more complex, it should be noted that the speech signal has a property to be non-stationary. A normal speaker never pronounces the same alphabet two times identically because the speed and the period of uttering can vary from one time to another. Moreover, when the vocal tract is altered, the speech signal changes, the inter-speaker variability is evident, the same thing for the pitch, intonation and accent that vary with sexes, social, regional and national origins [6-9].

11.2. Theoretical Background

A speech recognition system usually consists of front-end signal processing and back-end speech recognition modules. The front-end is based on a set of advanced feature extraction techniques, whereas the back-end module uses artificial intelligence approaches such as Feed Forward Back Propagation Neuronal Network (FFBPNN), Radial Basis Function Neural Network (RBF), Cascade-Forward Back Propagation Neuronal Network (CFBPNN), etc.

The speech signals are slowly timed varying signals (quasi-stationary). When examined over a sufficiently short period of time (5-100 ms), its characteristics are fairly stationary. However, if for a period of time the signal characteristics change, this reflects to the different speech sounds being spoken. The information in speech signal is actually represented by short-term amplitude spectrum of the speech waveform. This allows us to extract features based on the short-term amplitude spectrum from speech (phonemes).

The fundamental difficulty of speech recognition is that the speech signal is highly variable due to different speakers, speaking rates, contents and acoustic conditions. The feature analysis component of a speech recognition system plays a crucial role in the overall performance of the system. Many feature extraction techniques are available, they include:

- Mel-frequency cepstral coefficients (MFCC),

- The first-order temporal derivative coefficients of MFCCs (ΔMFCCs),

- Linear predictive analysis (LPC),

- Linear predictive cepstral coefficients (LPCC),

- Perceptual linear predictive coefficients (PLP).

11.2.1. Cepstral Coefficients

The speech signal varies permanently in time according to the movement of the vocal tract. Consequently, analysis must be processed on short slide overlapped windows as a speech signal, which is considered to be stationary in a short time interval. The speech signal is the result of the convolution in time domain of the source and the vocal tract (filter) [10]:

$$s(n) \;=\; e(n).h(n)_i, \tag{11.1}$$

where $s(n)$ is the filter output, $e(n)$ is the excitation signal and $h(n)$ is the impulse response of the filter. In order to replace the convolution by an addition operation, one passes to the log-spectral domain by the following equation:

$$\log\big(S(f)\big) \;=\; \log\big(E(f)\big) + \log(H(f)), \tag{11.2}$$

where $S(f)$, $E(f)$ and $H(f)$ are the Fourier transform of $s(n)$, $e(n)$ and $h(n)$ respectively.

The real Cepster of the speech signal is obtained by applying the inverse of discrete Fourier transform (IDFT) to equation (11.2), then separation of the source (excitation signal) and the vocal tract (Transfer function) is realized by a time windowing called 'Liftrage' resulting to Cepsral Coefficients. This stage is also called 'homomorphic analyses and it's widely spread in automatic speech recognition domain.

11.2.2. Mel Frequency Cepstral Coefficients (MFCC)

The MFCC are computed by discrete cosine transform of the power spectrum of the speech signal. It is based on the Mel scale, which models the perception of the speech by the human ear.

The Mel scale behaves linearly between zero and 1000 Hz and logarithmically above, so it spaces small values and approaches large values: the main advantage of MFCC coefficients is that they are uncorrelated.

To extract MFCC coefficients five steps are employed:

The first step is to pre-emphasis the speech signal by applying a high pass filter in order to increase the high frequency contribution. In fact, when spreading via air, the magnitude of speech signal reduces as the frequency rises. In order to compensate the attenuated speech signal, it is passed through a high-pass filter (finite impulse filter) to recover the signal.

In practice, we use simply a finite impulsion filter (1,-0.97). If *s(n)* is the speech signal and $s_p(n)$ is the pre-emphasized signal then:

$$s_p(n) = s(n) - 0.97\, s(n-1) \qquad (11.3)$$

The second step is to window the speech signal by overlapped Hamming windows. These windows are of little sizes (about 25 ms) and are used to reduce the discontinuity and to avoid the leakage effect and consequently to improve the analysis of the speech. The Hamming window is given by:

$$h_1(n) = \begin{cases} 0.54 - 0.46 \cos(2\pi n/N - 1) \; if \; 0 \le n \; \le N \\ 0 \; otherwise \end{cases}, (11.4)$$

where N is the size of the window.

This window was chosen since it generates fewer oscillations than other windows and has reasonable side lobe and main lobe characteristics, which are required for the DFT computation. The hamming window has effectively better selectivity for large signals and is commonly used is speech processing.

The third one is to compute the Discrete Fourier Transform of each windowed frame resulting in Short Time Discrete Fourier Transform (STDFT). The values derived from here are then grouped together in critical bands and weighted by a triangular filter bank counting M filters called 'Mel-Spaced filter bank'.

The Mel scale is given by the following equation:

$$f_{Mel} = 2595 \times \log(1 + f_{Hz}/700), \qquad (11.5)$$

where f_{Hz} is the frequency in Hz.

In the fourth step, the logarithm of the band passed frequency response is computed. Finally, the Discrete Cosine Transform (DCT) is applied on the found data which results in Mel Frequency Cepstral Coefficients [11].

Assume that $H_m(k)$ is the frequency magnitude response of the mth filter of Mel filter bank, where k is the discrete frequency index in the digital domain. The filter output of the mth filter X_m can be expressed by:

$$X_m = \sum_{k=0}^{N/2-1} |S(k)|^2 \, |H_m(k)| \; 1 \le m \le M \qquad (11.6)$$

The Mel Frequency Cepstral Coefficients of the filtered information by the mth filter are represented by $c(m)$ as:

$$c(m) = DCT(\log(X_m)) \qquad (11.7)$$

11.2.3. The First-order Temporal Derivative Coefficients of MFCCs (ΔMFCCs)

ΔMFCCs are also known as differential coefficients. They correspond to the trajectories of the basic MFCCs coefficients over the time [12].

To calculate the delta coefficients, the following formula is used:

$$d_i = \frac{\sum_{n=1}^{N} n(C_{n+i} - C_{n-i})}{2 \sum_{n=1}^{N} n^2}, \qquad (11.8)$$

where d_i is the delta coefficient at frame i computed in terms of the corresponding basic Cepstral Coefficients C_{n+i} to C_{n-i}. A typical value for N is "2".

11.2.4. Linear Prediction Coding (LPC)

LPC is one of the most powerful speech analysis techniques and is a useful method for encoding quality speech at a low bit rate. The basic idea behind linear predictive analysis is that a specific speech sample at the current time can be approximated as a linear combination of past speech samples.

LP is a model based on human speech production. It utilizes a conventional source filter model, in which the glottal, vocal tract, and lip radiation transfer functions are integrated into one all-pole filter that simulates acoustics of the vocal tract. The principle behind the use of LPC is to minimize the sum of the squared differences between the original speech signal and the estimated speech signal over a finite duration. This could be used to give a unique set of predictor coefficients. These predictor coefficients are estimated every frame, which is normally 20 ms long. The predictor coefficients are represented by a_k. Another important parameter is the gain (G). The transfer function of the time varying digital filter is given by:

$$H(z) = \frac{G}{(1-\sum_{k=1}^{p} a_k z^{-k})},$$

(11.9)

where k = 1 to p, which will be 10 for the LPC-10 algorithm and 18 for the improved algorithm that is utilized [13].

11.2.5. Linear Predictive Cepstral Coefficients: LPCC

The LPCC feature extraction is based on the LPC analysis, which computes the Linear Predictive Coefficients, so the LPCC are calculated from the autoregressive modeling of the speech signal. They are very simple and well used since they allow a good representation of speech overlap vowels.

Each frame is represented by static coefficients: In general, thirteen or sixteen coefficients are usually used.

After pre-emphasizing and windowing the signal, the autocorrelation features are extracted then the Levinson Durbin is used for computing linear predictive coefficients (LPC) since the vocal tract is modeled by a digital all-pole filter [14]. Finally, the linear predictive Cepstral Coefficients (LPCC) for a speech frame are calculated by using the following formula:

$$\hat{v}[n] = \ln(G) \; for \; n = 0,$$

(11.10)

where G is the gain of the all-pole filter (the vocal tract).

$$\hat{v}[n] = a_n + \sum_{k=1}^{n-1} \hat{v}[k] \, a_{n-k} \; for \; 1 \leq n \leq p,$$

(11.11)

where $\hat{v}[n]$ is the nth linear predictive Cepstral Coefficient, p is the order of the LPC desirable analysis and a_n is the nth linear predictive coding coefficient computed with the Levinson-Durbin algorithm.

11.2.6. The Perceptually Based Linear Prediction Analysis (PLP and Rasta-PLP)

The PLP technique uses several operations inspired of perceptual data: that's to produce a hearing spectrum with the integration of few critical bands in the Bark scale, taking into account the isotone curve, compression of the spectrum in sound intensity and it is based on that of the LPCC.

We just add three steps such as:

- Integration of critical bands,

- Equal loudness pre-emphasis,

- Intensity-loudness conversion to simulate the power low of hearing.

The Rasta-PLP is based on the PLP method. It applies a regressive filter for analyzing and reducing noise [15]. Rasta-PLP is performed in few steps as shown in Fig. 11.1.

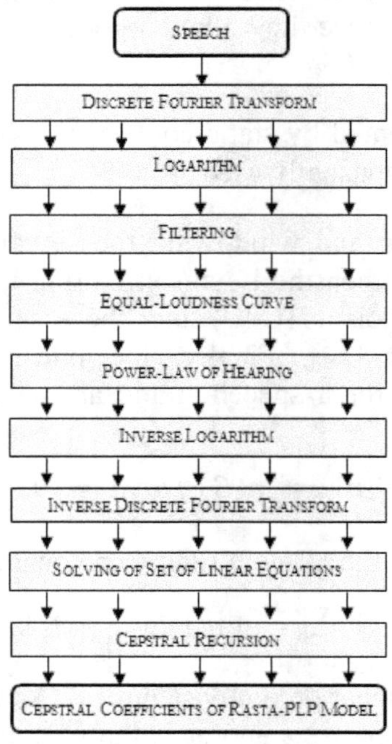

Fig. 11.1. Steps of Rasta-PLP.

11.2.7. The First-order Temporal Derivative Coefficients of PLPs (ΔPLPs)

The PLP feature vector describes only the power spectral envelope of a single frame, however differential coefficients give information about the dynamic evolution of the PLP coefficients over the time. ΔPLPs coefficients are computed similarly as in Equation (11.8).

11.2.8. Vector Quantization (VQ)

The vector quantization is a process of mapping vectors from a space vector to a finite number of regions in that space.

Here the LBG algorithm is used and implemented by the following recursive procedures [16]:

1. Design a 1-vector codebook: this is the centroid of the entire set of training vectors (hence, no iteration is required here),

2. Double the size of the codebook by splitting each current codebook Y_n according to the rule:

$$Y_n^+ = Y_n(1 + \varepsilon), Y_n^- = Y_n(1 - \varepsilon), \qquad (11.12)$$

   where n is varied from 1 to the current size of the codebook, and e is the splitting parameter (we choose e = 0.01),

3. Nearest-Neighbor Search: for each training vector, find the codeword in the current codebook that is closest (in terms of similarity measurement), and assign that vector to the corresponding cell (associated with the closest codeword),

4. Centroid Update: update the codeword in each cell using the centroid of the training vectors assigned to that cell,

5. Repeat Steps 3 and 4 until the average distance falls below a preset threshold,

6. Repeat Steps 2, 3 and 4 until a codebook size of M is designed.

11.2.9. Applying PCA

PCA is a method used to reduce the number of features used to represent data. The benefits of this dimensionality reduction include providing a simpler representation of the data, reduction in memory, and faster classification. The data is projected from a higher dimension to a lower dimensional space such that the error incurred by reconstructing the data in the higher dimension is minimized.

PCA is practically applied as the following algorithm [17]:

- Calculate the covariance matrix of the features on which we will apply PCA;

- Find the eigenvectors of the obtained covariance matrix;

- Extract diagonal of matrix as vector;

- Sort the variances in decreasing order;

- Project the original data set.

PCA algorithm is used after applying feature extraction techniques already mentioned in order to reduce the obtained feature matrix dimension corresponding to each word occurrence.

The projection of data with PCA approach generated, for each digit, a rate varying from 85 % to 89 % for the principal component and from 5 % to 9 % for the second component.

Thus, we obtained matrices of 13 rows and only 2 columns with a loss of information of about 7 % on average of all matrices. For all matrices, the two columns were concatenated in order to constitute one input vector for each digit, letter or word.

11.3. Arabic Digits Recognition

In this experiment, we investigated the feed forward back propagation neural network (FFBPNN) for the classification of two Maghrebian dialects: Tunisian and Moroccan.

The dialect used by the Moroccan speakers is called "La Darijja" and that of Tunisians is called "Darija". An Automatic Speech Recognition System is implemented in order to identify ten Arabic digits (from zero to nine). The implementation of our present system consists of two phases: The features extraction using a variety of popular hybrid techniques and the classification phase using the FFBPNN approach.

This experiment is performed in the following steps.

11.3.1. Speech Recording and Preprocessing

The speech corpus was developed with professional acoustical equipment: a digital Studer Professional Mixing Console On-air 2000 M2, a dynamic microphone MD 421 and a professional software. The speech was recorded in Mono wave files, at a sampling rate of 44100 Hz and coded in 16 bits.

Since Arabic dialect is under-resourced language, we prepared a proper corpus: where eight speakers: four Tunisians (2 males and 2 females) and four Moroccans (2 males and 2 females) pronounced the ten digits five times in their corresponding dialects (Tunisian or Moroccan dialect). The speech signal of each digit was stored in a proper wave file.

A trial consists in pronouncing all the digits by one speaker one time, so each speaker participates in the present corpus by five trials. Consequently, the digits corpus involves 40 trials, which counts 400 wave files.

The training corpus was built by 80 % of the entire digits corpus. The test corpus consisted of 20 % of the entire digits corpus which have not been in the training corpus. The validation corpus represents 20 % of the entire digits corpus and it involves data which have been in the training corpus.

Table 11.1 describes the SAMPA phonetic transcription of the ten digits in Tunisian and Moroccan dialects.

11.3.2. Applying FFBPNN

The obtained features were stored in a matrix, which is then composed of vectors corresponding to all the digits (one vector for each digit). This matrix was provided to the neural network as an input. In this experiment, FFBPNN has been trained in supervised mode. We used the binary code of 7 bits: (1 000 000) as a Target for all the vectors that represent the Tunisian dialect and a code of (0 100 000) for that of the Morrocan dialect.

We chose a number of neurons between 70 and 90 and the Tangent sigmoid "TanSig" activation function for the hidden layer. For the output layer, we chose seven neurons and the logistic sigmoid "LogSig" activation function. The learning algorithm was stochastic gradient descent and the used epochs have been varied between 23 and 41. The performance function is mean square error (MSE) and the training function is that of Levenberg-Marquardt 'Trainlm'. The remaining parameters were taken by default.

Table 11.1. SAMPA Phonetic transcription of the digits in both dialects.

Digits	Tunisia	Morocco
0	sfir	sifr
1	wa:Xid	waXd
2	Tni:n	zuz
3	tla:Ta	tlata
4	?arb?'a	Rb?'a
5	xamsa	xamsa:
6	Sitta	Stta
7	Sab?'a	Sb?'a
8	Tmanja	tmnja
9	Tis?'a	Ts?'ud

11.3.3. Results and Discussion

During the classification phase, the program continues running until one of the known multi-layer perceptron (MLP) stop criteria is reached. We notice then each time the corresponding error rates.

The stop criteria imply training stops early when any of these conditions occurs:

- The maximum number of epochs (repetitions) is reached.

- The maximum amount of time for training the FFBPNN is exceeded.

- The performance is minimized to the goal.

- The performance gradient falls below minimal gradient (min_grad).

- "mu" exceeds mu max, where mu is the learning rate.

- The validation performance has increased more than max_fail times since the last time it decreased (when using validation).

The parameters maximum number of epochs, maximum amount of time, goal, min_grad, mu max and max_fail time are chosen by the user.

During the whole experiment, we noticed that PLP followed firstly by ΔPLP and secondly by VQLBG has realized the best classification rate, which is 98.30 %.

PLP followed firstly by ΔPLP and secondly by PCA has occupied the second place in term of performances with 98.18 % classification rate. The stop criterion was "reaching min_grad".

In Table 11.2, the training error, the validation error, the test performance (classification success) and the computational time (Rec.time) taken by the FFBPNN are presented with each hybrid technique.

Table 11.2. Classification performance with FFBPNN.

Techniques	Training error (%)	Validation error (%)	Test Perf. (%)	Rec. time (s)	Epochs
PLP + ΔPLP + + PCA + FFBPNN	13.922e-15	2.148e-15	98.18	7159.920543	38
MFCC + ΔMFCC + + PCA + FFBPNN	753.987e-15	815.530e-15	96.94	7287.829331	41
PLP + ΔPLP + + VQLBG + FBPNN	2647.82e-15	11.669e-15	98.30	3628.540361	23
MFCC + ΔMFCC + + VQLBG + + FFBPNN	0.00446429	0.0018	97.07	5000.895744	31

In Fig. 11.2, the different lines blue, green and red correspond respectively to training error, validation error and test error curves when using PLP, ΔPLP, VQLBG and FFBPNN.

11.4. Arabic Letters Recognition

We investigate in this section the use of the feed-forward back propagation neural networks (FFBPNN) for automatic speech recognition of Arabic letters with their four vowels (Fatha, dhamma, Kasra, Soukoun). This investigation will constitute a fundamental step for the recognition of continuous Speech.

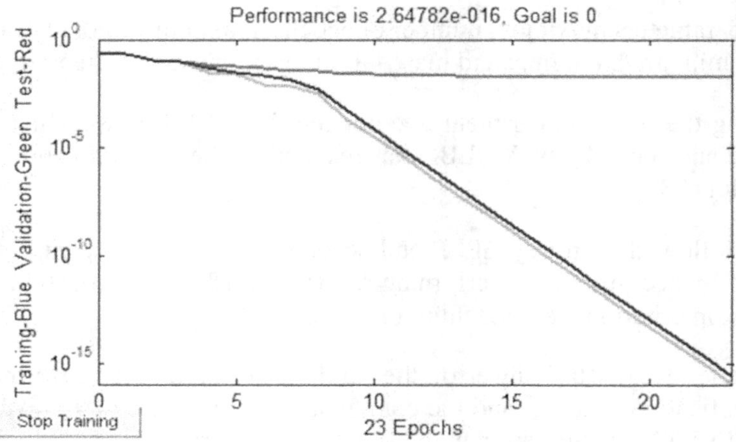

Fig. 11.2. Error rate curves with PLP, ΔPLP, VQLBG and FFBPNN.

Features were extracted from recorded corpus by using a variety of conventional methods such as Linear Predictive Codes (LPC), Perceptual Linear Prediction (PLP), Relative Spectral Perceptual Linear Prediction (RASTA-PLP), Mel Frequency Cepstral Coefficients (MFCC), Continuous Wavelet Transform (CWT), etc.

Here, several hybrid methods have been used too. Since the extracted features have large dimensionalities, they were reduced by conserving the relevant information with the Principal Component Analysis (PCA) technique. The recognition performance has been improved particularly when we use the PLP method followed by PCA technique.

The proposed speech recognition system consists of three modules according to their functionalities. The first module concerns the recording phase, which is followed by an enhancement procedure in order to obtain a best and intelligible quality of signal. In the second module, features are extracted and transformed reduced database. The last module concerns the recognizing phase, which includes training and testing processes.

11.4.1. Corpus Preparation

In this step, an experimental corpus was prepared for automatic recognition of Arabic letters. In fact, four speakers (two males and two females) have participated in the corpus design by uttering all Arabic letters (28) with their four vowels three times each one for the first case and then five times for the second case.

In the first case, the number of utterances of each speaker is equal to $28 \times 4 \times 3 = 336$ utterances. The total number of utterances for the four speakers was equal to 1344. Each utterance is stored in a separate wave file and each trial of each speaker stored in a separate sub-corpus.

Suppose for example that SPK1, SPK2, SPK3 and SPK4 are the four speakers, so SPK1 corpus is composed of three sub-corpora of 112 utterances each. The training corpus is composed of the two first trials of the four speakers ($SPK1_1$, $SPK1_2$, $SPK2_1$, $SPK2_2$, $SPK3_1$, $SPK3_2$, $SPK4_1$ and $SPK4_2$), so the number of files used here is equal to 896 files.

The validation corpus is composed of the second trial of SPK2 ($SPK2_2 = 112$ files) and the first trial of SPK3 ($SPK3_1 = 112$ files). Therefore, the total number of files in validation corpus is equal to 224 files.

The test corpus is composed of the third trial of SPK1 ($SPK1_3$) and the third trial of SPK4 ($SPK4_3$). Therefore, the total number of files in test corpus is equal to 224 files.

Thereby, the train corpus is composed of 80 % of the total corpus. The test corpus consists of 20 % of the total corpus that has not been included in the train corpus. The validation corpus is composed of 20 % of the total corpus from that has been included in the train corpus.

11.4.2. Features Extraction

Features extraction and analysis are described as the following steps:

1. Read file corresponding to each letter from its sub-corpus,

2. Remove silence and reduce noise from the obtained signal in order to improve quality and enhance the speech signal by applying the

algorithm of "Minimum Mean Square Error Short Time Spectral Amplitude Estimator" (MMSE-STSA),

3. Apply one of the feature extraction techniques which have been already mentioned above to the signal obtained in Step 2,

4. Apply PCA to the extracted features resulting from Step 3, in order to represent the letter with the minimum number of vectors,

5. Concatenate the obtained vectors in only one. The resulting vector will represent the speech signal for one letter. Our purpose from concatenating these vectors is to simplify computing and improve recognition performance,

6. Do the same steps for all Arabic letters,

7. Put all the final total vectors (these represent the total letters) obtained in Step 5 in one matrix. Each column in this matrix represents one letter,

8. Select from the obtained matrix the number of vectors that are designed to build the different corpora (training, validation and test) taking into account the size of each one. On the one hand, we have chosen 80 % of the obtained vectors in the latter matrix to construct the train corpus. On the other hand, 20 % are selected for the test corpus and 20 % among that of the train corpus to build the validation corpus.

Each corpus will be stored in a matrix that constitutes an input for the feed-forward back propagation neural networks.

11.4.3. Experimental Results and Discussion

The feature extraction techniques mentioned above have been applied to speech signal corresponding to each letter to provide matrices. The PCA algorithm is then applied in order to reduce the matrices dimensions.

All obtained vectors that represent the total letters are grouped in one matrix, which is provided to the Multilayer Perceptron MLP as inputs.

The number of neurons in the hidden layer has been varied between 50 and 130, the goal was G = 0.01. We let program prepared for our recognition system running until one of the known MLP stop criterions is reached and we note each time the corresponding error rates.

In the second experiment, each speaker is invited to utter each letter five times. This latter operation has significantly improved the recognition performance. We should note that when we concatenate feature vectors that represent the speech signal of any letter in one vector, we obtain a better result for speech recognition. The enhancement of the experimental corpus, by increasing the number of uttering letters from three to five times, has improved the recognition performance with all feature extraction techniques.

Compared to all used feature extraction methods tested in this work, the PLP technique occupies the first order in term of recognition performance and in term of computing time.

After different experiments, we have reached the following error rates as presented in Tables 11.3 and 11.4.

Table 11.4 shows that performance is far better improved when increasing the number of trials per person.

Table 11.3. Recognition performance using three trials per person.

Method	Training Error (%)	Validation Error (%)	Testing Error (%)	# of Epochs
MFCC + PCA	1.187189	0.897189	18.3939	930
ΔΔMFCC + PCA	0.991074	0.860687	30.4044	177
MFCC + ΔMFCC + + ΔΔMFCC + PCA	8.29687	9.33385	23.5392	232
PLP + PCA	0.978391	1.20843	12.6183	27
Rasta PLP + PCA	0.732753	0.715146	17.5906	17
LPCC + PCA	0.99792	1.02594	23.8582	83
CWT + PCA	3.30559	3.09105	26.1099	490
CWT + PLP + PCA	0.961214	0.783404	24.8872	36
PLP + CWT + PCA	7.48001	7.10607	21.6927	72
CWT + MFCC + PCA	0.987389	0.837862	27.5388	41
MFCC + CWT + PCA	4.48791	4.95848	23.2967	146
CWT + LPCC + PCA	1.40306	1.21173	32.2703	91

Table 11.4. Recognition performance using five trials per person.

Method	Training Error	Validation Error (%)	Testing Error	# of Epochs
PLP + PCA	0.992308	0.814672	*11.7432*	179
MFCC + PCA	0.890573	0.664166	13.1609	53
Rasta PLP + PCA	0.936744	0.819379	16.9822	30
LPCC + PCA	1.73818	1.72194	18.4507	271
MFCC + ΔMFCC + + ΔΔMFCC + PCA	6.93287	6.8629	20.0726	78

Figs. 11.3 and 11.4 describe the best obtained performances when using the PLP technique combined with PCA. This outperformance can be interpreted by the fact that the PLP technique adopts three essential properties, which are: (i) the integration of critical bands, (ii) the equal loudness pre-emphasis and (iii) the intensity-loudness conversion. With these aspects, the PLP becomes nearer to the human hearing than other techniques and consequently it allows obtaining robust and discriminatory parameters.

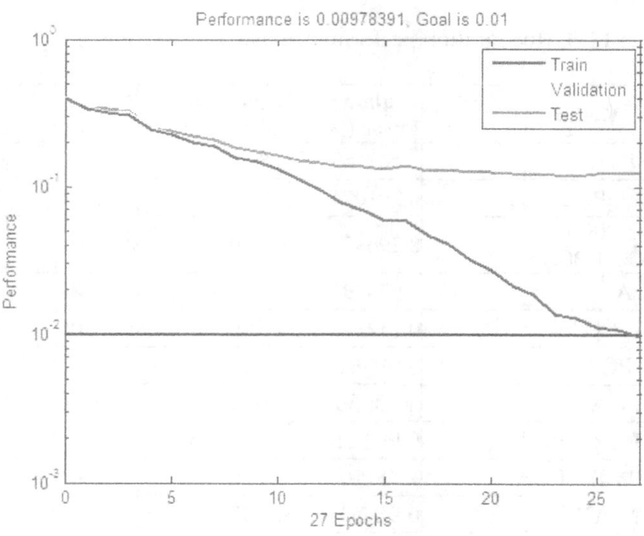

Fig. 11.3. Best performances by using PLP, PCA and FFBPNN techniques (three trials).

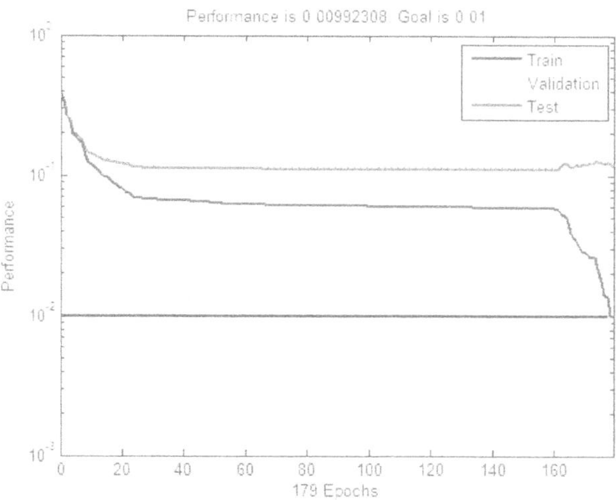

Fig. 11.4. Best performances by using PLP, PCA and FFBPNN techniques (five trials).

The same feature vectors (PLP and PCA), already used, were also computed as inputs for RBF neural networks. The obtained results show that RBF neural networks respond poorly when using large training vectors. The reached performances were respectively 587.056e-30 %, 261.71e-030 % and 27.98 % for training, validation and test. These results prove that FFBPNN is more efficient than RBF neural networks.

11.5. Arabic Words Recognition

In this section, we implemented a speaker-dependent speech recognition system for 11 standard Arabic isolated words. During the feature extraction phase, several techniques were used such as MFCC, PLP, Rasta-PLP and their first order temporal derivatives.

Principal component analysis was adopted in order to reduce the feature dimension. The recognition phase is based on the feed forward back-propagation neural network using two learning algorithms: the Levenberg-Marquardt "Trainlm" and the scaled conjugate gradient "Trainscg".

11.5.1. Design of the Experimental Corpora

To evaluate our recognition methods, an experimental corpus was developed. It consists of 20 speakers (10 males and 10 females). Each speaker pronounced each word five times.

In the second experiment, we divide the previous corpus of 20 speakers in four subcorpora (subcorpus 1 to subcorpus 4) of five speakers each. Therefore, the first subcorpus (subcorpus 1) contains the speech signal of the first speaker until the fifth speaker. The second subcorpus contains that of the sixth speaker until the tenth, etc.

In the third experiment, we also divide again the corpus of 20 speakers in two subcorpora (subcorpus 1 and subcorpus 2) each one contains the speech signal of ten speakers. Therefore, subcorpus 1 contains the speech signal of speaker 1 until speaker 10 and the subcorpus 2 contains that of speaker 11 until speaker 20.

Here, our work was conducted separately on 4 subcorpora of 5 speakers each, then on 2 subcorpora of 10 speakers each and finally on a corpus of 20 speakers.

The goal from the diversity of corpora is firstly to work with different amounts of databases to validate the proposed system performances and secondly to investigate the influence of database expansion on the recognition rate.

The training database for each corpus mentioned above is composed of the first four repetitions of each word by each speaker.

The validation database involves the first repetition of each word by each speaker.

The test database contains the fifth repetition of each word by each speaker. Therefore, when using the corpus of 20 speakers, the training database consists of 880 utterances ($4\times20\times11$), those of validation and test involves 220 utterances each ($1\times20\times11$). The training database is accordingly composed of 80 % of the initial corpus while the test and validation databases represent 20 % of the initial corpus.

Table 11.5 shows the used vocabulary.

Table 11.5. The writing of the used vocabulary.

Word index	Pronunciation	Arabic Writing	English Writing
1	Khalfa	خلف	Backward
2	Amam	أمام	Forward
3	Asraa	أسرع	Accelerate
4	Sir	سر	Walk
5	Istader	إستدر	Turn
6	Takaddam	تقدّم	Proceed
7	Tarajaa	تراجع	Push back
8	Tawakkaf	توقّف	Stop
9	Yamine	يمين	Right
10	Yassare	يسار	Left
11	Waraa	وراء	Back

11.5.2. Applying PCA

PCA algorithm was used after applying MFCCs or PLPs methods in order to reduce the obtained feature matrix dimension corresponding to each word occurrence. It should be noted that two cases were proposed when using PCA.

In the first case, we used a data input matrix e.g. of 13 rows (representing the cepstral coefficients) and a variable number of columns depending on the word size.

In the second case, we used the transpose matrix of the first case. For the two cases, matrices were projected on the two first principal components with an average information loss of 7 %.

After applying PCA algorithm, the obtained matrix in the first case is of 13 rows, which represent variables, and two columns, which represent the overlapped window constituting the observations related to an isolated word.

In the second case, the obtained feature matrix was of two columns, which represent two variables, and a number of lines depending on the size of a computed word.

In both cases, the two columns or two lines will be concatenated in order to constitute one input vector for each word.

Finally, datasets of three feature matrices was obtained. They represent training, test and validation data inputs.

11.5.3. Features Extraction

After pre-emphasizing and windowing the speech signal of each word occurrence, the already mentioned feature extraction techniques were applied separately and sometimes jointly to each speech frame. When MFCCs technique is applied, we used a filter bank of 40 filters where the first 13 are linear and the remained are logarithmic. One matrix of 13 coefficients that represents the extracted features is then obtained for each word. After applying ΔMFCCs a matrix with the same dimension is obtained too. This latter was concatenated with the static Cepstral Coefficients (MFCCs) matrix of the same word occurrence in order to form one matrix, which represents one word occurrence. When the PLP and ΔPLP techniques were applied, the same steps were adopted.

11.5.4. Applying FFBPNN

When applying FFBPNN, the three feature matrices already mentioned in the previous step fed FFBPNN input. The batch-training mode was adopted. Two learning algorithms were separately used: the Levinberg Marquardt (Trainlm) and the Scaled Conjugate Gradient "Trainscg".

When using the "Trainlm" algorithm, the following parameters were adopted: A target of seven bit code, a number of hidden layer neurons between 50 and 90 neurons, the "TanSig" activation function in the hidden layer, 7 neurons and the "Logsig" activation function in the output layer.

The performance function error was optimized to zero "MSE = 0" and the remained neural network parameters were taken by default.

When using "Trainscg", we conserved the latter adopted parameters and we changed the number of neurons in the hidden and output layers to 300 neurons and 55 neurons respectively, a code of 55 bits was used as a target for each word occurrence.

When using the matrix of the second case, only "Trainscg" learning algorithm was used since "Trainlm" did not support matrices of high lines dimension. These two learning algorithms were experimented in order to evaluate the effectiveness of each one when combined with FFBPNN.

The used approach in our work is described as follows:

1. Extract features of each word occurrence belonging to training corpus: A feature matrix is then obtained for each word occurrence.

2. Apply PCA (for the two cases mentioned above) and represent each word occurrence by two principal components. This reduces the previous matrix to two columns or two lines.

3. Concatenate the two previous columns or lines in order to represent each word occurrence by one vector of one column.

4. Store the obtained features corresponding to each occurrence of each word in one matrix in order to constitute the training database.

5. Apply the four previous steps to each word occurrence belonging to test and validation corpora in order to obtain test and validation databases.

6. Feed the FFBPNN with the three matrices corresponding to training, test and validation databases.

7. Choose the parameters of FFBPNN and start computation program until achieving one of the FFBPNN stop criterions.

8. Record the resulting curves and the three performances (training, test and validation).

11.5.5. Experimental Results

All experiments have been conducted as indicated above in two cases using separately two learning algorithms. We aim to study the effect of increasing databases amounts on the recognition rates. The training computational times were also examined with all the hybrid techniques. Three types of corpora were used during the experiments. The first corpus, the second one and the third were respectively based on five speakers, ten speakers and twenty speakers.

The first experiment using matrices of 13 rows and 2 columns.

In this case, the two learning algorithms were used separately. The obtained performances are shown below.

Tables 11.6 and 11.7 show the obtained error rates (training, validation and test) and the training computational times when using the five-speaker corpus. Hybrid techniques were used for features extraction and the two learning algorithms "Trainlm" and "Trainscg" during the recognition phase based on FFBPNN.

It is clear that "Trainscg" learning algorithm out-performs the "Trainlm" one. In Table 11.6, he best test error rate reached 0.26 % when using a combination of Rasta-PLP, PCA and FFBPNN techniques. However, the test error rate reached 0.05 % when using the "Trainscg" learning algorithm and a combination of Rasta-PLP, PCA and FFBPNN techniques.

Fig. 11.5 shows curves of the three best-recorded error rates (training, test and validation). They were obtained when using Rasta-PLP, PCA and FFBPNN with "Trainscg" learning algorithm. The test error rate reached 0.05 %.

Table 11.6. Error rates with FFBPNN based on "Trainlm" learning algorithm (5-speaker corpus).

Techniques	Training Error (%)	Validation Error (%)	Test Error (%)	Training Time (s)
MFCC + PCA + + FFBPNN	374.618e-16	481.18e-16	3.24	401.6
MFCC + ΔMFCC + + PCA + FFBPNN	636.777e-6	58442e-16	3.81	8383.0
PLP + PCA + + FFBPNN	678.773e-16	434.99e-16	1.66	278.8
PLP + ΔPLP + PCA + + FFBPNN	287.171e-16	3.1660e-16	0.88	1250.2
Rasta-PLP + PCA + + FFBPNN	1501.18e-16	1372.8e-16	0.26	295.7
RastaPLP + ΔRasta-PLP + PCA + + FFBPNN	24.7249e-16	44.827e-16	3.69	3168.1

Table 11.7. Error rates with FFBPNN based on "Trainscg" learning algorithm (5-speaker corpus).

Techniques	Training Error (%)	Validation Error (%)	Test Error (%)	Training Time (s)
MFCC + PCA + + FFBPNN	12316.4e-7	8068.1e-7	.10	14.9
MFCC + ΔMFCC + + PCA + FFBPNN	6383.41e-7	20517e-7	.97	9.9
PLP + PCA + FFBPNN	48.3053e-7	32.847e-7	.58	22.0
PLP + ΔPLP + PCA + + FFBPNN	58.5431e-7	40.915e-7	.47	11.4
Rasta-PLP + PCA + + FFBPNN	147.332e-7	162.11e-7	.05	14.9
RastaPLP + + ΔRasta-PLP + PCA + + FFBPNN	13.9349e-7	99.784e-7	.93	15.4

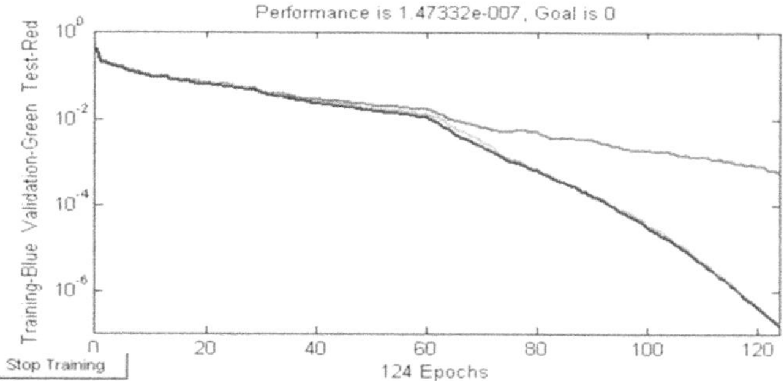

Fig. 11.5. Error rate curves when using RastaPLP, ΔPLP, PCA and FFBPNN with "Trainscg".

Tables 11.8 and 11.9 show the error rates and the training computational times when using a ten-speaker corpus with hybrid techniques and the "Trainlm" and "Trainscg" learning algorithms during the recognition phase based on FFBPNN.

The combination of Rasta-PLP, PCA and FFBPNN techniques has provided the best test error rate of 0.38 % when using "Trainlm" learning algorithm (Table 11.8) and 0.21 % when using "Trainscg" learning algorithm.

Table 11.8. Error rates with FFBPNN based on "Trainlm" learning algorithm (10-speaker corpus)

Techniques	Training Error (%)	Validation Error (%)	Test Error (%)	Training Time (s)
MFCC + PCA + + FFBPNN	356.428e-16	253.89e-16	2.81	711.3
MFCC + ΔMFCC + + PCA + FFBPNN	155.927e-16	420.39e-16	5.51	5290.3
PLP + PCA + + FFBPNN	893.54e-16	711.30e-16	0.58	749.3
PLP + ΔPLP + + PCA + FFBPNN	630.21e-16	386.58e-16	0.46	4155.4
Rasta-PLP + PCA + + FFBPNN	1407.7e-16	1246.2e-16	0.38	1015.1
RastaPLP + + ΔRasta-PLP + + PCA + FFBPNN	9238.77e-16	613.27e-16	2.54	2044.6

Table 11.9. Error rates with FFBPNN based on "Trainscg" learning algorithm (10-speaker corpus).

Techniques	Training Error (%)	Validation Error (%)	Test Error (%)	Training Time (s)
MFCC + PCA + + FFBPNN	0.0626659	496.93e-4	1.19	19.3
MFCC + ΔMFCC + + PCA + FFBPNN	948.771e-6	418.37e-6	3.36	31.7
PLP + PCA + + FFBPNN	874.56e-8	598.60e-8	0.85	47.6
PLP + ΔPLP + PCA + + FFBPNN	973.209e-8	598.13e-7	0.80	34.2
Rasta-PLP + PCA + + FFBPNN	201.712e-7	161.01e-7	0.21	29.1
RastaPLP + +ΔRasta-PLP + PCA + + FFBPNN	198.294e-7	167.91e-7	1.89	32.2

The Fig. 11.6 shows the obtained performance when using a combination of Rasta-PLP, PCA and FFBPNN with "Trainscg" learning algorithm. The test error rate reached 0.21 % and the training error reached 2017e-8 %. It is clear that we obtained a good fit since training error and validation error are close to each other.

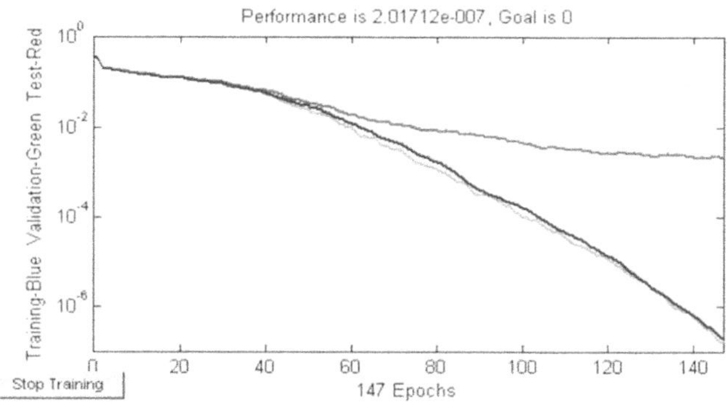

Fig. 11.6. Error rate curves when using Rasta-PLP, PCA and FFBPNN with "Trainscg".

Tables 11.10 and 11.11 show the error rates and the training computational times when using a 20-speaker corpus with hybrid techniques and the "Trainlm" and "Trainscg" learning algorithms during the recognition phase based on FFBPNN.

The combination of PLP, PCA and FFBPNN techniques has provided the best test error rate of 0.82 % when using "Trainlm" learning algorithm (Table 11.10). A best test error rate of 0.68 % is obtained when using PLP, ΔPLP, PCA and FFBPNN techniques with "Trainscg" learning algorithm.

Table 11.10. Error rates with FFBPNN based on "Trainlm" learning algorithm (20-speaker corpus).

Techniques	Training Error (%)	Validation Error (%)	Test Error (%)	Training Time (s)
MFCC + PCA + FFBPNN	834.577e-17	877.91e-17	3.61	1494.0
MFCC + ΔMFCC + + PCA + FFBPNN	904.884e-20	459.98e-20	4.80	4355.0
PLP + PCA + FFBPNN	524.175e-17	366.88e-17	0.82	931.8
PLP + ΔPLP + + PCA + FFBPNN	891.499e-17	912.80e-17	1.24	3301.5
Rasta-PLP + PCA + + FFBPNN	8156.32e-17	4.9643e-16	2.06	808.5
RastaPLP + ΔRasta-PLP + + PCA + FFBPNN	218.299e-9	376.14e-10	2.95	4523.4

Table 11.11. Error rates with FFBPNN based on "Trainscg" learning algorithm (20-speaker corpus).

Techniques	Training Error (%)	Validation Error (%)	Test Error (%)	Training Time (s)
MFCC + PCA + FFBPNN	7.79033e-6	917.21e-8	1.17	85.3
MFCC + ΔMFCC + + PCA + FFBPNN	486.301e-6	651.79e-4	1.23	52.9
PLP + PCA + FFBPNN	162.402e-6	690.45e-8	0.69	109.8
PLP + ΔPLP + PCA + + FFBPNN	974.074e-6	390.22e-8	0.68	124.8
Rasta-PLP + PCA + + FFBPNN	403.503e-6	582.19e-6	0.96	75.1
RastaPLP + ΔRasta-PLP + PCA + FFBPNN	671.323e-6	517.77e-5	1.28	70.3

The Fig. 11.7 shows the obtained performance when using a combination of PLP, ΔPLP, PCA and FFBPNN with "Trainscg" learning algorithm. The test error rate reached 0.68 % and the training error reached 97.407e-8 %.

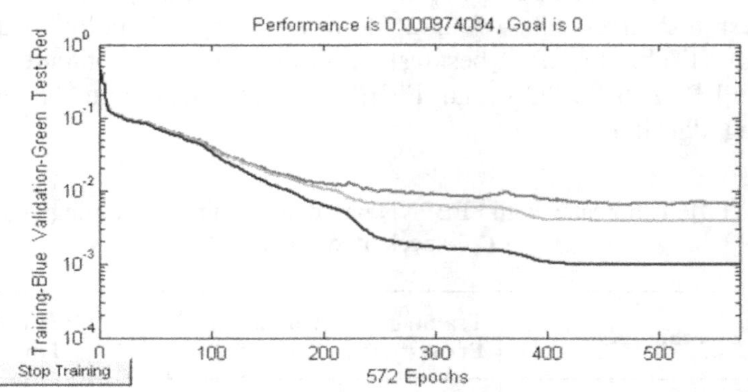

Fig. 11.7. Error rate curves when using PLP, ΔPLP, PCA and FFBPNN with "Trainscg".

The second experiment using matrices of n rows and 2 columns.

In the second case, all isolated-word matrices in the corpus are transposed. After applying PCA algorithm, the output matrices are of dimension (n×2). The n lines represent the overlapped window constituting a word and the two columns represent the two principal components of the obtained features after applying MFCC, PLP or Rasta-PLP.

The two columns are concatenated on a single vector of dimension 2n to feed the FFBPNN network.

All hybrid techniques mentioned above and the FFBPNN based on "Trainscg" learning algorithm are applied to the new corpora.

Tables 11.12-11.14 show error rates values obtained when using corpora of five speakers, ten speakers and twenty speakers respectively.

The combination of Rasta-PLP, PCA and FFBPNN techniques has provided the best test error rate of 1.87 % when using a five-speaker corpus (Table 11.12). A best test error rate of 3.68 % was obtained when we compute a combination of PLP, PCA and FFBPNN techniques on a ten-speaker corpus (Table 11.13). Table 11.14 shows that the best test error rate was of 3.41 % when we experimented a combination of Rasta-PLP, ΔRasta-PLP, PCA and FFBPNN.

Table 11.12. Error rates with FFBPNN based on "Trainscg" learning algorithm (5-speaker corpus).

Techniques	Training Error (%)	Validation Error (%)	Test Error (%)	Training Time (s)
MFCC + PCA + FFBPNN	639.012e-6	144.49e-6	3.09	29.4
MFCC + ΔMFCC + + PCA + FFBPNN	179.964e-6	170.86e-4	5.08	61.2
PLP + PCA + FFBPNN	66.2974e-5	106.70e-6	3.16	39.6
PLP + ΔPLP + PCA + + FFBPNN	344.217e-4	294.43e-4	5.13	106.0
Rasta-PLP + PCA + + FFBPNN	195.482e-6	159.49e-6	1.87	37.5
Rasta-PLP + + ΔRasta-PLP + + PCA + FFBPNN	683.171e-6	454.50e-5	3.47	53.1

Table 11.13. Error rates with FFBPNN based on "Trainscg" learning algorithm (10-speaker corpus).

Techniques	Training Error (%)	Validation Error (%)	Test Error (%)	Training Time (s)
MFCC + PCA + + FFBPNN	1279.42e-6	92793e-6	3.80	29.4
MFCC + ΔMFCC + + PCA + FFBPNN	358.22e-6	1941.1e-6	5.41	75.6
PLP + PCA + FFBPNN	331.123e-6	50.793e-6	3.68	91.0
PLP + ΔPLP + PCA + + FFBPNN	184.594e-6	1241.3e-6	4.78	132.2
Rasta-PLP + PCA + + FFBPNN	9159.51e-6	1536.9e-6	3.88	95.2
Rasta-PLP + +ΔRasta-PLP + PCA + + FFBPNN	331.055e-6	42.503e-6	4.37	91.7

Table 11.14. Error rates with FFBPNN based on "Trainscg" learning algorithm (20-speaker corpus).

Techniques	Training Error (%)	Validation Error (%)	Test Error (%)	Training Time (s)
MFCC + PCA + + FFBPNN	369.799e-7	38.967e-6	3.53	89.0
MFCC + ΔMFCC + + PCA + FFBPNN	7624.93e-7	6350.3e-6	4.43	169.6
PLP + PCA + FFBPNN	3855.35e-7	66659e-6	3.65	141.3
PLP + ΔPLP + PCA + + FFBPNN	228.443e-7	20.457e-6	4.30	286.9
Rasta-PLP + PCA + + FFBPNN	4020.35e-7	560.50e-6	3.36	201.0
RastaPLP + ΔPLP + + PCA + FFBPNN	624.907e-7	66.288e-6	3.41	116.7

The Fig. 11.8 shows the obtained performance when using a combination of Rasta-PLP, ΔRasta-PLP, PCA and FFBPNN with "Trainscg" learning algorithm. The test error rate reached 3.41 % and the training error reached 625 e-8 %.

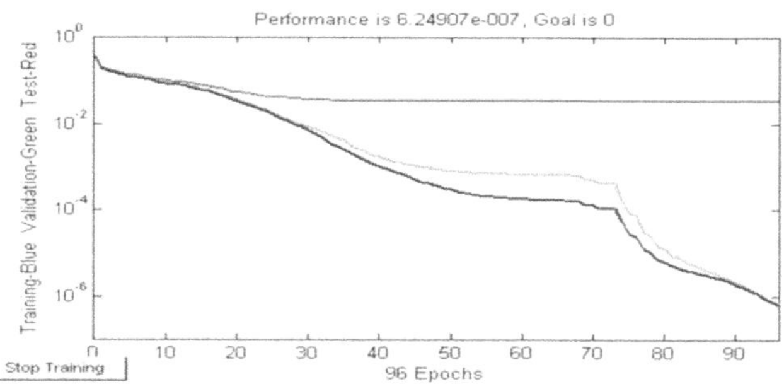

Fig. 11.8. Error rate curve when using RastaPLP, ΔRasta-PLP, PCA and FFBPNN with "Trainscg".

11.5.6. Results and Discussion

During this work, several combinations of features extraction techniques were investigated such as MFCC, PLP, Rasta-PLP and their first order temporal derivative.

To reduce the feature dimension of input matrices, PCA algorithm was applied to all isolated words in the corpus. In this regard, we experimented firstly PCA on features matrices and then on their transposes.

In the first case, we obtained matrices of dimension ($13{\times}2$), which we transformed on input vector of dimension 26. However, for the second case, the obtained matrices was of dimension of ($n{\times}2$), which we concatenated into an input vector of dimension 2n.

For the two cases, the hybrid techniques mentioned above and the FFBPNN based on "Trainlm" and "Trainscg" learning algorithms were investigated on different corpora (five-speaker, ten-speaker and twenty-speaker).

The input vectors of dimension ($13{\times}2$) obtained in the first case have provided good performances in training, test and computation time. It should be noted that "Trainscg" learning algorithm outperforms the "Trainlm" in terms of performance and computational time.

It is important to note that performances dropped when the number of speakers increases. Furthermore, the obtained performances in the first case were significantly better than in the second one. The use of PLP and Rasta-PLP feature extraction methods has led to better performances than the MFCC for the three corpora.

It should be noted too that in the second case, the use of input vectors of dimension 2n has increased the hidden neurons, the output neurons and therefore the computation time.

The best results were obtained with input vector of dimension 26 and "Trainscg" learning algorithm. They reached a test error rate of 0.05, 0.21 and 0.68 % when using corpora of five-speakers, ten-speakers and twenty speakers respectively.

References

[1]. K. A. D. Perera, R. A. D. S. Ranathunga, I. P. Welivyitigoda, R. M. Withanawasaw, Isolated word recognition, in *Proceedings of the International Conference on Information and Automation (ICIA'05)*, Colombo, Sri Lanka, 2005.

[2]. S. G. Sukminder, K. Dinesh, Isolated word recognition system for English language, *International Journal of Information Technology and Knowledge Management*, Vol. 2, Issue 2, 2010, pp. 447-450.

[3]. I. Zitounim, R. Sarikaya, Arabic diacritic restoration approach based on maximum entropy models, *Computer Speech and Language*, Vol. 23, 2009, pp. 257-276.

[4]. M. Elshafei, Toward an Arabic text-to-speech system, *Arabian Journal of Science and Engineering*, Vol. 16, Issue 4B, 1991, pp. 565-583.

[5]. D. E. Kouloughli, Sur la structure interne des syllabes «lourdes» en arabe classique, *Phonologie des Langues Sémitiques*, Vol. 16, Issue 1, 1986, pp 129-154.

[6]. C. Barras, Reconnaissance de la parole continue: Adaptation du locuteur et controle temporel dans les modeles de Markov caches, PhD Thesis, *Universite de Paris IV*, 1996.

[7]. R. Boite, M. Kunt, Traitement de la Parole, *Presse Polytechnique Romandes*, 1987.

[8]. O. Deroo, Modeles dependants du contexte et methodes de fusion de donnees appliquees a la reconnaissance de la parole par modeles hybrides HMM/MPL, PhD Thesis, Faculte Polytechnique de Mons, *Université de Mons*, 1998.

[9]. J. Genin, La parole et son traitement automatique Calliope, *Annales des Telecommunications*, Vol. 45, Issue 7-8, 1990, pp. 457-458.

[10]. L. Rabine, R. Schafer, Digital Processing of Speech Signals, *Prentice Hall*, 1978.

[11]. A. Zabidi, W. Mansor, L. Y. Khuan, R. Sahak, F. Y. A. Rahman, Mel-frequency Cepstrum coefficient analysis of infant cry with hypothyroidism, in *Proceedings of the 5th Int. Colloquium on Signal Processing & Its Applications*, Kuala Lumpur, Malaysia, 2009, pp. 204-208.

[12]. A. Srinivasan, Speech recognition using hidden Markov model, *Applied Mathematical Sciences*, Vol. 5, Issue 79, 2011, pp. 3943-3948.

[13]. J. R. Deller, J. H. L. Hansen, J. G. Proakis, Discrete-Time Processing of Speech Signals, *Wiley-IEEE Press*, 2000.

[14]. O. Cheng, W. Abdulla, Z. Sacic, Performance Evaluation of Front-end Processing for Speech Recognition Systems, Electrical and Computer Engineering Department School of Engineering, School of Engineering Report No. 621, *University of Auckland*, 2005.

[15]. H. Hermansky, N. Morgan, A. Bayya, Ph. Kohn, Rasta-PLP Speech Analysis, in *Proceedings of the IEEE Conference on Acoustics, Speech, and Signal Processing*, April 1992, Vol. 1.
http://www.icsi.berkeley.edu/pubs/techreports/tr-91-069.pdf

[16]. A. Ameen, R. Uma, R. Madhusudana, Speaker recognition system using combined vector quantization and discrete hidden Markov model, *International Journal of Computational Engineering Research*, Vol. 2, Issue 3, 2012, pp. 2250-3005.

[17]. J. Shlens, A Tutorial on Principal Component Analysis, Derivation, Discussion and Singular Value Decomposition, 2003.

Index

G

Gaussian membership, 218, 232
gesticon, 137, 139
gesture
   phrase, 132, 134, 135
   unit, 131
global best, 234, 235, 236
Gradient
   automatic differentiation, 60
   backpropagation, 76
green gas emission, 194
ground water, 196

H

Hanson robotics, 207
hazardous and solid waste, 196
HCSP, 19, 21, 23-25, 29, 36, 51-54
health monitoring, 188
hearing, 210
Heron's formula, 229
heuristic, 215
HRG structure, 134
human-machine interaction, 118, 121

I

imprecision, 207-211, 213
incremental, 205
inductive, 204
inertia weight, 216, 217
Infer, 26, 27, 30, 34
inferences, 204
informal Interaction, 117
information fusion, 117, 118, 123,
   127, 138
intelligence, 203, 204, 207, 208, 213,
   215
Intelligence, 203, 215
intensity, 206
intent, 119, 121, 125, 129, 131, 136-
   139
Internationalized Resource Identifier,
   147
interval arithmetic, 215
intrinsic orientation, 211
intuition, 204, 207
IRI, 147
iZplus, 54

K

knowledge, 203
knowledge engineering, 203

L

La Darijja, 302
language, 204-208, 210, 211
Law of Cosines, 222
Law of Sines, 221
law of tangents, 222
LBG algorithm, 301
learning, 18-25, 27, 32, 51, 54, 203
linguistic variable, 208
livestock, 192, 193, 194
localization, 203
LPC, 296, 298, 299, 306
LPCC, 296, 299, 300, 309, 310

M

machine learning, 205
Machines, 203, 204
manipulate, 203
manipulation, 206
mapping, 203
MATLAB
   fminsearch, 63
Matrix
   exponential map, 64
   rank, 63
maxima-minima, 212
MFCC, 295-297, 305, 306, 309-311,
   316-324
MiniZinc, 21, 51, 53
Mistral, 52
MLP, 304, 308, 309
Modern standard Arabic, 294
Modified Fast Marriage in Honey Bee
   Optimization Algorithm
   (MFMBO), 8-10, 170
Mollweide's identity, 223
monitoring, 271, 272, 288, 289
   socially oriented, 271, 272
      "preventive principle", 272
      computational forecasting
         method, 272, 275
      physical interpretation of the
         results, 272
monitoring process, 189